MW01490216

TRANSLATION STUDIES

TRANSLATION STUDIES

Critical Concepts in Linguistics

Edited by
Mona Baker

Volume III

Routledge
Taylor & Francis Group

LONDON AND NEW YORK

First published 2009
by Routledge
2 Park Square, Milton Park, Abingdon, OX14 4RN

Simultaneously published in the USA and Canada
by Routledge
270 Madison Avenue, New York, NY 10016

Routledge is an imprint of the Taylor & Francis Group, an informa business

Editorial material and selection © 2009 Mona Baker; individual
owners retain copyright in their own material

Typeset in 10/12pt Times NR MT by Graphicraft Limited, Hong Kong

All rights reserved. No part of this book may be reprinted or
reproduced or utilised in any form or by any electronic,
mechanical, or other means, now known or hereafter
invented, including photocopying and recording, or in any
information storage or retrieval system, without permission in
writing from the publishers.

British Library Cataloguing in Publication Data
A catalogue record for this book is available from the British Library

Library of Congress Cataloging in Publication Data
Translation studies / edited by Mona Baker.
p. cm. — (Critical concepts in linguistics)
Includes bibliographical references and index.
ISBN 978-0-415-34422-7 (set) — ISBN 978-0-415-34426-5 (v. 1) —
ISBN 978-0-415-34425-8 (v. 2) — ISBN 978-0-415-34424-1 (v. 3) —
ISBN 978-0-415-34423-4 (v. 4)   1. Translating and interpreting.
I. Baker, Mona.
P306.T7433 2009
418′.02—dc22
2008052775

ISBN10: 0-415-34422-0 (Set)
ISBN10: 0-415-34424-7 (Volume III)

ISBN13: 978-0-415-34422-7 (Set)
ISBN13: 978-0-415-34424-1 (Volume III)

Publisher's Note

References within each chapter are as they appear in the original
complete work

CONTENTS

CONTENTS

CONTENTS

ACKNOWLEDGEMENTS

The publishers would like to thank the following for permission to reprint their material:

Francis Jones for permission to reprint Francis R. Jones, 'Ethics, Aesthetics and *Décision*: Literary Translating in the Wars of the Yugoslav Succession', *Meta* 49, 4, 2004, pp. 711–728.

Domenico Jervolino for permission to reprint Domenica Jervolino, 'Il dono delle lingue. Per una filosofia della traduzione'; unpublished paper; translated by Angelo Bottone.

John Benjamins Publishing Company for permission to reprint Andrew Chesterman, 'Ethics of Translation', in Mary Snell-Horny, Zuzana Jettmarová and Klaus Kaindl (eds.), *Translation as Intercultural Communication* (Amsterdam: John Benjamins, 1997), pp. 147–157. www.benjamins.com

Sturrock, John. Writing Between the Lines: The Language of Translation. *New Literary History* 21:4 (1990), 993–1013. © New Literary History, University of Virginia. Reprinted with permission of The Johns Hopkins University Press.

Taylor & Francis Ltd for permission to reprint Lawrence Venuti, 'Translation as Cultural Politics: Regimes of Domestication in English', *Textual Practice*, 7, 1993, pp. 208–223. www.informaworld.com

Taylor & Francis Ltd for permission to reprint Carol Maier, 'Issues in the Practice of Translating Women's Fiction', *Bulletin of Hispanic Studies*, LXXV, 1, 1998, pp. 95–108. www.informaworld.com

St Jerome Publishing for permission to reprint Karen Bennett, 'Epistemicide!: The Tale of a Predatory Discourse', *The Translator*, 13, 2, 2007, pp. 151–169.

University of Massachusetts Press for permission to reprint Aleka Lianeri, 'Translation and the Establishment of Liberal Democracy in Nineteenth-Century England: Constructing the Political as an Interpretive Act', in Maria

Tymoczko and Edwin Gentzler (eds.), *Translation and Power* (Amherst and Boston: University of Massachusetts Press, 2002), pp. 1–24.

John Benjamins Publishing Company, Amsterdam/Philadelphia for permission to reprint Ian Mason, 'Discourse, Ideology and Translation', in Robert de Beaugrande, Abdulla Shunnaq and Mohamed H. Heliel (eds.), *Language, Discourse and Translation in the West and Middle East* (Amsterdam: John Benjamins, 1994), pp. 23–34. www.benjamins.com

Springer Science and Business Media for permission to reprint Susan Stan, '*Rose Blanche* in Translation', *Children's Literature in Education*, 35, 1, 2004, pp. 21–33. Copyright © 2004 Human Sciences Press, Inc.

Blackwell Publishing for permission to reprint Robin Queen, 'Du hast jar keene Ahnung': African American English Dubbed into German', *Journal of Sociolinguistics*, 8, 4, 2004, pp. 515–537. Copyright © 2004 Blackwell Publishing.

St Jerome Publishing for permission to reprint Marco Jacquemet, 'The Registration Interview: Restricting Refugees' Narrative Performances', in Mike Baynham and Anna De Fina (eds.), *Dislocations/Relocations: Narratives of Displacement* (Manchester: St. Jerome Publishing, 2005), pp. 197–220.

Blackwell Publishing for permission to reprint Brad Davidson, 'The Interpreter as Institutional Gatekeeper: The Social-linguistic Role of Interpreters in Spanish–English Medical Discourse', *Journal of Sociolinguistics*, 4, 3, 2000, pp. 379–405. Copyright © 2000 Blackwell Publishing.

Sage Publications, Inc for permission to reprint Galina B. Bolden, 'Toward Understanding Practices of Medical Interpreting: Interpreters' Involvement in History Taking', *Discourse Studies*, 2, 4, 2000, pp. 387–419. Copyright © 2000 by SAGE Publications.

John Benjamins Publishing Company, Amsterdam/Philadelphia, for permission to reprint Theo Hermans, 'The Translator's Voice in Translated Narrative', *Target*, 8, 1, 1996, pp. 23–48. www.benjamins.com

Taylor & Francis Ltd for permission to reprint Moira Inghilleri, 'National Sovereignty versus Universal Rights: Interpreting Justice in a Global Context', *Social Semiotics*, 17, 2, 2007, pp. 195–212. www.informaworld.com

The University of Minnesota Press for permission to reprint Naoki Sakai, 'The Subject of Translation/the Subject in Transit', extract from Introduction to *Translation and Subjectivity: On 'Japan' and Cultural Nationalism* (Minneapolis & London: University of Minnesota Press, 1997), pp. 11–17. Copyright © 1997 by the Regents of the University of Minnesota.

Duke University Press for permission to reprint Vicente L. Rafael, 'Translation in Wartime', *Public Culture*, 19, 2, 2007, pp. 239–246. Copyright 2007, Duke University Press. All rights reserved.

St Jerome Publishing for permission to reprint Maria Tymoczko, 'Ideology and the Position of the Translator: In What Sense is a Translator "In Between"?', in María Calzada Pérez (ed.), *Apropos of Ideology – Translation Studies on Ideology – Ideologies in Translation Studies* (Manchester: St. Jerome, 2003), pp. 181–205.

Disclaimer

The publishers have made every effort to contact authors/copyright holders of works reprinted in *Translation Studies (Critical Concepts in Linguistics)*. This has not been possible in every case, however, and we would welcome correspondence from those individuals/companies whom we have been unable to trace.

Part 8

TRANSLATION AS ETHICAL PRACTICE

ETHICS, AESTHETICS AND *DÉCISION*

Literary translating in the wars of the Yugoslav succession

Francis R. Jones

Source: *Meta* 49(4) (2004): 711–28.

Abstract

This is a participant-interpreter study of how issues of loyalty, ethics and ideology condition the action of a literary translator. A case-study is presented of the author's socio-ethical dilemmas and decisions while translating Bosnian, Croatian and Serbian literature into English during the 1990s. This aims both to contribute to the socio-cultural historiography of that period and to illustrate how a literary translator might perform in settings of acute socio-cultural conflict. The case-study observations are then used to explore the nature of the literary translator as a textual and social actor. The "constrained autonomy" of the literary translator is seen as having several key implications. Among these are: that all translating acts have ethical and socio-political repercussions; that partiality informed by awareness of the demands of the wider social web may often be a more appropriate stance than neutrality; that the power structures within which the literary translator acts are more important than target language or translating strategy per se in determining source-culture representation, and that time/workload/chance factors may also play a role here; and that confronting Derrida's *indécidable* is a defining feature of translator autonomy.

Introduction

The last decade and a half of the twentieth century saw a rapid and radical transformation of the European political space. The most traumatic of these transformations was that of former Yugoslavia, where a complex of extreme nationalist agendas and brutal anti-secessionist campaigns resulted in the deaths of a quarter of a million people and the expulsion of many more (for overviews, see e.g. Woodward, 1995; Silber & Little, 1997). Inevitably, the violent redrawing of political frontiers in the ex-Yugoslav space in the 1990s went along with an equally violent redrawing of cultural frontiers (Wachtel, 1998) – a process often informed by ethnically exclusive nationalisms which attempted to harness all aspects of culture to the greater glory of the *narod* (the people, the nation). But cultural frontiers are not mere abstracts – they run through people. Thus many former Yugoslavs have found their complex, multi-rooted identity forced into a dour monoethnic straitjacket (Miočinović, in press), or have found their cultural and personal loyalties painfully divided. Nevertheless, as the wars now begin to recede into the past and the new frontiers become taken for granted, there are gradual but increasing efforts to rebuild trust and reopen lines of cultural communication between states and communities in the region.

Before the mid-1980s, Yugoslavia was well-known internationally for its vibrant literature, much of whose strength derived from the variety of the cultural, historical and linguistic roots that fed it (see for example Miočinović, in press). The languages of the former Yugoslavia, however, are not widely read outside the region – even the most widely-spoken cluster of dialects that used to be known as Serbo-Croat and which I now call Bosnian[1]-Croatian-Serbian. This means that the literary translator played, and still plays, a prominent role in communicating that literature to the wider world.

Literary translators, however, are not only textual communicators: they are also individuals with relationships, loyalties and political/social ideologies of their own. Thus translators from the literatures of former Yugoslavia have not been immune to the fragmentation of personal and cultural loyalties, the need for socio-political commitment and the fact of hard ethical choices which the citizens of that region have had to face. The core of this article, in fact, is a case-study which explores how these issues affected the actions, states-of-mind and rationalisations of one literary translator out of Bosnian-Croatian-Serbian during the wars of the Yugoslav succession and its aftermath.

From a translation-studies viewpoint, though there has been much recent debate on the socio-ethical implications of literary translation (e.g. Venuti, 1995, 1998; Pym, 1997; Von Flotow, 1997; Zauberga, 2000; Davis, 2001; Munday, 2001: 126–160), the main focus has been on how translators transform text. The social action of literary translators, however, is often not only textual. It may also involve representing source writers and their culture – e.g. by working with the source writer and source-language informants, writing translator's introductions, negotiating with publishers, arranging readings, etc. (Jones, 2000). Nevertheless, there has been relatively little

4

discussion by translation-studies scholars of the socio-ethical principles underpinning literary translation as *both* textual *and* extra-textual action (*pace* Pym, Zauberga, ibid.), especially in terms of how they might affect real literary translators attempting to navigate real social contexts. Hence the present article also aims to further this discussion.

This study, therefore, has two purposes, which correspond to the two main sections which follow. The first is to contribute to the cultural historiography of 1990s ex-Yugoslavia (cf. e.g. Ali & Lifschutz, 1993; Cohen, 1998) by giving a first-person eye-witness account of how I, as an English-native literary translator from the region, attempted to navigate the conflicting claims of ethics and aesthetics, of personal and political loyalties during that time. Many of the issues I describe are known all too keenly by my fellow literary translators from the region, and some will almost certainly have bearing on the literary translator's experience in situations of inter-communal conflict and reconciliation elsewhere.

The harsh light of conflict, however, also illuminates some crucial social, ideological, ethical and interpersonal considerations which apply to literary translation in general, but which might otherwise remain unnoticed by the translator as subject. Thus my second aim is one of translation theory: to draw out these wider considerations within a framework which constructs the literary translator as a textual and social actor. Key questions addressed here are:

- To what extent can literary translators be seen as autonomous actors within their social and interpersonal setting?
- What implications does the case-study have for issues such as translator neutrality, translator power and translator ethics?
- What particular socio-ethical and ideological concerns are raised by the case-study, and how might these be resolved?
- How might power-structures of cultural representation condition the literary translator's action?
- Should irresolvable issues such as conflicting loyalties and "undecidable" decisions be seen as peripheral or central to any model of translator action?

The underlying framework within which these questions are set – that of the translator as textual and social actor – draws partly on "mainstream" areas of literary translation studies. One is that of translator creativity, where the debate is not so much about whether translators have independent creative rights and powers, as about what the nature of these rights and powers is, and what constrains them (Beylard-Ozeroff *et al.*, 1998; Boase-Beier & Holman, 1999; Hermans, 1999; Chang, 2000). Another is that of recent debates in post-colonialist and feminist translation theory which take as their basis the notion that translating, like writing, cannot take place in a socio-ethical void, and that translators therefore need to be aware of their role within wider social structures of representation, ideology and power (e.g. Venuti, 1995, 1998; Von Flotow, 1997; Zauberga, 2000).

I also draw on fields less commonly applied to literary translation. One is that of social-role and game theory, which defines and describes the various types of "go-between" role in social interaction (e.g. Goffman, 1970; Bailey, 1970; Goffman, 1971), and which Wadensjö (1998) uses to model the work of the community interpreter as a textual-social mediator. As I argue elsewhere (Jones, 2000, 2002), this can also model the role of the literary translator as a mediator between writer, publisher, readers and other involved parties. Another key theoretical strand is the ethics of deconstruction, as applied by Campbell (1998) to the Bosnian conflict of 1992–1995 and its representations outside the conflict zone itself, and by Davis (2001) to the act of translation. Two aspects are particularly useful to the present model. The first is deconstructionism's focus on "the call to the other" as a definer of human identity (Lévinas, in Campbell, 1998: 173–176; Derrida, in Davis, 2001: 92), a call which is an imperative but also an impossibility, because the other is both ultimately unknowable and multiple. This encapsulates the fact that the identity of the translator, as go-between *par excellence*, is dependent on others – such as the source writer and his/her enthusiasts and detractors in the source culture, the translator's helpers and informants, target-culture publishers, readers and critics. But it also shows that the needs, and wishes of these others can be impossible ever to determine fully, and may even clash – and the site of the resulting conflict is the translator's identity. The second key aspect is that of Derrida's concept of *décision*, which grounds the insoluble dilemma (*indécidabilité*) as a defining feature of human decision-making (Campbell, 1998: 184; Davis, 2001: 51). This is of particular relevance to the case-study which now follows, where, as we shall see, overt conflict between the translator's others brings one translator face to face with particularly sharp dilemmas.

Case-study: a literary translator in 1990s ex-Yugoslavia

Participant observation and objectivity

In this section, I provide my own narrative as a "participant-interpreter" (Campbell, 1998: 43–44) – i.e. as a literary translator from Bosnian-Croatian-Serbian during the conflicts of the 1990s and their aftermath. Before we start, however, some methodological caveats are in order. Firstly, the fact that I am both research subject and researcher makes it difficult to claim objectivity in my description of internal psychological states. Participant observation can be a powerful research tool – but it can only achieve the extemalisation necessary to interpret social-psychological events and roles, and generalise from them, if participant observers recognise their non-neutrality and incorporate it into their analytic method (cf. Holliday, 2002: 145–173). Secondly, when describing social relations, especially contemporary and recent ones, and especially ones of social division and conflict, there is no objective, Olympian vantage-point for the interpreter to occupy anyway. As Campbell argues in his review of English-language accounts of the Yugoslav break-up (1998: 53–78), observer-interpreters of contemporary events are also players in what they describe, for they shape the ground on which action or inaction takes place; and, in some views of historical method, even eye-witness accounts are shaped by narrative structures which witnesses use to make sense of what they tell (ibid: 40). Thus – as the opening paragraphs of this essay will already have made clear – I am patently not neutral in my account of external events and social relations, nor can I be. Thirdly, I am aware that wounds are fresh and deep in the region I describe. If any insensitive views or over-simplistic ideas on my part rub against wounds which the reader might have, I apologise for them in advance.

Background: literature, culture and the wars of the Yugoslav succession

It is worth starting with a sketch of key literary/cultural aspects of the Yugoslav break-up, for the wars of the 1990s ex-Yugoslav region were also culture wars, where cultural issues both informed ethno-political goals and were pressed into their service (Wachtel, 1998). In these wars, the key goal of the most aggressive nationalisms (primarily those of Serbia and Croatia, though none are completely innocent here) was one of cultural dominance – at its most extreme, taking the form of culturicide, as expressed in the dynamiting of mosques and the "other side's" churches, or even the deliberate destruction of whole historic town centres. Conversely, this means that the struggle for survival in the face of nationalist aggression (real or perceived) has also been seen by all parties to the conflict as a struggle for cultural survival.

These wars have also partially been literary wars. Firstly, because literature and nationalism are often closely intertwined – a phenomenon by no means unique to ex-Yugoslavia. Thus some roots of nationalism lie in literature – the Kosovo legend, for example, is originally a literary phenomenon.[2] Conversely, the manipulation of literature often plays a crucial role in the process of ethno-national identity formation by generating "pseudo histories" that create or reinforce national mythologies (Hudson, personal communication; cf. Banac, forthcoming). Thus what Banac (forthcoming) calls the construction of "the distorted and misconstructed past of nationalist ideology, with its stress on the continuity of victimhood and redemption, loyalty and treason" is enabled and reinforced in the case of Serbia (to continue the previous example) by the input of the Kosovo epics. And in any case, literature, as a key element of culture, inevitably gets drafted into any manufactured clash of cultures such as those manufactured before and during the break-up of Yugoslavia.

Moreover, literary figures have been deeply implicated in the most recent outbreaks of extreme nationalism. One of the key acts that prefigured the break-up of Yugoslavia by giving respectability to nationalist particularism was the 1986 draft Memorandum by the Serbian Academy, with the novelist Dobrica Ćosić as a prime mover (see e.g. Woodward, 1995: 71, 78); and two of the unholy trinity of Serbian Četnik leaders in the Bosnian wars of 1992–1995 (Radovan Karadžić[3] and Nikola Koljević) were also, respectively, a published poet and a professor of literature. This has led to the particularly unpleasant paradox of culture-creators instigating culturicide. Thus Karadžić and Koljević, in ordering the 1992 incendiary bombing of Sarajevo's National Library and Oriental Institute, did not so much try to impose "their" literature on others, but rather presided over the destruction of all literature, including their "own" Serbian literature stored in the National Library.

More recently, especially after the imposition of peace treaties and the death and removal of arch-nationalists Tuđman and Milošević respectively, there are signs that the nationalist wave (at least in its most extreme form: cf. Cigar, 2001) is beginning to subside at governmental level; and the voices calling for cultural cooperation across and within the new borders are becoming heard with more and more respect. Nevertheless, despite the best efforts of a committed and growing minority, in those territories which have been under the sway of extreme nationalist regimes there is a long way still to go before tolerance of other ethno-cultural groups and their world-views is the rule rather the exception among the population at large.

Personal history

It also would be useful to provide a little background to myself as subject. After several teenage holidays spent with ethnic Hungarian friends in the Vojvodina region of Serbia, I studied Serbo-Croat language and literature as part of my undergraduate degree in the UK. I then spent a year (1978–1979) as an exchange student at Sarajevo University, where I began translating the works of the Bosnian poet Mak Dizdar and the Serbian poet Ivan V. Lalić. These two poets have formed the mainstay of my literary translation work since then (Lalić, 1997; Dizdar, 1999), but I have also worked with other poets from the region, such as the Croat Drago Štambuk and the Serb Vasko Popa (Jones, 1994; Popa, 1997). More recently, I have become involved as a translation editor with the Sarajevo-based network International Forum Bosnia,[4] whose aim is to rebuild cultural and academic bridges in the ex-Yugoslav region (e.g. Mahmutćehajić, 1996; Lovrenović & Jones, 2001).

Literary translation and cultural-political loyalty

Let us now turn to the case-study narrative proper. As may be deduced from the personal history above, my main identification before the wars of the country's break-up was with Yugoslavia as a multi-cultural space, though with Bosnia and Serbia in particular. Nevertheless, during the Serbian (and later Croatian) onslaught on the emergent state of Bosnia and Herzegovina, my political loyalty lay with the latter. This loyalty was prompted and conditioned by four factors.

Firstly, like many foreign observers, I felt that *not* taking sides for Bosnia would simply have been immoral in the face of the brutality of the assault on the country, its people and its culture – a feeling strengthened by the fact that I had lived in Sarajevo for a year and thus felt considerable personal loyalty to the Bosnian cultural space. Thus I saw my translating of Bosnian and Herzegovinan literature – for example, the works of Mak Dizdar, a poet of major European stature – as an attempt to defend Bosnian and Herzegovinan culture by valorising it in the eyes of the outside world. And this motive – translating as an act of loyalty – has remained even in peacetime.

Secondly, my own idea of the culture I saw myself as trying to defend was far from neutral. I saw Bosnian and Herzegovinan culture as a complex and nuanced space whose vitality was (and is) based on an interplay between conflicting and common world-views, experiences and readings (Lovrenović, forthcoming), rather than the simplistic notion of separate "Bosniak" (i.e. Bosnian Moslem), "Croat" and "Serb" cultures which the nationalists were trying to promote. Thus translating Dizdar's *Stone Sleeper*, for example, implied supporting Dizdar's act of constructing a Bosnian identity through the country's medieval past – an identity (that of the heretic faithful, persecuted but impossible to exterminate) that is both uniquely Bosnian and applies equally to all its present-day inhabitants (Buturović, 2002):

> You know nothing about my wealth
> Hidden from your mighty eyes
> (You don't know that fate
> Has deemed
> And dealt me
> Much more
> Than
> You
> Surmise)
> You've decided to root me out at any price
> But nowhere will you find the real road
> To me
>
> > (from "Roads," Dizdar, 1999: 25)

Moreover, this act of defence or "ambassadorship" (Jones, 2000) did not only mean relaying a positive image of Bosnian culture. It also meant trying to combat negative images in the West of Bosnia as victim or Bosnia as a place of aggression and intolerance – images inevitably generated when media pictures of massacre and mayhem are followed by Western government and UN pronouncements about the impossibility of intervening between "warring factions" who were "all guilty" (cf. Cigar, 1998; Young, 2002). I felt that it was important to attempt to redress the balance by conveying an alternative image through translation – the image of Bosnia as a country with a high literary culture which could rank with any other in Europe.

A fourth aspect of this cultural-political engagement also meant stepping outside the realm of "high literature." During the war against Bosnia, I and many of my fellow translators felt there were not only literary images, but opinions and eye-witness reports which had to be transmitted urgently to the outside world, either by translating them directly or by editing translations made by source-language natives. Among my examples were the philosophical and political essays and newspaper columns of Rusmir Mahmutćehajić (e.g. Mahmutćehajić, 1996), which promoted inter-ethnic tolerance rooted in a shared religiosity as the unifying Bosnian idea, or the first memoirs from the?etnik concentration camps (Bosnević, 1993).

Using the metaphor of translation as cultural/political defence, how-ever, begs the question of defence where, against whom, and to what effect – otherwise it is no more than an intellectual conceit, offensive to those who did more concrete, physical acts of defence. In the literary and political translators' case, the place was primarily "the outside world," especially Western Europe and North America, where governments were striving not to intervene in the face of mounting evidence of genocide and culturicide (Cigar, 1998; Young, 2002). Here, translations, their publication and their public reading can probably best be seen as part of the gathering of popular pressure (small in comparison to the TV images of shelling and massacre relayed nightly into people's homes, but no less real) that eventually resulted in the USA's about-turn towards intervention in 1995.

But of course, though Western inaction before 1995 and its corollaries – support for an arms embargo and partition-based peace treaties – generated guilt through complicity, the prime agents of destruction were the cam-paigns of the nationalists and the views that underlay them. Here, it might seem that translation out of the language of the aggressors and victims can achieve even less. Nevertheless, validation via translation in the eyes of the outside world, especially through a world lingua franca like English, can provide the integrative model of Bosnian culture with an additional means with which it can try to win support or cement alliances – as happened through the distribution of the Dizdar translations via embassies and at inter-government meetings, for example.

Nowadays the physical fighting has stopped in Bosnia and Herzegovina, and the state's independence (albeit flawed by partition) is guaranteed by an international military and civil presence. Nevertheless, though crude nationalism is no longer respectable at official level, there is still a way to go before its ideas can be exorcised from many people's minds: indeed, exorcising these ideas is a key priority for many Bosnian intellectuals. Thus I have still felt the need to defend and promote the complexity and potential for tolerance in Bosnian culture, both via literary translation and the translation editing of works and discussions promoting inter-communal/ non-particularistic dialogue. But this again begs the question of what a literary translator can achieve here. Again, the answer is: not much alone. But if the translator is part of a wider drive for tolerance and for the rebuilding of cultural and intellectual contacts (as promoted, for example, by International Forum Bosnia), this wider drive may well have a chance of success, no matter how gradual.

Conflicting loyalties

So far, I have focused on loyalty towards Bosnia. Anti-nationalism, however, does not only mean defending the side one believes in – which is where my decisions became less easy. As a translator of South Slav (not just Bosnian) literature, even during the early 1990s, I felt that taking sides *for* Bosnian literature and culture should not mean that I was taking sides *against* literature written in Croatia and Serbia. That would have been ideological reductionism, falling into the nationalists' trap (at least, so my rationalisation went) – and thus I kept working with the Serbian and Croatian poets mentioned earlier.

Another reason to keep working with poets from throughout the Serbo-Croat region, even in the darkest times of the conflict, paralleled that mentioned earlier for Bosnian culture. This was the wish to defend a broad "post-Yugoslav" culture against simplistic cultural constructs which I saw as prevailing in the wider world – constructs which fit with a wider stereotype of the Balkans as Western Europe's uncivilised other which Todorova has labelled "balkanism" (1997: 3–20). Here the media images focusing on war and intolerance (concentration camps, shelled buildings, massacres and refugees) were usually well-meaning in their defence of the injustices committed against the Bosnians and the Kosovars. The cumulative picture they risked giving, however, was that of the ex-Yugoslav region as *tamni vilajet* – a "dark province" of ancient hatreds and nothing more.[5] This, I felt, should be countered by reminders that the region was also one of high culture, not merely one of victims and executioners – a region, like Bosnia itself, whose cultural richness I saw as stemming from the very diversity and complexity that the nationalists wished to expunge.

11

The question that one must ask here, however – and that I often asked – is whether it was ethically right for a translator to take such a stance at that time. In the early 1990s, nationalist agendas underpinned by notions of cultural exclusivity and superiority in Serbia and Croatia were powering, as I saw it, a drive to wipe out the culture and population of Bosnia. Seen in this light, might an Olympian stance of pan-Yugoslav fairness not be an act of hypocrisy or blindness as reprehensible as my government's insistence that aggressor and victim were equal? The following paragraphs detail the ethical, psychological and affective dilemmas which questions such as these generated.

To begin with, I feared that the publishing of my (and other translators') Serbian translations abroad might be propagandised by the nationalist regime in Belgrade, which was desperate for all the international credibility it could get – tempered by the fact that this may equally well have offered support to non-nationalist Serbian intellectuals. On a more personal level, there was the dilemma of whether to continue working with living writers of excellent texts (and/or personal friends) who supported or failed to oppose regimes which I felt to be hateful (a similar dilemma to that faced by many citizens of former Yugoslavia). My approach here tended to be: stay true to the texts, for that's where the writer speaks to the world (after all, there are examples in Anglo-American literary history as well of good poets having bad or ill-informed views).

A more dangerous issue arose when the very imagery which I was translating was used by nationalists to justify a campaign of hatred and genocide. An example was that of the Serbian atavistic images explored in Vasko Popa's *Uspravna zemlja* and *Vučja so* (Popa, 1973, 1980), such as the Kosovo myth or the figure of the wolf as tribal totem. When writing these poems, Popa was *positively* exploring his cultural roots, seeking pan-human archetypes through cultural particulars, in an age (the 1970s) when such explorations were relatively untainted. But a translator publishing in an age of rampant nationalism cannot claim the same innocence. Thus my editing/ translating of Popa's *Collected Works* (Popa, 1997) might have been seen as giving credibility (slight, perhaps, but no less slight than my earlier claim that I was defending Bosnian culture) to the murderous misuse of such imagery by Serbian nationalists: the Kosovo defeat of 1389 feeding a desire for revenge against the Bosnian and Kosovar Moslems six centuries later, for example, or White Wolves (*Beli vukovi*) supplying the name for an anti-Muslim death squad.

Alternatively, this imagery may risk reinforcing negative stereotypes of the region among an English-reading public – thus, for example, giving the impression that Popa was a narrow-minded nationalist. The *Glasgow Herald* review of Popa's 1997 *Collected Works* (Bold, year unknown) is telling here. Though Bold's text and the picture caption stress that "Serbian nationalism [. . .] has been synonymous with everything Popa opposed," the article is dominated by a large photograph of a forest of hands giving the Serb nationalist three-fingered salute – and images speak louder than words.

Publication in such cases, therefore, has its dangers. But what is one to do, as a translator – refuse to participate, or try to halt publication? Or is one then falling into another of the nationalists' traps, by agreeing that everything ever produced by a culture was produced for the greater glory of the *narod*, without room for alternative motives and readings? In the end, a key reason that I did *not* break with Serbian and Croatian poetry was that it would have meant breaking personal ties built up over many years. I tended to be very wary of building up new ties, however, except on the rare occasions when I felt that my translation work supported some sort of opposition to the nationalist mindset – as, for example, with an English-language issue of the Belgrade women's journal *Pro Femina* (Slapšak, 1997).

Conflicts of quality

Occasionally I found myself asked to translate poetry that I found rather sub-standard, but from a culture I feel I had to support. In retrospect, the choice seems relatively simple: refuse to translate, for a poor poem makes propaganda against its culture, not for it. Usually I did refuse – but was left with a sense that I should have supported, if not a culture, then a person with a message to tell. Sometimes, however, socio-political loyalty outweighed artistic judgment, as with my decision – when the outlook looked most dire for the Bosnian state – to translate an allegory (Latić, 1993) of the war against Bosnia:

> [. . .]
> Beside a thorn tree, all alone,
> a roe-deer grazed, not yet full-grown!
>
> Lovely it was, like a gift only dreamed,
> this pastoral scene – a wonder it seemed
> and yet it was smashed by a frantic roar,
> setting a pack of hounds on her spoor!
> [. . .]

A related issue – again, thankfully rare – was whether I should attempt to improve the literary quality of verse which I felt was worth translating for other reasons. The translator's default ethic of neutrality says one should translate a "not good, not bad" Bosnian poem, for example, into an English poem of similar quality. But if one's purpose is to further a cultural-political ideal, could strict neutrality not be seen as equally unethical? In actual fact, I often did improve such texts, but within clear limits, i.e. changing style but not content, turning obviously awkward or simplistic source-text phrasing and poetics into more stylish English phrasing and poetics, but leaving the central image and its development for the judgement of the target readers.

Conversely, one might ask whether verse of similar quality in support of a destructive ideology or by an evil poet should be *down*graded in translation. Such a descent, however – from promotion to smearing – would have been an ethical step too far. Moreover, the only reason I had for translating such work was to inform about "the other side." Thus, when Chris Agee, while writing the introduction to his edited collection of modern Bosnian poetry *Scar on the Stone* (1998), asked me to translate a poem by Radovan Karadžić in order to understand what sort of a poet could order the burning of libraries, I translated exactly what I saw. This – a second-division rather than fourth-division poem, moderately competently constructed round a rather soulless central conceit in an idiom thoroughly in keeping with contemporary South Slav poetics[6] – gave more telling insights into the character of the man (a moderately skilled opportunist in search of an identity, perhaps) than simple demonisation as "bad poet" would have given.

A coda to the issue of text quality is the fact that native-English-writing translators of Bosnian-Croatian-Serbian are very few in number. In my experience, this has two main consequences. Firstly, I have had to refuse many translation requests out of simple pressure of work and time. Conversely, when it comes to another role of many literary translators – that of spotting and supporting good up-and-coming writers, some may get overlooked. Thus, for example, when acting as an advisor and poetry scout for Chris Agee's *Scar on the Stone* collection, I only came across the work of two younger-generation Bosnian poets when it was already in press – Nermina Kurspahić and Jasna Šarnić, excellent poets who would also have helped equalise the gender imbalance in the collection (e.g. Šamić, 1986; Kurspahić, 1999).

At this point, it is important to reintroduce the issue of researcher reflexivity. This case-study has described a number of dilemmas and the routes which I chose through them. It is worth pointing out, however, that most of the latter were simply that: routes rather than intuitively satisfactory solutions. Even after I had taken a decision, a sense of inner conflict often remained. Thus, though I have tried where possible to take the necessary analytic distance in this article, the choice of case-study examples and the discussion that follows inevitably also reflect an affective drive to reconcile the dilemmas experienced and routes chosen with my political/ideological views and my persona as a translation professional.

Implications: translation as social/ethical action

Translators as social players

Given this final proviso, it is now time to step back from the personal and to examine what wider implications this narrative might have for the role of the literary translator, both in and beyond times of overt social conflict. To begin with, what *is* a literary translator? The person in the street would probably regard a translator as someone who simply enables a reader to experience a foreign-language text; and most literary translators, including myself, would almost certainly regard the core of their professionality as the duty to transmit the source text as accurately as possible. Translators are also social beings, however, as the present study has acutely highlighted. The very definition of "translator" presupposes at least one social other: the person who produces the source text. Thus, as this case-study has shown, personal relationships with source-text writers can be a powerful factor in shaping the literary translator's social action. Translators' identities and acts are also shaped by their wider social context: "the translating subject is constituted in a complex, heterogeneous system economic, social, sexual, racial, cultural" (Davis, 2001: 58). The present study has shown this linkage all too vividly in terms of source- and target-based culturo-political factors.

However, seeing literary translators as mere relayers of source-text meaning or slaves of social context seems overly deterministic, and is at odds with prevailing models of literary translation that see the translator as a creative agent (e.g. Beylard-Ozeroff *et al.*, 1998). The case-study indicates that the literary translator acts within a field shaped by a number of interdependent forces, both internal and external to the translator:

- **Self**: among the factors here are the translator's own psyche, personal history and motivations, political and ideological loyalties and views, ethical principles and conceptualisation of his/her own role, preferred translating tactics and strategies.
- **Source text**: its intrinsic features, such as difficulty/"translatability" or quality.
- **Significant others**: relationships with the source writer or his/her representatives (such as widow/er, official or unofficial agents), target publishers, editors and others (cf. Bush, 1998).
- The wider **social context** within which all the above operate. Among the factors operating here are: the political, social and literary-aesthetic features of the source culture, mutual images of and relationships between source and target culture, target-culture literary norms and norms of expected translator behaviour (Hermans, 1999: 72–90; Toury, 2000), time-lapse between source and target writing, source- and target-culture literary networks, relationships between interest-groups (such as source-culture regions/ethnicities), and the real-world consequences of translator decisions.

This implies seeing literary translation as constrained but autonomous social action (cf. Boase-Beier & Holman, 1999), with translators, as they work, constantly deciding between and evaluating their own text-transformation strategies within the opportunities and constraints of interpersonal contacts and the wider social context.

But is this model of literary translation specific to social settings of acute and aggressive intra-cultural and/or inter-cultural conflict, which demand especially urgent action by the translator whilst setting severe constraints on that action? I would claim that it is not. If nothing else, as feminist and Marxist theorists have pointed out, one cannot conceive of a social setting free from inter-group conflict. In less acute settings, however, the social constraints on the literary translator's action may be less visible. This echoes Davis' claim that "full awareness [that the translator is socially constituted] necessarily eludes the translator's consciousness" (2001: 58) – though here "necessarily" should almost certainly be replaced by "in unmarked situations." On present evidence, factors in the situation become marked and thus raised to the translator's awareness when they are linked to particularly salient outcomes – such as the political survival of a source state or the international recognition of a writer. Alternatively, such factors may be consciously perceived by the translator when they conflict – such as when the translator's relationship with a source writer conflicts with the translator's own ideology.

An analogy for the constrained autonomy of the literary translator is that of ambassadorship (Jones, 2000, 2002). In the social-game model of Goffman (1970; 1971; cf. Wadensjö, 1998), ambassadors (like translators) are players whose role is defined by their relationship to other players; though they can only act within the constraints of their brief, which is to represent their "party" in the best way possible, they have to make constant decisions about how to do so. Seeing literary translators as ambassadors also highlights the fact that many literary translators do more than just translate text. As the case-study indicates, they tend to be keen advocates for their source text, their source writer and for the literary source culture as a whole. They may have webs of literary contacts in the source and target culture, they may seek out or (more often) be approached by new writers, and they may have to find and work with publishers and editors, organise readings, etc. (cf. Jones, 2000). Thus translators form a key nexus in the web of literary and extra-literary patronage which determine the reception and even the form of a translated text (Lefevere, 1992, in Munday, 2001: 128).

Moreover, the analogy of literary translation as cultural ambassadorship helps to explain two crucial findings from the case-study. Firstly, ambassadors are not neutral. This study has indicated that the ethic of neutrality between parties to the communication, which is often seen as the translator/interpreter's default stance, may not always be the most appropriate ethic for the literary translator. Indeed, partiality might often be more appropriate. Secondly, with both ambassadors and literary translators, autonomy can give power over others. This is not only the power to interpret a text how one wishes, but also to choose whom to translate and whom not to translate – the gatekeeping function of literary translation (Jones, 2000; cf. Scollon & Scollon, 1983).

Ethics and ideology

If, as a translator, one claims not only autonomy but also partiality and power, it is crucial to have an awareness of the ethical and ideological implications of one's acts – indeed, literary translators should probably be seen as subject to the same responsibilities, concerns, dilemmas and risks as original writers (Pym, 1997: 65). Thus translators need to balance "their indebtedness and ultimate 'faithfulness' to their own circumstances and perceptions" against the "call to the wholly other" whom they represent and who forms their identity as translators (Arrojo, 1994, in Davis, 2001: 92; cf. Campbell, 1998). Moreover, this study has shown that, if the translator's partiality and ethical considerations are to coexist, then the call to the primary other (the source-writer or source-culture) must be tempered by a constant awareness of "the other other." In practical terms, this means taking account where possible of the interests of more parties than that of the source writer/culture. Examples of such interests might be those of related or overlapping source cultures, of other source-culture players, of target-culture players such as publishers and readers, and/or of fellow-translators and the normative frameworks they set (Lefevere, 1992, in Munday, 2001: 128; Pym, 1997; Bush, 1998; Venuti, 1998; Hermans, 1999: 72–90; Toury, 2000). Furthermore, in unmarked settings – as with the case of the translator's social embeddedness – ethical and ideological considerations may well remain below the level of conscious awareness, or not be conceptualised as ethical/ideological, until they conflict or the real-world stakes of action become raised.

The following paragraphs discuss key specific ethical and ideological issues raised by the case-study:

The first issue is that of the conflict between the calls of Olympianism and *Realpolitik*. The former argues that translators should remain true to texts that are artistically good, even in tainted social circumstances of production and reception – such as a source culture hijacked by extreme nationalism – in the knowledge or hope that the culture will recover. The latter claims that a text cannot remain separate from and thus untainted by its social context. Thus, for example, a translator should refuse to translate works whose imagery is being exploited to justify genocide, no matter how innocuous that imagery might have seemed at the time of first writing. The study did not intrinsically favour one call before the other, though it indicated that other factors in the social game, such as relationships with key players, may well be what tips the balance.

The case-study also highlighted the gatekeeping role of the literary translator mentioned earlier. Here, we identified factors which affect gatekeeping decisions beyond the obvious ones of source-text quality and gatekeeper preference: translator workload and chance factors also play a key part, crucial though such decisions may be for a source writer's career. Once more, the specific social setting – that of many source writers with words to tell the world and few translators with time to give them a voice – has highlighted translator awareness of this issue, but it is one inherent in any translating "game" in the Goffman sense.

Thirdly, a common assumption in ideology-based approaches to translation studies is that translating into English risks being an act of McDonaldization – that is, of strengthening the world hegemony of Anglo-American values at the expense of those of the source culture (Jones, 2000; Venuti, 1995; Zauberga, 2000). The present study indicates that translating into English may equally well be a means for a "small" culture to gain a voice on the world stage (Jones, Zauberga, ibid.). In other words, English might enable such a culture to promote its own ideological values, even if they conflict with official and unofficial UK/US ideologies. A key example here is the translator's drive to deconstruct the target-culture images of Bosnia as *tamni vilajet* – images constructed to justify non-intervention – and to replace them with the Bosnian state's self-image of unity in diversity; these images were then deliberately used by other source-culture players to promote Bosnia's cultural and political independence (cf. Mahmutćehajić, 1996). The case-study, in fact, supports Zauberga's observation (2000) that target language is almost, certainly less important in terms of a text's ideological effect than the power and loyalty structures of those engaged in the translating process.

Another issue is that of altering source-text content, as exemplified in the case-study in the discussion about the stylistic "improvement" of Bosnian poems. In contemporary theoretical accounts, such acts of "translation as rewriting" (Lefevere, 1992, in Munday, 2001: 127–131) to conform with target-culture ideological drives and aesthetic norms are usually seen a clear breach of translator ethics – a notorious and often-quoted example being that of Edward FitzGerald's orientalist rewriting of Omar Khayyam (ibid.). Thus normalising or domesticating a quirky or culturally unfamiliar source text for the sake of target-language fluency or reader-friendliness is widely regarded as suppressing source-text/source-culture identity (e.g. Venuti, 1995; Allén, 1999; Berman, 2000). And, of course, what one person sees as improvement another may see as desecration – as in the case of FitzGerald and Omar Khayyam, where FitzGerald's tactic is now decried by translation commentators. Other views are possible, however. Certain "interventionist" branches of feminist translation theory, for example, allow the altering even of core semantics for purposes of gender ethics (Von Flotow, 1997: 24–30). Alternatively, literary translators polishing target-text poetics may be seen as performing a similar role to literary editors, few of whom would see their advice to authors as unethical; or to community interpreters working between a doctor and a refugee patient, who would see their job as to help the two parties to communicate and not merely to transpose words (Carr *et al.*, 1997; Wadensjö, 1998). In the end, I do not claim that the stylistic editing which I carried out was necessarily the better course. However, it does show that the strategy of improvement/normalisation/domestication, ethically high-risk though it may be, need not necessarily suppress source-text/writer/ culture identity, and may even be used to promote it. Thus, in source-culture representation terms, one may cautiously conclude that the ideologies, loyalties and power structures in the wider social setting of translation (Lefevere, 1998) might again be more crucial than the translating strategy per se.

Décision

A constant leitmotiv in this study has been that of dilemmas of translator choice, where any outcome brings as many problems as it solves. Moreover, the translation-theory discussions above have often merely confirmed the existence of rival options, with no indications as to which may be the better path. A potential way out of this impasse is offered by the deconstructionist concept of *décision*. *Décision*, to Derrida, is an act that necessarily involves confronting a dilemma: "only when faced with an impossible decision – one for which a pre-existing 'right' choice is not 'presented' – do we decide" (Davis, 2001: 51). Moreover, the fact of having to decide between undecidable options lies at the basis of the constrained autonomy that typifies all human action, including that of the translator: a "decision that didn't go through the ordeal of the undecidable would not be a free decision, it would only be the programmable application or unfolding of a calculable process" (Derrida, 1990, quoted in Davis, 2001: 94).

Similarly, *indécidabilité* may be seen as a defining rather than an interfering factor in ethical choice. Firstly because *décision*, as mentioned, presupposes a set of potential outcomes that seem equally valid. Secondly, because, if we gloss ethical responsibility as responsiveness to the call of the other, we can never know the exact nature of that call ("Ethics would begin with the realisation that the other is [. . .] precisely that which exceeds, my grasp and powers": Critchley, 1999, in Davis, 2001). Thirdly, the entry of a second other, whose agenda may – especially at times of overt social conflict – oppose that of the first other, turns a simple ethical imperative into a situation of ethical *indécidabilité*: "I cannot respond to the call [. . .] of another without sacrificing the other other" (Derrida, 1992/1995, in Davis, 2001: 94–95; cf. Lévinas, in Campbell, 1998: 177–179).

Seen in this light, the fact of having to confront apparently insoluble textual, interpersonal and ethical dilemmas is not an aberration in the work of literary translators. It is what defines their status as creative agents rather than interlingual copyists.

19

Conclusion

Individuals have complex sets of loyalties – to home-town, to family, to friends, to past, to state, to faith – which (despite what the nationalists tell us) are rarely coterminous. This applies to literary translators too, one of whose sets of loyalties is to the country, culture and texts they spend a large amount of their life translating and representing. Even in "normal" times this has repercussions for how literary translators perform their identities as textual and cultural ambassadors – in terms of what they translate and how, and what they choose not to translate, and why. But in times and places of acute social conflict, loyalties clash and ethical dilemmas multiply for all social actors, including translators. This is exacerbated by specific features of the literary translator's social role – that of cultural ambassadorship coupled with bi-cultural responsibility (towards both writer and reader, towards both source and target cultures: Pym, 1997), for example, or that of cultural gatekeeper.

There are no easy solutions to the problems outlined here. Though attempting to solve the insoluble may well be a defining feature of translator action, a principle of maximum awareness of ethical implications together with one of least harm to other players may serve as initial guidelines ("points de repère": Pym, 1997: 69) when making hard decisions. Beyond this, however, it may be best for us, as translators, to accept the maxim that *nous avons tons les mains sales* – and the dirtier the situation, the dirtier our hands. And thus use them to do what we feel is the least wrong, so that, hopefully, the good effects might outnumber the bad.

Looking specifically at the ex-Yugoslav region, physical conditions finally seem to be returning, no matter how hesitantly, to some sort of normality. To intellectuals and cultural actors from the region, the key priority now is to re-establish an open and pluriform model of culture within and between the ex-Yugoslav states. In this, an important concern is to link regional processes into the wider processes of European and world culture. The aim here is not only to validate and strengthen the drive towards an open and pluriform regional culture, but also so that the ex-Yugoslav cultures may continue to energise and inspire cultures outside the region. Literary translators, as part of a social web involving writers, publishers, cultural organisers, readers and other actors in the literary process, have a crucial role to play here.

Acknowedgements

I would like to thank Robert Hudson, Hanneke Jones, Chris Perriam and Allan Turner for their invaluable advice and feedback on this article's structure and content.

Notes

1 For reasons of conciseness, I usually shorten the proper term "Bosnia(n) and Herzegovina(n)" to "Bosnia(n)."
2 This tells of the glorious defeat of the Serbian armies in 1389 by the Ottoman conqueror. Among the key elements are the Serbian Prince Lazar being given the choice of a heavenly before an earthly kingdom (and choosing the latter, thus bringing defeat but sainthood), and his betrayal by the turncoat Vuk Branković. It derives from the cycle of Serbian folk epics collected by the philologist Vuk Karadžić in the early nineteenth century.
3 Radovan Karadžić was particularly proud of his status as poet, and claimed kinship with Vuk Karadžić through their common Montenegrin origins (Robert Hudson, personal communication) – minor and exiguous though the status and kinship actually were.
4 Homepage <http://www.ifbosna.org.ba:92/>, accessed April 22, 2002.
5 The *tamni vilajet* is the folk-tale land of the dead. Its balkanist image, implying mayhem as mystically endemic to the region, was often used by nationalists to deter foreign intervention and conceal the fact that such mayhem was a deliberate tool of their policies. The writer Dževad Karahasan, however, has powerfully pointed out – in the TV panel discussion "Angažiranje i umjetnost (Engagement and art)," Sarajevo Studio 99, October 1st 2001 – that the primordial chaos of the *tamui vilajet* was the raw material from which the world was created. Thus the image can equally well construct the region's complexities and diversities as a source of creative power.
6 As the only poem ("Doppelgänger") by Radovan Karadžić included in a pre-war anthology of contemporary Bosnian poetry, it was presumably one of his best. Here is my translation in full:

> I'm waiting for you beside the church.
> The old bells are mute.
> The raindrops beat into my silence.
> Then a beggar passed by.
> Like a soul back from Lethe.
> Neither man nor child. But he
> Resembled me.
>
> Despite this,
> In his pocket, nothing else to give.
> Except a pencil to write this.
>
> Then that vanished too.
> And he passed on.
> Resembling me to a tee.
>
> And you left with him.
> Splashes of rain lave
> My eyes.
> And peace slams down
> On my darkness,
> Like a stone on a grave.

References

AGEE, C. (ed.) (1998): *Scar on the Stone: Contemporary Poetry from Bosnia*, Newcastle, Bloodaxe.

ALI, R. and L. LIFSCHUTZ (eds.) (1993): *Why Bosnia? Writings on the Balkan War*, Stony Creek, CT, Pamphleteer's Press.

ALLÉN, S. (1999): *Translation of Poetry and Poetic Prose*, Proceedings of Nobel Symposium 110, Singapore/New York/London, World Scientific.

BAILEY, F. G. (1970): *Stratagems and Spoils: A Social Anthropology of Politics*, Oxford, Blackwell.

BANAC, I. (forthcoming): "The Weight of False History," in LOVRENOVIĆ, I. and F. R. JONES (eds.), *Reconstruction and Deconstruction*, Special issue of Forum Bosnae.

BERMAN, A. (2000): "Translation and Trials of the Foreign," Source text first published 1985, Translated by Lawrence Venuti, in VENUTI, L. (ed.), *The Translation Studies Reader*, London, Routledge, p. 284–297.

BEYLARD-OZEROFF, A., KRÁLOVÁ, J. and B. MOSER-MERCER (eds.) (1998): "Translators' Strategies and Creativity," Benjamins Translation Library 27, Amsterdam, Benjamins.

BOASE-BEIER, J. and M. HOLMAN (1999): "Introduction: Writing, Rewriting and Translation: Through Constraint to Creativity," in BOASE-BEIER, J. and M. HOLMAN (eds.), *The Practices of Literary Translation*, Manchester, St. Jerome.

BOLD, A. (year unknown): *Triumph of a rough beast.* Review of Collected Poems, by Vasko Popa, Anvil Press, Glasgow HeraldPage and date unknown.

BOSNEVIĆ, O. (1993): *The Road to Manjaća*, Translated by Francis R. Jones, In Rabia Ali and Lawrence Lifschutz, eds.: Why Bosnia? Writings on the Balkan War. Stony Creek, CT: Pamphleteer's Press.

BUSH, P. (1998): "Literary Translation" in BAKER, M. (ed.), *Routledge Encyclopaedia of Translation Studies*, London, Routledge.

BUTUROVIĆ, A. (2002): *Stone Speaker: Medieval Tombs, Landscape and Bosnian Identity in the Poetry of Mak Dizdar*, New York, Palgrave.

CAMPBELL, D. (1998): *National Deconstruction: Violence, Identity and Justice in Bosnia*, Minneapolis, University of Minnesota Press.

CARR, S., R. ROBERTS, DUFOUR, A. and D. STEYN (eds.). (1997): *The Critical Link: Interpreters in the Community*, Amsterdam, Benjamins.

CHANG, N. F. (2000): "Towards a Macro-Polysystem Hypothesis," *Perspectives: Studies in Translatology* 8–2, p. 109–123.

CIGAR, N. (1998): "Paradigms and U.S. policymaking for Bosnia (1992–1995)," Paper presented at the International Forum Conference on the Bosnian Paradigm, Sarajevo.

CIGAR, N. (2001): *Vojislav Koštunica and Serbia's Future*, London, Saqi, The Bosnian Institute.

COHEN, R. (1998): *Hearts Grown Brutal: Sagas of Sarajevo*, New York, Random House.

DAVIS, K. (2001): *Deconstruction and Translation, Translation Theories Explained*, Manchester, St. Jerome.

DIZDAR, M. (1999): *Kaineni spavač / Stone Sleeper*, Translated by Francis R. Jones. With Afterwords by Rusmir Mahmutćehajić and Francis R. Jones, and graphics by Dževad Hozo, Source text originally published 1973, Sarajevo, Kuća bosanska.

GOFFMAN, E. (1970): *Strategic interaction*, Oxford, Blackwell.

GOFFMAN, E. (1971): *The Presentation of Self in Everyday* Life, First published 1959, Harmondsworth, Penguin.

HERMANS, T. (1999): "Translation in Systems: Descriptive and System-Oriented Approaches Explained," *Translation Theories Explained*, Manchester, St. Jerome.

HOLLIDAY, A. (2002): *Writing and Doing Qualitative Research*, London, Sage.

JONES, F. R. (1994): "Poems by Ivan V. Lalić and Drago Štambuk," Contemporary Criticism 16, p. 105–125.

JONES, F. R. (2000): "The Poet and the Ambassador: Communicating Mak Dizdar's Stone Sleeper," *Translation and Literature* 9–1, p. 65–87.

JONES, F. R. (2002): "Translating spiritual space-time: recreating Kameni spava? in English," Appendix, in BUTUROVIĆ, A. (ed.), *Stone Speaker: Medieval Tombs, Landscape and Bosnian Identity in the Poetry of Mak Dizdar*. New York, Palgrave, p. 165–180.

KURSPAHIĆ, N. (1999): *Skoro će i tebi kraj (And Soon it'll be Over with You)*, Biblioteka Novo pismo, Sarajevo, Ljiljan.

LALIĆ, I. V. (1997): *Fading Contact*, Translation of Smetnje na vezama, 1975, Translated by Francis R. Jones, London, Anvil.

LATIĆ, D. (1993): "Bloody morning," Translated by Francis R. Jones, in ALI, R. and L. LIFSCHUTZ (eds.), *Why Bosnia? Writings on the Balkan War*, Stony Creek, CT, Pamphleteer's Press, p. 114–115.

LEFEVERE, A. (1998): "Acculturating Bertolt Brecht," in BASSNETT, S. and A. LEFEVERE (eds.), *Constructing Cultures: Essays on Literary Translation*. Clevedon, Multilingual Matters, p. 109–122.

LOVRENOVIĆ, I. (forthcoming): "The Voices of Sarajevo's Night," Translated by Maja Lovrenovi? and Robert Hudson, in LOVRENOVIĆ, I. and F. R. JONES (eds.), *Reconstruction and Deconstruction*, Special issue of Forum Bosnae.

LOVRENOVIĆ, I. and F. R. JONES (eds.) (2001): *Life at the Crossroads*, Special issue of Forum Bosnae 11.

MAHMUTĆEHAJIĆ, R. (1996): *Living Bosnia*, Translation of Živa Bosna, Translated by Slovenka Beus and Francis R. Jones, Ljubljana, Oslobodjenje International.

MIOČINOVIĆ, M. (in press): The Pluriform South Slav Identity: Controversy and Destruction, in LOVRENOVIĆ, I. and F. R. JONES (eds.), *Reconstruction and Deconstruction*, Special issue of Forum Bosnae.

MUNDAY, J. (2001): *Introducing Translation Studies: Theories and Applications*, London, Routledge.

POPA, V. (1973): *Uspravna zemlja (Earth Erect)*, Belgrade, Nolit.

POPA, V. (1980): *Vučja so (Wolf Salt)*, Belgrade, Nolit.

POPA, V. (1997): *Collected Poems*, Translated by Anne Pennington, revised and expanded by Francis R. Jones, with introduction by Ted Hughes, London, Anvil.

PYM, A. (1997): "Pour une Éthique du Traducteur," *Pédagogie de la Traduction*, Artois / Ottawa, Artois Presses Université / Presses de l'Université d'Ottawa.

SCOLLON, S. and R. SCOLLON (1983): *Face in interethnic communication*, in RICHARDS, J. C. and R. SCHMIDT (eds.), *Language and Communication*, London, Longman.

SILBER, L. and A. LITTLE (1997): *Yugoslavia: Death of a Nation*, New York, Penguin.

SLAPŠAK, S. (ed.) (1997): *Women's Literature and Culture*, Special issue of Pro Femina.

ŠAMIĆ, J. (1986): *Iz biljež aka Babur-š aha (From the Notes of Babur Shah)*, Sarajevo, Svjetlost.

TODOROVA, M. (1997): *Imagining the Balkans*, New York, Oxford University Press.

TOURY, G. (2000): "The Nature and Role of Norms in Translation," Revised version of 1978 article, VENUTI, L. (ed.), *The Translation Studies Reader*, London, Routledge, p. 198–211.

VENUTI, L. (1995): *The Translator's Invisibility: A History of Translation*, London, Routledge.

VENUTI, L. (1998): *The Scandals of Translation*, London, Routledge.

VON FLOTOW, L. (1997): "Translation and Gender: Translating in the 'Era of Feminism.'" *Translation Theories Explained*, Manchester, St. Jerome.

WACHTEL, A. B. (1998): "Making a Nation, Breaking a Nation: Literature and Cultural Politics in Yugoslavia," *Cultural Memory in the Present*, Stanford, CA, Stanford University Press.

WADENSIÖ, C. (1998): *Interpreting as Interaction*, London, Longman.

WOODWARD, S. L. (1995): *Balkan Tragedy: Chaos and Dissolution after the Cold War*, Washington, DC, The Brookings Institution.

YOUNG, H. (2002): *It's Sick to Ignore our Part in the Making of Milosevic*, Guardian, London, <http://www.guardian.co.uk/Archive/Article/0,4273,4355675,00.html>, accessed February 20, 2002.

ZAUBERGA, I. (2000): *Rethinking Power Relations in Translation*, Across Languages and Cultures 1-1, p. 49–56.

THE GIFT OF LANGUAGES

Towards a philosophy of translation

Domenico Jervolino

Source: 'Il dono delle lingue: per una filosofia della traduzione'; unpublished paper (2009); translated by Angelo Bottone.

This paper introduces a number of fundamental topics in my research, which is oriented towards a philosophy of translation inspired by the phenomenological-hermeneutical thinking of Paul Ricoeur, my teacher and friend, who passed away on 20 May 2005. It is to his memory that I wish to pay homage here.

1. Language and diversity of languages

Contemporary philosophy has in many ways acknowledged the central role of language. Language is the living discourse within which both man's capability of saying and the possibility that things are spoken about are realized.

In its broader sense, language is therefore the reciprocal disclosure of man and world. From the perspective of a phenomenological hermeneutics, language is the first prerequisite of any form of interpretation, since only what is linguistically mediated can be interpreted. This should not be understood to mean that linguistic expressions are the sole object of interpreting or that interpreting is restricted to the sphere of language: language, in the latter case, would become a sort of cage. That which is mediated linguistically is anything that language allows us to say something about, that is, everything that is other-than-language, that which is talked about, listened to, written or read ... What is at stake in interpretation is precisely this other-than-language; one can further characterize it as the totality of 'things' or phenomena that surround us and that manifest themselves in our experience of life. Among these things are our own selves and others: those others to whom we speak and about whom we speak. Language is thus the inauguration of a meaningful life, and we may rightly consider it as a *lumen naturale* which enlightens each individual who comes into this world and is responsible for making every phenomenon visible to the world.

But language does not exist outside a plurality of historical languages, and this plurality seems tantamount, *prima facie*, to disempowerment and inevitable fragmentation. Thousands of languages, dead languages as well as living ones, and among the dead languages those that disappeared leaving no trace of their existence. In this hiatus between the unity of language and the plurality of languages, translation becomes a philosophical question.

Only recently, in proportion to the long cycles of history, and more precisely since the 1940s, have the practice and the study of translation become a field of research for a large range of disciplines, a field which has variably designated itself as 'the theory of translation', *traductologie* (in French), 'the science of translation' or, more cautiously, in English, 'translation studies'. The lack of agreement on its name clearly suggests the existence of different approaches, as well as disciplines (linguistics, semiotics, cognitive science, literary theory, poetics, hermeneutics, . . .): instead of a single discipline, the field seems to delineate an interdisciplinary area of study. In any case, there is growing awareness of the importance of the phenomenon of translation and the need for engaging with it theoretically. Given that my interest in this phenomenon proceeds from the perspective of hermeneutics and hermeneutical phenomenology, and since translation, in its various forms, is unquestionably a 'hermeneutic practice', my working hypothesis is that thinking about this practice is productive not only for understanding translation itself, but also for achieving a deeper understanding of the meaning of interpretation and of phenomenology.

From the methodological perspective within which I place myself, there is no gift of the phenomenon except in the gift of language, nor any gift of language outside the diversity of languages. Humboldt had already paid attention to this diversity at the beginning of the nineteenth century, as well as to the 'family resemblance' that pertains among languages – since every language is already identified as a language, when considered as a whole and within their dialectical tension languages constitute the presuppositions that inform the work of translation. Language, languages and translation therefore enter into the very heart of the constitution of sense.

The diversity of languages has long been considered an obstacle, a difficulty, even a damnation or a curse, in that it obstructs the unity of human discourse and free communication among men. This is the most common interpretation of the myth of Babel. But a more accurate and modern exegesis has seen instead, in the divine intervention depicted in the myth, the sanction given to a plurality that is essential to humanity; the titanism of the planned tower being more consistent with the idea, also recurrent in the history of linguistic thinking, of a unique and uniform language. The destruction of the Babel project could therefore be interpreted as a blessing rather than a curse.[1] The benediction of Babel, read in this way, would

26

prefigure the Pentecostal gift of languages – as in the famous passage of the *Acts of Apostles*, which exalts the Utopia of a transparent communication among speakers of different languages – and this is similar to an achieved synthesis between the universal and the particular.

Nevertheless, if this synthesis is considered in terms that are congruent with the finite nature of humans, it can only be seen as a difficult and always precarious and partial outcome of a practice such as that of translation. Biblical and theological meditation can show the purpose of a reconciled humanity, again unified while preserving its constitutive diversities. Without recourse to a variety of genres, we can postulate some kind of convergence between philosophical and theological or biblical discourse, between this poetical horizon and the ethical dimension that is integral to the difficult task that requires humanity to build itself as one and plural.

I must add that the full complexity of translation becomes clear once translation from one language to another becomes a paradigm of translation in a broader sense, that is, of mutual understanding within the same linguistic community. In this broader sense, to speak is always already to translate, even when one is speaking one's own native language or when one is speaking to oneself.[2] In each case, the encounter with the other cannot be avoided.

The gap between a hypothetical perfect language and the concreteness of a living language is felt again and again in verbal interaction: it is always possible to say the same thing in a different way. Now, to say something in a different way, to say it in other terms, is exactly what a translator does as he or she moves from one language to the other. These two halves of the concept of translation clarify each other and present again the enigma and richness of the relationship with the Other.

2. The gift of languages

The word 'gift' – in its most general meaning, taken from ordinary language – can be used in at least three meanings in our discourse: the first with respect to phenomena or, if you prefer, to life; the second with respect to language, where phenomena manifest themselves as capable of being said; and the third with respect to the plurality of languages, where language itself becomes real.

Language is a gift because we find ourselves alive, open to the appearance of the world (in other words, able to grasp it). It is a gift because phenomena appear capable of being said, in that they are already said and can be expressed in a different way. It is a gift because they appear in their capacity to be said in many languages that we can understand; they reveal themselves in their possibility, even in their effectiveness, which we can only very partially achieve, starting from our own language, which was given to us for free.

I believe we can talk of a 'gift' in all three of these cases, just as we can say that life is a gift. This comment can be further specified and deepened – it implies in all forms, even in the most ordinary use of the term, the notions of gratuity, of passivity, of receptivity.

If the giving of phenomena can never disregard language, this does not mean one should limit oneself to the characteristics and peculiarity of every language; it means realizing that language expresses experience and that all languages, even though they are different, have the power to translate one into the other. This is therefore not a pure phenomenology but a hermeneutical phenomenology, a linguistic phenomenology that interprets the gift and the giving. These three forms of giving – life, language and languages – refer one to the other and sustain themselves reciprocally. I think it is important to stress that the third form presupposes and clarifies the former two: the gift of life (which is the essential openness to the world as phenomenon, as it appears to us) and the gift of language as a *logos*, thanks to which we are living beings with the capacity of speech. In the gift of the mother tongue these two aspects (to have a world and to have the ability to describe it) converge, but our being within a world which is common to all talking beings is also implicit, thanks to the fact that every different 'tongue' belongs to the universe of language and thanks to the translatability, in principle, of all languages. The mother tongue, in this case, does not close us into an exclusive ethnic belonging but opens us, in principle, to the whole of humanity.

3. Translation and the plural unity of human discourse

Here are a number of topics relating to the linguistic and anthropological problem of translation within the context of an open philosophical debate: language as an inescapable characteristic of the finite and bodily condition of man, the constitution of sense in the phenomenon–language relationship, the tension between universality and finitude that comes out of this constitutive duality of what is human, and, finally, translation as a moment in which it is possible to dissipate that tension and as a paradigm of the different forms of interaction and communication among people.

In this way, translation becomes a privileged moment of a reconstruction of the plural unity of human discourse that opens the way to *an ethics of hospitality and of conviviality*. The gift of language and of languages becomes a paradigm of gratuity that corrects the contemporary obsession with the general commodification of lifeworlds and that offers us a glimpse of a possible basis for the social bond, from a perspective of solidarity and of solicitude towards others.

Translation, thus, is also an ethical challenge. The modern Self is bound more closely than one might like to admit to the violent encounter with the Other outside Europe. These encounters, including the discovery and conquest of other continents, confront us with problems of translation in its most tragic meaning. We remember that the year 1492 was both the year in which the Americas were discovered (and their conquest was begun), and the year in which Granada was conquered (completing the Christian *Reconquista* of Spain) and the Jews were expelled, signifying the expulsion from the European self – or at least the identity of a certain part of Europe – of the 'other': one specific 'other', however, that remains silently present despite its absence.

Five centuries later, in the context of globalization and where great opportunities but also great dangers and suffering for the whole of humanity come to the fore, today, more than ever, we need a 'strong thought' to sustain this commitment and direct this research. One thorny issue is finding a radical alternative to violence, which dominant ideology and political practice have too often considered to be an obligatory route. This has been the case even for those who oppose the current social system. Such an alternative cannot remain a mere aspiration for people of good will but must have a theoretical foundation and be borne out in praxis.

There is no denying that a view that is limited to describing reality can find a thousand reasons to reaffirm the sad knowledge that *homo homini lupus* (man is a wolf to man). However, must this man, who is naturally aggressive against other men, be ruled by the iron fist of a hard and terrible power such as the mythical Leviathan? And the discordant voices, which reply with the ancient poet Terentius: *homo homini deus* (man is a god to man), do they belong only to the poetic imagination, or may they also inspire the practical wisdom that guides actions in everyday life? And may they also inspire that form of action that enacts the reasoned methods of self-government by which human beings manage their own lives and which we call politics?

4. Reciprocal recognition as a basis for the social bond

The modern paradigm of politics, grounded in the idea that the concentration of power in the hands of the sovereign can generate *de malo bonum* (the collective advantage of peace, security and social order), must today be called into question. This paradigm seems unable to fulfil the needs of humanity in the age of globalization.

The challenge, instead, is to think of a non-violent basis for the social bond. Following *Parcours de la reconnaissance* (2004), one of Ricoeur's last works, the idea of linking the great Hegelian theme of the struggle for recognition of subjects to that of the economy of the gift seems to me to be potentially seminal. The struggle among subjects does not necessarily fall within an irreducible aggressiveness; from the conflict a reciprocal recognition can arise.

This Hegelian theme is well known (it is the famous theme of the dialectic of master and slave in the 1807 *Phenomenology of the Spirit*). The master needs the slave and depends on him to satisfy his need, so that at the end there is no difference between the two consciousnesses. Thus, in the *Phenomenology*, which is a sort of philosophical novel, Hegel decides to move to a discussion of Stoicism. In Stoicism the emperor and the slave are both philosophers, they both say 'we think'. However, this lack of differentiation between the two blurs reality; so Hegel then moves from Stoicism to scepticism. This way of thinking is fascinating for the resources of intelligence Hegel draws upon, but its weakness is that it not only remains confined within a dialectic of mere ideal figures, but also leads to a kind of cul-de-sac – according to the Hegelian language – to a kind of endless claiming, an *unhappy conscience* that is never satisfied and looks for without ever finding itself.

The search for identity and recognition is inescapable, but the conflict between subjectivities is not the end of the matter. Reciprocal recognition can be sought somewhere else, in the gift. In fact, as the extensive literature of anthropological studies has made evident, starting with Marcel Mauss, in primitive societies the gift and its return generate a complex net of social relationships. Why must the gift be returned? The anthropologists' answer is that the gift symbolizes a magic power that has to be circulated. This is an insufficient answer that would condemn discourse on the gift to remaining in the sphere of pre-modernity. What must be sought, instead, is a non-magical sense of the gift, which is neither more nor less than reciprocal recognition. I give a gift because I give something of myself and I expect to be recognized by the one I give my gift to. The gift is still a symbol, but not in a magical sense; rather it is a symbol of a humanity that is expressed in the other and myself, in our reciprocal relationship.

The exemplary gift is then one that has no price – like Socrates, who, unlike the Sophists, used to teach for free the truth that has no price. In other words, we could say that it is what belongs to the group of *common goods* of humanity, which do not belong only to the physical order (for example the water we drink or the air we breathe, more generally the environment that constitutes the basis – threatened today – of a 'good life' on the planet earth, and the basis of essential and non-commodifiable rights like health, for ourselves and future generations), but also to the moral order, like truth and language.

5. Mother tongue and linguistic hospitality

We could then also say that what constitutes the social bond is the gift *of languages* that allows us to become part of the human consortium in the twofold form of the gift of the mother tongue and the reciprocal gift of languages (these two forms are strangers each to the other) – a gift that becomes real through *translation*, thanks to the practice of *linguistic hospitality*.

30

It is an original *gift*, in that it is given for free, before any social contract, the moment we enter into human existence: it is evident that to establish a contract we need to understand each other. We are talking here of something that comes first in a transcendental sense, as an *a priori* condition of possibility. This coming first does not imply a naïve view of cohabitation but, rather, clashes with the painful fact of violence and domination, and in its coming first affirms an equal share of dignity – in principle – for all human beings, offering a basis for the possibility that speech can oppose violence and domination. This coming first does not deny conflict, nor does it aim to eliminate it; its ambition – which is lofty and simple at the same time, without guaranteeing success but being morally necessary to cultivate a hope for a sense of human cohabitation – is to allow the conflicts of life to be dealt with non-violently. It is to *oppose*, using an expression that evokes Kant, *the radical evil*, which is violence operating in history, and to claim, against this violence, the moral dignity of humans, the humanity of humans as living beings provided with a *logos*.

This original gift is given to us in the form of a mother tongue. The mother tongue is the place where consciousness is born; it is no mere set of instrumental signs. In the mother tongue words embody reality itself; through it the world is born into our conscience. Nevertheless, we cannot stop here. The relationship between consciousness and language, the same metaphor of language as a *verbal body* of thought used by Husserl and the French existential phenomenology of language, allows us to go deeper.

In fact, we *are and we are not* our body, we conform to our mother tongue, but at the same time it has its own relative autonomy. Language is placed between the world and us, with everything that this implies, i.e. to say and not to say, the possibility of equivocation and deception, a world of implicit or hidden meanings that need to be reactivated and rediscovered. This *ambiguity* of language, which has its roots in our mother tongue, makes it possible for us – who are born to the world thanks to it – to also stand back from it. We always can and have to distance ourselves. Our consciousness of the world, and of ourselves, is not only a given but has to be reconquered. There is a space here, I think, for the work of interpretation but also for an ethic of responding to the gift we have received.

The mother tongue, which is my verbal body, does not shut me in. Rather, it opens me to other languages, to humanity and to history. Here we find a justification for translation, one that a unilateral emphasis on the mother tongue would risk making impossible.

At the same time I think we should shun any 'mystical' conception of language. It is not language that talks in us; man talks. In the Christian conception of Incarnation (*Verbum caro factum est*) we find again the strongest expression of the radical humanity of language. Language throws us outside ourselves; in some sense it forces us to lose ourselves, living the experience of estrangement in order to find an authentic relationship with reality and alterity. Thus, our words really become the route to hope.[3]

The free gift of language and of languages that permits us to have access to the world and to meet the other, thereby completely fulfilling ourselves, directly corresponds to the debt of expressing and developing our humanity within and through language.

6. Translation and the renewal of the phenomenological method

On the basis of the considerations I have outlined here, I think we can affirm that translation helps us to reconsider the phenomenological method.

According to Ricoeur, the three fundamental theses of phenomenology are:[4]

1 Meaning is the most comprehensive category of phenomenological description.
2 The subject is the bearer of meaning.
3 Reduction is the philosophical act which permits the birth of a being for meaning.

These three theses, as presented above, are listed in the order of their discovery. If we read them in the opposite order, they follow the order of their founding.

My hypothesis is that all three of these theses can be clarified when we test them against the diversity of languages and against translation.

Let us start from the third one, reduction: if we consider that every language is like a world, then to reduce or distance ourselves from a language, methodologically neutralizing it, is exactly what happens when we deal with a foreign language (and with every other language considered as a language of otherness). Explained in these terms, reduction loses its potential as a fantastic and impossible operation of exiting the world. It becomes possible and necessary to reach that particular level that enables understanding among different people. It thus becomes possible to reach that transcendental humanity that is the basis for people speaking a language in which they were born to consciousness, as well as for being able to understand other human beings speaking different languages.

This has clear implications for the conception of the subject that is always embodied in a world through the mediation of a language; but all particular worlds eventually belong to a common world, and our subjectivity exists in the communion with all the real and possible subjects, recognized in their essential and peculiar identity.

The subject of a hermeneutical phenomenology is never an isolated ego but is the self, as a contingent, finite, bodily being that coincides with our concrete condition as suffering and acting human beings. We are required to realize ourselves in the praxis of a whole life, in the reciprocity of the intersubjective relationship, and to find a place in the world and in history. The essential core of our life and our search for an identity in which our struggle and desire to live are expressed, which Ricoeur calls the 'original affirmation', must then undergo an enormous and never final process of translation and translations, of all sorts, which is tantamount to the telling of our own stories, with the infinite web of our actions and passions, with the work of mourning and memory that such an undertaking requires, with its always renewed challenges and the joy that it can bestow on us.

Finally, meaning is neither the will to say, belonging to a subject without relationships, nor the access to a world of separate essences. It is, on the contrary, the space opened up by translation in order to compare and allow our perspectives on the world to be communicated.

In this way a phenomenological hermeneutics of translation can help us to realize that humanity, just like language, exists only in the plural mode.

Notes

The original Italian title of this paper is *Il dono delle lingue. Per una filosofia della traduzione.* It was presented, in English translation, at the 2nd Meeting of the OPO (Organization of Phenomenological Organizations), 15–20 August 2005, in Lima, Peru.

1 See François Marty, *La Bénédiction de Babel. Vérité et communication*, Cerf, Paris, 1990.
2 Examination of the problems of translation quickly reveals that *traductio dicitur multipliciter* (translation is said in many ways). Awareness of this multiplicity of senses emerges from several sources. One of these sources is certainly Roman Jakobson's distinction between intralinguistic, interlinguistic and intersemiotic translation : cf. Roman Jakobson, *On Linguistic Aspects of Translation*, in R. Brower (ed.), *On Translation*, Harvard University Press, Cambridge (Mass.) 1959, pp. 232–239. We must also remember the emphasis that George Steiner placed on translation in a broader sense: cf. *After Babel. Aspects of Language and Translation*, Oxford University Press, Oxford and New York 1975, 1998 (third edition). Italian students of hermeneutics know that the distinction between the broad and narrow senses of translation was not ignored by scholars like Emilio Betti, whose principal sources for questions related to the concepts of language and translation are Humboldt and Schleiermacher. Cf. Emilio Betti, *Teoria generale della interpretazione*, edited, corrected and enlarged by G. Crifò, Giuffré, Milano 1990, vol. II, pp. 660–694.
3 I refer here to Plato, *Philebus* 40a, quoted by Pierre Thévenaz in his *L'Homme et sa raison*, La Baconnière, Neuchâtel 1956, vol. II, p. 72. Thévenaz is a virtually unknown author, a contemporary of Ricoeur, who died prematurely in 1955. In his original version of existential phenomenology, he discusses the subject of language as a 'verbal body'. See my volume *Pierre Thévenaz e la filosofia senza assoluto*, Studium, Rome 2003.
4 Cf. Paul Ricoeur, *Le Conflit des interprétations*, Seuil, Paris 1969, pp. 242–257. (English trans., Northwestern University Press, Evanston 1974, pp. 246–263. [Tr.])

40

ETHICS OF TRANSLATION

Andrew Chesterman

Source: Mary Snell-Horny, Zuzana Jettmarová and Klaus Kaindl (eds) (1997) *Translation as Intercultural Communication*, Amsterdam: John Benjamins, pp. 147–57.

Traditional discussions of ethics in translation studies have dealt with a rather motley set of questions. These have generally been concerned either with the duties of translators or with their rights. Typical issues have been:

(a) the general concept of loyalty, to the various parties concerned;

(b) the acceptable degree of freedom in the translating process, plus the issue of whether translators have the right or duty to change or correct or improve the original (cf. the ethics debate in the 1994 ITI Proceedings [Picken 1994], and e.g. Robinson 1991);

(c) linked to both these, the argument about the translator's invisibility, understood as an ideal of neutrality or anonymity and recently challenged by many scholars;

(d) whether translators have the right to refuse to translate a text they find "unethical" (a right encoded in codes of translational ethics in some countries);

(e) what rights translators have regarding translations as intellectual property, e.g. compared with the rights of original authors (e.g. Venuti 1995).

(f) There has been some discussion of the translation commissioner's power and ideology in initiating the selection of texts to be translated: see e.g. Lefevere (1992) on patronage. Issues have also been raised concerning the relation between translators and the various authoritative bodies who legislate or otherwise determine the positions to be taken within a given culture concerning the above questions (e.g. Pym 1992).

I propose a rather different view of translation ethics, based not on the concepts of duty or right but on that of value. Both duties and rights are secondary notions: they depend on notions of value, which are therefore primary. The framework I shall describe governs actual translation action after the point when a translator has agreed to do a translation. That is, it excludes issue (d) above, which I take to be more a matter of personal ethics generally, not translation ethics in particular. The framework also excludes issue (e), which comes into play after a translation has been submitted. And also excluded are commissioner's ethics (cf. issue (f) above), and the wider questions of cultural dominance and subservience. True, commissioner and translator may sometimes coincide in the same person; yet in this case we can still distinguish between the initiator's ethics of text selection and the translator's ethics governing the act of translation itself. For convenience, I shall include "team of translators" under the singular term "translator"; I shall not therefore discuss here the additional ethical issues of cooperative translation by committee.

My starting point is in deontic logic, that branch of philosophy that deals with normative concepts. Translation studies since Toury (1980, and most recently 1995) has been increasingly interested in norms and in applications of the theory of action, and the approach to an ethics of responsibility which I shall outline below fits in well with current concerns in translation theory.

Deontic logic makes a basic distinction between three levels of concepts: *praxeological* concepts (concepts such as choice, decision, desire, freedom, will, that have to do directly with actions); *normative* concepts (norms); and *axiological* concepts (values). Deontic actions (those the agent feels "ought" to be done) are governed by norms, and norms themselves are governed by values. A norm, after all, is accepted as a norm because it embodies or manifests or tends towards some value. Values are thus examples of regulative ideas.

Actions have to do with changes in states of affairs. An action may either be *productive*, in that it brings about such a change; or it may be *preventive*, in that it prevents the occurrence of a change that would otherwise have taken place. (For a formalized presentation of these and other deontic points, see e.g. von Wright 1968.) Corresponding to these two classes of action there are also two classes of non-action (i.e. of omission or forbearance): *leaving* a state unchanged (no productive action), and *letting* a change take place (no preventive action).

An analysis of the concept of change can be based on three elements: (a) the initial state of affairs, before any action A; (b) the end state, after A has taken place; (c) the hypothetical state, which would have prevailed if A had not taken place.

A translator (or team of translators, *passim*) is someone who effects changes of certain kinds in certain slates of affairs, a decision-making agent. The translator's task at every decision point is simply to make a comparison between two states: the predicted end state (or: the most likely end state) resulting from A and the hypothetical state resulting from not-A, and act according to the result of this comparison. This comparison is a *value judgement*: of two states, which comes closest to manifesting or promoting a given value or values? Deontic logic accepts that such judgements are not automatic, and not universal either: every deciding agent is a unique human being in a unique personal life-situation with a unique state of knowledge and cognition, with a unique personal history. Norms may be shared by a community, a profession or a culture; so may their underlying values; but the understanding and application of these norms and values in decision-making is inescapably individual. In Gadamerian terms, we could say that this deontic logic recognizes not only the influence of the constraint of tradition, but also that every individual has a personal horizon. Decisions (such as translation decisions) are not made in a void, but in a particular life-situation. (Hence, of course, no two translations of a given text need ever be the same: cf. Quine [1960] and the indeterminacy argument.)

So: what are the values underlying translation decisions? In deontic logic, values are concepts that govern and underlie norms. The suggestion I shall put forward is built on the analysis of translation norms I have proposed elsewhere (Chesterman 1993). Assume first that translation activity is governed by four fundamental kinds of norms:

(a) *Expectancy norms*: a translator should translate in such a way as to conform to readership expectations about the translation product. Being thus product norms, expectancy norms are logically prior to the three process norms that follow; the point of process norms, after all, is to guarantee that the quality of the outcome of a process meets people's expectations.
(b) The *relation norm*: a translator should act in such a way that an appropriate relation is established and maintained between the source text and the target text.
(c) The *communication norm*: a translator should act in such a way as to optimize communication, as required by the situation, between all the parties involved.
(d) The *accountability norm*: a translator should act in such a way as to be accountable to all the parties involved.

I suggest that each of these norms is governed by a primary ethical value; "primary", because there is some obvious overlap between the values, and because the correspondences between norms and values are not absolute but relative. The correspondences nevertheless seem striking enough to be worth noting, and may at least provoke further thought.

Clarity

Expectancy norms are primarily governed by the value of *clarity*. This is of course an old rhetorical value, and not special to translation as such. Recall the Gricean maxim of manner, and Leech's "Clarity Principle" (1983). Popper ([1945] 1962:307f.) takes clarity to be the basic value of any linguistic communication, since without it rational communication in social life becomes impossible. By this token, clarity is a genuine ethical principle, not just a linguistic one.

True, clarity can of course be interpreted differently in different cultures; and postmodernists may be suspicious of the concept's desirability, or even of its possibility. Yet I will stick my neck out and claim that clarity will survive as an ethical linguistic value long after the postmodernist textual anarchists are dead and buried. It could be argued that one aspect of clarity is aesthetic, and that beauty and clarity are closely related, but I will not pursue this point here. Another related concept is that of relevance: clients or recipients of a translation certainly expect a translation to be done in such a way that the resultant text is relevant to their needs or expectations. Relevance, however, is more a technical value than an ethical one; as a technical value, it pertains both to the expectancy norms and to the relation and communication norms: recall the wordings "an *appropriate* relation" and "as required by the situation" in the definitions for the relation and communication norms, above — the notion of relevance is already inherent there.

In terms of productive action, the clarity value may justify translation strategies that enhance psycholinguistic processing, such as a choice of iconic vs. non-iconic versions. In terms of preventive action, the clarity value may justify translation strategies that seek to avoid ambiguity or unnecessary obscurity etc. During the editing process, the clarity value is particularly to the fore.

Paradoxically perhaps, the clarity value may also justify the breaking of expectancy norms. Values are prior to norms, after all. And if reader expectations concerning a particular text-type are indeed that the translation will be clumsy, virtually unreadable gobbledygook, then a translator who decides to over-ride these expectations and produces a clear and readable text is breaking this norm for a very good reason: in order to approximate more closely to an underlying value (or values).

Truth

Of my four basic norms, the relation norm is the only one that deals exclusively with translation, for the others are of course relevant to other kinds of communication too. The value behind this norm has traditionally been defined as fidelity or faithfulness or loyalty, and this in turn has usually been interpreted as some kind of equivalence — to the original text, the author's intention, the original effect, etc. However, equivalence itself is then usually defined in terms of identity or sameness, which has meant that the translator is typically bound to fail to achieve it.

I emphasize that the relation norm is a linguistic one, between two texts (not between a person and a text, as suggested by terms like fidelity and loyalty — see below), one of which is some kind of representation of the other. I suggest that the value underlying this relation is that of *truth*. Roughly speaking, we say that something is true if it corresponds to reality. "Truth" in this sense is a quality characterizing a relation between, say, a proposition and a state of affairs. The proposition is not "the same as" the state of affairs it describes, but the relation between the two can nevertheless be a true one, not false. The truth relation has many forms: passport photos bear "a true likeness", a report of an event can be "true", a photocopy can be "a true copy", and so on. Similarly, translations can relate to their originals in many different ways, each of which can be called a "true resemblance" (recall Wittgenstein's family resemblances). A translation will be rejected by the target community (or by the client) if it is not considered to bear any kind of "true" resemblance to the original (or, the text in question will simply not be called a translation).

In deontic logic, the truth relation is perhaps best represented in terms of preventive action. In a given state of affairs, unwanted change must be prevented as far as possible. A relation of some kind must be maintained between the two texts, and it must be one that the receiving culture (the one in which translations are defined as translations) accepts as being "true" in some appropriate way. Whatever the relation is, it must not be false. (Compare the Gricean maxim of quality, that one should forbear from saying what one knows is false.)

Douglas Robinson's provocative book *The translator's turn* (1991) has a long section on translation ethics that has precisely to do with this truth relation. What Robinson is arguing is that there is indeed a vast variety of relations that can validly subsist between a source text and its translation, and that translators should be aware of the full range of possibilities. The point is stressed also by Toury (1995), and in descriptive translation studies generally.

One of Robinson's more extreme examples is that of Jordan's Cotton Patch New Testament, which places the text in the context of the black liberation movement. This translation strategy means that the target text is often what might be called "very free indeed", containing many additions and semantic alterations. But the text has nevertheless been accepted by the target culture as a translation of a kind, and Jordan states his aims and translational principles quite openly. There is thus no theoretical reason why the relation norm should not be met in this way, for the relation between source and target has *de facto* been accepted as *a* possible true one. Mention might also be made here of so-called feminist translations (cf. e.g. Lotbinière-Harwood 1991), which also offer a new understanding of what can constitute a true relation.

The test of the translation pudding is always in the eating, not in some theoretical preconception: to the extent that a translation is accepted by the target community as being valid, the relation it establishes between source and target is *de facto* one possible true one. Such acceptance may of course vary widely across periods, cultures and sub-communities, and even between individual readers. Translators are free to translate how they feel (to paraphrase Robinson); but their professional and financial survival will depend on the degree to which their mode of translating is accepted by their clients and readers, i.e. on the degree to which translators conform to the expected norms. This is also the pragmatic answer to the injunctions of scholars such as Newmark that translators should always neutralize sexist language: yes, in principle one might agree. But if a client nevertheless insists on sexist language, you either have to bite the bullet or simply decline to translate certain texts at all. The path taken will also depend on the status of the translator in question, and on the status of the translator profession in the cultures concerned.

Trust

Clarity is a value pertaining to the quality of a text itself. Truth (here) is a value pertaining to the relation between two texts, source and target. The third value, underlying the accountability norm, pertains to a relation between people: *trust.*

In Steiner's (1975) hermeneutic motion, trust represents the first stage: the translator (or initially the client, in fact) must trust that the original is worth translating. This is followed by aggression (into the source text) and incorporation (of the translation into the target culture), and finally by restitution. This last seems to be the only point at which ethics enters the process: restitution is necessary in order to redress the balance, to balance the books between source and target. However, it is not clear how the translator is to achieve this redressing of the balance: restitution comes across rather as something that simply happens, in that the very fact of translation endows the original text with a greater value. Steiner's translation ethics, and his view of trust, seem unnecessarily narrow.

It is worth comparing the concept of trust with that of loyalty. Loyalty is commonly used in two ways in translation theory: to describe the translator's relation to the original writer or the source text, and also the relation to the target readership (e.g. Nord 1991:29). In our deontic framework, the relation with the source text is governed by the value of truth, which I take to be a quality of the relation between that which represents and that which is represented; in translation, this is an intertextual value. Trust, on the other hand, is an interpersonal value.

One point of difference between trust and loyalty concerns the relative status of the people involved. To be loyal to something or someone is to maintain firm support, friendship or service. Yet this something or someone is often understood to be "higher" than whoever is being loyal: one speaks of being loyal to the king, of an army being loyal to the government, of being loyal to a cause. Loyally is commonly thought of as allegiance, as duty to a liege or master. Its prevalence in translation studies perhaps goes back to the days when the source text and/or its writer were raised on a pedestal above all the other factors involved in translating, with the translator in a servant's role. Trust, on the other hand, describes something more like a relation between equals, and specifically between people. As a translator, I trust that the original writer has something to say that is worth translating (cf. Steiner's point, above); I also trust that the client will pay me; and I trust that my own readers will read my translation in good faith, trusting in turn that there is "something there".

More importantly, whereas loyalty is presented as a requirement of translators alone (not the other parties in the communicative act), trust is a value that must be subscribed to by all parties concerned. The client must trust the translator, and so must the original writer if he or she is present; so must the readers. Without such mutual multidirectional trust, communication fails. In fact, trust is precisely the value which motivates loyal behaviour: one is loyal in order not to lose trust; it is not the case that one trusts in order not to lose loyalty. Trust is therefore the underlying and primary value here.

This is where Pym (1992) makes a central contribution to translational ethics. Taking a sociological perspective, Pym is interested in extending the cope of translation ethics to include broader questions, such as who decides what shall be translated and who validates the norms governing translation action in a particular culture; who accredits licensed translators, for instance? Pym's basic argument is that translators have a higher loyalty than to source or target organs: the whole accountability of professional translators is grounded in the profession itself, in other professionals. Translators check each other's work, drawing on past translations for guidance. They derive their norms from the existing professional context, but the profession itself is not bound to a particular culture. Like the international scientific community, translators are a community that survives via its own system of checks and balances: we validate each other. In Pym's words: "Translators' prime loyalty must be to their profession as an intercultural space" (1992:166).

If we then ask why a translator must be accountable in the first place to the profession, the answer is of course trust. Trust is the glue that holds the system together. Translators, in order to survive, must be trusted as translators. They will be trusted (a) if the profession is trusted, (b) if they are deemed to be *bona fide* members of the profession, and (c) if they have done nothing to forfeit this trust.

Trust is typically lost rather than gained: one's default reaction is to trust someone unless events undermine this. In deontic action theory, then, we can again make use of the concept of preventive action: we aim to translate in such a way as to prevent a change in the default slate of affairs in which trust exists. Initiation into the profession, perhaps via a special examination or the like (administered usually by other professionals who are presumably trusted in turn both by the profession and by society at large), counts as establishing the trust, and the purpose of the accountability norm is to set a standard so that this trust will be maintained. In other words, we seek to leave the status of trust unchanged, or at least unimpaired.

The value of trust is directly relevant to the translator's visibility. It used to be argued, by some, that the translator should be invisible, a window through which the original could shine unimpeded. But if you accept that trust is one of the fundamental values of translation ethics, visibility often seems more important than invisibility. It goes without saying that a translator's name should always be mentioned, as a minimum degree of visibility; but translator's prefaces to longer literary translations are also valuable, particularly when the translator is seeking to challenge rather than conform to readers' expectations (as in the examples mentioned in the previous section).

Pym associates the importance of loyalty to the profession with the aim of translation as such. The translator profession exists in an intercultural space, and the aim of translation is simply to improve intercultural relations. In terms of the trust value, this could be paraphrased as "creating more trust".

Understanding

The fourth value, underlying the communication norm, is *understanding*. Like the other three, I take this too as an ethical value, particularly in the light of the analysis offered by Ebeling (1971), in which understanding virtually becomes a manifestation of, or metaphor for, love. Like trust, understanding also has to do with relations between people.

Ebeling offers a hermeneutic theory of translation, a theory embedded in what he calls a theological theory of language and centred around the concept of understanding. His starting point is the speaker's right to speak (*Ermächtigung*). For a translator, this means that I start any translation task with the question: do I have the right to translate this? And then: will my readers trust that 1 have the right to translate it? (My client *de facto* does seem to trust me, at least.)

The second element in Ebeling's analysis is responsibility (*Verantwortung*): speakers (translators) are responsible for saying the right word at the right time, and for knowing when to remain silent. A third key concept is the speaker's need to challenge the hearer to understand (*Verstehenszumutung*). And finally there is the understanding itself (*Verständigung*), which is the goal of all communication, the value that makes communication worth attempting: empathy, love.

In terms of action theory, we could say that the goal of a translational action is to produce understanding, to effect a change of state from non-understanding to understanding. Formulated thus as productive action, this may sound trivial; it also raises queries about the possibility of complete understanding anyway. But a formulation in terms of preventive action allows a more realistic and also more fruitful approach. In terms of preventive action, we seek to promote the value of understanding by reducing or minimizing misunderstanding.

This is refreshingly non-utopian: we acknowledge that misunderstanding cannot be eliminated entirely, that total absolute communication is impossible, that horizons can never fuse completely, only overlap to varying degrees. This approach is in fact an application of Popper's inverse utilitarianism: seek not the way of greatest happiness but that of least suffering. As science proceeds by eliminating false theories, so social advancement is best effected piecemeal, via the gradual elimination of defects, argues Popper (e.g. 1972). As regards the value of understanding, we might extend Popper's view to cover "communicative suffering": a translator would then seek to minimize this, rather than to attain some impossible ideal.

Communicative suffering is of two main types. One is qualitative, having to do with misunderstanding as such, as a consequence of ambiguity, obscurity, confusing style etc.; this brings us back to the value of clarity. The other is quantitative, having to do with the number of "understanders": to reduce misunderstanding in this sense is to increase the number of (potential) receivers of the original message. It is often pointed out that translation automatically extends the potential number of receivers of a message, thereby decreasing quantitative misunderstanding. Nystrand (1992) explores this notion further, with respect to all writers, not just translators.

One corollary of this general argument would be that translators should be aware of whether they are translating for native or also non-native readers of the target text: this may affect their translation strategies, choice of lexis and idiom, etc. To exclude readers, albeit non-native readers, might even be construed as denying them their right to understand.

The four values of clarity, truth, trust and understanding thus suggest a basis for a fairly comprehensive translation ethics. An approach from deontic logic further suggests that it is useful to think of translation not just as productive action but also as preventive action. Deontic logic furthermore offers the possibility of a formalized description, if such is deemed desirable.

Whatever the ethical framework, since translators are, by definition, agents of change, it is instructive to wonder about the values that guide the norms we follow. What right do we have to interfere with the state of the world? What values shall we rank higher than the value of the trees that will be killed for the sake of our texts?

References

Chesterman, Andrew. 1993. From 'is' to 'ought': translation laws, norms and strategies. *Target* 5 (1), 1–20.

Ebeling, Gerhard. 1971. *Einführung in theologische Sprachlehre*. Tübingen: Mohr.

Leech, Geoffrey. 1983. *Principles of pragmatics.* London: Longman.

Lefevere, André. 1992. *Translation, rewriting and the manipulation of literary fame.* London: Routledge.

Lotbinière-Harwood, Susanne de. 1991. *Re-belle et infidèle. La traduction comme pratique de réécriture au feminin / The body bilingual. Translation as a rewriting in the feminine.* Montréal/Toronto: Les éditions du remue-ménage / Women's Press.

Nord, Christiane. 1991. *Text analysis in translation.* Amsterdam / Atlanta, GA.: Rodopi.

Nystrand, Martin. 1992. Social interactionism versus social constructivism: Bakhtin, Rommetveit and the semiotics of written text. In: A. H. Wold (ed.) *The dialogical alternative. Towards a theory of language and mind.* Oslo: Scandinavian University Press, 157–173.

Picken, Catriona (ed.) 1994. *Quality — assurance, management, control* (ITI Conference 7, Proceedings). London: ITI.

Popper, Karl R. [1945] 1962. *The open society.* London: Routledge and Kegan Paul.

Popper, Karl R. 1972. *Objective knowledge. An evolutionary approach.* Oxford: Clarendon Press.

Pym, Anthony. 1992. *Translation and text transfer.* Frankfurt am Main: Lang.

Quine, Willard van O. 1960. *Word and object.* Cambridge, Mass.: MIT Press.

Robinson, Douglas. 1991. *The translator's turn.* Baltimore: Johns Hopkins University Press.

Steiner, George. 1975. *After Babel.* London: Oxford University Press.

Toury, Gideon. 1980. *In search of a theory of translation.* Tel Aviv: Porter Institute.

Toury, Gideon. 1995. *Descriptive translation studies and beyond.* Amsterdam: Benjamins.

Venuti, Lawrence. 1995. Translation, authorship, copyright. *The Translator* 1 (1), 1–24.

von Wright, Georg H. 1968. *An essay in deontic logic and the general theory of action* (Acta Philosophica Fennica 21). Amsterdam: North-Holland.

Part 9

MODES AND STRATEGIES

41

WRITING BETWEEN THE LINES

The language of translation

John Sturrock

Source: *New Literary History* 21(4) (1990): 993–1,013.

A translation is a substituted text which keeps no further company with its source once it has been published; after that it stands alone, patently derivative but a text in its own right. As books, translations differ from original texts only on the title page, where it is advertised that this work is a translation, made from language x by translator y.[1] Its status of translation may or may not be borne in mind by readers as they read. Generally, it is not; readers hope not to be reminded as they go that what they are reading is (only) a translation. The translator whose prose is not sufficiently smooth to pass for indigenous will be faulted, and accused of writing "translationese," which counts against him as a professional failure. In complaining of the awkwardness or "unnatural" phrasing distinctive of "translationese," we take as a premise that in good translation the source must not show through. What follows here is an extended questioning of the soundness of this premise.

Because published translations exist in physical independence of their source, they are only ever collocated with it by rare individuals on rare occasions: when there is a translation prize to be given, perhaps, or when a translated author checks the foreign version of his work for gross infidelity. At most other times, the translator's work is taken on trust, the source from which he has been working having been definitively shelved so far as its new audience is concerned. There are interesting exceptions, however, when the convention of independence is broken and a translation is published in the presence of its source, in order to make metalinguistic points about the technique or the theory of translation. A treatise on translating, for instance, will quote or make up specimen sentences from at least two languages, through the intelligent examination of which degrees of bilingual synonymy or equivalence may be established.

But beyond the banal and fragmentary instances such as manuals of translation provide, more elaborate juxtapositions can be made: in the form of *en face* translations of longer, continuous texts. *En face* translations differ markedly according to whether they are of prose or verse. In the case of prose their use is narrowly illustrative; they are merely fuller, more palatable versions of the textbook, teaching random or recurrent lessons in how best to translate between the languages involved. In their format they tend toward literature inasmuch as they are of complete texts and not broken sentences; but they remain anonymous, the translator himself claiming to be nothing more than a pedagogue or the impersonal conduit through which one language has been turned (has turned itself?) into another.

En face translations of verse are very different. They come in two kinds: translations of verse into prose and of verse into verse. *En face* translations of verse into prose aim at literalism and since literalism is my main theme in this essay I shall for now withhold further reference to them. *En face* translations of verse into verse by no means display the exemplary correspondence with their originals that the modest teacher of prose translation looks for. On the contrary; the translation of verse into verse is undertaken by poets and is therefore a less self-effacing activity than the translation of prose. The poetic translator wishes to identify himself by the virtuosity of his translations, and in order to do that must take the risk of printing the original poems alongside his own versions of them. If we know something of the language he is translating from we can compare the two poems and admire his talent, or not (though the comparison is not made directly between source and version, only indirectly between the translator's version and *our own* hypothetical alternative to it). I have implied that the *en face* translator-poet prints his source out of vanity, in order to prove his skill; in fairness, let me concede that he may also supply it out of guilt, since the peculiarly high standing we accord to poetry as a literary genre means that in translation a greater guilt attaches to the occlusion of a poetic source than of a prose one, so the *en face* format may also be taken as a public confession on the part of the translator that he is engaged on an inescapably damaging literary exercise, and that to print his source is the least he can do if he is to reassure us that originals may be supplanted by their translations but never finally erased.

The *en face* translation is not a *method* of translation, it is merely an unusual format for it. The format will have effects on the translator who adopts it, who knows that he is for once being invigilated and may find this either inspiring or inhibiting, a spur either to pedantry or ostentation. When source and translation are printed together *en face*, the source comes first: that is, it is given the formal precedence of the lefthand page of a spread, whether or not we choose to read it before reading the poet's version on the page opposite. The degree of symmetry between the two texts will depend on whether the translator has attempted to keep to the line lengths, stanza scheme, and so on, of his original, but one might in general say that the facing layout, or confrontation of two typographically distinctive texts, *represents* iconically the act of translation, conceived of as the matching of one text to another. Source and translation are in apposition, but they do not meet or mingle. Between them is the "gutter," or the empty space that runs down the center of any page spread, and this wordless hiatus I shall take also to be valuably representative, of the radical grammatical and semantic divide between any two natural languages. The *en face* format does us then a twofold service, first in bringing the source of a translation back materially into view, and second in enforcing a certain separateness so that we are not tempted rashly to conflate them.

In an *en face* translation, however, finished text confronts finished text; the translation that we are given to read is an end product, it shows no trace of the activity of translation, in the difficult course of which the translator can be assumed to have tried out and abandoned other versions of words and sentences before settling on his final version. The *en face* format represents the achievement of translation, not its process, and in it the translator's fumblings show no more than do those of the author of his source. In this respect source and translation keep their distance from one another too decorously, as if it were no business of the reader to be allowed to see anything of the work which requires to be done in the turning of one text into another. The blank space of the "gutter" is a little too blank.

There is another format for translation which represents it more completely and dramatically as a process: the interlinear format, in which source and translation appear one above the other, a line at a time. This is an exceedingly uncommon format actually to meet with in print. The paired sentences of translation textbooks do not rank as interlinear translations because unless they extend over several lines they have no effect on the eye of interlinearity. Interlinearity requires verse or prose sequences long enough for the format to be appreciated for the typographically eccentric thing it is, with a deeper than usual space inserted between successive lines of print to make room for the translation. Whether the translation appears above or below the source hardly matters, though the "natural" setting for the translation, as coming after the source, would surely be in superscript, like the changes or insertions we make to what we write. But what is important is that the translation should be understood as appearing *between* the lines. We all of us know how to *read* between the lines; the practice of interlinear translation is one of writing between the lines. It might seem that reading and writing between the lines must somehow be alike, but paradoxically they are practices leading in opposite directions. When we "read between the lines" we take what we read in other than a literal sense, in compliance with certain conventions of the language which enable us to decode the text's deliberately "hidden" or secondary meaning; literalism is specifically bypassed. But the whole purpose of "writing between the lines" is, on the contrary, to display literalism, to translate with a rare fidelity to the word-forms of the source; it is translation at its most explicit: "... the more literal translation is seen as more literally a translation," as W. V. Quine aphoristically has it.[2]

It is translation also at its most provisional, for whatever is written or printed *between* the lines on the page, and normally in a different typeface, is not granted the definitive status of what appears *on* the lines. The interlinear translation is asking to be, if not expunged, then certainly transcended before it is held worthy of taking up a dignified position on the line; its subordinate place is in part determined by our ineradicable prejudice against literalism. But whether it be actually realized, in the pages of a book, or whether it remain as a concept, interlinear translation exemplifies the most familiar and deep-rooted model of translation, as a linguistic process divisible into two stages: a first stage in which the translator travels from his source to a "literal" translation of it, and a second stage in which this first, temporary version is suitably edited so as to make a finished, publishable one. This is not an empirical model, in the sense of being descriptive of what must occur in any given act of translation; but it does square with the experience known to translators, of passing from a first, quickly found translation of a word or phrase, deemed to be inadequate because of its literalism or formal proximity to a too-influential original, to a revision judged on reflection to be more "natural." To revert for a moment to the *en face* translation of verse: the two-stage model is perfectly illustrated by the occasional practice of offering *successive* versions of poems in translation, the first made in prose or at best blank verse by a translator without literary ambitions but expert in the foreign language and striving to be literal, the second a finished poem, made by a poet who may not even know the source language but has based himself on the prose "crib," rather as if this were his dictionary. In all such flights from literalism, the translator relegates his source to one more remove from himself, since the revised version of his translation is just that: a revision of what he (or his helper) has already thought of or written down. The translator in fact has shifted his stance, from a source-oriented to a reader-oriented practice of translation, and this is a shift which frequently leads to a remarkable libertarianism among those theorists of the subject who take the reception of a translation to be of more importance than its fidelity. Eugene Nida and Charles Taber, for example, who approach translation from the standpoint of Bible translators engaged in an apostolic endeavor, are so firmly wedded to the two-stage model as to envisage the doctrinally qualified Bible translator producing his literal version and then if need be calling in a "stylist" to "fix it up."[3] This general sequence, of an ultraclose translation being handed over for cosmetic surgery, is one followed daily in publishing houses across the world, where translations are subject to the same editorial procedures as other texts, and are freely "naturalized" with little or no consultation with either their source or their translator. As a way of redirecting the heathen into the paths of a

Protestant godliness Nida and Taber's method may work miracles, but as a general recipe for translation its pragmatism is offensive; it is surprising, what is more, to find it coming from translators who have for their source the peculiarly authoritative word of God, which surely deserves better than to be so casually "fixed up."

But then sustaining the assumption that as a process translation advances beyond an unprintable literalism into a successful literariness is a second assumption: that in the course of this advance the meaning of the source has been preserved intact. The commonest defence of "freedom" in translation has always been that nothing is lost by way of meaning in the revision of the literal version but that something has been gained by way of style. When Nida and Taber and their collaborators "fix up" the scriptures for mission-ary use the word of God is assumed to survive unscathed; it has merely been made more easily intelligible and more appropriate to its new audience than had the translation process been arrested at its more primitive stage. (That "intelligibility" is a virtue Nida takes for granted; he is a modernist in these matters, who would have the Bible sound as unambiguous as is compatible with its unusual textual prestige.)

Traditionally, the arguments against literalism in translation have been far more vigorous and effective than those which find for literalism. It is only in the later twentieth century, with the intrusion into the theory of translation of philosophers of language, that literalism has acquired a new standing, not as yet as a characteristic considered to be desirable in the translator's finished product, but as a uniquely revealing index to the prob-lematic nature of translation itself. The translator who is adjudged a literalist remains an incompetent, just like the computers with which experiments in translation have been going on for many years and around which there has grown up a corpus of contemptuous anecdotes, all of them celebrating the machines' inability to disambiguate and hence to avoid grotesque "literalisms" that a human translator would intuitively reject. But the literary world's easy confusion of literalism with a presumptuous machine's failure to dis-tinguish between homonyms is one more sign of the prejudice against it as a mode of translation.

It is essential, in fact, to step outside any merely literary context when starting to theorize about translation, since literary translation has a vested interest in ignoring the philosophical problems that underlie its practice. The high service which the interlinear format does us is to complicate matters, by drawing our attention to the between-ness of any act of trans-lation and by denying us the illusion of its immediacy; translation *is* a process, even though not one that should be so simplistically divided as it has been into the two distinct, hierarchical stages of literalism and fluency. For an example of interlinear translation in use I go to the academic dis-cipline that has done more than any other in recent years to fix attention on the question of translation: to ethnography. In some quarters ethnography has come to be seen as specifically concerned, no longer with the disingenuous description of other cultures, but with their "translation" into a form comprehensible to ourselves.[4] An explicit "translation" of an alien society's customs, rites, and beliefs is no longer mistakeable for the "real" thing, it is a version or account of another culture familiarized for us through the agency of a translator, himself now more fully sensitive to his own inescapable ethnocentrism.

Or perhaps we should say glotto-centrism, because what is at stake here is ethnography's dependence for its data on linguistic contact between the ethnographer and those users of the local language picked out as his "informants." It is paradoxical that a discipline which has done so much to increase knowledge in the West of the world's languages and their structure should so often have presented its findings about other societies and cultures without any serious analysis of the means by which these had been gathered. Informants must inform and do so either in their own language or in that of the visiting ethnographer or in whatever third, common tongue is available to the two parties. Ethnography as published hinges on the fullness, intelligibility, and truthfulness of a whole series of verbal exchanges in the course of which the ethnographer is initiated into a language not his own. When the time comes for this process to be reversed, and for his enquiries to be reformulated as a "translation," the ethnographer cannot be granted the same degree of license in respect of his source as we grant to literary translators; his professional name is to be made otherwise than the poet's, by the closest conceivable approximation to the source rather than by florid departures from it. Here then is the best imaginable setting in which to look more closely at. the actual process of translation.

Happily, one of the great masters of twentieth-century ethnography was unusually conscious of the language problem: Bronislaw Malinowski. Malinowski was himself a Pole who had had to learn to speak and to write in English, no bad preparation for his work in the Trobriand Islands. In the second, theoretical volume of his study called *Coral Gardens and their Magic* he makes good use of the interlinear model of translation in order to recapitulate the history of how he himself has come to understand the culture of the islanders who are his subject there. It is a model involving not two languages but three, not just the Kiriwinian spoken locally and English, but Kiriwinian, English, and a third, intermediate language, which I shall call the language of translation. Here is Malinowski's own short account of the form in which he has chosen to publish his examples of native usage: "We shall have in the first place to produce the texts, phrases, terminologies and formulae in native. Then we shall have to face the task of translating them. A word for word rendering is necessary to give a certain direct feeling for the language, which a free translation can in no way replace. But the literal translation is not sufficient because . . . such a translation simply never makes sense."[5] Interlinear translation is here identified with a "word-for-word" translation, the only appropriate setting for which, if it is to be projected at all, is in that strict collocation with the source which interlinearity alone permits. With the "native" component of this model we need not I hope be concerned, beyond to say that what Malinowski gives of Trobriand usage has been transcribed into our own phonetic script, and a language without writing thus textualized in a form unknown to its speakers; as readers of it we are at the mercy of the transcriber since we have no way of knowing whether his forms and word divisions represent fairly those grasped by speakers of Kiriwinian or whether they have been decided upon for his own advantage. However, it is the purpose of the word-for-word rendering that is of interest, rather than whether "word-for-word" is an accurate description of it (there can in truth be no such thing as a word-for-word translation of more than a few words at a time because no two natural languages are structurally close enough to allow it). Its purpose, Malinowski tells us, is "to give a certain direct feeling for the [native] language"; but what sort of feeling can this be? It is the feeling quickly induced in leaders whose native language is English that the grammatical and semantic categories employed by these islanders are not as our own. The "certain direct feeling" for Kiriwinian is conveyed *in* English, of a strange, interlinear kind, but with a view to exhibiting the non-Englishness of local thought processes. Let me quote one of Malinowski's more straightforward examples of how he proceeds by way of his interlinear language from native utterance to "free" translation:

Waga bi-la,   i-gisay-dasi, boge   i-katumatay-da wala
canoe he might go they see us already they kill us   just
were a canoe to sail, they would see us then they would kill us
directly

(*CG* 14)[6]

We can take it as read that this "free" translation is entirely satisfactory; it makes a passable English sentence approved of by its author-translator, which is the only test we are in a position to apply to it. But what of the provisional, interlinear version of the native utterance, the preparatory work as it were out of which the final free version is to be constructed? It uses familiar English words but not in an order we can approve or quite make sense of; it promises a meaning but fails to deliver one. It calls for the expert's revision. The justification of this ill-formed string of English words is that it correlates as precisely as possible with the native string. The alienation effect of Malinowski's interlinear language starts to work straight away, when he uses the English nominal *Canoe* without either a definite or an indefinite article in front of it (and without the capital letter it has oddly and misleadingly been given in the native version; the same goes for the punctuation, of two commas, supplied in the source yet withdrawn from the English translation where it could alone belong). The canoe has subject position (or what English recognizes as such) in both the native and the interlinear sentence, but in the interlinear version a subject pronoun is introduced also, again infringing the grammatical norms of English; this is on the ground that verb forms in Kiriwinian must include a personal pronoun and that native noun forms incorporate a gender. Malinowski's auxiliary verb form *might* represents the translation of the prefixed *b-* which, as he explains, when added to the personal pronoun *i*, alters the character of the Kiriwinian verb in a variety of ways, making it "very roughly" into a future form, or conveying "the idea of potentiality," or else assimilating it to our own imperative. The English *might* has been chosen to represent this congeries of formal possibilities, whose diversity it takes Malinowski several lines to describe.

I shall not pursue the commentary on this particular interlinear version; like all the other such versions it bears out his earlier promise that "such a translation simply never makes sense." But *must* an interlinear translation fail to make sense, or does it fail because the translator requires it to? In Malinowski's case one might well ask how far his literal versions of native word forms are determined by their (spoken) source and how far they represent the choice of a translator set on making his case at whatever cost. The technique of translation followed in *Coral Gardens and their Magic* is that to which many of us were exposed long since in school, in the handling of classical languages. In England it was known as the "construe" (in American schools, I'm told, as the "trot"), and it involved the same double act of translation, of first a "word-for-word" version of some Latin or Greek sentence and then an improvement of this into an acceptably fluent and meaningful English sentence. This was only ever an oral exercise; the interlinear version was spoken, never written down. The stock teacher's question prompted by its obvious inadequacy as English was "And what does that mean?" The proper performance of the "construe" thus entailed producing a literal translation which failed *conspicuously* to make sense; the clever pupil who rushed things and passed straight to fluency was penalized for having missed out a necessary stage of the translation process. The dispensable literal version was intended to demonstrate a formal grasp of the source sentence, in its grammatical as well as its semantic structure: to demonstrate that you knew how Latin or Greek worked formally; and the effect of being made to take this initiatory step was one of alienation followed by recovery as the quiddities of Latin were replaced by those of an acceptable English. It is a nice irony that Malinowski should follow this ancient pedagogic practice so closely in *Coral Gardens and their Magic* because, as someone professionally engaged in the encounter with alien but living languages, he has some severe things to say in that book about the "typical philologist, with his firm belief that a language becomes really beautiful and instructive—ethically, logically and aesthetically valuable—when it is dead" (*CG* viii).

Whether it is used in the schoolroom or in the ethnographer's accounts of his fieldwork, the word-for-word translation is a pedagogic contrivance, not a recognizable empirical stage in the process of translation. It is a model marked "for display purposes only." In its flagrant inadequacy or incompleteness it points beyond itself, to the "free" or "natural" translation to come, the one that we accept as a well-formed sentence of our language. Malinowski produces his own finished translations by a systematic rewriting of the interlinear ones, first by means of a "grammatical commentary" on the native utterances in question, partly evidenced in the hyphenated form in which he prints these, the better to identify Kiriwinian word classes and morphology; and then by "a contextual specification of meaning," in the course of which various kinds of vagueness and ambiguity in the interlinear rendering will be resolved and its inarticulate English words integrated syntactically. The procedure as a whole bears out Malinowski's empirical theory of meaning, according to which "words are part of action and they are equivalent to actions, so that their meaning may be defined in terms of experience and situation" (*CG* 9). Thus, if we are to understand effectively what his Trobriand informants have earlier told him, we need the guidance of the ethnographer, whose own acquired knowledge of the indigenous culture will pad out the skeletal indications of the interlinear version. This is a traditional enough view of the translator's task, as being to ensure that his source is fully understood, if necessary by the glossing or analysis of certain obscure moments of it. The translator is by the nature of things an exegete, called upon to provide what the most weighty of the earlier theorists in England gave as his first Principle of Translation: "a complete transcript of the ideas of the original work."[7] Malinowski's three-part model of translation in *Coral Gardens* takes on a mimetic, even a diegetic quality for thus summarizing his own experience in the field, where an original state of incomprehension faced with a native language little if at all known to him was over time replaced by knowledge based on the definitions and elaborations of key terms elicited by the questions he put to his informants.[8] And so it is with us, as readers of Malinowski: the native utterances are beyond us and will largely remain so, since we have nothing to gain by learning them. Their inclusion shows, however, that this ethnographer is both more scrupulous and more methodical than the majority of his colleagues, whose normal practice was to cite, not whole sentences or sequences of sentences from native informants, but only certain key terms, chosen either because they were picturesque or because they were peculiarly "untranslatable" and thus very well illustrative of the difficulties facing the ethnographer. With Malinowski these difficulties are dramatized in the form of his interlinear English, intended to reproduce native utterances that he himself characterizes as "telegraphic." As the typical example I have given shows, it lacks those connectives which we can be sure will be added, to make the sentence fully intelligible, once he goes on to give us the "free" translation. Why in the interlinear version does he leave these out? Because, he writes, "I want the reader to have as close a reproduction as possible of the bald clipped juxtapositions of the Kiriwinian language" (*CG* 27). That is, he wants his natives to sound not only strange but, relative to our own linguistic expectations, naive, when the asyndetic nature of what they say to him suggests a simple incapacity to recognize the logical relations between successive elements of the utterance. We can assume that the Kiriwinian language does not impress its native users as asyndetic, but that Malinowski wishes his own impression of that language as a stranger to be taken as a quality inherent in it. If we judge its scope and potentialities as being fairly conveyed in the interlinear translations, Kiriwinian is bound to appear a crude, even contemptible linguistic instrument; but then we might bring to mind a second laconic saying of Quine's, to the effect that "Wanton translation can make natives sound as queer as one pleases."[9]

The interlinear translation as practiced by Malinowski, or by generations of teachers of classical languages, is not permitted to reproduce a natural language in a fluent form; rather, it approximates to those intermediary languages such as pidgin which have developed in like contexts in order practically to bridge the gap between existing languages. But as with pidgin, the inference is that one of these languages, our own, is both lexically richer and syntactically more advanced than the other, to confer with whose users in a middle tongue thus demands an intellectual sacrifice on our part. Malinowski's middle tongue is intended to be neither one language nor the other, but English masquerading as Kiriwinian. The rules which he follows in constructing it aim at the decontextualization of the native utterances.[10] These he had first heard and recorded in a context which made them perfectly intelligible; that is, they were spoken to him on a given occasion by one or more local individuals as he pursued a particular line of enquiry. As printed on the page, however, utterances tend to revert to sentences, even when they occur in discursive sequences. The meaningful gestures and intonations of the informants have been lost, along with whatever other circumstances of the moment helped to determine their discourse or interchange with their visitor. The situation Malinowski finds himself in is that endured by any translator: he has a text in front of him which asks, if it is to be adequately translated, to be referred to a context. The ethnographer of course is fortunate beyond other translators, since the very thing he knows *is* that context, which, the bad interlinear moment once past, he can restore by the fullness of his commentary, expanding on the empirical evidence as cited until it becomes a synthesis of what he has learned over months or years in the field.

But how does decontextualization work, what must Malinowski get up to between the lines in order to show us how badly we need him? His method is, wherever possible, to give one English term for one native term, and the same English term for the same native term; these English terms thus function not yet as translations but as what he calls "mnemonic counters" or else "aides-mémoires." As such they bring to mind—to Malinowski's mind, not to ours, ignorant as we are of Kiriwinian—the native term while making that term seem mightily rigid in its English meaning; only once it is "contextualized" is that rigidity dissolved and the Kiriwinian signifier shown to be a semantically very flexible item indeed. Malinowski's "mnemonic counters" do the reputation of his natives much disservice at the interlinear level. Wholesale changes take place between the interlinear and the "free" stages of the translation. In the example I have quoted, the interlinear, pidginlike phrase "canoe he might go" (who does not hear echoes there of "Mr Kurtz he dead"?) becomes in free translation "were a canoe to sail," where the stopgap auxiliary *might* has given way to a refined conditional clause *were . . . to*—this is overdoing things, since Malinowski is translating sentences that were *spoken* to him and "Were a canoe to . . ." belongs decisively to the written register of English. *Canoe* is now naturalized for us by the addition of an indefinite article; the generic verb *go* has been narrowed down to the contextual *sail*; and so on throughout Malinowski's examples. The transition from *go* to *sail* is especially provocative; on what authority, one wants to know, did he decide that the native verb form *-la* should be generalized in the sense of *go* before its eventual specification as *sail*? Because this Kiriwinian verb has multiple uses, and thus potentially many contexts of use; *go* is therefore offered as its "prime" meaning. But prime for whom? The interlinear *go* is an imposition of the translator's, since the natives seem to lack the generic concept precisely mappable onto English as "go," having instead a different categorization of the semantic field roughly determinable as that of *movement away from*. What Malinowski hopes to achieve by this method of imposed generalization is to get his readers to "think in native," only with English terms. That is a contradictory ambition, as the duplicities of his interlinear translations show. But Malinowski errs only in asking too much of such a format, in mistaking it indeed for a distinct *method* of translation.

Interlinear translation is a peculiarly seductive format because it promises to actualize in front of us that hypothetical language between languages which common-sense models of the translation process have always presumed to exist. Common sense in the matter of translation is resolutely Platonist, Platonism being here the philosophical belief that meanings are entities independent of and thus transcendent of the sentences of the various natural languages in which we encounter them. Platonists have a solution to the problem of translation; natural languages may have few or no signifiers in common but they can still share their signifieds, so that identical meanings can be carried by different sentences in different languages. These transcendent entities are thus capable of materialization in many, perhaps in all natural languages, and the translator's task is to identify them in his source and transfer them from there to a second language. Thus common

57

sense's most quotable advocate in English, Samuel Johnson, wrote of translators that "he, therefore, will deserve the highest praise, who can give a representation at once faithful and pleasing, who can convey the same thoughts with the same graces, and who, when he translates, changes nothing but the language."[11] "Nothing but the language" sounds well enough, until one sets to asking what is there *except* the language. Or better, what is there once a translation has been made except for the two texts, the source and the version? Only the Platonist is willing to posit between these a third, abstract, or conceptual something, not itself a text presumably but distinguishable from both the texts we have, and usable as a reference by which to estimate their degree of synonymy.

But what if we disallow this convenient abstraction, or "language of thought," which coincides with no one natural language yet informs them all? Contemporary philosophies of language, whether European or Anglo-American, are strongly against it. We have learned from the tough-minded nominalists, from Quine and Jacques Derrida, to be disbelieving of anything claimed as existing *between* languages, and disbelieving, by extension, of any theory which supposes that the process of translation involves a passage through a "pure," sign-less, intermediate language. A rigorous empiricism allows us only two languages, a source language and a target language,[12] with no common denominator, a concept which profoundly alters the way in which we think about translation. The question of what translation is has been reformulated. Instead of naively supposing that translators are in the semantic haulage business, occupied in moving certifiably identical meanings from language to language, we can now only ask whether two sentences in two different languages "mean the same," and that is to be decided at best approximately by evaluating their respective functions within their own language. The empiricist has no need of the substantive *meaning*, a more than dubious reification that easily leads our minds astray. In his canonical essay on "Two Dogmas of Empiricism" Quine calls meanings into question as "obscure intermediate entities, which may well be abandoned."[13] Meanings are not referents, not physical things outside language, as translators know all too well, since what a translator trying to understand a text in another language is employed to provide is sequences of words of his own language, not a collection of objects referred to in the original. The only legitimate answer to the question of what a certain sentence means is another sentence of the same (or in the case of translation, a second) language. This process of semantic substitution or refinement is potentially endless, and the conception of translation may itself be redefined as being among what Quine calls "the synonymy of literary forms."

There are meaninglike entities it would be well to get rid of from any theory of translation at the textual level too: those commonly known as the "sense" of a text. The "sense" is a meaning writ large, a meaning somehow conceived of as pervading the entirety of the text under discussion. It is noticeable, however, that the "sense" of a passage or, more mysteriously still, of a whole text is almost always what a translator is held by his critics to have *failed* to give us; it is an entity remarkable for its elusiveness, even though we must presume that whoever complains of the "sense" of the source text having gone missing in the translation is able to produce evidence of its presence in the original. But then the "sense" has ever stood opposed to that other entity, the "literal meaning" of a text, and the translator who is taken to task for being too literal is also the one who has no hope of capturing the "sense." The notion of a "sense" simply reintroduces the crucial notion of freedom as the prerogative of the translator, and in its higher, more ethereal form it becomes the "spirit" of the text, that vitalizing entity forever opposed to the inertia of the "letter." As entities "sense" and "spirit" alike transcend the text and lift us again on to that utopian plane of "pure" translatability, where the privileged translator can enter into immediate communication with his source without having to suffer the all too obviously mediate pains of literalism.

On that higher plane, amidst the green and easeful landscape of transcendental signifieds, the radical indeterminacy of translation argued for by Quine no longer holds; should a rabbit pop suddenly out of its scrape and a passing native exclaim "Gavagai!", the inquisitive English-speaker will be able to establish beyond doubt that this item of the vernacular has an identical meaning to his own exclamation of "Gosh, a rabbit!" and is not in fact some other wayward response to the same stimulus. Quine's indeterminacy thesis is after all so radical that it leaves us unable to determine even the stimulus, which is a labile "event" itself occurring outside language and therefore open to different determinations in different languages. It is disconcerting for any translator to be brought to see that even "events" in the world are language dependent, that there are, as Quine insists, no predetermined "facts of the matter." There is thus nothing "out there" on which a source and its translation can be said to fix with an absolute synonymy of reference.

From a different philosophical direction, Derrida has done as much as Quine to prove the indeterminacy of translation, and to bring us to share in his own deep enjoyment of knowing that there can be no final arresting of the semantic flux. For him also there is no intelligible escape from natural language. The question of translation pervades his writings, as it must, since were translation possible in its "pure" form, then his own philosophy of language and of meaning would collapse. The lesson of Derrida's anti-Platonism goes to the limit: it is that "pure" translation, or the integral transfer of meanings from language to language, is not possible because it is not thinkable, since we have no way of establishing that it has taken place. In what language could the matter finally be determined? Misconceptions arise over translation because of the "iterability" of linguistic signs, whose constant reappearance or repetition leads us to assume their "ideality," as essences which transcend their various manifestations. This misconception was one with which Derrida took early and definitive issue in the thought of Husserl, whom he charged with determining Being itself as ideality, or repetition, and History as "the transmission and reactivation of the origin."[14] His own philosophy of an absolutely strict, progressive temporalization, allowing no possibility of a "pure," Proust-like identification of a stimulus in the present with the "same" stimulus in the past, undermines Husserlian notions of the ideality of natural language forms and hence of their perfect iterability. As an empiricist resistant to any notion whatsoever of the intelligible transcendence of actual language events, Derrida thus cannot allow that "pure" translation is feasible, suggesting that we stick instead to talk of "transformation," which is a less ambitious idea: "We shall not have and never in fact have had to do with any 'carrying' of pure signifieds which the signifying instrument—or 'vehicle'—leaves virgin and unscathed, from one language to another, or within one and the same language."[15] For Derrida each actual manifestation of a sign or signs is a historical event in time and space and necessarily distinct from every other such manifestation; he will not allow any slack-minded lapse into what he witheringly calls "the indigence of an indefinite iteration."[16]

In the face of nominalism as uncharitable as this, what to say of the interlinear mode of translation, which purports to find forms of words that will plot a convincing route between one language and another across the semantic void that seems definitively to separate them? I shall say that in this ultraskeptical environment of thought the notion of interlinearity, and the notion of literalism which is linked with it, is more valuable than ever. Pyrrhonists such as Quine and Derrida do not seek to prevent translation from continuing, as an activity central to the diffusion of knowledge and culture; nor will the practicing translator be deterred or depressed by learning of the theoretical impossibility of "pure" translation. We have something called "translation" even if we cannot be sure exactly what it is. What these philosophers have done is to fix the theorist of translation's mind on that obscure region where it should remain fixed, on between-ness, or the region sardonically referred to by Derrida as the "entr'expression." Interlinearity does so fix the mind. It sets us to puzzling over what occurs in the act of translation at such times as the translator feels himself to be between languages; or to questioning, more radically still, whether the words "between languages" are themselves comprehensible.

Loaded experiments such as that conducted by Malinowski in *Coral Gardens and their Magic* do at least show that an interlinear language, in the form of an English that has gone native, cannot make sense. His may look an extreme case, of someone attempting to mediate between two wildly incompatible natural languages. Had he been doing his fieldwork in Provence or the Tyrol rather than in furthest Melanesia, Malinowski's task would have been simpler and his interlinear translations of his native informants'

French or German no doubt a great deal closer to a well-formed English than are his versions of Kiriwinian. But the difference is one of degree, not of kind; there could never *not* be a space between two languages in which to insert interlinear translations and by doing so to characterize the failure of those languages to match up either formally or semantically.

The interlinear mode of translation has virtues, moreover, whatever one cares to believe as to the existence of an abstract or "pure" language of thought. If, *contra* the nominalists, that hypothesis be allowed, then an interlinear language may attempt to indicate its hypothetical forms, as Malinowski tried to indicate them, by a process of decontextualization. Such an enterprise today might call on the support of Chomskyan grammarians, whose researches into syntax have led them to postulate structures, if not "beyond" then "below" the empirical level of actual language use, to invoke in extreme cases such new denizens of the linguistic deep as "presentential structures of a more abstract kind."[17] If these underlying structures are universal, or common to the species, they can be called in to underpin the common-sense belief that human thought processes follow certain rules by the fact of their being human, or biologically conditioned; which being so, at some suitably abstract level "languages" might be claimed to be ideally intertranslatable. But that level turns out to be of a degree of abstraction or mathematization such that we might refuse to recognize it as a language at all; moreover, the problem of by what criteria to identify beyond argument one such structure with another seems to remain unsolved. Nevertheless, the assertion of a rationalist philosopher of language like Jerrold Katz that "each human language community has the same stock of possible thoughts"[18] will be of encouragement to those who persist in thinking that translation is determinable.

Katz's vertiginous hypothesis, of "the same stock of possible thoughts," is very close to the sly and mind-numbing fantasy thought up by Borges in his story of "The Library of Babel," whose title overtly declares it to be a contribution to the theory of translation. But Borges's library, unlike Katz's theory of language, has no room for abstractions; it is the dreadfully extended space in which all "possible thoughts" have for once been materialized (as well as a very great many sequences of signifiers which are not thoughts at all). The Library is, however, for all its size, language dependent, containing as it does only the possible combinations (restricted by certain arbitrary rules of combination laid down by Borges) of the material signs of a particular writing system. Somewhere in the stacks of the Library of Babel are all the thoughts possible in whatever natural languages share that writing system; and, if you are an idealist, you may properly claim that certain volumes in the library, and certain bits of other volumes, constitute the "pure" translations one of the other. The volume that is lacking, however, is one containing the extralinguistic proof that this "purity" of translation is absolute.

61

But if "pure" translation is not even conceivable, it remains desirable: desirable because inconceivable is what Derrida is saying. Whatever we achieve in translation falls short of an ideal of synonymy that is itself ineffable, the ineffable being the romantic, Derridian version of Quine's more scientific category of the indeterminate. But faced with this ultimate indeterminacy, or antifoundationalism, we can still engage in the work of translation shored up by the assumption that human beings of different cultures and environments are sufficiently alike psychologically for their languages to approximate to each other; let our common behavior be, as Wittgenstein suggests, that "system of reference by means of which we interpret an unknown language."[19] In the real world we seldom if ever have to "interpret an unknown language"; so-called "radical" translation, from languages of which we know nothing at all (not even the fact that they are "languages": suppose *gavagai* were to turn out to be the only sound Quine's native informant was able to make, to any stimulus at all?), is itself a hypothetical activity, a philosopher's device for severing the metaphysical links which we might otherwise believe to guarantee the ideal communicability of thoughts between natural languages, and for establishing each individual language as autonomous in respect of every other.

Languages may converge but not merge; it is in the act of translation that their apartness manifests itself. Or it is there that it should do so. And yet we hold that act of translation the most successful which contains no evidence at all of the apartness of languages, but only of a source text flawlessly naturalized, which is to say finally occluded. There is no hint of interlinearity in the translations that are the most prized and applauded, because interlinearity would be "translationese" and who is ever heard speaking up for that? Someone should speak up for it; the case for "translationese" is that it could represent, if intelligently used, an honorable refusal on the part of a translator seamlessly to indigenize his source; it could make visible the between-ness in which he is trapped. The translator who is caught between the lines expects to make his escape in the direction of his own language and away from the source; were an interlinear "translationese" permitted to him it would mean that he could pay his respects to his source rather than to his eventual reader. "Translationese" as we know it is involuntary and all that is read into it is the incompetence of the translator, together with the neglectfulness of his editor. A voluntary "translationese," systematically followed, would be something else, a drawing of our attention to the irrevocably mediate status of the language of translation. An interlinear language does not have to be as patronizingly primitive as that employed by Malinowski; it need only allow certain "purely" untranslatable characteristics of the syntax and lexicon of the source to show through in the translation. Interlinear English will always be English but not an *altogether* familiar English, its abnormalities being so designed as to acknowledge the derivative nature of what we are reading.[20]

Translators know very well how much their sources lose on their passage into another language; a greater tolerance of literalism in translation would bring some ease to their consciences and restore the lost balance between the claims to ultimate respect of the source and the brazen imperatives of the market. Much day-to-day translation may be hackwork, of sources themselves perishable whose integrity is thought scarcely worthy of defence. But the principles of translation derive not from this low kind of translation but from the highest kind, from the translation of masterworks whose claims to integrity are paramount and certainly come before any assuagement of the tastes of readers. If it is ever to be recognized as an ideal in translation, interlinearity can only start at the top, as its greatest advocate in the modern age recognized. For Walter Benjamin, translation, in its doomed striving to fuse one language with another, offers us in its flounderings the mystical "prospect" of a pure language beyond languages; it displays the complementarity of languages, and does so all the more powerfully if the first language can be seen to be still present in the second, or else visible through it. How more compellingly to rest the case for interlinearity than on Benjamin's splendid architectural trope: "For if the sentence is the wall before the language of the original, literalness is the arcade."[21]

Notes

1 This is the standard practice, though publishers do depart from it and publish translations either anonymously or even without indicating that they are translations. Translations of the more academic sort may also carry footnotes supplied by the translator, and marked as being by him, where he feels the need to explain or justify some element of the text. Similarly, there are translations which declare themselves as such by giving the original form of certain key terms in parentheses after the translated forms, or by leaving key terms untranslated. These practices serve as at least intermittent reminders that what we are reading has an original "behind" it.

2 W. V. Quine, "Meaning and Translation," in *On Translation*, ed. Reuben A. Brower (Cambridge, Mass., 1959), p. 169.

3 Eugene A. Nida and Charles R. Taber, *The Theory and Practice of Translation* (Leiden, 1982), p. 157.

4 Or more often, their "interpretation." The late Sir Edward Evans-Pritchard, a pupil of Malinowski's, was very influential in establishing this point of view among British ethnographers, and a Festschrift presented to him at the end of his career had the title *The Translation of Culture*. Quoting Evans-Pritchard on the "semantic difficulties" faced by ethnographers, Sir Edmund Leach goes on to write: "The social anthropologist in the field devotes his efforts to trying to understand, not just the spoken language of the people with whom he interacts, but their whole way of life. That, in itself, is a problem of translation, of finding categories in his own ways of thought which can be fitted to the complex of observed facts which he records. But that is only the beginning. Having, as he hopes, gained 'insight' into what he has observed, he then has the further task of translating that insight into a language which his readers, who have not shared his personal experience, might reasonably be expected to understand." Leach goes on to

conclude that "Social anthropologists are bad novelists rather than bad scientists." Sir Edmund Leach, *Social Anthropology* (Oxford, 1982), p. 53.

5 Bronislaw Malinowski, *Coral Gardens and their Magic* (London, 1935), II, 10–11; hereafter cited in text as *CG*.

6 The "free" versions of the native utterances are given by Malinowski in the first descriptive volume of the work rather than in conjunction with the interlinear versions, so that comparison of the two is made rather laborious.

7 A. F. Tytler. Lord Woodhouselee. *Essay on the Principles of Translation* (London, 1907), p. 9.

8 Malinowski touches several times on his dealings with native informants among the Islanders in *A Diary in the Strict Sense of the Term* (London, 1989). He seems to have had greater success with and greater trust in the men he talked with. Of the women he writes: "I try to talk to them: they run away or tell lies" (p. 140). But he does not say how he knew he was being lied to, nor indeed why he should have been so trusting of the men.

9 W. V. Quine, *Word and Object* (Cambridge, Mass., 1960), p. 58.

10 I am trying to observe the usual distinction between an *utterance* and a *sentence*, the first being the verbatim record of a realization of the second, which belongs to the grammar of the language.

11 Samuel Johnson, *The Idler*, Nos. 68–69 (London, 1759), p. 120.

12 These are the terms customarily used by theorists of translation. The term *target language* is not only ugly but seems to place the translator in some extra- or else prelinguistic state where he must remain until such time as he has succeeded in finding the right words to match those in the source language. The notion of having a "target" at which to aim in translating implies that the right form of words is already "there" if only one can find it. Only where is "there"?

13 W. V. Quine, "Two Dogmas of Empiricism," in his *From a Logical Point of View* (New York, 1963), p. 22.

14 Jacques Derrida, *La Voix et le Phénomène* (Paris, 1967), pp. 58–59, and passim, my translation.

15 Jacques Derrida, *Positions* (Paris, 1972), p. 31, my translation.

16 Jacques Derrida, *Edmund Husserl's 'Origin of Geometry': An Introduction*, tr. John P. Leavey, Jr. (Stony Brook, 1978), p. 102.

17 John Lyons, *Semantics* (Cambridge, 1977), p. 393. Talk of "pre-sentential structures" can be interestingly compared in this same very lucid and comprehensive book with Professor Lyons's invocations of a "propositional" language. E.g., "We want to be able to say . . . that the sentences 'It is raining', 'It was raining' and 'It will be raining' all express the same proposition (namely, 'It be raining')" (p. 469). "It be raining," however, is a sentence of English famously characteristic of yokels, and understood by everyone to be an ill-formed, bucolic version of "It is raining." Do the yokels in fact know something about language that we don't, if they are thus able to speak propositionally?

18 Jerrold J. Katz, "Effability and Translation," in *Meaning and Translation*, ed. F. Guenthner and M. Guenthner-Reutter (London, 1978), p. 219.

19 Ludwig Wittgenstein, *Philosophical Investigations* (Oxford, 1953), p. 82.

20 An example of the hybrid "language" this would call for is the one adopted by Ernest Hemingway in some of the dialogue of *For Whom the Bell Tolls*, where one or more of the speakers is Spanish and presumed to be speaking his native tongue. The following exchange, for example: "'To me, now, the most important is that we be not disturbed here,' Pablo said. 'To me, now, my duty is to those who are with me and to myself.'—'Thyself. Yes.' Anselmo said. 'Thyself now since a long time. Thyself and thy horses. Until thou hadst horse thou wert with

us. Now thou art another capitalist more'" (Ernest Hemingway, *For Whom the Bell Tolls* [Harmondsworth, 1955], pp. 18–19). The point is not whether Hemingway did what he was trying to do well but the fact that he should even have attempted it. "Translated" dialogue of this kind is sure to irritate many readers, particularly those who know no Spanish and are therefore unable to see the rationale for such alien forms of English. It would be interesting to know whether the Spanish translator of *For Whom the Bell Tolls* took the author's cues and translated the "Spanish" dialogue accordingly.

21 Walter Benjamin, "The Task of the Translator," in *Illuminations*, tr. Harry Zohn (London, 1970), p. 79. Benjamin's exalted view of interlinear translation, as being the highest kind of all, clearly owes much to the example in German literature of Goethe, who likewise esteemed it above all other modes of translation. The filiation between these two thinkers is brought out by George Steiner, in *After Babel: Aspects of Language and Translation* (Oxford, 1975), in his account of Goethe, see pp. 256–60. Goethe, incidentally, recognized that interlinear translations would be very unpopular with readers.

42

TRANSLATION AS CULTURAL POLITICS

Regimes of domestication in English

Lawrence Venuti

Source: *Textual Practice* 7 (1993): 208–23.

> A metalanguage is always terrorist.
> Roland Barthes
> (trans. Richard Howard)
>
> All violence is the illustration of a pathetic stereotype.
> Barbara Kruger

I propose these two epigraphs as an extravagant but pointed metaphor for translation. The statement from Roland Barthes concludes his incisive 1961 review of Michel Foucault's *Histoire de la folie*.[1] For Barthes, Foucault's history shows that madness is the discourse of reason about unreason, and this discourse, apart from the physical exclusions of exile, imprisonment, and hospitalization which it makes possible, also excludes the discourse of unreason about unreason, hence reducing the object of which it professes knowledge. In Barthes's conclusion, a metalanguage, a second-order discourse that takes a prior signifying system as its object, is found to be reductive and exclusionary and thus likened to terrorism, violent action that is both intense and damaging, that intimidates and coerces, usually in the service of social interests and political agendas, often under the aegis of reason or truth. The epigram from the artist Barbara Kruger was part of a 1991 installation, in which the accusatory aphoristic statements that distinguish her photomontages were painted across the walls and floors of the Mary Boone Gallery in New York.[2] Here violence is likened to a metalanguage: it is action with the function of representation, a second-order discourse illustrating a prior stereotype, which can be seen as pathetic in its destructiveness, its reductive and exclusionary relation to a person or social group. Violence is the enactment of a cultural discourse that already constitutes a conceptual or representational violence. Reflection on translation in the context of Barthes's and Kruger's statements undoubtedly cheapens violent action, trivializing its serious physical and psychological costs, its brutal materiality. But such reflection will also illuminate the discursive conditions of violence by attending to the material effects of another metalanguage, the power of translation to (re)constitute and cheapen foreign texts, to trivialize and exclude foreign cultures, and thus potentially to figure in racial discrimination and ethnic violence, international political confrontations, terrorism, war.

The violence of translation resides in its very purpose and activity: the reconstitution of the foreign text in accordance with values, beliefs and representations that pre-exist it in the target language, always configured in hierarchies of dominance and marginality, always determining the production, circulation, and reception of texts. Translation is the forcible replacement of the linguistic and cultural difference of the foreign text with a text that will be intelligible to the target-language reader. This difference can never be entirely removed, of course, but it necessarily suffers a reduction and exclusion of possibilities – and an exorbitant gain of other possibilities specific to the translating language. Whatever difference the translation conveys is now imprinted by the target-language culture, assimilated to its positions of intelligibility, its canons and taboos, its codes and ideologies. The aim of translation is to bring back a cultural other as the same, the recognizable, even the familiar; and this aim always risks a wholesale domestication of the foreign text, often in highly self-conscious projects, where translation serves an imperialist appropriation of foreign cultures for domestic agendas, cultural, economic, political.

Thus, the violent effects of translation are felt at home as well as abroad. On the one hand, translation wields enormous power in the construction of national identities for foreign cultures and hence can play a role in racial and ethnic conflicts and geopolitical confrontations. On the other hand, translation enlists the foreign text in the maintenance or revision of literary canons in the target-language culture, inscribing poetry and fiction, for example, with the various poetic and narrative discourses that compete for cultural dominance in the target language. Translation also enlists the foreign text in the maintenance or revision of dominant conceptual paradigms, research methodologies, and clinical practices in target-language disciplines and professions, whether physics or architecture, philosophy or psychiatry, sociology or law. It is these social affiliations and effects – written into the materiality of the translated text, into its discursive strategy and its range of allusiveness for the target-language reader, but also into the very choice to translate it and the ways it is published, reviewed, and taught – all these conditions permit translation to be called a cultural political practice, constructing or critiquing ideology-stamped identities for foreign cultures, affirming or transgressing discursive values and institutional limits in the target-language culture. The violence wreaked by translation is partly inevitable, inherent in the translation process, partly potential, emerging at any point in the production and reception of the translated text, varying with specific cultural and social formations at different historical moments.

The most urgent question facing the translator who possesses this knowledge is: What to do? Why and how do I translate? Although I have construed translation as the site of multiple determinations and effects – linguistic, cultural, ideological, political – I also want to indicate that the translator always exercises a choice concerning the degree and direction of the violence at work in his practice. This choice was given its most decisive formulation at the beginning of the nineteenth century by the theologian and philosopher Friedrich Schleiermacher. In an 1813 lecture on the different methods of translation, Schleiermacher argued that 'there are only two. Either the translator leaves the author in peace, as much as possible, and moves the reader towards him; or he leaves the reader in peace, as much as possible, and moves the author towards him.'[3] Admitting (with qualifications like 'as much as possible') that translation can never be completely adequate to the foreign text, Schleiermacher allowed the translator to choose between a domesticating method, an ethnocentric reduction of the foreign text to target-language cultural values, bringing the author back home, and a foreignizing method, an ethnodeviant pressure on those values to register the linguistic and cultural difference of the foreign text, sending the reader abroad.

Schleiermacher made clear that his choice was foreignizing translation, and this has led the French translator and translation theorist Antoine Berman to treat Schleiermacher's argument as an ethics of translation, concerned with making the translated text a place where a cultural other is manifested – although, of course, an otherness that can never be manifested in its own terms, only in those of the target langauge, and hence always already encoded.[4] The 'foreign' in foreignizing translation is not a transparent representation of an essence that resides in the foreign text and is valuable in itself, but a strategic construction whose value is contingent on the current target-language situation. Foreignizing translation signifies the difference of the foreign text, yet only by disrupting the cultural codes that prevail in the target language. In its efforts to do right abroad, this translation method must do wrong at home, deviating from native norms to stage an alien reading experience.

I want to suggest that in so far as foreignizing translation seeks to restrain the ethnocentric violence of translation, it is highly desirable today, a strategic intervention in the current state of world affairs, pitched against the hegemonic English-language nations and the unequal cultural exchanges in which they engage their global others. For the fact is that only 2–3 per cent of the books published in the US and UK each year are translations, whereas foreign titles, many from English, count for as much as 25 per cent (or more) of the books published annually in other countries.[5] And yet for-eignizing translation has always been marginalized in Anglo-American culture. This method is specific to certain European countries at particular historical moments: formulated first in German culture during the classical and romantic periods, it has recently been revived in a French cultural scene characterized by postmodern developments in philosophy, literary criticism, psychoanalysis, and social theory that have come to be known as 'poststructuralism'.[6] English-language translation, in contrast, has been dominated by domesticating theories and practices at least since the seven-teenth century.

In 1656, Sir John Denham prefaced *The Destruction of Troy*, his version of the second book of the *Aeneid*, with the remark that 'if *Virgil* must needs speak English, it were fit he should speak not only as a man of this Nation, but as a man of this age.'[7] Denham saw himself as presenting a naturalized English Virgil. He felt that poetic discourse in particular called for domest-icating translation because 'Poesie is of so subtle a spirit, that in pouring out of one Language into another, it will all evaporate; and if a new spirit be not added in the transfusion, there will remain nothing but a *Caput mortuum*' (p. 65). The 'new spirit' Denham 'added' to Virgil belonged to Denham ('my Art', 'my self'), and he was acutely aware that it was specifically English, so that domestication was a translation method laden with nationalism, even if expressed with courtly self-effacement:

> if this disguise I have put upon him (I wish I could give it a better name) fit not naturally and easily on so grave a person, yet it may become him better than that Fools-Coat wherein the French and Italian have of late presented him.
>
> (p. 65)

Domestication became the preferred method for English-language poetry translation by the end of the seventeenth century, when it received its authoritative formulation in John Dryden's *Dedication of the Aeneis* (1697). 'I have endeavoured to make Virgil speak such English,' wrote Dryden, 'as he would himself have spoken, if he had been born in England, and in this present age.'[8] In Dryden's wake, from Alexander Pope's multi-volumed Homer (1715–26) to Alexander Tytler's systematic *Essay on the Principles of Translation* (1791), domestication dominated the theory and practice of English-language translation in every genre, prose as well as poetry. William Guthrie, for example, in the preface to his version of *The Orations of Marcus Tullius Cicero* (1741), argued that 'it is *living Manners* alone that can com-municate the Spirit of an Original' and so urged the translator to make 'it his Business to be as conversant as he cou'd in that Study and Manner which comes the nearest to what we may suppose his Author, were he now

69

to live, wou'd pursue, and in which he wou'd shine.'[9] Hence, Guthrie cast his Cicero as a member of Parliament, 'where,' he says, 'by a constant Attendance, in which I was indulg'd for several Years, I endeavour'd to possess myself of the Language most proper for this translation.'

It is important not to view such instances of domestication as simply inaccurate translations. Canons of accuracy and fidelity are always locally defined, specific to different cultural formations at different historical moments. Both Denham and Dryden recognized that a ratio of loss and gain inevitably occurs in the translation process and situates the translation in an equivocal relationship to the foreign text, never quite faithful, always somewhat free, never establishing an identity, always a lack and a supplement. Yet they also viewed their domesticating method as the most effective way to control this equivocal relationship and produce versions adequate to the Latin text. As a result, they castigated methods that either rigorously adhered to source-language textual features or played fast and loose with them, that either did not sufficiently domesticate the foreign text or did so by omitting parts of it. Following Horace's dictum in Ars *Poetica*, Denham 'conceive[d] it a vulgar error in translating Poets, to affect being *Fides Interpres*', because poetic discourse required more latitude to capture its 'spirit' in the target language than a close adherence to each foreign word would allow. But he also professed to 'having made it my principal care to follow [Virgil]', noting that 'neither have I any where offered such violence to his sense, as to make it seem mine, and not his'. Dryden similarly 'thought it fit to steer betwixt the two extremes of paraphrase and literal translation', i.e. between the aim of reproducing primarily the meanings of the Latin text, usually at the cost of its phonological and syntactical features, and the aim of rendering it word for word, respecting syntax and line break. And he distinguished his method from Abraham Cowley's 'imitations' of Pindar, partial translations that revised and, in effect, abandoned the foreign text. The ethnocentric violence performed by domesticating translation rested on a double fidelity, to the source-language text as well as to the target-language culture, but this was clearly impossible and knowingly duplicitous, accompanied by the rationale that a gain in domestic intelligibility and cultural force outweighed the loss suffered by the foreign text and culture.

By the turn of the nineteenth century, a translation method of eliding the linguistic and cultural difference of the foreign text was firmly entrenched as a canon in English-language translation, usually linked to a valorization of transparent discourse. In 1820, a translator of Aristophanes, John Hookham Frere, unfavourably reviewed Thomas Mitchell's versions of *The Acharnians* and *The Knights*, their principal 'defect' being 'the adoption of a particular style; the style of our ancient comedy in the beginning of the 16th century'.[10] Frere faulted Mitchell's use of an archaic literary and dramatic discourse, English Renaissance comedy, because the language of translation ought, we think, as far as possible, to be a pure, impalpable and invisible element, the medium of thought and feeling, and nothing more; it ought never to attract attention to itself; hence all phrases that are remarkable in themselves, either as old or new; all importations from foreign languages and quotations, are as far as possible to be avoided ... such phrases as [Mitchell] has sometimes admitted, '*solus cum solo*', for instance, '*petits pates*', &c. have the immediate effect of reminding the reader, that he is reading a translation, and ... the illusion of originality, which the spirited or natural turn of a sentence immediately preceding might have excited, is instantly dissipated by it.

(p. 481)

Frere advocated a fluent strategy, in which the language of the translation is made to read with a 'spirited or natural turn', so that the absence of any syntactical or lexical peculiarities produces the illusionistic effect of transparency, the appearance that the translation reflects the foreign writer's intention ('It is the office, we presume, of the Translator to represent the forms of language according to the intention with which they are employed') (p. 482) and therefore the appearance that the translation is not in fact a translation, but the original, still within the foreign writer's control, not worked over by the translator. Fluency produces an individualistic illusion, in which the text is assumed to originate fundamentally with the author, to be authorial self-expression, free of cultural and social determinations. Since fluency is here a translation strategy, it can be considered a discursive sleight of hand by which the translator domesticates the foreign text, causing its difference to vanish by making it intelligible in an English-language culture that values easy readability, transparent discourse, and the illusion of authorial presence.

And, once again, the domestication enacted by a fluent strategy does not necessarily result in an inaccurate translation. In 1823, the anonymous reviewer of William Stewart Rose's *Orlando Furioso* recommended this strategy in the pronouncement that

the two characteristics of a good translation are, that it should be *faithful*, and that it should be *unconstrained*. Faithful, as well in rendering correctly the meaning of the original, as in exhibiting the general spirit which pervades it: unconstrained, so as not to betray by its phraseology, by the collocation of its words, or construction of its sentences that it is only a copy.[11]

Fluency can be associated with fidelity because it means foregrounding the conceptual signified in the translation, checking the drift of language away from communication, minimizing any play of the signifier which calls attention to its materiality, to words as words, their opacity, their resistance to immediate intelligibility, empathic response, interpretive mastery. What the fluent strategy conceals with the effect of transparency, what it makes seem faithful, is in fact the translator's interpretation of the foreign text, the signified he has demarcated in the translation in accordance with target-language cultural values. The fluent translation is seen as 'rendering correctly the meaning of the original' because it constitutes an interpretation that conforms or can be easily assimilated to those values, not only the valorization of 'unconstrained' language, but also the understanding of the foreign text or literature that concurrently prevails in the target culture.

In Frere's case fluency entailed a linguistic homogenization that avoided 'associations exclusively belonging to modern manners' as well as archaism, that removed as many of the historically specific markers of the foreign text as possible by generalizing or simply omitting them. The translator will,

> if he is capable of executing his task upon a philosophic principle, endeavour to resolve the personal and local allusions into the genera, of which the local or personal variety employed by the original author, is merely the accidental type; and to reproduce them in one of those permanent forms which are connected with the universal and immutable habits of mankind.
>
> (p. 482)

Frere rationalized these admitted 'liberties' by appealing to a 'philosophic principle':

> The proper domain of the Translator is, we conceive, to be found in that vast mass of feeling, passion, interest, action and habit which is common to mankind in all countries and in all ages; and which, in all languages, is invested with its appropriate forms of expression, capable of representing it in all its infinite varieties, in all the permanent distinctions of age, profession and temperament.
>
> (p. 481)

In Frere's view, a fluent strategy enables the translation to be a transparent representation of the eternal human verities expressed by the foreign author.

The principle on which Frere's translation theory rests is liberal humanism, in which subjectivity is seen as at once self-determining and determined by human nature, individualistic yet generic, transcending cultural difference, social conflict, and historical change to represent 'every shade of the human character'. Frere's theory may appear to be democratic in its appeal to what is 'common to mankind', to a timeless and universal human essence, but it actually involved an insidious domestication that allowed him to imprint the foreign text with his conservative sexual morality and cultural elitism. He made plain his squeamishness about the physical coarseness of

Aristophanic humour, its grotesque realism, and felt the need to explain it away as inconsistent with the author's intention: the 'lines of extreme grossness' were 'forced compromises', 'which have evidently been inserted, for the purpose of pacifying the vulgar part of the audience, during passages in which their anger, or impatience, or disappointment, was likely to break out' (p. 491). Hence, 'in discarding such passages,' Frere asserted, 'the translator is merely doing that for his author, which he would willingly have done for himself' – were he not 'often under the necessity of addressing himself exclusively to the lower class' (p. 491). Frere's advocacy of a fluent strategy was premissed on a bourgeois snobbery, in which the moral and political conservatism emerging in early nineteenth-century English culture resulted in a call for a bowdlerized Aristophanes that represented the 'permanent' class divisions of humanity, what Frere described as 'that true comic humour which he was directing to the more refined and intelligent part of his audience' (p. 491).[12] For Frere, 'the persons of taste and judgment to whom the author occasionally appeals, form, in modern times, the tribunal to which his translator must address himself' (p. 491).

Fluency is thus a discursive strategy ideally suited to domesticating translation, capable not only of executing the ethnocentric violence of domestication, but also of concealing this violence by producing the illusionistic effect of transparency. And it is this strategy that, with very few exceptions (the Victorian archaism of Francis Newman and William Morris, for example, or the modernist experiments of Ezra Pound and Louis and Celia Zukofsky), has continued to dominate the theory and practice of English-language translation to this day. Perhaps the clearest indication of this dominance is Eugene Nida's influential concept of 'dynamic' or 'functional equivalence' in translation, formulated first in 1964, but restated and developed in numerous books and articles over the past twenty-five years. 'A translation of dynamic equivalence aims at complete naturalness of expression,' states Nida, 'and tries to relate the receptor to modes of behavior relevant within the context of his own culture.'[13] The phrase 'naturalness of expression' signals the importance of a fluent strategy to this theory of translation, and in Nida's work it is evident that fluency involves domestication. As he has recently put it, 'the translator must be a person who can draw aside the curtains of linguistic and cultural differences so that people may see clearly the relevance of the original message.'[14] This is of course a relevance to the target-language culture, something with which foreign writers are usually not concerned when they write their texts, so that relevance can be established in the translation process only by replacing source-language features that are pot recognizable with target-language ones that are. Thus, when Nida asserts that 'an easy and natural style in translating, despite the extreme difficulty of producing it . . . is nevertheless essential to producing in the ultimate receptors a response similar to that of the original receptors' (*Science*, p. 163), he is in fact imposing the English-language valorization of transparent discourse on every foreign culture, masking a basic disjunction between the source- and target-language texts which puts into question the possibility of eliciting a 'similar' response.

Like earlier theorists in the Anglo-American tradition, however, Nida has argued that dynamic equivalence is consistent with a notion of accuracy. The dynamically equivalent translation does not indiscriminately use 'anything which might have special impact and appeal for receptors'; it rather 'means thoroughly understanding not only the meaning of the source text but also the manner in which the intended receptors of a text are likely to understand it in the receptor language' (*One Language*, pp. vii–viii, 9). For Nida, accuracy in translation depends on generating an equivalent effect in the target-language culture: 'the receptors of a translation should comprehend the translated text to such an extent that they can understand how the original receptors must have understood the original text' (ibid., p. 36). The dynamically equivalent translation is 'interlingual communication' which overcomes the linguistic and cultural differences that impede it (ibid., p. 11). Yet the understanding of the foreign text and culture which this kind of translation makes possible answers fundamentally to target-language cultural values while veiling this domestication in the transparency evoked by a fluent strategy. Communication here is initiated and controlled by the target-language culture, and therefore it seems less an exchange of information than an imperialist appropriation of a foreign text. Nida's theory of translation as communication does not adequately take into account the ethnocentric violence that is inherent in every translation process – but especially in one governed by dynamic equivalence.

As with John Hookham Frere, Nida's advocacy of domesticating translation is explicitly grounded on a transcendental concept of humanity as an essence that remains unchanged over time and space. 'As linguists and anthropologists have discovered,' Nida states, 'that which unites mankind is much greater than that which divides, and hence there is, even in cases of very disparate languages and cultures, a basis for communication' (*Science*, p. 2). Yet the democratic potential of Nida's humanism, as with Frere's, is contradicted by the more exclusionary values that inform his theory of translation, specifically Christian evangelism and cultural elitism. From the very beginning of his career, Nida's work has been motivated by the exigencies of Bible translation: not only have problems in the history of the Bible translation served as examples for his theoretical statements, but he has written studies in anthropology and linguistics designed primarily for Bible translators and missionaries. Nida's concept of dynamic equivalence in fact links the translator to the missionary. When, in *Customs and Cultures: Anthropology for Christian Missions* (1954), Nida asserted that

> a close examination of successful missionary work inevitably reveals
> the correspondingly effective manner in which the missionaries were

able to identify themselves with the people – 'to be all things to all
men' – and to communicate their message in terms which have
meaning for the lives of the people,

he was echoing what he had earlier asserted of the Bible translator in *God's
Word in Man's Language* (1952): 'The task of the true translator is one of
identification. As a Christian servant he must identify with Christ; as a
translator he must identify himself with the Word; as a missionary he must
identify himself with the people.'[15] Both the missionary and the translator
must find the dynamic equivalent in the target language in order to establish
the relevance of the Bible in the target culture. But Nida permits only
a particular kind of relevance to be established. While he disapproves of
'the tendency to promote by means of Bible translating the cause of a particular theological viewpoint, whether deistic, rationalistic, immersionistic,
millenarian, or charismatic' (*One Language*, p. 33), it is obvious that he
himself has promoted a reception of the text centred in Christian dogma.
And although he offers a nuanced account of how 'diversities in the back-
grounds of receptors' can shape any Bible translation, he insists that
'translations prepared primarily for minority groups must generally involve
highly restrictive forms of language, but they must not involve substandard
grammar or vulgar wording' (ibid., p. 14). Nida's concept of dynamic equivalence in Bible translation goes hand in hand with an evangelical zeal that
seeks to impose on English-language readers a specific dialect of English as
well as a distinctly Christian understanding of the text.

To advocate foreignizing translation in opposition to the Anglo-
American tradition of domestication is not to do away with cultural political
agendas. Clearly, such an advocacy is itself an agenda. The point is rather to
develop a theory and practice of translation that resists dominant target-
language cultural values so as to signify the linguistic and cultural difference
of the foreign text. Philip Lewis's concept of abusive fidelity can be taken as
a first step in such a theorization: it acknowledges the equivocal relationship
between the foreign text and the translation and eschews a fluent strategy in
order to reproduce in the translation whatever features of the foreign text
abuse or resist dominant cultural values in the source language.[16] Abusive
fidelity directs the translator's attention away from the conceptual signified
to the play of signifiers on which it depends, to phonological, syntactical,
and discursive structures, resulting in a 'translation that values experimenta-
tion, tampers with usage, seeks to match the polyvalencies or plurivocities
or expressive stresses of the original by producing its own' (p. 41). Such a
translation strategy can best be called resistancy, not merely because it avoids
fluency, but because it challenges the target-language culture even as it
enacts its own ethnocentric violence on the foreign text.

The notion of foreignization can alter the ways translations are read as
well as produced because it assumes a concept of human subjectivity that is

very different from the humanist assumptions underlying domestication. Neither the foreign author nor the translator is conceived as the transcendental origin of the text, freely expressing an idea about human nature or communicating it in transparent language to a reader from a different culture. Rather, subjectivity is constituted by cultural and social determinations that are diverse and even conflicting, that mediate any language use, and that vary with every cultural formation and every historical moment. Human action is intentional, but determinate, self-reflexively measured against social rules and resources, the heterogeneity of which allows for the possibility of change with every self-reflexive action.[17] Textual production may be initiated and guided by the producer, but it puts to work various linguistic and cultural materials which make the text discontinuous, despite its appearance of unity, and which result in meanings and effects that may exceed the producer's intention, creating an unconscious that is at once personal and social, psychological and ideological. Thus, the translator consults many different target-language cultural materials, ranging from dictionaries and grammars to texts, discursive strategies, and translations to values, paradigms, and ideologies, both canonical and marginal. Although intended to reproduce the source-language text, the translator's consultation of these materials inevitably reduces and supplements it, even when source-language cultural materials are also consulted, and their sheer heterogeneity leads to discontinuities in the translation that are symptomatic of its ethnocentric violence. Discontinuities at the level of syntax, diction, or discourse allow the translation to be read as a translation, revealing the strategy at work in it, foreignizing a domesticating translation by snowing where it departs from target-language cultural values, domesticating a foreignizing translation by showing where it depends on them.

This method of symptomatic reading can be illustrated with the translations of Freud's texts for the *Standard Edition*, although the translations have acquired such unimpeachable authority that we needed Bruno Bettelheim's critique to become aware of the discontinuities.[18] Bettelheim's point is that the translations make Freud's texts 'appear to readers of English as abstract, depersonalized, highly theoretical, erudite, and mechanized – in short "scientific" – statements about the strange and very complex workings of our mind' (p. 5). Bettelheim seems to assume that a close examination of Freud's German is necessary to detect the translators' scientistic strategy, but the fact is that his point can be demonstrated with no more than a careful reading of the English text. Bettelheim argues, for example, that in *The Psychopathology of Everyday Life* (1960), the term 'parapraxis' reveals the scientism of the translation because it is used to render a rather simple German word, *Fehlleistungen*, which Bettelheim himself prefers to translate as 'faulty achievement' (p. 87). Yet the translator's strategy may also be glimpsed through certain peculiarities in the diction of the translated text:

I now return to the forgetting of names. So far we have not exhaus-tively considered either the case-material or the motives behind it. As this is exactly the kind of parapraxis that I can from time to time observe abundantly in myself, I am at no loss for examples. The mild attacks of migraine from which I still suffer usually announce themselves hours in advance by my forgetting names, and at the height of these attacks, during which I am not forced to abandon my work, it frequently happens that all proper names go out of my head.[19]

The diction of much of this passage is so simple and common ('forgetting'), even colloquial ('go out of my head'), that 'parapraxis' represents a con-spicuous difference, an inconsistency in word choice which exposes the translation process. The inconsistency is underscored not only by Freud's heavy reliance on anecdotal, 'everyday' examples, some – as above – taken from his own experience, but also by a footnote added to a later edition of the German text and included in the English translation:

This book is of an entirely popular character; it merely aims, by an accumulation of examples, at paving the way for the necessary assumption of *unconscious yet operative* mental processes, and it avoids all theoretical considerations on the nature of the unconscious.

(p. 272n)

James Strachey himself unwittingly called attention to the inconsistent diction in his preface to Alan Tyson's translation, where he felt it necessary to provide a rationale for the use of 'parapraxis': 'In German "*Fehlleistung*", "faulty function". It is a curious fact that before Freud wrote this book the general concept seems not to have existed in psychology, and in English a new word had to be invented to cover it' (p. viii n). It can of course be objected (against Bettelheim) that the mixture of specialized scientific terms and commonly used diction is characteristic of Freud's German, and there-fore (against me) that the English translation in itself cannot be the basis for an account of the translators' strategy. Yet although I am very much in agreement with the first point, the second weakens when we realize that even a comparison between the English versions of key Freudian terms easily demonstrates the inconsistency in kinds of diction I have located in the translated passage: 'id' vs. 'unconscious'; 'cathexis' vs. 'charge', or 'energy'; 'libidinal' vs. 'sexual'.

Bettelheim helpfully suggests some of the determinations that shaped the scientistic translation strategy of the *Standard Edition*. One important con-sideration is the intellectual current that had dominated Anglo-American psychology and philosophy since the eighteenth century: 'In theory, many topics with which Freud dealt permit both a hermeneutic-spiritual and a positivistic-pragmatic approach. When this is so, the English translators nearly always opt for the latter, positivism being the most important English philosophical tradition' (p. 44). But there are also the social institutions in which this tradition was entrenched and against which psychoanalysis had to struggle in order to gain acceptance after the Second World War. As Bettelheim concisely puts it, 'psychological research and teaching in American universities are either behaviorally, cognitively, or physiologically oriented and concentrate almost exclusively on what can be measured or observed from the outside' (p. 19). For psychoanalysis this meant that its assimilation in Anglo-American culture entailed a redefinition, in which it 'was perceived in the United States as a practice that ought to be the sole prerogative of physicians' (p. 33), 'a medical specialty' (p. 35), and this redefinition was carried out in a variety of social practices, including not only legislation by state assemblies and certification by the psychoanalytic profession, but the scientistic translation of the *Standard Edition:*

> When Freud appears to be either more abstruse or more dogmatic in English translation than in the original German, to speak about abstract concepts rather than about the reader himself, and about man's mind rather than about his soul, the probable explanation isn't mischievousness or carelessness on the translators' part but a deliberate wish to perceive Freud strictly within the framework of medicine.
>
> (p. 32)

The domesticating method at work in the translations of the *Standard Edition* sought to assimilate Freud's texts to the dominance of positivism in Anglo-American culture so as to facilitate the institutionalization of psychoanalysis in the medical profession and in academic psychology.

Bettelheim's book is of course couched in the most judgemental of terms, and it is his negative judgement that must be avoided (or perhaps rethought) if we want to understand the manifold significance of the *Standard Edition* as a translation. Bettelheim views the work of Strachey and his collaborators as a distortion and a betrayal of Freud's 'essential humanism', a view that points to a valorization of the concept of the transcendental subject in both Bettelheim and Freud. Bettelheim's assessment of the psychoanalytic project is stated in his own humanistic versions for the *Standard Edition*'s 'ego', 'id', and 'superego': 'A reasonable dominance of our I over our id and above-I – this was Freud's goal for all of us' (p. 110). This notion of ego dominance thinks of the subject as the potentially self-consistent source of its knowledge and actions, not perpetually split by psychological ('id') and social ('superego') determinations over which it has no or limited control. The same assumption can often be seen in Freud's German text: not only in his emphasis on social adjustment, for instance, as with the concept of the 'reality principle', but also in his repeated use of his own experience for analysis; both represent the subject as healing the determinate split in its own consciousness. Yet in so far as Freud's various psychic models theorized the ever-present, contradictory determinations of consciousness, the effect of his work was to decentre the subject, to remove it from the transcendental realm of freedom and unity and conceive it as the determinate product of psychic and familial forces beyond its conscious control. These conflicting concepts of the subject underlie different aspects of Freud's project: the transcendental subject, on the one hand, leads to a definition of psycho-analysis as primarily therapeutic, what Bettelheim calls a 'demanding and potentially dangerous voyage of self-discovery . . . so that we may no longer be enslaved without knowing it to the dark forces that reside in us' (p. 4); the determinate subject, on the other hand, leads to a definition of psycho-analysis as primarily hermeneutic, a theoretical apparatus with sufficient scientific rigour to analyse the shifting but always active forces that con-stitute and divide human subjectivity. Freud's texts are thus marked by a fundamental discontinuity, one which is 'resolved' in Bertelheim's human-istic representation of psychoanalysis as compassionate therapy, but which is exacerbated by the scientistic strategy of the English translations and their representation of Freud as the coolly analysing physician.[20] The inconsistent diction in the *Standard Edition*, by reflecting the positivistic redefinition of psychoanalysis in Anglo-American institutions, signifies another, alternative reading of Freud that heightens the contradictions of his project.

It can be argued, therefore, that the inconsistent diction in the English translations does not really deserve to be judged erroneous; on the contrary, it discloses interpretive choices determined by a wide range of social institu-tions and cultural movements, some (like the specific institutionalization of psychoanalysis) calculated by the translators, others (like the dominance of positivism and the discontinuities in Freud's texts) remaining dimly per-ceived or entirely unconscious during the translation process. The fact that the inconsistencies have gone unnoticed for so long is perhaps largely the result of two mutually determining factors: the privileged status accorded the *Standard Edition* among English-language readers and the entrenchment of a positivistic reading of Freud in the Anglo-American psychoanalytic establishment. Hence, a different critical approach with a different set of assumptions becomes necessary to perceive the inconsistent diction of the translations: Bettelheim's particular humanism, or my own attempt to ground a reading of translated texts on a foreignizing method of translation that assumes a concept of determinate subjectivity.

In many translations, however, the discontinuities are readily apparent, unintentionally disturbing the fluency of the language or deliberately estab-lishing the linguistic heterogeneity that distinguishes a resistant strategy. Literary translations, in particular, often bear prefaces which announce the translator's strategy and alert the reader to the presence of noticeable stylistic peculiarities. But perhaps translations in other disciplines should also contain prefaces that not merely describe the problems posed by the foreign text and the translator's solutions, but rationalize the global strategy developed and implemented by the translator, including the specific kind of discourse chosen for the translation and the specific interpretations assigned to key concepts. Such prefaces will ultimately force translators and their readers to reflect on the ethnocentric violence of translation and possibly to write and read translated texts in ways that seek to recognize the linguistic and cultural difference of foreign texts. What I am advocating is not an indiscriminate valorization of every foreign culture or a metaphysical concept of foreignness as an essential value; indeed, the foreign text is privileged in a foreignizing translation only in so far as it enables a disruption of target-language cultural values, so that its value is always strategic, depending on the cultural formation into which it is translated. My goal is not an essentializing of the foreign, but resistance against ethnocentrism and racism, cultural narcissism and imperialism, in the interests of democratic geopolitical relations. Hence, my project is the elaboration of the theoretical, critical, and textual means by which translation can be studied and practised as a focus of difference, instead of the homogeneity that widely characterizes it today. Once the violence of translation is recognized, the choices facing the writers and readers of translated texts become clear – however difficult they are to make.

Notes

1 Roland Barthes, 'Taking sides', in *Critical Essays*, trans. Richard Howard (Evanston, Ill.: Northwestern University Press, 1972) pp. 163–70.

2 Barbara Kruger, Mary Boone Gallery, 5–26 January 1991.

3 Friedrich Schleiermacher, 'On the different methods of translating', in *Translating Literature: The German Tradition from Luther to Rosensweig*, ed. and trans. André Lefevere (Assen: Van Gorcum, 1977), pp. 67–89.

4 Antoine Berman, *L'épreuve de l'étranger: Culture et traduction dans l'Allemagne romantique* (Paris: Gallimard, 1984). See also Berman's 'La traduction et la lettre, ou l'auberge du lointain', in *Les Tours de Babel: Essais sur la traduction* (Mauvezin: Trans-Europ-Repress, 1985), pp. 31–150, especially pp. 87–91. Schleiermacher's theory, despite its stress on foreignizing translation, is complicated by the nationalist cultural programme he wants German translation to serve: see my article 'Genealogies of translation theory: Schleiermacher', in *TTR: Traduction, Terminologie, Rédaction: Etudes sur le texte et ses transformations*, vol. 4, no. 2 (1991), pp. 125–50.

5 See the annual statistics for the American publishing industry presented by Chandler B. Grannis in *Publishers Weekly*, 19 September 1989, pp. 24–5, 9 March 1990, pp. 32–5, and 8 March 1991, pp. 36–9. For the British statistics, see *Whtttaker's Almanack* for the years 1986 to 1991. The volume of translations published annually in a European country like Italy can be gauged from Herbert R. Lottman, 'Milan: A world of change', *Publishers Weekly*, 21 June 1991, pp. s5–s11.

6 I discuss the impact of French poststructuralism on translation theory and practice in the introduction of my anthology, *Rethinking Translation: Discourse,
   Subjectivity, Ideology* (London and New York: Routledge, 1992) pp. 1–17. The
   present article develops theoretical issues set forth in that introduction. Although
   I am theorizing translation from within Anglo-American culture, the foreign
   theoretical discourses I put to work considerably complicate my 'home' position,
   creating possibilities for cultural critique and resistance. In a previous article
   – 'The translator's invisibility', *Criticism*, 28, (1986), pp. 179–212 – I offer an
   assessment of current English-language translation that is indebted as much to
   Althusserian Marxism as to poststructuralism.

7 Sir John Denham, 'Preface' to *The Destruction of Troy*, in *English Translation
   Theory, 1650–1800*, ed. T. R. Steiner (Assen: Van Gorcum, 1975), pp. 64–5.

8 John Dryden, 'Dedication of the *Aeneis*,' in *English Translation Theory*,
   pp. 72–4.

9 William Guthrie, 'Preface' to *The Orations of Marcus Tullius Cicero*, in *English
   Translation Theory*, pp. 96–9.

10 John Hookman Frere, Review of Thomas Mitchell's translation of *The Comedies
   of Aristophanes, Quarterly Review*, 23 (July 1820), pp. 474–505.

11 Review of William Stewart Rose's translation of *Orlando Furioso, Quarterly
   Review*, 30 (October 1823), pp. 40–61.

12 For the emergence of moral and political conservatism in early nineteenth-
   century England, see Maurice J. Quinlan, *Victorian Prelude: A History of English
   Manners, 1780–1830* (New York: Columbia University Press, 1941) and Lawrence Stone, *The Family, Sex and Marriage in England, 1500–1800* (New York:
   Harper & Row, 1977).

13 Eugene A. Nida, *Toward a Science of Translating, with Special Reference to
   Principles and Procedures Involved in Bible Translating* (Leiden: Brill, 1964),
   p. 159. Further references to this work will be indicated by *Science*.

14 Jan de Waard and Eugene A. Nida, *From One Language to Another: Functional
   Equivalence in Bible Translating* (Nashville: Thomas Nelson, 1986), p. 14. Further references to this work will be indicated by *One Language*.

15 Eugene A. Nida, *Customs and Cultures: Anthropology for Christian Missions*
   (1954; reprinted South Pasadena, Calif.: William Carey Library, 1975), p. 250;
   God's World in Man's Language (New York: Harper & Brothers, 1952), p. 117.

16 Philip E. Lewis, 'The measure of translation effects', in *Difference in Translation*,
   ed. Joseph Graham (Ithaca, N.Y.: Cornell University Press, 1985), pp. 31–62.

17 These remarks assume Anthony Giddens' concept of agency in *Central Problems
   in Social Theory: Action, Structure, and Contradiction in Social Analysis* (Berkeley
   and Los Angeles: University of California Press, 1979), especially ch. 2.

18 Bruno Bettelheim, *Freud and Man's Soul* (New York: Knopf, 1983).

19 Sigmund Freud, *The Psychopathology of Everyday Life*, trans. Alan Tyson, ed.
   James Strachey (New York: Norton, 1960), p. 21.

20 The same contradiction appears in Freud's own reflections on the therapeutic/
   hermeneutic dilemma of psychoanalysis in *Beyond the Pleasure Principle* (1920),
   trans. James Strachey (New York: Norton, 1961), p. 12:

> Twenty-five years of intense work have had as their result that the
> immediate aims of psychoanalytic technique are other today than they
> were at the outset. At first the analyzing physician could do no more
> than discover the unconscious material that was concealed from the
> patient, put it together, and, at the right moment, communicate it to
> him. Psychoanalysis was then first and foremost an art of interpreting.

Since this did not solve the therapeutic problem, a further aim quickly came in view: to oblige the patient to confirm the analyst's construction from his own memory. In that endeavor the chief emphasis lay upon the patient's resistances: the art considered now in uncovering these as quickly as possible, in pointing them out to the patient and in inducing him by human influence – this was where suggestion operating as 'transference' played its part – to abandon his resistances.

It will be noted that although Freud intends to draw a sharp distinction in the development of psychoanalysis between an early, hermeneutic phase and a later, therapeutic phase, his exposition really blurs the distinction: both phases require a primary emphasis on interpretation, whether of 'unconscious material' or of 'the patient's resistances', which in so far as they require 'uncovering' are likewise 'unconscious'; in both 'the analyst's construction' can be said to be 'first and foremost'. What has changed is not so much 'the immediate aims of psychoanalytic technique' as its theoretical apparatus: the intervening years witnessed the development of a new *interpretive* concept – the 'transference'. It is also worth pointing out that this characterization of psychoanalysis as primarily therapeutic occurs in a late text that is one of Freud's most theoretical and speculative. Bettelheim's characterization of psychoanalysis, the basis for his rejection of the *Standard Edition*, smooths out the discontinuities in Freud's texts and project by resorting to a schema of development (like Freud himself): 'The English translations cleave to an early stage of Freud's thought, in which he inclined toward science and medicine, and disregard the more mature Freud, whose orientation was humanistic, and who was concerned mostly with broadly conceived cultural and human problems and with matters of the soul' (p. 32).

43

ISSUES IN THE PRACTICE
OF TRANSLATING
WOMEN'S FICTION

Carol Maier

Source: *Bulletin of Hispanic Studies* LXXV(1) (1998): 95–108.

The paragraphs that follow began their existence as a talk, similarly titled, given at the Institute of Translation and Interpreting International Colloquium on 'The Practices of Literary Translation', held at the University of East Anglia in September 1996.[1] That talk in its turn drew upon thoughts and notes accumulated in the course of translating María Zambrano's *Delirio y destino*.[2] Such thoughts and notes are, of their nature, difficult to order: bulletins from a front where the translator works with a general strategy, but with one that she questions and refines as the work goes on. Translation in a case like this cannot be assessed from that reflective distance at which one might contemplate a completed project: it can only be discussed as practice, as activity. In this instance too, the difficulties are compounded by the need to address, clearly and concisely, an interaction that was inherently complex. The principal goal of this essay is to encourage translators to consider the question of gender with regard to translation practice. This question, however, is bound to raise the related issues of how we are to understand and use the key terms 'translation' and 'woman'.

In part (a) of this essay, therefore, I will discuss these questions as they have arisen repeatedly in my own work and recent reading. Part (b) will outline several loosely-defined approaches to addressing them in practice; in part (c) I will offer examples of how each approach might be applied and what strategies it might promote within a broadly common context. None of these approaches, however, will be presented as exemplary. The objective is not to prescribe, but to illustrate how translators employ an approach to gender as they practise, even if that approach is unacknowledged, and to suggest ways they might employ their approaches knowingly.[3] I would hope too that the comments offered here on gender and sexuality might suggest analogies with other aspects of identity, such as political affiliation, which translation can call into question.

(a) Issues

How does one talk about 'translation'—without relying too heavily on either theory or individual practice? This is a particularly troubling question. It is surely not the case that one must be a practising translator to speak theoretically about translation nor is it reasonable to ask that all practising translators be theorists. It remains a matter for concern, though, that too few translators, even those who teach and write about translation are willing to attempt this discussion. My own experience as both a teacher and a translator, has constantly involved the need to comment on my translations—to answer student questions, for example, or to think through and articulate the decisions made in my practice. To respond adequately in such situations, a translator must be able to work at least to some degree, as both theoretician *and* practitioner. In other words, translators should be able to articulate their approaches, albeit in simple terms, using examples from their work when appropriate, but without allowing their working explanations to become a mere defence of their own methods and solutions. Most translators have been trained either as practitioners *or* as theoreticians—if they have been trained at all—yet many if not most translators also teach or explain their work to others, even if not in a formal academic setting. This coexistence of a lack of training with the need both to talk about translation and to train translators suggests that currently one of the most pressing tasks for translators is to grapple with the dichotomies they have inherited as 'natural'. Hence, the present treatment becomes an essay in working around—if not out of—the dichotomies that polarize translation theory and practice as well as those pertaining to the genders.

Although 'translation' is used to refer to many different activities in a wide variety of contexts,[4] the term will be used here to refer specifically to an activity in which a literary work—in the case which most directly concerns me, a novel—is rewritten in a different language. This activity, however, is far less restricted than it may seem at first. Not only does it invariably involve—through consultation and collaboration—more than a single individual, it also occurs as one of many simultaneous, overlapping activities: most immediately perhaps the commercial (and at times academic) activity required for the support and dissemination of the translator's work, and the translator's own self-definition and 'dissemination', whether as an academic, a free-lancer, or creative writer. Additional activities could be cited, and the interconnections between translation and other forms of re-writing have been well documented by not a few theorists. My conversations with translators and my reading of their commentaries lead me to believe, however, that, narrow as it is the somewhat broader-than-usual definition of translation offered here would not be operative for many practising translators. Their remarks indicate that their attention is fixed primarily, if not exclusively, on re-writing in the most conventional sense.

The second issue can be stated simply as 'What is woman?'. Consider the response Judith Butler received when she asked for a show of hands by all the people in an audience of more than four hundred who thought of themselves as women and not a single hand was raised.[5] One scarcely needs to repeat that experiment in order to validate a single observation: unqualified, 'woman' is not a reliable, stable point of departure for either the discussion or the practice of translation of work from any genre. On the contrary, one finds repeatedly that neither authors nor characters—and certainly not readers—conform to any fixed understanding of 'woman', even though they are defined as women by themselves or others. Perhaps more importantly, one frequently finds that even when 'woman' can be used appropriately, to use it as a single form of definition is to exclude other definitions that may be equally or more determinant. As Lisel Mueller has suggested in her prose poem *Triage*, 'To speak of one thing is to suppress another',[6] and to describe an individual as a woman is to describe only in terms of gender, to suppress definitions of race, class; nationality, vocation or religious affiliation, to cite just a few. Recently translation theorists and practitioners have begun to explain their use or refusal of 'woman' with respect to related words such as 'feminine' or 'feminist', but they have not explicitly questioned the actual practice of using a single word to define an individual work or life—even in discussions about what it means to be a woman in one place as compared to another.[7]

(b) Strategies

It will make much sense, then, to refrain from offering even such a general definition of 'woman' as was proposed for 'translation', but rather to discuss the term in relation to individual translational approaches. These latter are not put forward here as a set of fixed categories but as elements in a continuum, the parts of which can be separated only arbitrarily for a particular purpose.

(1) The first approach might be characterized as 'no deliberate approach', and associated with a 'null' strategy or with direct translation of the kind often referred to as 'literal'. This might well be the approach of many translators, both to translating women's fiction and to translation in general. It is the absence of a deliberately formulated method. The absence of an acknowledged approach does not necessarily imply carelessness, however, nor is it purely negative. Many highly successful

translators discuss their work by detailing problems and solutions but without defining principles. They often express a refusal to work analytically, affirming instead 'spontaneity' or 'creativity'. For such 'null' strategists 'What is woman?' would not be a question, and there would be no definition of 'woman'. The translator would not feel a need for one.

(2) At the opposite end of the continuum, would lie what might be termed a 'feminist' approach to 'woman'. The term 'end' is in some ways inapposite here: the continuum is not so much linear as circular, because a feminist approach to translation circles back to resemble 'no deliberate approach' in two important ways. First, like the absence of an approach, feminist translation is usually not concerned with a definition of 'woman'. Rather, feminist translators generally employ 'woman' without question, although like other feminist theorists, they have begun to use both 'feminism' and 'woman' in a less global sense and with an increasing recognition that those terms cannot and should not be 'transferred' without 'translation'.[8]

Second, the work of feminist translators also arises from a simultaneous affirmation and refusal, in this instance the refusal and affirmation implicit in Rachel DuPlessis' explanation of feminist writing as the infusion of vanguard 'theoretical practices with urgent and continuous confrontations with the political and representational oppression of wome/an, with an eye to enacting their end'.[9] Some feminist translators, such as Susanne de Lotbinière-Harwood have focused this refusal-affirmation even more precisely by affirming women writers through a refusal to translate work written by men, often choosing to translate only explicitly feminist texts. They are well aware of the perspective that guides their work, and they often discuss their strategies in detail. These strategies are applied both at the lexical level of a text—in the translation of pronouns, for example—and in terms of the text as a whole, where feminist strategies concern footnotes and commentary, and at times they lead a translator to claim a text by intervening in one way or another, for example, inserting a translator's remarks (or person) in the text itself, or even eliminating passages the translator considers non-feminist.[10]

(3) Between such deliberate and frequently explicit intervention and the close adherence to a text associated with 'no deliberate approach' one finds varying degrees of attention to 'woman'. It is possible to think of these degrees primarily with respect to a translator's identification or definition of her, or his, own work—in other words to associate them with translators who either identify themselves as women or work with authors identified as women. For two principal reasons the term 'woman-identified' seems apt here. First, it is inclusive enough to span both ends of our continuum; and this is important because of the

non-absoluteness which is manifested even at the two extremes—in recent discussions by feminists themselves about the impossibility of applying their own feminist principles globally, and in gender-related comments even on the part of translators who claim to have no interest in 'theory'. And second, because 'woman-identified' allows for a straight-forward definition of one's work based on the identification of the translator's or the author's gender.

Both of these reasons retain their force for me. Yet, in seeking to define my own work as a translator, I have come increasingly to find 'woman-identified' a less appropriate term. Among many other explana-tions, three experiences in particular have led me to rethink its use.

The first was my discovery of Casandra Reilly, the protagonist of Barbara Wilson's novel *Gaudí Afternoon*.[11] Reilly's explanation that she is neither a woman nor a man because 'I'm a translator' brought my doubts about 'woman-identified' into clear focus. As long as one identifies one's practice with a single, fixed gender identity, that prac-tice may bridge gender definitions but will probably not prompt their interrogation.

No doubt Cassandra Reilly's words had this impact because of the uncertainties about gender identification associated with a second experience—translating two authors identified as men: Ramón del Valle-Inclán and Severo Sarduy. In the case of Valle-Inclán, my endeavour to investigate—through translation—the 'feminine', as it appears in *La lámpara maravillosa*, led me to consider the inseparability of a feminine and a masculine language or use of language, and the complex inter-action between gender and other identities determinant in Valle-Inclán's writing. I was intrigued, for example, by the consistent ambivalence in his use of words usually associated with one sex or another, and by Salvador de Madariaga's portrayal of Valle-Inclán as a 'feminine' writer because of his Galician heritage.[12] The translation of Sarduy's *Escrito sobre un cuerpo* provoked a different but not unrelated uncertainty. How does one refer pronominally, for example, to an author whose introductory self-description portrays a 'palandrija . . . vestida de rojo' but whose simulation of the feminine aims to surpass the duality of a copy or image ('que lo mismo sea lo que no es')?[13] At the same time, however, when an author's work clearly indicates an unstable gender identification, or dis-identification, can a translator fairly consider work by that writer as either man- or woman-identified?

The third experience concerns a different although closely related element of many translation projects—scholarly editing. The issue arose in relation to my English version of *Delirio y destino*, by María Zambrano. The book is a novelized autobiography that deals primarily with Zambrano's coming of age as a philosopher in the years immedi-ately preceding the Spanish Civil War. Although it was written in the early 1950s, *Delirio y destino* was not published until shortly before Zambrano's death. At the time of publication, excisions and corrections were made to the typescript, many of which were realized by a male cousin of Zambrano. One and perhaps several other men also contributed significantly to the editing at a time when Zambrano was unable to participate actively herself. I became gradually aware that my translation of *Delirio y destino* would require informed, deliberate editing, which was bound to address the role gender might have played when the book was prepared for publication. Zambrano had remained the woman author, but it seemed clear that many of the excisions and corrections made by men compromised or even obscured her work.[14]

(4) This obscuring of women authors in the production of texts prompts the definition of a fourth approach. It is a reminder that to identify primarily as a woman either oneself or an author whose writing one translates may obscure other determinant identities. In addition, such an identification employs as fixed a definition that recent work in many disciplines has shown to be contingent and impermanent. More and more, then, I have come to think of working not as a woman-identified translator, but as one who questions, even interrogates gender definitions— one who can hold 'natural' definitions of gender in abeyance, attempting to identify one's practice as a translator in a way that is open to and can thus interact with whatever gender identity (or other identity) a translator might encounter. It would be appropriate to think of this approach as 'woman-interrogated' because it involves an endeavour to work less from confidently held definitions than from a will to participate in re-definitions, to counter the restrictions of a gender-based identity by questioning gender as the most effective or the most appropriate point of departure for a translator's practice.

But, one might ask, would such a refusal not paralyse a translator and make necessary decisions impossible? How might a translator work interrogatively with 'woman'?

My own experience makes it easy to answer the first of those two questions unequivocally: it would not. Some, perhaps even many translators may find it unacceptable to refuse the conventional definitions that guide their practice. For me as a translator, the need to hold my own gender identification in abeyance presents a challenge—sobering but welcome. Moreover, thinking about gender interrogatively promotes a fuller appreciation of the translator's responsibility not only with respect to the identity of an author but also to the task of representing that author's work in a more informed and deliberate manner.

This paradox of an experience at once 'sobering' and 'welcome', might be explored further. When I read Cassandra Reilly's words, I realized that indeed the opportunity to represent, to perform in collaboration with another identity was one of the aspects of translation I found most rewarding. I remembered that for a long time I had thought of translation in terms of a performance associated less with definitiveness than with change, even with ephemerality—a performance closely related to the performativity discussed more recently by Butler with respect to gender.[15] As Butler has explained, this understanding of 'performative' carries the double meaning of 'dramatic' and 'non-referential'.[16] Consequently, it implies an activity both challenging and disquieting because, as Eve Kosofsky Sedgwick has noted, it 'carries the authority of two quite different discourses, that of theater on the one hand, of speech act and deconstruction on the other'.[17] It also implies an ambivalent position (although in such a situation that word can be used only relatively), in which a practitioner—in this case a translator—offers an interpretation or performance that is inevitably contingent on many factors, not the least of which is the translator's own notion of 'identity'.[18]

Such contingency can of course prompt a sense of impotence, since it can lead to the feeling that one works without any possibility of agency. At the same time, however, it can also prompt a sense of responsibility not unrelated to power, especially if one accepts performativity's paradox and endeavours to exploit it, bearing in mind particularly that representation is inherent in translation, and not only in a theatrical context. For to translate an author is to represent that author in a new language and tradition, and such representation involves agency. It soon became evident that despite the lack of recognition they receive consistently, translators are not at all powerless. On the contrary, as both practitioners and theoreticians in diverse fields have begun to document, translators are often very powerful with respect to authors and their work.[19] Not only do they decide which works they translate and how responsibly they carry out their translations, their understanding of gender-related issues (including their feelings about their own gender identifications as well) to a large extent determines an author's appearance in another language. Some years ago, I began to translate the poetry of Ana Castillo, for example, because I admired Castillo's insights and her use of language, but also because I identified with her as a woman. It was soon evident to me, however, that for Castillo the gender bond I sensed did not exist, or it existed only minimally. The fact that she was a woman was crucial to her, but when it came to the publication of her work in English translation, she identified herself first and foremost as a Chicana. This meant that gender, while inseparable from class or ethnicity, could also be distinguished from them, and for her it was not the most salient factor. Or it was not the salient factor in her relationship with a translator who was not a Chicana but an Anglo academic whose experiences of gender-related oppression, painful as they may have been, could not provide the basis for a mutual identification between the two women.[20]

(c) Examples

Castillo's guarded response was instructive, because it highlighted the limits of gender-related definitions and the translator's responsibility as an author's 'representative' in English. Once translation is understood, practised, or experienced as a representation that simultaneously destabilizes and defines, it becomes impossible to ignore the extent to which a translator (or an editor, or a publisher) has attempted to direct readers to a particular aspect of a text, prompted them to hold their own thinking about gender in abeyance, or encouraged them to reflect on the inconclusive and even potentially threatening nature of the mediation that is operative in all translation. This returns us to the second of our two questions about practice: how might one practise translation in a way that destabilized rather than reinforced notions of identity, even as one was defining a text? In this case, how might one translate 'woman' interrogatively? The question is not easy to answer because, I suspect, the very claim that one translates 'interrogatively' makes an exclusive adherence to any one method impossible. I also suspect that it makes a 'woman-interrogated' approach as inappropriate for some situations as it is appropriate for others. Furthermore, it raises the larger, although no less important issue of the extent to which a translator can direct a reader's attention.[21] These reservations, however, are not framed as a way of avoiding the immediate question raised here. The three situations discussed below, by way of concluding, all offer possible translation strategies corresponding to each of the approaches previously outlined. These examples, derived from different, though integrally related aspects of my translation of María Zambrano's *Delirio y destino*, are deliberately chosen from a project still in progress in order to minimize whatever allegiance I might feel to my working versions.

The first example concerns the translator's initial definition of a writer. Envisage the following: a translator wants to translate a novel and offers a prospective publisher a first brief sentence of description. The author is unknown in the translator's native language; the author's name, photograph and biography indicate that the author is a woman; and the novel offers a harsh critique of oppression in the author's country where women are among the most victimized. How would a translator describe the author in this situation? The translator who followed 'no deliberate approach', who proceeded unquestioningly, as it were, would probably describe this writer as a woman, although the definition might well also include other identifications. A feminist translator, on the other hand, would be less apt to offer a spontaneous definition and might well opt for 'feminist' rather than 'woman', since 'feminist' qualifies 'woman' further, placing the word in a more politicized context, albeit in an imprecise one. A 'woman-identified' translator would definitely opt for one word or the other, and that choice would depend on the translator's position with respect to feminism and on the project the translator had formulated, however tentatively. A 'woman-interrogated' translator would want to throw the term 'woman' into question and would probably work differently from any of the others and consider the possibility of not referring to the writer's gender at all. This translator might rely on the author's name or another factor to indicate gender. The issue scarcely arose in my own experience with *Delirio y destino*, because that initial description of Zambrano—as 'a Spanish woman'—was formulated at a time when I was only beginning to question the viability of 'woman-identified translation'.

The second example also concerns the use of 'woman', but it relates to a lexical decision made in the actual 'translation' of *Delirio y destino.* This concerned the word *española* as it appears in the subtitle: 'Veinte años en la vida de una española'. What would a woman-interrogated translator do here? What this translator did in her interrogation was to think long and hard about the implications of choosing 'Spanish woman' as opposed to 'Spaniard'. In my first draft of the book I had translated *española* as 'Spanish woman'. But further reflection made it evident that in so doing I had followed 'no deliberate approach' and used the word that came 'naturally', relying on my knowledge that *española* indicates both 'Spaniard' and 'female'. The importance of gender-related issues in *Delirio y destino* was unmistakable, as was Zambrano's life-long resistance to the historical idealization of women she found so crippling. It seemed clear too that both a feminist translator and a woman-identified one would choose 'Spanish woman', because both would find it imperative to stress Zambrano's gender. This decision is certainly defensible but my own eventual 'woman-interrogated' version is 'Twenty years in the life of a Spaniard'. *Española*, though in its adjectival use literally translated as 'Spanish', here indicates a female Spaniard without specifying gender and without adjectivizing 'Spaniard'. 'Spaniard' does not specify female, but neither does it exclude that connotation. The gender of Zambrano's protagonist is soon apparent to the reader; and although it is valid, useful and necessary to discuss that protagonist as a woman, I do not believe one can fairly say that Zambrano presents her protagonist more as 'a (Spanish) woman' than as 'a (female) Spaniard'. On the contrary, the protagonist explains in detail that one sets aside all personal 'identities' in order to participate as fully as possible in certain moments in history. For this reason, if for no other, there is more than enough justification for choosing 'Spaniard', which also reflects Zambrano's own affirmation-refusal during the 1920s and 1930s.[22]

My final example can also be discussed in terms of actual experience as a woman-interrogated translator. It concerns the supplementary materials that accompany a translation. Will the translation include such supplementary materials and if it will, what will they be? To this question there may be as many answers as there are translations. It acquires a more specific focus, though, in terms of those instances in which a translator has a say in how the question is answered. This becomes the case especially in a translator-initiated project, when the translator also works to some degree as an editor and therefore can consider the question of supplementary materials from the moment the translation is planned. In such an instance, supplementary materials are an integral part of a 'translation', although not all translators address them as such (or at all), even if the translator decides against their inclusion. Given a say, a translator who has 'woman' in mind will have an answer to this question and it will be a deliberate, well-considered answer.

A translator with 'no deliberate approach' could often arrive at a decision without giving much thought to 'woman' at all. If 'woman' were a factor which seemed to call for such supplementary matter, it would be because something about the author's life or work made its inclusion appear 'natural'. Whether or not these materials did appear would depend on what seemed appropriate to the translator or on what others involved in the project might request or expect.

For a feminist translator, the question of supplementary materials would be crucial because of the opportunity they offer a translator to comment, as editor, on the work of both author and translator and to stress the relation between that work and feminist principles and practice. For example, in her introduction to a Spanish edition of three of Zambrano's plays, Elena Laurenzi, an Italian feminist identifies and studies Zambrano's work in feminist terms. She cites in evidence passages from several of the author's books. Stressing Zambrano's lifelong commitment to 'una crítica consciente y un desafío a la institucionalidad masculina de la cultura',[23] she at times obscures the equally strong commitment to what the writer describes as a 'neutrality' that is neither masculine nor feminine because it is 'más acá de la diferencia existente entre hombre y mujer, ya que del pensamiento se trata'.[24] A woman-identified translator would probably be equally concerned with supplementary information, although the materials deployed would probably be oriented less specifically toward 'feminism'—however the translator understood that term—than toward gender and its relation to the project as a whole.

The same could be said for a woman-interrogated translator, although only to a degree, because the translator would want to make it clear that in the realization of the project 'woman' had served less as a fixed point of departure than as a literal question. Supplementary materials might include an explanation of the translator's use or refusal of 'woman' as a determining factor in the project, an element of commentary on the translator's approach, or even a discussion of the limits inherent in a translator's efforts to supplement a text through commentaries, documentation or insertion.

In its eventual English version, *Delirium and Destiny*, for example, will include an essay about Zambrano's life and work, a translator's introduction and a glossary of terms related to Spanish history and culture. Her work as a philosopher involved her not merely in abstracting from what she referred to—adapting José Ortega y Gasset's word—as her 'circumstances' but in an active engagement with them, whereby she continually questioned the sense of 'woman' in history and society. Hence, I have sought to present her, as a Spaniard who was also, simultaneously, and in alphabetical order, a daughter, an exile, an ex-wife, a lover, a man, a philosopher, a sister, a student, a wife, a woman and a writer—as a complex human being. And indeed, that list has to include 'man', because on more than one occasion Zambrano made it clear that she had deliberately used *hombre* rather than *humano*.[25] In these instances I have used 'man' in the English. To have done otherwise, (followed current usage and used 'humankind' or 'humanity', for example) would have been to suppress the continuous tension, both between man and woman and within the human, that is present throughout *Delirio y destino*, and to dilute Zambrano's own effort to define 'human'.[26] It would also have been to suppress an analogous challenge in English, allowing readers to feel comfortable with Zambrano's words but preventing them from approaching both those words themselves and her struggle to redefine them.

That rather paradoxical affirmation of 'man', then, indicates that a set of new definitions of 'woman' might not be the appropriate conclusion here. Instead, three final suggestions may encourage others to carry this line of thinking further. First, translating women's fiction emerges as a translator's rewriting of fiction written by a woman, as 'woman' is defined by the translator with respect to a particular instance of translation. Secondly, in view of the current need for a more developed translation pedagogy and criticism, such rewriting is best realized and discussed interrogatively by calling attention to the complexity and contingency of 'woman' and 'translation' and by encouraging readers to reconsider—to engage in the translation of—both the familiar definitions of those terms and their own relation to them. Thirdly, an excellent way for translators (as well as readers, teachers, reviewers, and literary critics) to begin to engage in an interrogative discussion of gender is by considering the approaches and strategies that guide their practice and articulating those approaches and strategies clearly.

Notes

1 The talk was delivered on 9 September 1996. The Colloquium was organized in collaboration with the British Centre for Literary Translation and the Translators Association. The present essay follows the text of that talk closely, although I have edited it considerably, expanded several sections and developed some of the examples. My thanks to Peter Bush and the conference organizers for the invitation and to the Faculty and staff at the University of East Anglia, in particular Christine Wilson, the conference administrator.

2 María Zambrano, *Delirio y destino* (Madrid: Mondadori, 1989). The translation will be published as *Delirium and Destiny* by SUNY Press in the Autumn of 1998.

3 In this context, see the discussions by Harveen Sachdeva Mann, '*Bharat mein Mahila Lekhana*, or Women's Writing in India: Regional Literatures, Translation, and Global Feminism', *Socialist Review*, XXIV (1994), No. 4, 151–72, especially pp. 164–68 and Karen Van Dyck, 'Introduction to Translation and Deterritorialization', *Journal of Modern Greek Studies*, VIII (1990), No. 2, 173–82.

4 In contexts as diverse for example, as mysticism and Cultural Studies. In forming my own definition, I have drawn on Gideon Toury's discussion of the 'notion of an "assumed translation"' (Gideon Toury, *Descriptive Translation Studies and Beyond* [Philadelphia: John Benjamins, 1995], 31–35) and on Theo Hermans, 'Toury's Empiricism Version One', *The Translator*, I (1995), No. 2, 215–23, especially pp. 220–21.

5 Cited in Tom Frank, 'Textual Reckoning', *In These Times* (27 May 1996), 22–24, at p. 22.

6 Lisel Mueller, 'Triage', *Waving from the Shore* (Baton Rouge, LA: Louisiana State U. P., 1989), 51.

7 See, for example, Françoise Massardier-Kenney's 'redefinition of these terms with respect to gender ('Toward a Redefinition of Feminist Translation Practice', *The Translator*, III [1997], No. 1, 55–69, especially pp. 31–35); also Luise von Flotow, *Translation and Gender: Translating in the Era of Feminism* (Manchester: St Jerome Publishing, 1997) which suggests a need for redefinition with respect to gender—in particular, 'Future Perspectives', 89–94. Even when redefined in this way, however, 'gender' continues to impose an inevitable unification—as Hawkesworth points out, albeit arguably (Mary Hawkesworth, 'Confounding Gender', *Signs*, XX [1997], No. 3, 648–85; see also the exchange that follows Hawkesworth's article). However, the work of some novelists and theorists, many of them lesbian, convincingly suggests the impossibility of simple definitions (see, for example, Judith Halberstam, 'FM2: The Making of Female Masculinity', *The Lesbian Postmodern*, ed. Laura Doan [New York: Columbia U. P., 1994], 210–28, especially pp. 210–11). In this context, it is important to point out, as Françoise Massardier-Kenney and I noted in our work for 'Gender and/in Literary Translation', in *Translation Horizons: Beyond the Boundaries of 'Translation Spectrum'*, ed. Marilyn Gaddis Rose, Translation Perspectives IX (Binghamton, NY: Center for Research in Translation, SUNY Binghamton, 1996), 225–42, that the specifically lesbian identification of many translators and theorists indicates 'that a particularly necessary and promising area of study involves the interaction of translation and homosexuality' (239, n. 11).

8 Hari Kunzru, review of *The European Studies Journal, TLS* (25 November, 1994), 30. Many other examples could be cited. For two of them, see Nanette Funk and Magda Mueller's *Gender Politics and Post-Communism: Reflections from Eastern Europe and the Former Soviet Union* (New York: Routledge, 1993), in particular the comments in Funk's 'Introduction: Women and Post-Communism', 3–4; and Sherry Simon's 'Missed Connections: Transporting French Feminisms to Anglo-America', *Gender and Translation: Cultural Identity and the Politics of Transmission* (New York: Routledge, 1996), 86–110.

9 Rachel Blau DuPlessis, *The Pink Guitar: Writing as Feminist Practice* (New York; Routledge, 1990), 191.

10 See Barbara Godard, 'Theorizing Feminist Discourse/Translation', in *Translation, History and Culture*, ed. Susan Bassnett and André Lefevre (London: Pinter Publishers, 1990), 87–96, and 'A Translator's Journal', in *Culture in Transit: Translating the Literature of Quebec*, ed. Sherry Simon (Montreal: Véhicule Press, 1995), 69–82; Susanne de Lotbinière-Harwood, *Re-belle et Infidèle. La traduction comme practique de réécriture au feminin/The Body Bilingual. Translation as a*

Rewriting in the Feminine (Quebec: Les Éditions du Remue-Ménage/Women's Press, 1991), and 'Geo-graphies of Why', in *Culture in Transit*, 55–68; Carol Maier and Françoise Massardier-Kenney, 'Gender and/in Literary Translation'; Massardier-Kenney, 'Toward a Redefinition of Feminist Translation Practice'; and Simon, *Gender and Translation*; also von Flotow, *Translation and Gender*.

11 Barbara Wilson, *Gaudí Afternoon* (Seattle, WA: Seal Press, 1990).

12 See Madariaga's description of Valle-Inclán as a faithful, if not thoroughly reliable representative of 'el espíritu gallego', which he links to a poetry not only distinct from the Castilian tradition but also 'tres veces femenina' (*Semblanzas literarias contemporáneas* [Barcelona: Editorial Cervantes, 1924] 188).

13 Severo Sarduy, *La simulación: ensayos generates sobre el barroco* (Mexico/Buenos Aires: Fondo de Cultura Económica, 1987), 54. I refer here to the following translation: *Written on a Body*, trans. Carol Maier (New York: Lumen Books, 1989).

14 In this regard, two essays were particularly helpful: Alexandra Barratt, 'Feminist Editing: Cooking the Books', *AUMLA (Journal of the Australasian Modern Languages Association)*, LXXIX (May 1993), 54–57, and Susan Kirkpatrick, 'Toward Feminist Textual Criticism', in *The Politics of Editing*, ed. Nicholas Spadaccini and Jenaro Talens (Minneapolis: Univ. of Minnesota Press, 1992), 125–38.

15 Carol Maier, Translation as Performance: Three Notes', *Translation Review*, XV (1984), 7–8; Judith Butler, 'Performative Acts and Gender Constitution: An Essay in Phenomenology and Feminist Theory', *Performing Feminisms: Feminist Critical Theory and Theatre*, ed Sue-Ellen Chase (Baltimore: Johns Hopkins U. P., 1980), 270–82.

16 Butler, 'Performative Acts', 273.

17 Eve Kosovsky Sedgwick, 'Shame and Performativity: Henry James's New York Edition Prefaces', in *Henry James's New York Editions: The Construction to Authorship*, ed David McWhirter (Stanford, CA: Stanford U. P., 1995), 206–39, 312–14, at p. 207.

18 It is important to stress that 'identity' is used here principally in the context of translation practice. This practice is neither opposed to nor separable from a translator's own gender identification as an individual, but neither are the two identical. One can practise translation interrrogatively and simultaneously identify oneself with respect to one gender or the other. For a discussion of this distinction that has useful and provocative implications for translation, see Pamela L. Caughie, 'Let it Pass: Changing the Subject Once Again', *PMLA*, CXII (1997), No. 1, 26–39.

19 With respect to translation as discussed in this essay, see for example, Gayatri Chakravorty Spivak, most recently 'The Politics of Translation', in *Destabilizing Theory: Contemporary Feminist Debates*, ed. Michéle Barrett and Anne Phillips (Stanford, CA: Stanford U. P., 1992), 177–200 and her 'Translator's Preface' and 'Afterword', in *Imaginary Maps: Three Stories by Mahasweta Devi* (New York: Routledge, 1995), xxiii–xxix and 197–205. In addition, such discussions as those in Lawrence Venuti's 'Margin', in *The Translator's Invisibility: A History of Translation* (New York: Routledge, 1995), 187–202 and Matthew Howard's article on Jorge Luis Borges ('Stranger than *Ficción'*, *Lingua Franca* [June–July 1997], 40–49) show that the invisible are not always powerless.

20 I have discussed my translations of Castillo's poetry in greater detail in 'Notes After Words: Looking Forward Retrospectively at Translation and Hispanic and Luso-Brazilian Feminist Criticism', in *Cultural and Historical Grounding for Hispanic and Luso-Brazilian Feminist Literary Criticism*, ed. Hernán Vidal (Minneapolis: Institute for the Study of Ideologies and Literature, 1989), 625–53.

21 For a discussion of this larger issue with respect to gender, see von Flotow, *Translation and Gender*, 77–88. Spivak's comments in her 'Translator's Preface' and Butler's *Excitable Speech: Politics of the Performative* (New York: Routledge, 1997) address the question in a broader, more theoretical context.

22 I should note here that the published version of *Delirium and Destiny* will very likely carry yet another different translation, because I believe that an even more interrogative solution might well be a transfer of *una española* exactly as it occurs in Spanish.

23 Elena Laurenzi, *María Zambrano: nacer por sí misma*, trans. Raquel Hidalgo (Madrid: Horas y Horas, 1995), 17.

24 María Zambrano, 'A modo de prólogo', in *Obras reunidas* (Madrid: Aguilar, 1971), 10. Laurenzi also cites this passage (*María Zambrano*, 17).

25 See, for example, *Delirio y destino*: '. . . y si es hombre, entonces, humano si se prefiere así' (226).

26 Lesley Harman makes and comments on a similar decision to use the male pronoun in *The Modern Stranger: On Language and Membership*, cited by Janet Wolff, *Resident Alien Feminist Cultural Criticism* (New Haven: Yale U. P., 1995), 7.

Part 10

DISCOURSE AND IDEOLOGY

44

EPISTEMICIDE!

The tale of a predatory discourse

Karen Bennett

Source: *The Translator* 13(2) (2007): 151–69.

Abstract

English academic discourse, which emerged in the 17th century as a vehicle for the new rationalist/scientific paradigm, was initially a vehicle of liberation from the stifling feudal mind-set. Spreading from the hard sciences to the social sciences and on to the humanities, it gradually became the prestige discourse of the Anglophone world, due no doubt to its associations with the power structures of modernity (technology, industry and capitalism); today, mastery of it is essential for anyone wishing to play a role on the international stage. The worldview that this discourse encodes is essentially positivist; it privileges the referential function of language at the expense of the interpersonal or textual and crystallizes the dynamic flux of experience into static, observable blocs, rendering the universe passive, inert and devoid of meaning. Despite its obvious limitations for dealing with a decentred, multi-faceted, post-modern reality, its hegemonic status in the world today is such that other knowledges are rendered invisible or are swallowed up in a process of 'epistemicide'. This paper examines this process from the point of view of the translator, one of the primary gatekeepers of western academic culture. Drawing on surveys carried out in 2002 of Portuguese academics working in the humanities, it attempts to discover just what happens to the very different worldview encoded in traditional Portuguese academic discourse during the process of translation, and goes on to discuss the political and social consequences of the ideological imperialism manifest in editorial decisions about what counts as 'knowledge' in today's world.

Part I

"Once upon a time, many years ago in England, a new discourse was born. His parents were both very old at his birth, and poor, because, although they were of illustrious lineage, they had since fallen on hard times. Moreover, the kingdom was ruled at that time by a tyrannical old discourse who claimed to have been put there by God, and who cruelly suppressed any that challenged his word. Consequently, the new baby discourse had to be nurtured with care and in secret, for fear he would be silenced before he was strong enough to fend for himself.

With time, however, he grew strong and tall and began to gather supporters. He organized forays against the tyrannical king in the name of justice, freedom and equality, and gradually started to gain control of territories in the land. The old ruler was eventually overcome and went into exile abroad, where he could do no more harm. The young discourse found himself in control of the country . . ."

As we can see, the subject matter that I wish to broach in this paper does not necessarily have to be presented in the conventional academic way. Indeed, with its clear chronological development, elements of suspense, and the moral twist that will surely come at the end, the topic lends itself particularly well to the kind of narrative treatment that we might associate with the fairy tale or parable. However, no researcher in their right mind would dream of seriously submitting a tale like this to an academic journal such as *The Translator* without at least signalling their awareness of the irregularity, as I have done, with distancing devices such as inverted commas and italics. For such journals, and the scholars who read them, have very clear cut expectations as to how the fruits of academic endeavour should be presented. Guidelines are provided for contributors to ensure that they keep within accepted style parameters, and there is a team of referees and editors on hand to exclude any that do not make the mark. Consequently, authors who fail to comply run the risk of being considered incompetent and scientifically illiterate.

Yet knowledge has not always been configured in the same way as it is today. Until a few centuries ago in Western culture, and still today in many others, the narrative form, alongside others which we today associate with 'literary' rather than 'factual' genres, was considered a perfectly valid way of transmitting the collective wisdom of a community. It was only after the Enlightenment, with its elevation of reason at the expense of the emotions, and with the growing status of the natural sciences, that a split took place between Fact and Fiction and literary forms were deprived of any 'cognitive authority' (White 1997:23). Thus began the reign of the discourse that Venuti (1995:5) calls the 'authoritative plain style', the predatory discourse of my title and the one employed routinely by academics and, more pertinently, by academic *translators* across the English-speaking world.

Today, this discourse is not used for academic writing alone but for factual writing of any kind. Indeed, it is so entirely ubiquitous and so apparently transparent that most people who have been brought up in Anglophone culture do not even notice it is there. As White (1997:22) has pointed out, proficiency in it is felt to constitute basic literacy and is essential for success in many walks of life. Consequently, the teaching of it is lucrative business. Courses in academic writing for undergraduates and foreigners are offered in almost all institutions of higher education; style manuals are churned out by the thousand; and some countries have even introduced literacy programmes designed to foster such skills in primary schools.

Yet, while the hegemony of this discourse seems, if anything, to be consolidating, its claims to be structurally and historically the only appropriate vehicle for knowledge in the modern world have started to be seriously challenged. Far from reflecting reality in a plain, unprejudiced way, its neutrality has been shown to be linguistically construed (Halliday 1998, 1993b, Ding 1998, Martin 1989, 1993a, 1993b, Wignell 1998, among others), and its aspirations to universalism have been undermined by historical studies that describe how it developed in a particular social context to fulfil a particular purpose (Atkinson 1998, Halliday 1993a, 1993c, Ding 1998, etc.).[1] Moreover, as Swales (1990:22) has pointed out, the whole notion of 'discourse' and 'discourse community' is a circular one; the community is defined as those who share certain discourse habits and functions, while skill in the prescribed discourse is a prerequisite for being taken seriously by the discourse community. Academic discourse is thus revealed, from the outset, to be a self-referential self-justificatory practice that determines what may legitimately be considered as knowledge, as Kress (1988:7) has argued:

> Discourses are systematically-organised sets of statements which give expression to the meanings and values of an institution. Beyond that, they define, describe and delimit what it is possible to say and not possible to say . . . with respect to the area of concern of that institution, whether marginally or centrally. A discourse provides a set of possible statements about a given area, and organizes and gives structure to the manner in which a particular topic, object, process is to be talked about. In that it provides descriptions, rules, permissions and prohibitions of social and individual actions.

Discourses thus encode ideology. They encapsulate a particular vision of the world in their very structure and determine what may be thought and said by the communities using them. Their aim is ultimately totalitarian (*ibid.*):

> A metaphor which I use to explain the effects of discourse to myself is that of a military power whose response to border skirmishes is to occupy the adjacent territory. As problems continue, more territory is occupied, then settled and colonized. A discourse colonises

101

the social world imperialistically, from the point of view of one institution.

When the discourse in question is a vehicle of knowledge, as is the one we are studying here, then the kind of territorial expansion that Kress describes amounts to 'epistemicide'. This sounds nasty – and indeed it is, as we realize when we stop to think about it. For the way that a particular culture formulates its knowledge is intricately bound up with the very identity of its people, their way of making sense of the world and the value system that holds that worldview in place. Epistemicide, as the systematic destruction of rival forms of knowledge, is at its worst nothing less than symbolic genocide.

The term 'epistemicide' was coined by the Portuguese sociologist Boaventura de Sousa Santos in his General Introduction to the multi-volume project *Reinventing Social Emancipation. Toward New Manifestos* (2005) to describe one of the more pernicious effects of globalization upon developing countries. However, we do not have to go as far afield as the Third World to find evidence of epistemicide. It is committed every day even within the boundaries of Europe, as this paper is designed to show. And it is we, the translators operating at the interface of cultures, who are responsible for dealing with those 'border skirmishes' that Kress so eloquently describes. To complete his metaphor, we are the border police, parading up and down with our guns and our dogs, and casting harsh spotlights into the linguistic foliage to flush out any unwanted ideology that might be trying to slip in unseen.

Epistemicide works in a number of ways. Knowledges that are grounded on an ideology that is radically different from the dominant one (as in the case of many of the Third World knowledges that Boaventura foregrounds) will by and large be silenced completely. They will be starved of funding, if the hegemonic power controls that aspect (and in the European Union this is increasingly the case); they will remain unpublished, since their very form will be unrecognizable to the editors of journals and textbooks; and they are unable to be taught in schools and universities, thus ensuring their rapid decline into oblivion.

Knowledges that are not so distant as to warrant automatic annihilation, having some historical or cultural overlap with the dominant one, are instead bullied or cajoled into an acceptable shape. This is where the translator comes in. Our job is, essentially, to present the alien knowledge in a form that will enable it to be assimilated into one or another of the ready-made categories existing for the purpose, which means ensuring that it is properly structured, that it makes use of the appropriate terminology and tropes – in short, couching it in the accepted discourse.[2]

It is when the underlying ideology of the original is very different from the dominant one that the process of translation may be said to be epistemicidal.

102

This is, to my mind, the situation that takes place in countries like Portugal and Spain on a daily basis. The knowledge that is produced in the humanities in these countries is, I believe, configured quite differently from English discourse in similar fields. Consequently, the process of making a text suitable for publication in the English-speaking world often involves not only the elimination of characteristic lexical features and ornament, but also the complete destruction and reconstruction of the entire infrastructure of the text, with far-reaching consequences as regards the worldview encoded in it.

The process may be illustrated with Example 1, the first paragraph of a musicology article, which was submitted to me for translation in 2006 with a view to publication in an English-language specialist journal. A literal, interlinear translation is given to assist the reader:

Example 1: From 'Representação Gráfica como Manifestação de Estilo' by Vasco Negreiros: original and literal translation

Diante de quern o lê ou escreve, o termo 'estilo' rasga um vertiginoso campo aberto.
Before anyone that reads or writes it, the term 'style' tears a vertiginous open field.

Isto dever-se-á tanto ao facto de envolver uma quantidade ilimitada de dados
This is due both to the fact of involving an unlimited quantity of data

dificilmente mensuráveis,
difficultly measurable,

não passíveis de uma organização inteiramente satisfatória,
not susceptible to completely satisfactory organization

na perspectiva do musicólogo, como, na do intérprete,
in the perspective of the musicologist, as, in that of the performer,

por despertar, enquanto 'palavra-faísca', intensas lembranças
by arousing, as 'spark-word', intense memories

de experiências contrastantes na sua trajectória musical e pessoal.
of contrasting experiences in his/her personal musical trajectory.

Para tal, o músico toma como referência não só a prática de repertório
For this, the musician takes as references not only the practice of repertoire

---

103

e a literatura especializada que conhece, como também a sua observação de
and the specialized literature that s/he knows, but also his/her observation of

outras modalidades de arte e até de vivências
other forms of art and even of experiences

não exclusivamente ligadas ao ofício artístico,
not exclusively connected to the artistic craft,

ainda que muitas vezes a revelação daí advinda se cinja unicamente
although many times the revelation that comes from this is only girdled

à perturbação de certezas anteriores, reacendendo o processo,
to the perturbance of previous certainties, rekindling the process,

inserido-o numa busca infindável — à procura dos estilos
inserted into an endless quest – in search of styles

e da sua relação com cada urn, ou até do estilo próprio, no caso do compositor —,
and his/her relation with each one, or even an own style, in the case of the composer

sendo esta uma trajectória individual e intransferível, ainda que partilhada.
this trajectory being individual and untransferrable, although shared.

Despite the fact that the text as a whole is a largely analytical discussion of the effects produced by different kinds of musical notation and describes an entirely tangible experiment in graphic reproduction, the discourse used in this introduction clearly subscribes to a neo-romantic idealistic view of the creative process. Terms such as 'word-spark', 'rekindle', 'revelation', 'endless quest', etc., evoke Romantic discourse on divine inspiration, while even relatively banal notions are expressed in emotionally violent language (e.g. 'tears open'; 'vertiginous', 'arousing intense memories').

The syntax is also anything but clear and linear, with a sprouting of subordination that defies translation into a language like English. The last sentence in particular illustrates very well the Portuguese tendency to cultivate verbal foliage that, to English eyes, only obscures the main trunk of the argument. The translation, therefore, does not merely replace one chain of signifiers in Portuguese with another in English. In order to make this text acceptable within the target discourse, I have had to undertake some quite serious alterations that have repercussions on the underlying ideology.

Example 1a: 'Graphic Representation as a Manifestation of Style' by Vasco Negreiros: English translation

To anyone using it, the term 'style' is a bewilderingly broad concept. For the musicologist, it is not easy to categorize and measure; while, for the musician, it is likely to be associated with intense personal memories of different situations experienced over the course of a musical career. The musician gets around the problem in performance by relying on current practice and specialist literature concerning the repertoire in question, and also possibly by consulting other art forms, including those that are not exclusively artistic – even though the effect of this may be merely to unsettle any previous preconceptions he or she once had and stimulate further quest.

The flamboyant emotive terms of the original have mostly been replaced by more matter-of-fact equivalents, while familiar-sounding collocations from the target discourse ('broad concept'; 'not easy to categorize and measure'; 'current practice'; 'unsettle preconceptions', etc.) have been introduced in order to assimilate the text to target discourse expectations. As regards the syntax, the last sentence has been quite radically pruned in order to make the argument more linear, and elsewhere the information has been reorganized in the interests of clarity and cohesion. In places, connections have been made more explicit by the introduction of new elements.

Example 2 below, an abstract in the area of architecture, is also grammatically alien to English academic discourse but in a different way from Example 1. Instead of an elaborate syntax heavy with subordination, this text asserts its poeticality with short verbless sentences that are deliberately elliptical. It also maintains suspense by deferring any mention of location or purpose for several paragraphs:

Example 2: Abstract – 'Architecture': Original and literal translation

Lugar mágico, paisagem grandiosa sobre a Foz do Tejo, Lisboa, as pontes e as margens.
Magical place, magnificent landscape over the mouth of the Tagus, Lisbon, the bridges and the banks.

Entre cidades sim, no sentido geográfico do termo e mais precisamente no
Between cities yes, in the geographical sense of the term and more precisely in the

---

> sentido morfogenético do mesmo entre a cidade «em movimento» que
> é Lisboa e
> *morphogenetic sense of the same between the city "in movement" that is*
> *Lisbon and*
>
> a cidade emergente que é Almada. Mas sobretudo entre cidades
> *the emerging city that is Almada. But above all between cities*
>
> no seu sentido mais profundo e só aparentemente oculto.
> *in its deeper and only apparently occult sense.*

The translation in Example 2a therefore fills in the gaps by introducing verbs and linking the clauses in a more conventional way. The place is also explicitly identified right at the beginning, which makes the discourse more concrete and less poetic:

Example 2a: 'Architecture': Translation

Almaraz is a magical place, with a magnificent landscape that extends over the mouth of the Tagus and across Lisbon, its bridges and river banks. It is located between cities, not only geographically, but also in the morphogenetic sense of being between the city 'in movement' that is Lisbon and the emerging city that is Almada. But it is also between cities in a much deeper sense, a sense that it is only apparently hidden.

In both of these cases, therefore, the Portuguese text has been substantially altered in order to bring it into line with the norms of the equivalent discourse in English. The alterations were necessary because the texts would not have been comprehensible to the English reader otherwise, and as such would not be acceptable for publication in an English language journal. However, during the process of domestication the underlying ideological framework has been largely abolished, to be replaced by the positivist structure inherent to English academic discourse. It is this that allows us to consider this process as epistemicide.

Part II

". . . The old discourse, whom the young pretender had usurped, had believed whole-
heartedly in the value and power of the human spirit. This was not surprising, as
his father's ancestors had been Scholastics, who spent all their time poring over the
scriptures, while his mother, Rhetoric, had inherited from her own family a great

106

respect for words. Indeed, for this old king, the only knowledge worth having lay in words, which he believed to be divine. And it was clear that not everyone could master their secrets. Many long years of training in Latin grammar, rhetoric and dialectic were required before a man could even begin to consider himself knowledgeable. So the lower classes, who could not even write their own language, let alone Latin, had necessarily to be told what to believe by the priests and friars – the old discourse was quite sure of that!.

However, at the time our young discourse was born, new ideas were starting to come into the country from abroad and were stirring up unrest. These new ideas said that God was in everyone, that men were therefore equal, and could learn for themselves and that they didn't need the priests to explain it all to them. There were murmurs in some quarters that in fact all the learned words of the old discourse were mere gobbledygook, designed to keep the people enthralled, and that they could learn more about the world by observing what they saw before their very eyes than by studying ancient texts.

Also, at around the same time, some of the common people had started to get rich through trade and they were keen to educate their children. They needed someone to defend their interests against the old king, who kept the power and the wealth and the knowledge in the hands of his aristocratic relatives.

And so they rallied around the new young discourse, who became their hero, championing their cause against the corrupt old regime . . ."

English academic discourse emerged out of the scientific paradigm that first began to take shape in England in the 17th century (Halliday 1993a), gradually spreading to the social sciences and humanities over the course of the next three hundred years (Wignell 1998, Halliday and Martin 1993:16). The 'scientific revolution', as it has come to be known, represented a major shift in attitudes and values. For not only did the focus of knowledge pass from man's symbolic systems to the outside world, a whole new methodological approach of induction (combining the rational and the empirical) gradually took over from the Aristotelian system of deduction, which had been the basis of university education until then. The copious eloquence and elegant rhetoric valued by the Christian humanists now fell out of fashion, and instead a terse plain style was cultivated as the only appropriate vehicle for the new knowledge (no doubt reflecting the Protestant distrust of ornament and symbols as much as their desire to discover the truth about the world around them).[3]

The first stirrings in this direction can perhaps be traced back to Francis Bacon, who, in *The Advancement of Learning* (1605), argued against the tendency of the scholastics to 'study words and not matter'. However, the linguist Michael Halliday (1993a:57) locates the true birth of scientific discourse in the writings of Isaac Newton, in which processes were systematically reconstrued as things for the first time, chiefly by means of the linguistic device of **nominalization**. This had the ideologically significant result of transforming subjective dynamic experience into static objective fact by the effective removal of the observer, a process reinforced by the appearance of the **passive** at around the same time (see Ding 1998). Thus, with these two resources a framework was established for the transmission and propagation of a positivist philosophy, which would gradually replace the old anthropocentric theory of knowledge in the English speaking world.

With the growing status of the natural sciences, the new kind of impersonal discourse acquired prestige and began to spread to other areas. Its associations with the bourgeoisie, which in the 17th century was the social class in the ascendancy, also linked it firmly to the structures of wealth and power in the new social configuration. Thus began the process of colonization of other disciplines, beginning with the social sciences (Wignell 1998), and moving on to all areas of knowledge in western society, even to less tangible domains like literature and art criticism.

Today it has become what Halliday (1993b:84) calls 'the discourse of modernity', used whenever factuality is asserted and authority claimed. And although numerous internal differences exist between disciplines and genres – as has been pointed out by descriptive linguists such as Hyland (2000), Swales (1990) and Flowerdew (2002:29) – there is clearly a common structure and ideology underlying them all, as becomes obvious when we take a step backwards to view these texts from outside our culture. Indeed, the hundreds of style manuals currently on the market for foreign students and undergraduates are remarkably consistent as regards the precepts they transmit, revealing very little disciplinary variation.[4] These therefore can provide a framework for claims about the general principles underlying English academic discourse.

These principles may be summed up as follows: the discourse needs to be above all clear and coherent, and based upon a structured rational argument supported by evidence; the language should be generally impartial and objective, with fact clearly distinguished from opinion, and there should be general caution and restraint about all claims made; current theory will be incorporated through citation and referencing. The text should be organized into sections with a clear introduction, development and conclusion, each of which should be subdivided into paragraphs, and there will be a hierarchical organization on all these levels (general statement of theme, followed by development, etc). In terms of style, the prose should be lucid, economical and precise, avoiding vagueness, verbosity and circumlocution, and will make use of complete sentences with straightforward syntax. Impersonal structures, such as the passive and nominalized forms, will predominate in many disciplines, and there will be an absence of figurative language (though this is less marked in the humanities), allowing the focus to fall firmly upon the object of study. There will also be a predominance of material or existential processes,[5] reflecting a preoccupation with statements of fact and descriptions of actions.

Portuguese, in contrast, has no hegemonic academic discourse that can be said to cover all production of knowledge.[6] The discourse of the hard sciences is essentially calqued from the English (it is the same in all respects, ranging from text structure and syntax to technical terminology), but, as we move across the social sciences to the humanities, we start to notice a change. The style becomes more elaborate, less transparent, increasingly difficult to read (by Anglo Saxon standards); the vocabulary becomes rich and literary, and we start to see the appearance of figures of speech which, to the English eye, would perhaps be more appropriate in literary genres. When we reach the extreme end of the spectrum, in literary and cultural studies, art or architecture, the prose is frequently so different from the English that translation within the genre becomes well nigh impossible.

The following extract (a work of literary criticism about the essays of Eduardo Lourenço, taken from a reputable Portuguese journal) is a particularly good example of this more extreme style. Clarity of exposition and logical reasoning are clearly not objectives here, for the text revels in ambiguity, deliberately setting up paradoxes and analogical relations and using language in a non-referential way. The syntax is highly complex, with a meandering main clause that is constantly being interrupted by circumstantial information; and there is also a high degree of abstraction that is scarcely digestible by the English language (e.g. 'tragicity', 'Portugalness'; 'messianity'). There are also very few of the material processes that are so predominant in English academic prose, and instead most are relational or existential.[7]

Example 3. Varela, M. H. (2000) 'Rasura e reinvenção do trágico no pensamento português e brasileiro. Do ensaísmo lúdico ao ensaísmo trágico', in *Revista Portuguesa de Humanidades* 4 (UCP, Braga). Original and literal translation.

O ensaísmo trágico de Lourenço, [sic] parece em parte decorrer da sua própria tragicidade de ensaísta, *malgré lui*,
Lourenço's tragic essayism seems in part to arise out of his own tragicity as an essayest, 'malgré lui',

como se esta posição de *metaxu* do pensamento português, entre o *mythos* e *logos*, projectada no papel do crítico
as if this position of 'metaxu' of Portuguese thought, between 'mythos' and 'logos', projected onto the role of critic

que tragicamente parece assumir, entre o sistema impossível e a *poiesis* estéril, o guindasse para um lugar / não lugar
which he tragically seems to assume, between the impossible system and the sterile 'poiesis', hoists him to a place / non-place

109

> de indecibilidade trágica, ao mesmo tempo que, inserido no fecha-
> mento de um pensar saudoso, na clausura
> *of tragic undecidability, at the same time as, inserted into the closure of*
> *a yearning thought, in the confinement*
>
> de uma historicidade filomitista, mais do que logocêntrica, se debate
> na paradoxia de uma portugalidade sem mito,
> *of a philomitist historicity, more than logocentric, struggles in the*
> *paradoxalness of a Portugalness without myth,*
>
> atada à pós-história de si mesmo, simultaneamente dentro e fora dela.
> *bound to the post-history of itself, simultaneously inside and outside it.*

Defining the boundaries of this academic discourse is made difficult by the fact that it is not systematically taught nor has been the object of any kind of linguistic analysis. However, the prestige that it clearly enjoys in the home culture belies any facile assumption that it is merely deficient writing. A vast number of published examples of it exist in Portuguese journals, and an oral version, full of rhetorical flourishes, can frequently be heard in lecture halls across the country. The responses I received to a survey of Portuguese researchers in the humanities undertaken in 2002[8] also confirmed that the Portuguese perceive this to be a separate discourse with distinct characteristics in relation to English. Ninety-one per cent of respondents claimed to consciously alter their discourse when writing for publication in English and described English academic prose as more succinct, logical and linear; more oriented to the outside world; more objective; clearer and less verbose, and plainer in terms of diction.

The reasons for these differences become clear when we remember that the Scientific Revolution did not take place uniformly around the globe. In the Catholic countries of southern Europe, the scholastic tradition was main-tained long after it had been overturned in the Protestant countries of the north; and in Spain and Portugal in particular, education systems controlled by Jesuits and feudal pre-industrial economies maintained by conservative political regimes ensured that Enlightenment values never really took hold. This meant that the old anthropocentric worldview was able to persist for much longer.

Knowledge, understood as philosophy, was thus to be found in words, the tools of the soul. Verbal abundance and linguistic complexity were valued as signs of inner worth,[9] and knowledgeable texts were expected to be beautiful artifacts, rather than transparent windows onto some outer reality. A certain obscurantism may also have been cultivated for political

reasons, as Timmermans (2002:214) points out, since one of the main purposes of this prose was often to "impress and impose" (*ibid.*:218),[10] a
dimension that was particularly evident in conservative Catholic circles from
the 19th century and during the fascist regimes of the 20th.

It is not surprising, then, that traces of this tradition are still to be seen
in the linguistic attitudes and discourse habits of many scholars operating in
the humanities today. Since the rupture between fact and fiction never really
happened here, as it did in the Anglo-Saxon world, academic writing in the
humanities has continued to promote a more holistic view of knowledge,
one in which subjectivity is actively promoted rather than suppressed and in
which the emotional response plays as much of a part as rational argument
and close observation. Indeed, writing is largely viewed as an art, rather
than as a mechanical skill, and therefore often appears to be endowed with
a kind of sacred aura (proportional to the status of its author) that discour-
ages critical analysis or stylistic tampering. Hence, journals in these fields
rarely indulge in the kind of extensive editing of articles that is common in
the Anglophone world, nor do we see much systematic dissection of texts
in subjects such as Literary Studies or History; instead, a literary work may
be used (as in the above extract) as a starting point for further philosophical
reflection, which will itself be presented in abundant flowing poetic prose in
which meanings are not controlled in the interests of clarity but proliferate
profusely.

This is not to say that the scientific paradigm was without its champions
in Portugal and Spain. Associated as it was with the values of socialism,
liberalism and positivism, it has historically drawn its supporters from the
political left and represented a modernizing tendency in a highly religious
and conservative society. Consequently, the plain objective discourse associated with it is perceived by many as a tool of democracy and progress and
cultivated as a way of achieving these political ideals.

There are others in Portuguese society, however, that resent the hegemony
of English in the world and view the encroachment of the scientific paradigm as a form of cultural imperialism. Without necessarily subscribing to
reactionary politics, they often experience the rationalization and object-
ivization of reality as a kind of reductionism that is inadequate to explain
the complexities of human experience. This was clearly revealed by some
of the responses to my survey, in which English academic discourse was
described as 'less elegant' or 'less refined' than Portuguese, with a 'rigid
structure' and 'impoverished vocabulary'. One sociologist was particularly
damning: "English discourse is impoverished and dogmatic. The questions
raised at the outset are simplistic, and formulated in such a way as to
require a YES/NO type of response, based upon mathematical models that
tell us very little about reality. This is how they legitimize their science,
grounding it in the logic of positivism".

Part III

"Once the young discourse had seized power in England and sent the old king away into exile, he started to gain more confidence. He helped his people to become rich and powerful, and they rewarded him with their loyalty and support. He gradually became convinced that he himself was in possession of the truth about men and things.

This feeling grew so strong in him that after a while, he started to think that he had a mission to enlighten the poor benighted creatures in foreign lands, who pledged allegiance to other kings. Thus, he set about organizing a series of crusades overseas. These were remarkably successful, for by now he was very rich and powerful, and the subjects of other nations were in awe of his wealth and wanted to partake of it. He had no difficulty in winning over a large part of the world, which voluntarily came and bowed at his feet, begging to be granted entry into his kingdom.

But some of these new subjects that kneeled before him still bore the vestments and insignia of the old king, the one he had usurped, while others were garbed in strange attire of the kind he had never seen before. Hence, he laid down the law; to gain access to his kingdom and all the wealth and glory that was therein, newcomers must don the local apparel or be turned away at the gates.

Some protested that this was an unjust law. But our discourse truly believed that his word was right and good, and so he began to systematically suppress all who refused to obey. In the name of freedom and justice, he set about destroying all opposition . . ."

One of the most salient facts that emerged from the survey of Portuguese academics I undertook in 2002 was the profound need that they feel to publish their work abroad. Seventy-nine per cent of respondents had already published in English, and most of those who had not voluntarily offered an explanation as to why (e.g. still a junior researcher; works with languages other than English, etc.).

Almost all those who had already published in English claimed to take account to some extent of the differences between the discourse habits when preparing their original versions; that is to say, they systematically practised a form of self-censorship before their text even got into the hands of the translator. They were generally aware of the ideological significance of the alterations made, but accepted the situation in order to further their own academic career – or even favoured it on the grounds of increased rigour.[11]

As for those more extreme examples of Portuguese discourse (such as the extract in Example 3), which are clearly committed to a completely different scholarly tradition, these are unlikely to get translated into English at all, unless at the behest of a Portuguese journal or institution.[12] Portuguese academics are today sufficiently aware of what is going on beyond the boundaries of their country to hesitate before submitting a text to a journal for which it is radically unsuitable; instead, they may attempt to publish it in Brazil, or, in some cases, have it translated into Spanish or French, which are not only linguistically closer but also share a similar epistemological tradition.

The normalizing tendency of English academic discourse and its determination to extinguish all rivals is thus all too clear. But the extent of the phenomenon becomes even more obvious if we take a look at the various English-language journals on the market devoted to Portuguese language and culture, which, in Portugal, is the area of study most immune to English influence. What is immediately clear from a perusal of journals such as *Portuguese Studies* (Department of Portuguese, King's College, London), *Portuguese Literary and Cultural Studies* (Centre for Portuguese Studies and Culture, University of Massachusetts, Dartmouth) or the *E-Journal of Portuguese History* (www.brown.edu/Departments/Portuguese_Brazilian_Studies/ejph) is that contributors are clearly expected to present their articles in impeccable English academic style.

So, even though the subject matter is Portuguese and most of the contributors and editors are too, the traditional Portuguese way of configuring knowledge has been quite spectacularly extinguished in these journals. Lured by the prospect of an international readership and the prestige that comes from publishing abroad, the authors of these articles have voluntarily agreed to collaborate with the hegemonic power in repackaging their culture for foreign consumption. In doing so, they are unwittingly silencing their own collective voice. That is the real tragedy of epistemicide.

Part IV

So how does the story end?

I'm afraid, dear Reader, I do not know, for it hasn't ended yet. Our discourse is today very rich and powerful, and he controls most of the western world. Many people from other parts of the globe are dazzled by him and so he attracts new supporters every day, who want to partake of his power and wealth. But he has lost supporters too, people who have become disillusioned with his methods and his conclusions.

There have started to be murmurs in some quarters that his words do not mean much any more, that they are gobbledygook designed to keep people in thrall. Others are angry that he has trampled all over the human spirit and installed a regime that cares about nothing save money and material possessions.

And so around the boundaries of his kingdom, small groups of protesters are mobilizing, some of them in the name of the god that he denounced so many years ago, others with different agendas. They don't yet have the strength to mount a serious attack against him and are reduced to guerrilla tactics on the fringes of his empire. But they are growing stronger by the day . . .

Notes

1 Other challenges to the truth claims of science have come from the sociology of science, ethnomethodology, semiotics, etc. See Potter (1996) for an overview.

2 This process has been extensively explored by translation theorists since the 1970s. For example, Toury (1978) and Lefevere (1985) describe how translation choices are inevitably conditioned by ideological and material constraints operating within the target culture, while Evan-Zohar (1979, 1990) discusses how these are affected by the ever-shifting balance of power within the polysystem.

3 Although it is not easy to determine which came first, social or ideological change, the Protestant Reformation, with its doctrine of 'the priesthood of all believers', was clearly an important factor in promoting the paradigm shift that we have come to know as the Scientific Revolution. Robert Merton (1970/2001), the sociologist/historian of science, argues in a seminal text that science, like capitalism (with which it has always been closely associated) had its roots in Puritanism, a fact which may well explain the continuing emphasis on clarity and plainness in academic discourse.

4 This claim is based upon a review of the style manuals available at a Birmingham book store, undertaken in 2004. Cf. for example: Fairburn, Gavin and Christopher Winch (1996) *Reading, Writing and Reasoning: A Guide for Students*, Open University Press; Cottrell, Stella (2003) *The Study Skills Handbook*, Palgrave Study Guides; Hennessy, Brendan (2002) *Writing an Essay*, How To Books Ltd; Barrass, Robert (1996) *Students Must Write*, Routledge; Oliver, Paul (1996) *Writing Essays and Reports*, Hodder & Staughton; Pirie, David (1985) *How to Write a Critical Essay*, Routledge.

5 In Systemic Functional Grammar, Material Processes are basically verbs of Doing, involving an Actor that interacts with the material world, while Existential Processes represent something that exists or happens (as in 'there is' constructions). These may be contrasted with Behavioural, Mental, Verbal and Relational Processes (for a full description, see Halliday 1994:106–143).

6 Academic discourse is not systematically taught in Portuguese, and until very recently, the only style manuals that existed were concerned with 'literary' writing or traditional rhetoric. As regards available models, Portuguese academic journals publish a wide range of styles (even within a single publication or issue), no doubt reflecting the various conflicting epistemological influences on the culture, as described below.

7 This passage was analyzed in detail in Bennett (2006).

8 The questionnaire was sent to all researchers listed as members of national research centres in the areas of the humanities and social sciences by the Foundation of Science and Technology (www.fct.mct.pt), the body responsible for funding research work in Portugal. 537 questionnaires were sent out electronically and 156 responses were received in the following fields: Anthropology, Architecture, Economics, Education, Geography, History, Linguistics, Literary Studies, Musicology, Philosophy, Psychology, Sociology and Other (this latter category corresponded to people from more scientific fields who, for some reason, were listed as working in these areas).

9 In the Classically-inspired Christian humanist tradition, language was perceived as a civilizing force, a God-given faculty, which could move men to virtue and bring about peace, justice and liberty. Hence, eloquence was cultivated as an educational discipline and literary ideal.

10 Bourdieu and Passeron (1965, 1994:19–20) make a similar point about French academic discourse.

11 It should be pointed out that many of the researchers questioned in fact used positively-charged adjectives such as 'depurado' 'expurgado' ('purified', 'cleansed', 'purged') to describe English academic discourse and made comments such as "it obliges us to think more clearly"; "I cannot hide in a forest of language as I do in Portuguese").

12 A certain amount of English translation that takes place in Portugal is solicited and financed by Portuguese institutions that wish to attract a wider audience for their own publications. In this kind of situation, there is clearly less need to adapt the text to the norms of the target culture, and the translation is likely to be much more source-text oriented.

References

Atkinson, Dwight (1998) 'Integrating Multiple Analyses in Historical Studies of Scientific Discourse: the Philosophical Transactions of the Royal Society of London 1675–1975', in John T. Battalio (ed.) *Essays in the Study of Scientific Discourse: Methods, Practice and Pedagogy*, Stamford & London: Ablex, 139–65.

Battalio, John T. (ed.) (1998) *Essays in the Study of Scientific Discourse: Methods, Practice and Pedagogy*, Stamford & London: Ablex.

Bennett, Karen (2006) 'Critical Language Study and Translation: the Case of Academic Discourse', in João F. Duarte, Alexandra Assis Rosa and Teresa Seruya (eds) *Translation Studies at the Interface of Disciplines*, Amsterdam & Philadelphia: John Benjamins, 111–27.

Bourdieu, Pierre and Jean-Claude Passeron (1965/1994) 'Language and Relationship to Language in the Teaching Situation', in Pierre Bourdieu, Jean-Claude Passeron and Monique de Saint Martin (eds) *Academic Discourse: Linguistic Misunderstanding and Professorial Power*, Stanford: Stanford University Press, 1–34.

Ding, Dan (1998) 'Rationality Reborn: Historical Roots of the Passive Voice in Scientific Discourse', in John T. Battalio (ed.) *Essays in the Study of Scientific Discourse: Methods, Practice and Pedagogy*, Stamford & London: Ablex, 117–35.

Even-Zohar, Itamar (1979/1990) 'Polysystem Studies', *Poetics Today: International Journal for Theory and Analysis of Literature and Communication* 11(1): 8–51.

Flowerdew, John (ed.) (2002) *Academic Discourse*, London & New York: Longman.

Halliday, Michael A. K. (1993a) 'On the Language of Physical Science', in Michael A. K. Halliday and Jim R. Martin (eds) *Writing Science: Literacy and Discursive Power*, Pittsburgh: University of Pittsburgh Press, 54–68.

—— (1993b) 'Some Grammatical Problems in Scientific English', in Michael A. K. Halliday and Jim R. Martin (eds) *Writing Science: Literacy and Discursive Power*, Pittsburgh: University of Pittsburgh Press, 69–85.

—— (1993c) 'The Construction of Knowledge and Value in the Grammar of Scientific Discourse: Charles Darwin's "The Origin of the Species"', in Michael A. K. Halliday and Jim R. Martin (eds) *Writing Science: Literacy and Discursive Power*, Pittsburgh: University of Pittsburgh Press, 86–105.

—— (1994) *An Introduction to Functional Grammar*, London: Edward Arnold; second edition.

—— (1998) 'Things and Relations: Regrammaticising Experience as Technical Knowledge', in J. R. Martin and Robert Veel (eds) *Reading Science: Critical and Functional Perspectives on Discourses of Science*, London & New York: Routledge, 185–235.

—— and Jim R. Martin (eds) (1993) *Writing Science: Literacy and Discursive Power*, Pittsburgh; University of Pittsburgh Press.

Hill, Christopher (1965/1997) *Intellectual Origins of the English Revolution Revisited*, Oxford: Oxford University Press.

Hyland, Ken (2000) *Disciplinary Discourses: Social Interactions in Academic Writing*, Harlow: Longman.

Kress, Günther (1988) *Linguistic Processes in Sociocultural Practice*, Oxford: Oxford University Press.

Lefevere, André (1985) 'Why Waste our Time on Rewrites? The Trouble with Interpretation and the Role of Rewriting in an Alternative Paradigm', in Theo Hermans (ed.) *The Manipulation of Literature: Studies in Literary Translation*, London & Sydney: Croom Helm, 215–43.

Martin, Jim R. (1989) *Factual Writing: Exploring and Challenging Social Reality*, Oxford: Oxford University Press.

—— (1993a) 'Technicality and Abstraction: Language for the Creation of Specialized Texts', in Michael A. K. Halliday and Jim R. Martin (eds) *Writing Science: Literacy and Discursive Power*, Pittsburgh: University of Pittsburgh Press, 203–20.

—— (1993b) 'Life as a Noun: Arresting the Universe in Science and Humanities', in Michael A. K. Halliday and Jim R. Martin (eds) *Writing Science: Literacy and Discursive Power*, Pittsburgh: University of Pittsburgh Press, 221–67.

—— and Robert Veel (eds) *Reading Science: Critical and Functional Perspectives on Discourses of Science*, London & New York: Routledge.

Merton, Robert K. (1970/2001) *Science, Technology and Society in Seventeenth-Century England*, New York: Howard Fertig.

Potter, Jonathan (1996) *Representing Reality: Discourse, Rhetoric and Social Construction*, London, Thousand Oaks & New Delhi: Sage Publications.

Rose, David (1998) 'Science, Discourse and Industrial Hierarchy', in Jim R. Martin and Robert Veel (eds) *Reading Science: Critical and Functional Perspectives on Discourses of Science*, London & New York: Routledge, 236–65.

Santos, Boaventura de Sousa (2005) 'General Introduction', in Boaventura de Sousa Santos (ed.) *Democratizing Democracy: Beyond the Liberal Democratic Canon*, Vol. I of *Reinventing Social Emancipation. Toward New Manifestos*, London: Verso, xvii–xxxiii.

Swales, John M. (1990) *Genre Analysis: English in Academic and Research Settings*, Cambridge, New York & Melbourne: Cambridge University Press.

Tawney, Richard Henry (1922/1938) *Religion and the Rise of Capitalism*, West Drayton: Penguin.

Timmermans, Benoît (1999/2002) 'Renascimento e Modernidade da Retórica', trans, from the French by Maria Manuel Berjano, in Michel Meyer, Manuel Maria Carrilho and Benoît Timmermans (eds) *História da Retórica* [*History of Rhetoric*], Lisbon: Temas e Debates, 83–223.

Toury, Gideon (1978) 'The Nature and Role of Norms in Literary Translation', in James S. Holmes, José Lambert and Raymond van den Broek (eds) *Literature and Translation: New Perspectives in Literary Studies*, Leuven: Acco, 83–100.

Venuti, Lawrence (1995) *The Translator's Invisibility: A History of Translation*, London & New York: Routledge.

Weber, Max (1930/1992) *The Protestant Ethic and the Spirit of Capitalism*, trans. T. Parsons, New York & London: Routledge.

White, Hayden (1997) 'The Suppression of Rhetoric in the Nineteenth Century', in Brenda Deen Schildgen (ed.) *The Rhetoric Canon*, Detroit: Wayne State University, 21–31.

Wignell, Peter (1998) 'Technicality and Abstraction in Social Science', in Jim R. Martin and Robert Veel (eds) *Reading Science: Critical and Functional Perspectives on Discourses of Science*, London & New York: Routledge, 297–326.

45

TRANSLATION AND THE ESTABLISHMENT OF LIBERAL DEMOCRACY IN NINETEENTH-CENTURY ENGLAND

Constructing the political as an interpretive act

Alexandra Lianeri

Source: Maria Tymoczko and Edwin Gentzler (eds) (2002) *Translation and Power*, Amherst and Boston: University of Massachusetts Press, pp. 1–24.

The representation of other cultures in the signifying codes of a historical community is increasingly described by contemporary theorists as a process of interpretation or cultural translation.[1] The idea that our knowledge of cultures is neither unmediated nor neutrally articulated in scientific discourses, but remains contingent on the conceptual potential and social conditions of its own historical production, has resulted in the use of a metaphorical conception of translation as a theoretical alternative to the notion of representation as faithful reproduction of an original semiotic unit. Within the framework of this "interpretive turn" manifested in philosophy, as well as in cultural and social theory, Clifford Geertz described anthropological writings as "interpretations" of cultures, "fictions," not in the sense that they are imaginative thought experiments but in the sense that they are "something made," "fashioned," within the conceptual structures of the target community (1973:15). Starting from a more politicized theoretical perspective, James Clifford not only drew attention to the inherently translational character of disciplines, such as ethnography and anthropology, but also emphasized the transient, socially constructed truthfulness of their interpretive meaning, whose objectivist claims are in the full sense of the word ideological and "made possible by powerful 'lies' of exclusion and rhetoric" (1988:38–4,

1986:7). Such works have problematized traditional conceptions of transparency and the scientific neutrality of cultural representations by arguing both theoretically and through empirical studies that "writing" about other cultures necessarily takes place from a cultural and social perspective and on behalf of a political one.

A parallel discussion in the field of literary theory and cultural studies has employed the notion of interpretation in order to challenge the univocality of textual and, more particularly, literary meaning. Already anticipated by Mikhail Bakhtin's concept of *heteroglossia*,[2] which pointed out the plurality of social voices inscribed in literary texts, the idea that meaning cannot be reduced either to the individual intentions of its author or to the linguistic codes of a one-dimensional and static original context has been argued by theorists as diverse in their methodological and ideological positions as Fredric Jameson, Stanley Fish, and Jacques Derrida. Although it is not the intention of this work to impose a false unity among theoretical agendas ranging from Marxism to poststructuralism, it must be emphasized that what these writers suggest—if only as an initial theoretical presupposition— is a negative postulate: that meaning cannot be determinatively and finally defined, but exceeds definitions by being constantly (re)interpreted and (re)constructed within the diversified conceptual frameworks and sociocultural conditions of its constituting communities.

A postulate as revolutionary as this did more than disperse the romantic notion of interpretation as the revelation and empathetic reexperiencing of individual world perspectives. It was also directed against a fundamental hermeneutic assumption, prevalent as much in Friedrich Schleiermacher's romanticism and Wilhelm Dilthey's historicism, as in the radicalization of hermeneutic theories articulated by Martin Heidegger and Hans-Georg Gadamer: that intercultural interpretation can create the potential for true disclosures of historical meaning through a process of acquiring new conceptual frameworks, systems of relevance, and semantic relations, and hence by rising to "a higher universality that overcomes [one's] own particularity but also that of the other" (Gadamer 1989:305). The idea of hermeneutic fidelity, which was intended to provide the human sciences with an interpretive method that would claim equal authority and validity with the explanatory methods of natural sciences, was deemed to be equally idealist as its Cartesian predecessors. The valorization of a totalizing conception of meaning inscribed in the idea of historical truthfulness, the assertion of the social and political neutrality of cultural languages, and the prioritization of a universalized tradition of world conceptions, as both the presupposition and the ultimate end of the hermeneutic process, became the focus of a rigorous critique, predominantly inspired by the work of poststructuralism, Marxism, feminism, and postcolonial theories.

While this critique was taking place within the fields of philosophy, anthropology, cultural studies, and literary theory, the hermeneutic model, as

Edwin Gentzler has pointed out, became in the 1970s one of the basic targets of historically oriented translation research (1993:76–77). In this framework, a wide range of scholars, including James Holmes, Gideon Toury, André Lefevere, Theo Hermans, Susan Bassnett, Lawrence Venuti, and José Lambert, developed a theoretical vocabulary that called into question notions of interpretive faithfulness and sought to relate translation production to the cultural systems and norms, social institutions, and ideological convictions of historical communities.[3] What is more, translation studies introduced into this vocabulary a radicalized notion of interpretation, whose roots can be traced to the historicization of understanding effected by Gadamer's thought since the 1960s but whose development was dissociated from the idealism of the hermeneutic tradition, by seeking to relate conceptual and interpretive choices to the broader historical conditions of the target society.

Thus translation studies scholars employed the hypothesis that the understanding of a text does not entail the elimination but the use of historical presuppositions and "prejudices,"[4] in order to describe the determinative role played by the translator's conceptual horizon, cultural position, and social context in the process of rewriting the source text. This process was no longer assumed to imply the rediscovery of a univocal original meaning, but to manifest, as Bassnett indicates, the multiplicity of the source text's meanings and the need for a disengagement from the idea of the translator as a betrayer of an already given original (1996:11). The absence of a static and ahistorical meaning of a text was further explored by José Lambert and Clem Robyns in relation to the translated text itself. In an article that advances a productive dialogue between translation studies and the problematic of contemporary philosophy and semiotics, Lambert and Robyns suggest that translation can be understood as a historical product of a chain of interpretations. The translated text, they argue, should not be seen as the final component of a static dichotomy but as a sign in itself, subjected to other interpretations, whose formation is related to the interaction of different codes and normative models in the target society (Lambert and Robyns, forthcoming).

This dual function of interpretation, at both the level of production of translation and the level of its reception and reproduction by subsequent readership, is examined here on the basis of translations of the ancient Greek concept of *democracy* in nineteenth-century England. This case study demonstrates that translation can be described as the actualization of a series of interpretive acts, which include at once past translation choices and present historiographic accounts of translation writing.[5] These acts are neither reducible to a mere conceptual construct nor the direct and predictable outcome of social structures, which are established in themselves, irrespective of the ways in which their very reality is linguistically perceived and conceptualized in the target context. As a constitutive part of historical

120

social formations, rather, translations develop as both a product of social realities and a means to make sense of, endorse, or seek to transform these realities. They delimit a space in which social agents can understand, defend, justify, control, but also criticize historical social structures and relations, and pursue alternatives to them. From this perspective, translations, as the following case study indicates, stand as much in a relation of accordance with, as in a relation of tension and opposition to, the social context that constitutes their precondition.

Translations of the concept of *democracy* in England developed from the sixteenth century onward as a reaction to absolutist forms of politics and as an endorsement of the liberal-democratic ideals that sustained the establishment of England as a modern bourgeois society. Translations acted to legitimize an emerging political system that was intimately related to the historical advancement of industrial capitalism. Particularly in the late eighteenth and early nineteenth centuries, socioeconomic changes—including the Industrial Revolution, the establishment of capitalist production, urbanization, and the shaping of the bourgeois and working classes—created the potential for Britain's transition from a feudal, predominantly religious society that believed in the aristocracy and the God-given power of kings, to a modern industrialized nation-state.

Challenging previous social structures, translations provided new social models for an audience that was ideologically heterogeneous and that still lacked a sense of its social and political identity. The process entailed transformation and manipulation of the source texts, relating democracy to an abstract ideal of individual freedom and equality (employed as an equivalent of the Greek notion of citizenship), and defining democratic politics as a system of contestable social hierarchies. This ostensibly consistent ideological discourse was, however, simultaneously interrupted and fragmented by conceptual gaps, tensions, and contradictions that are inscribed in the translated texts and related to their historical context. Translation became the symbolic code for the representation of an imaginary historical tradition that connected nineteenth-century politics to Athenian democratic institutions. It altered preexisting systems of ethical and political judgment and reconceptualized, thereby actualizing, nineteenth-century political reality on the basis of new structures, norms, and models of political thought. Far from being an impoverished reproduction of the "real" original meaning of *democracy*, translation contributed to the constitution of a new political order and its stabilization as a social and political unity.

Translation and the shifting image of the concept of democracy

One of the most significant images of Athenian democracy was included in Thucydides' *History*. As Thucydides writes, when fifth-century Athens came to the end of the first year of the Peloponnesian war, Pericles, political and military leader of the city, delivered his famous "Funeral Speech," which presented a glorifying image of the Athenian polity. The speech began by defining the name and features of this polity:

καὶ ὄνομα μὲν διὰ τὸ μὴ ἐς ὀλίγους ἀλλ' ἐς πλείονας οἰκεῖν δημοκρατία κέκληται.

(Book 2, section 37)

Charles Foster Smith translates this passage in the following fairly literal way:

It is true that our government is called a democracy, because its administration is in the hands, not of the few, but of the many.

(1956:323)

Smith's translation suggests that in a democracy, government is administered not by a privileged minority, but by the majority of the people, "the many." It therefore relates democracy to what Anthony Arblaster has described as the basis of democratic institutions: "the idea of popular power, or a situation in which power and perhaps authority too, rests with the people" (1993:8)[6]

From such a perspective, a different translation of Thucydides' *History*, written by Thomas Hobbes in 1629, appears to distort the real image of the Athenian polity:

We have a form of government . . . which, because in the *administration* it hath *respect not to a few, but to the multitude*, is called a democracy.

(1843:8.191, my emphasis)

The essence of democracy in this translation is found not in the power of the people but in the fact that government has regard to the multitude ("hath respect . . . to"), that is, it has consideration for the majority in the administration of social issues.[7] In other words, people do not govern themselves but their views and interests are taken into account by the government. A translation mistake, one might argue, if one could afford to ignore its constant repetition until at least the end of the nineteenth century.

Hobbes's work, which was reprinted three times from the seventeenth to the mid-eighteenth century, was succeeded in 1753 by William Smith's translation. Smith suggested the following rewriting of the passage:

. . . our form [of government] as committed not to the few, but to the whole body of the people is called a democracy.

(1831:1.167)

Smith does not relate democracy to the multitude but to the society as a whole, that is, to the well-being and interests of both the social elite and the majority. This choice does not, however, entail a conception of democracy as a form of self-government, insofar as it establishes again a strict division between the government of a society and the people.

This denial of what many of us would tend to recognize as the core of Athenian democracy, namely the sovereignty and equality of the people, becomes more meaningful when related to conceptions of democracy before the twentieth century, when political consensus in Western thought was based, as Crawford Brough Macpherson notes, on negative appraisals of democratic constitutions: "Democracy used to be a bad word. Everybody who was anybody knew that democracy, in its original sense of rule by the people or government in accordance with the will of the bulk of the people, would be a bad thing—fatal to individual freedom and to all the graces of civilized living" (1966:1). For the translators in question, democracy— defined as a form of government bestowing power and authority on the majority—was not an institution that established political liberty and social justice but, rather, a menace to social order and coherence, threatening prosperity and cultural development alike.

A series of negative appraisals of democracy dating back to the sixteenth century constituted a significant political heritage for this interpretive tradition, which was first manifested in Thomas Elyot's 1531 description of Athenian democracy as a "monster with many heads," lacking stability and social coherence (1883:1.9–10), and later consolidated by Hobbes's translation of Thucydides. Hobbes described the ancient author as "most hostile to democracy," noting that social order and consistency would be damaged by following the demagogically susceptible political judgment of the common people (1843:xvi–xvii). The same position underwrote the translations of the Scottish historian John Gillies. More specifically, Gillies's 1797 translation of Aristotle's *Politics* was introduced as an attack on government based on consent, even as Aristotle's description of man as a "political animal" was interpreted as an indication of the "natural" disposition of men to form political societies based on the authoritative power of monarchy and the strict separation between the main body of citizens and their government (1813:2.3–6). In the same spirit, Gillies's translations of Lysias and Isocrates claimed to present an illustration of the unhappiness generated by republican polity and the turbulent life in "democracies" (1778:1.lxii–lxiii), and his *History of Ancient Greece* (1786) pointed out "the incurable evils inherent in every form of Republican polity" and "the inestimable benefits" of "hereditary Kings and the steady operations of well-regulated Monarchy" (1792:1.iii). Likewise, William Mitford's *History of Greece* (1778) stressed the "uncertainty and turbulence of democratic rule" and the evident undermining of the Athenian democracy by the "want of one supreme authority" whenever the city encountered serious problems and difficulties (1835:1.326, 2.104–5).

Translations and rewritings of classical democracy from the sixteenth until the late eighteenth century seem to have been defined by the denial of any value to democracy, as well as the tendency to dissociate classical culture from institutions establishing the liberty, equality, and sovereignty of the Athenian citizens. Though none of these works bestowed a definitively positive value on the concept of *democracy*, the central issue regarding the period following Hobbes's translation is that representations of classical Athens provided a context, within which democracy was spoken about—a field for discussion, which sought to illuminate the political features of Athenian society through historical writings and to reproduce the cultural and intellectual voices that grew out of democratic institutions through the translation of classical texts. Such a proliferation of discourses, as Michel Foucault (1990) has emphasized, cannot merely be examined as a negation of democratic principles. For apart from asserting the dangers of democracy or, more accurately, irrespective of the expression of negative or positive appraisals, these writings acted to introduce *democracy* into the political thought of their time and determined, among other factors, its subsequent range of meanings and significance. In this sense these writings constituted the conceptual frameworks within which democracy was revived and accepted as a positive concept and a legitimate form of government during the next centuries.

One can identify two interrelated notions evoked by these works: that of the individual and that of social hierarchies. Hobbes's translation, which was considered to have a deep and lasting influence on the development of the philosopher's thought and language,[8] expressed a concept that was scarcely established in his contemporary political discourses but that was to become the central assumption of liberal democratic thought in the next centuries: the concept of the *subject*, who is able to contemplate and discuss social matters and has the right to be a *citizen* of a state. This idea was most clearly conveyed by the translation of the debates that took place in the Athenian Assembly and that constitute a significant part of Thucydides' books. These debates portray a model for political organization based on reasoned discussion and deliberation among (male) citizens, who are given full freedom to speak and decide on issues of public concern, while being considered in this context as moral and political equals. The translation of these passages did not simply record the speeches and dialogues of the source text. Rather it functioned metonymically, as an evocation of the broader social and political life of classical Athens.[9] In other words Hobbes's translation did not merely transfer the source text as a historical document but presented a model for political institutions and social organization as well.

In this capacity Hobbes's work became an integral part of a wider seventeenth-century problematic about the legitimacy of religious authorities, the status of monarchic power, and the feudal system of property rights. Written only thirteen years before the outbreak of the English civil war in

1642, in a context that was marked by radical economic and social changes (including the passage from feudalism to a capitalist mode of production and the subsequent constitution of the bourgeois classes, represented in the House of Commons), this evocation of democratic polity set up the traits of a political model that could fulfill the needs of the newly emergent bourgeoisie to contest previously established hierarchies and articulate a range of values and ideals that would legitimize its social position and power. The key concept in this process was that of the *individual*: the "self-conscious" human being, who does not automatically subject himself [sic] to a social condition prescribed by God (and materialized by the representatives of God on earth) but can freely formulate his own political opinion and will. It was because of this radical idea of "individuality," which was further elaborated in the *Leviathan*, that Hobbes can be described, in Foucault's terms, as a "founder of discursivity," who set up, in conjunction with his main theoretical opponent, John Locke, the "rules of formation" of liberal democratic discourses (Foucault 1977b:131).

Hobbes's individuals were essentially self-interested, uncultivated, and unable to solve by themselves social conflicts and oppositions. Hence their freedom had to be surrendered to the power of a sovereign governor. Yet this move of subjection could only be legitimized once individuals *decided* to establish this power and *agreed* to obey it.[10] What is more, this form of sovereign government was no longer the expression of the will of God. It was described in the *Leviathan* (1651) as "representative" of the will of the people (Hobbes 1968:220). This conception of representation, which bestowed controlled political freedom on the social body but implied simultaneously the exclusion of the people from political constitution and government, dictated the transformation of one of the most renowned features of Athenian democracy in Hobbes's translation: the direct participation of all citizens in the public affairs of the city. The Athenian citizens, as Thucydides writes, were all equally responsible for the political government of the city:

ἔνι τε τοῖς αὐτοῖς οἰκείων ἅμα καὶ πολιτικῶν ἐπιμέλεια καὶ ἑτέροις πρὸς ἔργα τετραμμένοις τὰ πολιτικὰ μὴ ἐνδεῶς γνῶναι· μόνοι γὰρ τόν τε μηδὲν τῶνδε μετέχοντα οὐκ ἀπράγμονα, ἀλλ᾽ ἀχρεῖον νομίζομεν, καὶ αὐτοὶ ἤτοι κρίνομέν γε ἢ ἐνθυμούμεθα ὀρθῶς τὰ πράγματα.

(Book 2, section 40)

A "literal" translation of this passage by Charles Foster Smith reads as follows:

And you will find united in the same persons an interest at once in private and in public affairs, and in others of us who give attention

125

chiefly to business, you will find no lack of insight into political matters. For we alone regard the man who takes no part in public affairs, not as one who minds his own business, but as good for nothing; and we Athenians decide public questions for ourselves or at least endeavour to arrive at a sound understanding of them.

(1956:329)

Hobbes translated the passage as follows:

Moreover there is in the same men, a care both of their own and the public affairs; and a *sufficient knowledge* of state matters, *even in those that labour with their hands.* For we only think *one that is utterly ignorant therein,* to be a man, not that meddles with nothing, but is good for nothing. *We likewise weigh what we undertake, and apprehend it perfectly in our minds.*

(1843:8.194, my emphasis)

The most striking transformation of the source text by Hobbes is found in the rendering of the phrase "μόνοι γὰϱ . . . νομίζομεν," which says that the Athienian people considered a man who did not participate in politics to be worthless and incompetent, into a much milder renunciation of apolitical men as "utterly ignorant" of public affairs. Hobbes's position was further sustained by the translation of the phrase "καὶ ἑτέϱοις . . . γνῶναι," which says that people who are chiefly involved in work (πϱὸς ἔγα) have "no lack of insight into political matters," (Smith 1956:329) by the statement that there is "sufficient knowledge of state matters, even in those that labour with their hands." Hobbes's translated phrase not only diminishes the involvement of the Athenian people in politics by suggesting that citizens have merely "sufficient knowledge" of political issues but also introduces the idea that those "that labour with their hands"—thus presumably those least likely to be involved in politics—are in possession of this knowledge. A final change can be found in the translation of the last phrase of the passage, which says that "we Athenians decide public questions for ourselves" (Smith 1956:329). Hobbes's translation does not bestow a political connotation on this statement. It describes, instead, a process of intellectual evaluation and apprehension, which is not related to "public questions" and political decisions, as is the case in the source text.

If Hobbes was reluctant to recognize individual sovereignty, Locke, at the end of the seventeenth century, employed the concept of *man* to celebrate the rationality of individuals as well as their natural property of "Lives, Liberties, and Estates" and the obligation of political government to protect this property (Locke 1988:350). The work of both of these thinkers was appropriated by the founders of the American constitution and became the basis of the ambivalent disposition of American revolutionary thought toward

Athenian democracy. Despite some general appeals to classical antiquity, the founding of the United States of America manifested a self-distancing of republican thought from "purely" democratic affiliations, on the grounds that the exercise of political power by the commons would violate the principle of mixed government and endanger individual liberty and rights. "Pure democracies," as Madison wrote in *The Federalist* in 1788 (no. 10), "have ever been spectacles of turbulence and contention; have ever been found incompatible with personal security or the rights of property; and have in general been as short in their lives as they have been violent in their deaths" (Hamilton, Madison, and Jay 1970:45). The notion of *republic* was thereby explicitly distinguished from the idea of bestowal of power on the people. As Russell L. Hanson has argued, "whereas a democracy represented rule *by* the 'commons' or *demos*, a republic was ruled *in* common *for* the commonweal" (1985:77). The establishment of this semantic distinction allowed for the dissociation of the American Revolution from the connotations of anarchy and political instability related to democratic polity,[11] and it also determined the subsequent reconceptualization of democracy as a form of government whose power is established by and should be accountable to the governed, but whose main aim is not the realization of the self-institution of a social community but the protection of the rights of *individuals* to life, liberty, and the pursuit of happiness. This was a conception of happiness that was more identified with narrow individualistic interests than with collective prosperity or a condition of social equality.

Democracy began to be described in positive terms once it ceased to evoke ideals of materialized social equality and was, instead, related to a liberal form of polity: a political system that established basic civil rights (freedom of speech and political association, and security of life and property), formal legal equality, and parliamentary representation.[12] These newly evoked rights, which had already been asserted during the French Revolution in 1789 by the *Déclaration des droits de l'homme et du citoyen* (*Declaration of the Rights of Man and the Citizen*), gave voice to contemporary bourgeois demands by evoking Man as the ontological hallmark and ultimate end of political practice. Although inspired in certain respects by the ideals of the American Revolution, the promise of the *Declaration* for liberty, equality, and justice was novel. It favored the establishment of a fully extended liberal democracy and implied the formal dissociation of social and cultural distinctions from the right to political participation. The French conception of the nation as identified with the whole of the people was not merely radical, it was revolutionary. Yet it was simultaneously an ideal that was rendered unrealizable by those very principles that enabled its formulation: an understanding of democracy as a matter of legal and political administration that was presumably strictly dissociated from the unequal positions from which social agents were able to participate in social institutions and politics. That is to say, a conception of democracy that subsumed freedom and equality to an ideological attempt at securing and strengthening the hierarchical social structures of modern bourgeois societies.

Altering norms, translations, and politics: the establishment of liberal democracy

From the beginning of the nineteenth century, British interest in classical culture and politics was remarkably intensified.[13] Hobbes's translation was reprinted five times and Smith's translation six times during the century. A significant proportion of these publications were initiated and/or endorsed by utilitarian thinkers, although several of Hobbes's translations were edited under the auspices of Jeremy Bentham, the political philosopher who together with James Mill, formulated the basic principles of nineteenth-century English liberalism (Held 1996:95), in Macpherson's terms the "founding model for democracy for a modern industrial society" (1977:43). Bentham, James Mill, and the utilitarians in general, as David Held suggests, developed one of the clearest justifications for the liberal democratic state, which creates the conditions necessary for individuals "to pursue their private interests without the risk of arbitrary political interference, to participate 'freely' in economic transactions, to exchange labour and goods on the market and to appropriate resources privately" (1996:95). In the context of this turn, the meaning of *democracy* no longer evoked the notions of equality and political sovereignty. Liberal democracy, as Macpherson explains, has been a system "by which people can be *governed*," that is, made to do things they may not otherwise do and refrain from things they otherwise may have done. So long as this government is not controlled by the people themselves, "democracy . . . is then a system by which power is exerted by the state over individuals and groups." Most significant, a democratic government exists to uphold and enforce a certain kind of society and, therefore, a certain range of relations among individuals, a certain set of rights and claims that people have on each other, both directly and indirectly through their rights to property. These relations, as Macpherson argues, are relations of power: they stem from the conditions of social, economic, and cultural inequality that are established in capitalist societies, while acting, in turn, to nourish and strengthen these conditions (1966:4, cf. 35–45).

Parallel and interrelated to the change in political theorizing in nineteenth-century England was the development of a wider interest in classical Greece,[14] which was sustained by the increasingly dominant position of Greek studies in the educational institutions of the period. Oxford and Cambridge shifted the emphasis of classical learning from Latin to Greek and established the study of Greek literature as an educational requirement for every degree, while schoolmasters such as Samuel Butler, B. A. Kennedy, and Thomas Arnold advanced a new conception of Greek culture in the public schools by emphasizing the need to relate classical learning to contemporary interests, instead of pursuing a traditional study of texts only as models of style (Clarke 1959:74–127). This idea was explicitly expressed in Thomas Arnold's statement that fifth-century Athens belonged more to modern than to ancient history, that "the history of Greece . . . is not an idle inquiry about remote ages and forgotten institutions, but a living picture of things present, fitted not so much for the curiosity of the scholar, as for the instruction of the statesman and the citizen" (1835:3.xviii, xxii).

In this framework translators of classical Greek texts advanced an endorsement, but also a transformation, of classical conceptions of democracy, which oscillated between authoritarian social ideals and the convictions of an enlightened and liberal politics. The first translation of Thucydides' *History* during this period was written by S. T. Bloomfield in 1829. Unlike both Hobbes and Smith, Bloomfield was not directly opposed to democratic politics. He rather presented his work as an endorsement of the *"happily-attempted mixture* of aristocracy and democracy . . . embodied" in the British constitution (Bloomfield 1829:vi, original emphasis). From this perspective, his translation rewrote Pericles' definition of democracy as follows:

> From the government being administered, not for the few, but for the many [our institution] is denominated a democracy.
>
> (1829:366–67)

Hobbes's rendering of "the many" by the term *multitude* is missing from this translation and will not appear again in translations of the passage. What is more, Bloomfield did not describe democracy in Smith's terms, as a government that makes political decisions in accordance with the interests of the society as a whole. In Bloomfield's work, a democratic government is claimed to be administered *"not* for the few, but for the many." That is to say, democracy is not only posited in a social context in which the aims of the few are opposed to those of the many but also seeks to prioritize the latter over the former.

Bloomfield's emphasis on this opposition expresses a significant change in European conceptions of society and politics, which was crystallized in the English context after the French Revolution. Before 1789, English intellectuals and political theorists were able to perceive and represent their immediate reality in terms of social conflict but, nevertheless, believed that it would be possible to resolve this conflict by moderate reforms, which would establish a political alliance between the traditional aristocracy and the middle classes without being threatening to the existing status quo. The outbreak of the French Revolution, the September massacres of 1792, the execution of Louis XVI in 1793, and the images of the Terror dispersed this idea.[15] From the beginning of the nineteenth century, conceptions of democracy indicated an understanding of Western societies as fragmented and divided; as structured on the basis of conflictual rather than harmonious and reconcilable interests. This realization did not, however, entail an immediate acceptance of democratic ideas. Quite the contrary: Bloomfield's translation repeated the distinction between the government and the governed established by the works of Hobbes and Smith, and it further denied that classical Athens was *really* a democratic polity. The translation of the passage in question was qualified by a footnote, which suggested that Pericles' description "might be a good definition of the Athenian government as far as it was *supposed* to be" (original emphasis). Yet the Athenian polity was only "a democracy in name." "In fact" it was "a modification of aristocracy called elective monarchy" (Bloomfield 1829:367).

As the century progressed, the tear of the people and of revolution became weaker and Bloomtield's characterization of the Athenian polity was not repeated until the end of the century. Classical democracy instead became the central reference for liberal and utilitarian thinkers, in whose writings Athenian society was transformed from an object of fear and denial into a model for imitation. This turn was substantially advanced by *A History of Greece*, a significant publication written by George Grote (1846–56). In this work Grote presented extensive translated passages in order to sustain his appraisal of democratic Athens, and he also employed translation in the formation of his historical vocabulary, describing, for example, Pericles as the "prime minister" of the Athenian Assembly and Athenian politics as characterized by oppositions between the "conservative party" and the party of "reformers" (1888:4.454). As a result Athenian democracy was perceived as the equivalent of English society and politics and lost its previous connotations of anarchy and injustice. John Stuart Mill wrote two eulogizing reviews (1846, 1853) of Grote's *History*. He praised Grote for representing democracy as the real basis of Athenian progress and further described the Greeks as the "originators of political freedom and the grand exemplars and sources of it to modern Europe." "The battle of Marathon," Mill argued, "even as an event in English history is more important than the battle of Hastings" (1978: 316, 273).

But what did democracy mean for these writers? And how did translations of ancient Greek texts serve to sustain its meaning? J. S. Mill's appraisal of Athens was justified by the quotation of a further translation of Thucydides, which had been made by Grote himself and had been included in his *History*. This work defined democracy as follows:

> It [our constitution] is called a democracy, since *its permanent aim tends towards the Many and not towards the Few.*
>
> (Grote 1888:5.67, my emphasis)

The translation transforms the original phrase "καὶ ὄνομα . . . κέκληται" into the rather vague assertion that democracy is a form of government whose "permanent aim tends towards the Many and not towards the Few." This translation differs from Hobbes's work because it recognizes the majority as the "aim" of democratic government, whereas Hobbes restricted democratic processes to a government's "consideration" of the needs of the multitude. Yet it also follows its predecessors, by suggesting that this "aim" would not be sought by "the many" but by a social institution that is strictly separated from the social body of citizens: that is, the government. In the middle of the nineteenth century, Henry Dale wrote a similar translation of the source text: "In name, from its not being administered for the benefit of the few, but of the many, it [our form of government] is called a democracy" (1848:112). Subsequently, Richard Crawley's translation defined the Athenian polity as founded on a government "whose administration . . . favours the many instead of the few" (1876:1.121).

Neither the source text nor the history of classical Athens could justify such a division. Athenian democracy was administered on the basis of direct participation of citizens in the Assembly, which decided all significant political issues, from legislation to finance and military matters. In the context of the Assembly, Athenian citizens were considered as moral and political equals, and were all responsible for the government of the city.[16] It follows that in the source context the concept of *democracy* conveyed the idea of direct, free, and equal participation of all citizens in the institution of public affairs. This meaning was not reproduced in the translations.

After the first decades of the nineteenth century, this transformation crystallized into a significant change in the meaning of the concept, which implied that democracy was at once dissociated from ideas of social equality and the collective self-institution of a society, and intrinsically related to the notion of individual liberty: the freedom to participate in elections and articulate political opinions publicly, as well as the liberty to pursue one's goals and secure one's rights in the context of civil society. These forms of liberty were described in Crawley's introduction to his translation as the main features of the Athenian democracy. As he stated, the reader of his work could find in the presentation of Athens "the *political freedom* which he glories in, and the *social liberty* which he sometimes sighs for" (Crawley 1876:1.xi, my emphasis). Equality thereby became understood as electoral equality (political freedom) and equality of opportunity (social liberty): the right of all people to compete for the attainment of social status, political power, and economic growth, irrespective of their initial social position or rank.

It was precisely this understanding of democracy that enabled Grote to state in his translation that the Athenian city did not bestow political and constitutional power on the people but, rather, enabled social advancement and chose only those citizens of "real worth" as governors. As the source text reads:

... μέτεστι δὲ κατὰ μὲν τοὺς νόμους πρὸς τὰ ἴδια διάφορα τᾶσι
τὸ ἴσον, κατὰ δὲ τὴν ἀξίωσην ὡς ἕκαστος ἔν τῳ εὐδοκιμεῖ οὐκ
ἀπὸ μέρους τὸ πλέον ἐς τὰ κοινὰ ἢ ἀπ' ἀρετῆς προτιμᾶται.

(Book 2, section 37)

A "literal" translation of this passage by Charles Foster Smith reads:

... yet while as regards the law all men are on an equality for the
settlement of their private disputes, as regards the value set on them
it is as each man is in any way distinguished that he is preferred to
public honours, not because he belongs to a particular class, but
because of his personal merits.

(1956:323)

Grote translated the passage as follows:

As to private matters and disputes, the laws deal equally with every
man; while in regard to public affairs and to *claims of individual
influence, every man's chance of advancement* is determined not by
party favour *but by real worth*, according as his reputation stands in
his own particular department.

(1888:5.67, my emphasis)

Grote's translation maintained the meaning of the first phrase of the passage, which refers to the equality of citizens before the laws as regards private
disputes. The rest of the passage was substantially transformed by the
employment of the concept of *individual influence*, which is absent from
the source text, and the use of the phrase "every man's chance of advancement is determined ... by real worth," which rewrote the source-text idea
that every man's chance of attaining a position of political responsibility is
determined by his ability to perform the particular task. Both of these choices
stem from an understanding of democracy as the establishment of freedom
for competition and "social advancement." They could not have made sense
in a context in which political participation was open to all citizens and
entailed no special privileges or profit as was the case in the Athens of
Thucydides' text.[17]

But more than this, Grote suggested the negation of the source text's
idea that all members of a democratic community have both the right
to and obligation of equal participation in politics. The Athenian political
model was based on the assumption that men could fulfill themselves only
in and through the *polis*, on the maxim that the "virtue of the individual
is the same as the virtue of the citizen" (Jaeger 1965:2.157). This decisive
trait of classical democracy was testified, as has been argued, by Thucydides'
description of the Athenian citizen as a man who "participates" in the

132

institution of the city (Book 2, section 40). Grote translated this passage as follows:

> The private citizen, while engaged in professional business, *has competent knowledge on public affairs.* For we stand alone in regarding the man who keeps aloof from these latter not as harmless, but as useless. Moreover *we always hear and pronounce on public matters when discussed by our leaders, or perhaps strike out for ourselves correct reasoning about them.*
>
> (1888:5.69, my emphasis)

Unlike Hobbes, Grote maintained the idea that the Athenians regarded as useless any man who abstained from public affairs. Yet Grote's rewriting of the last phrase of the passage, which states that "we Athenians decide public questions for ourselves" (C. F. Smith 1956:329), effected a significant transformation of the source text. The Athenians were presented in the translation as having a passive role in the determination of political issues, as a community that listens and chooses but does not actively plan a certain politics. It hears and endorses but does not participate in political discussions. No aspect of the source text could legitimize such a division between the "leaders" of the city and the people who abstain from political deliberation. Furthermore, even when Grote acknowledged that Athenian citizens could *perhaps* formulate for themselves correct political reasoning, he changed the source text by adding the word "perhaps," which presented this case as a rather unlikely one and acted to cast doubt on and qualify the role of the people in the institutions of Athenian politics. To say that the body of citizens was capable of advancing "correct" political reasoning implied that the appraisal of this correctness was made on the basis of standards that did not originate within this social body. Yet for the Athenians, it was precisely the Assembly, the main body of citizens, that was responsible for drawing the line between "correct" and "incorrect" opinions on political matters.

The rewritings previously discussed did more than dispute the validity of negative appraisals of democratic institutions, they provided a context for the construction of a liberal conception of democracy, which emphasized the need for the hierarchical organization of social communities, the liberty of individuals from excessive state power, and the establishment of formal equality of opportunity, based on a presumably free competition and meritocracy. This conception, which set up the key political features of modern bourgeois societies, contested the authoritarian organization of feudal monarchies and asserted that human beings are the only legitimate source of political judgments. Thus it ostensibly left no room for the justification of inequality and power relations. At the same time, however, it posited an abstract conception of these human beings as individuals who stood for humanity, lacking specific social and cultural characteristics. This abstraction enabled the ensuing qualification of these individuals as cultured, educated, Western European, white, middle-class, and male subjects. What followed was the ability of these subjects to judge political matters "better" than the rest of the people, have a rationally justified political authority, and impose their historically declared civil rights—"liberty, equality, and estate"—as the indisputable "democratic" values of humanity. These values silenced the historical dependence of liberty and equality on the actual economic, social, and cultural inequalities of modern bourgeois societies, and they constructed a new conception of secular authority as the necessary and desirable complement of democratic processes. It was precisely this interrelation of democracy and authority that created the context for a final turn in translations of democracy after the middle of the nineteenth century. This new line of interpretation was profoundly influenced by Matthew Arnold's thought and represented classical culture as an alternative to individualistic ethics, excessive commercialism, and lack of authoritative power.

A model for social assent: Ancient Greek culture as a unifying social force

Arnold was not hostile to democracy. Along with many of his contemporary thinkers, he had realized its inevitable establishment and its compatibility with the political interests of the nineteenth-century bourgeoisie, which for him was the only potential successor of a corrupt, politically incapable, and culturally degraded aristocracy. Yet he did not visualize a society based on social equality and self-institution. Instead, he described inequality as a "natural" feature of societies and sought to establish the presuppositions for an explicitly authoritative model of government, which could harmonize social conflicts and oppositions under the unifying power of the state. The latter was not, however, defined by him as a source of oppression and unjustifiable power relations but as the embodiment of a higher cultural authority, which was presumably dissociated from partisan interests and was able to guide the society as a whole (Arnold 1993:102–25; 1962:7–8, 20–21).

Two main aspects of Arnold's thought seem to have influenced the translation of Pericles' description of classical democracy toward the end of the nineteenth century: (1) the conviction that the majority could possibly attain a ruling political position and (2) the creed that such a prospect should be controlled by the intervention of a higher political authority. Hence Benjamin Jowett's translation of the passage in question reads as follows:

It is true that we are called a democracy, for the administration is in the hands of the many and not of the few. *But* while the law secures equal justice to all alike in their private disputes, *the claim of excellence is also recognised*; and when a citizen is in any way

134

distinguished, he is preferred to the public service, not as a matter
of privilege but as the reward of merit.

(1881:1.117–18, my emphasis)[18]

Unlike all previous translations, Jowett renders the source-text idea that
democracy is a polity by which political power is "in the hands of the many
and not of the few." Yet his work immediately disputes the existence of
democracy in classical Athens ("it is true that we are called a democracy
... but ..."). A democracy, in Jowett's view, lacks the means to recognize
excellence, whereas the classical city only established equality before the law,
simultaneously electing an "aristocracy of merit" that was put at the service
of the state.

Jowett proceeds to translate Pericles' assertion that all citizens "participate" in politics, suggesting that an Athenian citizen is fairly aware of
political issues. As he writes,

An Athenian citizen does not neglect the state because he takes
care of his own household; and even those of us who are engaged
in business have a *very fair idea of politics*. . . . and if *few are
originators, we are all sound judges of a policy.*

(1.119, my emphasis)

This translation changes the source text's representation of Athenian
citizens as actively engaged in the political institution of the city and introduces a rigid distinction between "originators" of a policy and "judges" of
political matters. Both ideas, as has been demonstrated, are absent from
the source text.

Jowett's translations did not evolve in opposition to Mill's and Grote's
conceptions of liberal democracy. Mill's initial doubt regarding the political
ability of the "common" people was bound to be transformed into an idealization of secular authority in the context of the late nineteenth century. By
then, the liberal promise of endless social and cultural progress, unrestricted
pursuit of individual interests, and unprecedented maximization of human
happiness seemed to many unrealizable and incompatible with the establishment of basic civil rights, equality, and social coherence in the context of
bourgeois societies. This promise was crushed under the weight of its own
presupposition that democracy implies the liberty to pursue "individual
interests" in a society constructed by social inequalities and power relations.
It was eroded and undermined by its own internal contradictions and inconsistencies: the glorification of human subjects that was paired with their
immediate division into political authorities and "the common people"; the
idealization of cultural progress and the simultaneous reduction of culture
into a means for individual advancement; and the exaltation of political
justice and moral values in a discourse that recognized no other human

purpose or value apart from the accretion of private profit, growth of social status, and accumulation of capital.

Did the polity of ancient Athens contain an illusory potential? Was the radicalness of translating Greek democracy as a positive concept a deceiving political promise? Was translation simply a means for justifying a society structured on the basis of injustice, actual inequality, and power differentials? The answer to these questions cannot be one-dimensional. Classical political thought itself resists final concretizations by being variably interpreted and transformed throughout modern European history. Nineteenth-century English translators played a determining role in this process by articulating the optimistic enchantment of the period with the ideal of political reason and the belief in human progress. Their view challenged a long tradition of monarchic politics and endorsed at once the values of freedom, equality, and political justice, and an idealization of social inequality, human exploitation, and asymmetrical power relations. Their interpretation of the concept of democracy had a historical afterlife that continued to form Western political thought until World War I and entered a process of semantic alteration only after the actual collapse of humanist idealism materialized in Berlin and Hiroshima. This afterlife, which witnessed colonialism, political totalitarianism, and the imperialistic discourses of advanced capitalism, often turned back to the nineteenth-century liberal concepts of *natural human divisions, civil rights*, and *secular authority* for its own ideological legitimization. Yet, it was precisely the liberal interpretive framework that also established the value of democratic ideals, thus providing the means for radical critiques of its ideology and the conception of political alternatives to it. If nineteenth-century conceptions of classical democracy established a historical "interpretant" that claimed a unique validity in modern political discourses, this interpretant was not internally coherent and unified.[19] Its semantic concretization was the product of plural and internally opposed conceptualizations of democracy, which cannot be reduced to a single and unitary "original" meaning but established a sequence of differentiated interpretations that constituted the contemporary complexity and contestability of the concept.

Notes

1 I am very much indebted to Maria Tymoczko, Susan Bassnett, Joanne Collie, and Yorgos Avgoustis for valuable suggestions and comments on this work.
2 On Bakhtin's use of the concept, see especially the chapter "Discourse in the Novel" in *The Dialogic Imagination* (1981:259–422).
3 For a historical account of the work of these writers in the context of contemporary translation research, see Gentzler 1993.
4 On the issue, see Gadamer 1989:277–307.
5 For a further discussion of historiographic translation analysis as a form of interpretation and translation, see Hermans 1999:68–69.

6 Smith's translation of this passage and the ones that follow are offered more as a guideline to the reader with no knowledge of Classical Greek, rather than as an ultimate accurate rendering or as a translation that manages to escape interpretive bias. The translation of Pericles' definition of democracy continues to be a highly debated issue among contemporary scholars and continues to give rise to a wide range of interpretations. An indicative example of this disparity of readings is offered by comparing Smith's translation of this passage to that of Rex Warner: "Our constitution is called a democracy because power is in the hands not of a minority but of the whole people" (1972:145).

7 On the negative connotations of the word *multitude*, see Williams 1988:192–97.

8 On the issue, see Rossini 1987:303.

9 For a discussion of the metonymic function of translation, see Tymoczko 1999: 41–61.

10 For a further discussion of this issue, see Held 1996:76–78.

11 For a further discussion of this issue, see Roberts 1994:186.

12 As Raymond Williams points out, this move involved a substantial deradicalization of democratic thought. It implied the dissociation of democracy from connotations of popular power and thus its distancing from a political system in which the interests of the majority are both exercised and controlled by the majority itself (Williams 1988:96).

13 The increase of translations from ancient Greek into English after the late eighteenth century is striking. As the bibliographical survey of F. M. K. Foster (1918) indicates, the total number of translations up to 1780 was 312, whereas book-length translations published from 1780 to 1900 reached 1259.

14 As Frank Turner points out, the extensive nineteenth-century concern with ancient Greece was a relatively novel phenomenon in European thought, for until the late eighteenth century, most Europeans thinkers conceived their culture as Roman and Christian in origin, having only an indirect relation to classical Greece. The search for new cultural roots in Greek antiquity assumed major intellectual significance in both Europe and America during the nineteenth century. It was manifested as an unprecedented enthusiasm for Greek cultural production and exercised a deep influence on the development of literature, arts, scholarly discourses, and—I would add—translation (Turner 1981:1–14).

15 For a further discussion of the impact of the French Revolution on British scholarly and literary circles, see Dawson 1993:50–53.

16 This point does not imply that classical democracy was not formed on the basis of an exclusionist politics. "The many" in classical Athens were still the minority of the population of the city because women and slaves were deprived of any political rights. Slaves were not citizens, and Athenian free women were regarded as "citizens" only in order to legitimize their citizen-sons, having no right to participate in politics themselves. For a further discussion of "citizenship" and "participation" in classical Athens, see Sinclair 1988:24–135.

17 For the Athenians, to be in positions of political responsibility was not equivalent to the idea of *personal* advancement or influence. The members of the Athenian *Voulē*, a body of five hundred citizens who were responsible for the administration of issues that were not discussed in the *Ecclēsia*, were elected by lot. Their position was considered as predominantly administrative, had a relatively low salary, and did not entail the attainment of political power, since all important decisions on public matters had to be endorsed by the *Ecclēsia*. Participation in the supreme court of justice, the *Hēliaia*, was open to every Athenian citizen over the age of thirty. The *Ecclésia* had the absolute right to force citizens to leave public positions, if they were deemed to be unfit for their responsibilities.

What is more, no citizen had the right to attain a position in the public administration more than once or—in the case of participants in the *Voulē*—twice in his lifetime. This law prohibited the association of such positions with the fulfillment of political ambitions of individuals. For further discussion of these issues, see Glotz 1929.

18 Jowett's point is made explicit in the notes accompanying the translation in which he explicates the meaning of the passage: "though we bear the name of democracy, this name is an *inadequate* description of the Athenian commonwealth. For before the law all men (including the [few]) are equal, while at the same time *there is an aristocracy of merit* at the service of the state" (1881:2.106, my emphasis).

19 For the notion of "interpretant," see Lambert and Robyns forthcoming.

Bibliography

Arblaster, Anthony (1993) Democracy. Buckingham: Open University Press. First edition 1987.

Arnold, Matthew (1962) Democratic Education, ed. R. H. Super. Ann Arbor: University of Michigan Press.

—— *(1993) Culture and Anarchy and Other Essays*, ed. Stefan Collini. Cambridge: Cambridge University Press.

Arnold, Thomas (ed.) (1835) The History of the Peloponnesian War by Thucydides, 3 vols. Oxford: James Parker.

Bakhtin, Mikhail (1981) The Dialogic Imagination, ed. Michael Holquist, trans. Caryl Emerson and Michael Holquist. Austin: University of Texas Press.

Bassnett, Susan (1996) "The Meek or the Mighty: Reappraising the Role of the Translator" in Román Álvarez and M. Carmen-África Vidal (eds.) *Translation, Power, Subversion.* Clevedon: Multilingual Matters, 10–24.

Bloomfield, S. T. (trans.) (1829) The History of Thucydides: Newly Translated into English and Illustrated with Very Copious Annotations, Exegetical, Philological, Historical and Geographical. London: Longman, Rees, Ormen, and Brown.

Clarke, Martin Lowther (1959) Classical Education in Britain 1500–1900. Cambridge: Cambridge University Press.

Clifford, James (1986) "Introduction: Partial Truths" in James Clifford and George E. Marcus (eds.) *Writing Culture: The Poetics and Politics of Ethnography.* Berkeley: University of California Press, 1–26.

—— *(1988) The Predicament of Culture: Twentieth-Century Ethnography, Literature, and Art.* Cambridge: Harvard University Press.

Crawley, Richard (trans.) (1876) History: The History of Herodotus; The History of the Peloponnesian War [by] Thucydides, 2 vols. London: J. M. Dent.

Dale, Henry (trans.) (1848) The History of the Peloponnesian War by Thucydides: A New and Literal Version. London: Henry Bohn.

Dawson, Paul Martin Stuart (1993) "Poetry in an Age of Revolution" in Curran Stuart (ed.) *The Cambridge Companion to British Romanticism.* Cambridge: Cambridge University Press, 44–73.

Elyot, Thomas (1883) The Boke Named The Governour, ed. Henry Herbert Stephen Croft, 2 vols. London: Kegan Paul. First edition 1531.

Foster, Finley Melville Kendall (1918) English Translations from the Greek: A Bibliographical Survey. New York: Columbia University Press.

Foucault, Michel (1977b) "What Is an Author?" *Language, Counter-memory, Practice: Selected Essays and Interviews,* ed. and trans. Donald F. Bouchard and Sherry Simon. Ithaca: Cornell University Press, 113–38.

—— *(1990) The Will to Knowledge.* Vol. 1. of *The History of Sexuality.* Harmondsworth: Penguin.

Gadamer, Hans-Georg (1989) Truth and Method, trans. Joel Weinsheimer and Donald G. Marshall. London: Sheed and Ward. First edition 1975.

Geertz, Clifford (1973) "Thick Description: Toward an Interpretative Theory of Culture" *The Interpretation of Cultures: Selected Essays.* London: Fontana, 3–30.

Gentzler, Edwin (1993) Contemporary Translation Theories. London: Routledge.

Gillies, John (trans.) (1778) The "Orations" of Lysias and Isocrates, 2 vols. London: J. Murray.

—— *(1792) The History of Ancient Greece, Its Colonies, and Conquests from the Earliest Accounts till the Division of the Macedonian Empire in the East Including the History of Literature, Philosophy, and the Fine Arts,* 3d ed., 2 vols. London: A Strahan and T. Cadell. First edition 1786.

—— *(trans.) (1813) Aristotle's Ethics and Politics Comprising His Practical Philosophy,* 2 vols. London: T. Cadell and W. Davies. First edition 1797.

Glotz, Gustave (1929) The Greek City and Its Institutions trans. N. Mallison. London: Kegan Paul.

Grote, George (1888) A History of Greece from the Earliest Period to the Close of the Generation Contemporary with Alexander the Great, 12 vols. London: John Murray. First edition 1846–56.

Hamilton, Alexander, James Madison, and John Jay (1970) The Federalist or The New Constitution. London: J. M. Dent. First edition 1787–88.

Hanson, Russell L. (1985) The Democratic Imagination in America: Conversations with Our Past. Princeton: Princeton University Press.

Held, David (1996) Models of Democracy, rev. ed. Cambridge: Polity Press and Blackwell.

Hermans, Theo (1999) Translation in Systems: Descriptive and System-oriented Approaches Explained. Manchester: St. Jerome.

Hobbes, Thomas (trans.) (1843) The History of the Grecian War, Written by Thucydides, Translated by Thomas Hobbes, in William Molesworth (ed.) *The English Works of Thomas Hobbes of Malmesbury,* vols. 8–9. London: John Bohn. First edition 1629.

—— *(1968) Leviathan,* ed. Crawford Brough Macpherson. Harmondsworth: Penguin. First edition 1651.

Jaeger, Werner (1965) Paedeia: The Ideals of Greek Culture, trans. Gilbert Highet, 3 vols. Oxford: Blackwell. First edition 1939.

Jowett, Benjamin (trans.) (1881) Thucydides Translated into English with Introduction, Marginal Analysis, Notes and Indices, 2 vols. Oxford: Clarendon Press.

Lambert, José, and Clem Robyns (forthcoming) "Translation" in Roland Posner, Klaus Robering, and Thomas A. Sebeok (eds.), *Semiotics: A Handbook on the Sign-Theoretic Foundations of Nation and Culture.* Berlin: de Gruyter.

Locke, John (1988) Two Treatises of Government. Cambridge: Cambridge University Press. First edition 1690.

Macpherson, Crawford Brough (1966) The Real World of Democracy. Oxford: Oxford University Press.

—— (1977) *The Life and Times of Liberal Democracy*. Oxford: Oxford University Press.

Mill, John Stuart (1978) *Essays on Philosophy and the Classics*, in J. M. Robson (ed.) *Collected Works of John Stuart Mill*, vol. 11. Toronto: University of Toronto Press.

Mitford, William (1835) *History of Greece*, rev. ed., 10 vols. London: T. Cadell. First edition 1778.

Roberts, Jennifer Tolbert (1994) *Athens on Trial: The Antidemocratic Tradition in Western Thought*. Princeton: Princeton University Press.

Rossini, Gigliola (1987) "The Criticism of Rhetorical Historiography and the Ideal of Scientific Method: History, Nature and Science in the Political Language of Thomas Hobbes" in Anthony Pagden (ed.) *The Languages of Political Theory in Early-Modern Europe*. Cambridge: Cambridge University Press, 303–24.

Sinclair, Robert K. (1988) *Democracy and Participation in Athens*. Cambridge: Cambridge University Press.

Smith, Charles Forster (trans.) (1956) Thucydides, *History of the Peloponnesian War*, vol. 1. Loeb Classical Library. Cambridge: Harvard University Press.

Smith, William (trans.) (1831) *History of the Peloponnesian War by Thucydides*, 2 vols. London: Valpy. First edition 1753.

Thucydides (1956) *History of the Peloponnesian War*, trans. Charles Foster Smith, 4 vols. Loeb Classical Library. Cambridge: Harvard University Press.

Turner, Frank M. (1981) *The Greek Heritage in Victorian Britain*. New Haven: Yale University Press.

Tymoczko, Maria (1999) *Translation in a Postcolonial Context: Early Irish Literature in English Translation*. Manchester: St. Jerome.

Warner, Rex (Trans.) (1972) Thucydides, *History of the Peloponnesian War*, rev. ed. London: Penguin.

Williams, Raymond (1988) *Rewards: A Vocabulary of Culture and Society*, rev. ed. London: Fontana.

46

DISCOURSE, IDEOLOGY AND TRANSLATION

Ian Mason

Source: Robert de Beaugrande, Abdulla Shunnaq and Mohamed H. Heliel (eds) (1994) *Language, Discourse and Translation in the West and Middle East*, Amsterdam: John Benjamins pp. 23–34.

Abstract

Using as a framework for analysis the categories of genre, discourse and text type proposed by Hatim and Mason (1990), this paper seeks to show how translators' decisions in composing the wording and arrangement (texture) of their texts may cumulatively project variant discourses and thus point to different underlying ideologies. Consciously or subconsciously, all text users, including translators, bring their own assumptions, predispositions, and general world-view to bear on their processing of text at all levels. Individual lexical choices, cohesive relations, syntactic organization and theme/rheme progression, text structure and text type are all involved in the construction of a text world that is offered to the reader. The translator, as both receiver and producer of text, has the double task of perceiving the meaning potential of particular choices within the cultural and linguistic community of the source text and deciding whether and/or how to relay that same potential, by suitable linguistic means, to a target readership operating in a different cultural context. These processes and the ways in which discourses, and thus ideologies, are projected are illustrated by reference to a source and target text produced to propagate the ideals of a large international organization. A new postscript compares the findings of this study, originally published in 1994, with more recent work in translation studies and poses some questions about the future of such investigations.

In a fascinating work of translation criticism, Bruno Bettelheim (1983) describes how the official English translators of Freud distorted the language – and hence the meaning – of their source text, principally through systematic lexical selections that had the effect of rendering their target text more clinical, more scientific and less subjective than Freud's original. Whereas Freud had nominalized German personal pronouns (*das Ich, das Es, das Über-Ich*) to represent central concepts of his work, his translators preferred Latin forms (*Ego, Id, Super-Ego*), appropriate – they no doubt reasoned – to a scientific treatise in English. The Graeco-Latin influence did not stop there; *Besetzung* (occupation) became in translation *cathexis*, *Fehlleistung* (erroneous performance) became *parapraxis*, *die Seele* (soul) and the corresponding adjective *seelisch* became *mind* and *mental*; and many more examples could be given. The choices made by Freud's official translators were strongly motivated. In line with the best practice of context-sensitive translators, they kept the target readership constantly in mind and had a clear sense of the language appropriate to a particular area of social activity. They strove to render the target text more abstract, more learned and more scientific in order to ensure that it would appeal to the Anglo-American medical/ scientific community and thus win acceptance for a set of ideas which, in the original, stemmed from a somewhat different European humanist tradition.

Thus, the translation gave rise to a perception of Freud – based on the Standard Edition of his works in English, through which he achieved worldwide renown – which is quite different from that of readers of the source text. In Joyce Crick's (1989) words, these translations made of Freud "the anatomist of the mind rather than the doctor of souls". Underlying the source text and the target text are two distinct ideologies, which Bettelheim identifies as humanism and behaviourism. For Peter Newmark (1991:59), Bettelheim "goes beyond neutrality when he insists on the translator's respect for the original, on values beyond culturally and socially-bound translation norms, on a respect for the 'literal truth'". Such an objection is unfortunate in implying that there can be a single, objectively defined meaning of a text, independent of both producer and receiver. But behind this issue lurks another more familiar one: where do the translator's loyalties lie? With the letter of the source text or with the expectations of the readers of the target text?

As Siân Reynolds (1991) relates, the controversy continues to rage in the preparation of the complete edition of Freud in French. While Jean Laplanche, co-editor and president of the terminology committee for the translation, speaks of "restoring Freud to Freud" by stripping away all of the accretions which have obscured the original text and by standardizing the vocabulary, others regret the terminological strait-jacket in which they feel the translation is being imprisoned. The end result, they fear, will be more the language of Laplanche than that of Freud. Moreover, the work may be posited on the outmoded notion of the attainability of a 'pure' translation carrying over a single definable body of meaning from source text to target text.

That such a monolithic view of meaning is erroneous is an underlying theme of this study, but one which has been ably argued elsewhere (e.g. Prince 1981) and will not be further elaborated here. Rather, our preoccupation in what follows will be with some of the questions raised by the issue of ideology in translation. How are ideologies to be objectively identified? Can they be pinned down in the use of discrete items of language? What should the translator's attitude be towards whatever is perceived to be the ideology of the source text? How far will the perceptions of the readers of the target text match those of the readers of the source text?

Tentative answers to questions like these can properly be attained only through systematic analysis of what goes on in the process of text production and reception. As will be argued here, words are invested with meaning by virtue of their use within a context and their exchange between users. In the multiple processes involved in translation (source text production, source text reception, target text production, target text reception), the meaning potential of items within the language system (Halliday 1978) is exploited by a variety of users, each within their own context and for their own purposes. In the particular case we shall consider, alternative world-views and discursive histories create divergent discourses and texts in a situation in which equivalence is normally assumed.

1. Terminology

Before outlining a model for analysis and then applying it to a text sample, it will be necessary to define certain of our terms – namely, discourse, text, and ideology. The terms discourse and text are frequently used to refer to any undifferentiated stretch of language performance, spoken or written, as for example in the expressions 'text linguistics' or 'discourse analysis'. This usage is standard and unproblematic. But the terms will be used here in narrower senses which require definition. The term **text** in the sense of Hatim and Mason (1990) refers to a unit of structure which is deployed in the service of an overall rhetorical purpose – e.g. to expound or to argue. Kress (1985), following Foucault (1971), uses the term **discourse** to refer to systematically organized sets of statements which give expression to the meanings and values of an institution.

Language users have their own discursive history: their previous experience of discourses which, in turn, shapes their own perception and use of discoursal features. Discourse is thus both institutional and individual and gives expression to users' attitudes towards any particular state of affairs. It is in this sense that the term is used here. As such, it is of course closely bound up with **ideology** – not in the commonly used sense of a political doctrine but rather as the set of beliefs and values which inform an individual's or institution's view of the world and assist their interpretation of events, facts and other aspects of experience.

2. A model for analysis

In examining ideology in translation, we shall be concerned with the constraints governing the production and reception of texts and the rhetorical
conventions of the cultural communities of source and target language.
The constraints may be considered as belonging to three categories: genre,
discourse and text. As semiotic categories, these are culture-specific in the
sense that different cultural communities may have evolved their own
intertextual conventions governing what constitutes a given genre, discourse
or text. Basil Hatim (e.g. 1991), whose work underlies this analysis, has
convincingly argued that there are cross-cultural differences in the use of
persuasive-strategies, giving rise, for example, to a preference in Modern
Standard Arabic for **through-argumentation** and in English for **counter-
argumentation**. Further, in an analysis of a translation into English of a
speech given by the late Ayatollah Khomeini (Hatim and Mason 1991), we
sought to show how systematic differences in Western and non-Western
generic, discoursal and textual conventions create considerable difficulties
for translators; and that whereas the strategy of relaying the unfamiliar
signals of genre and discourse in unmediated form to the target text reader
affords the latter the possibility of real insight into an unfamiliar text-world,
the translator's options are more constrained in the case of signals of text
structure. For example, a text-initial item such as English *Of course* or
French *Certes* (certainly) is a clear signal of a concession within a counter-
argumentative text structure. In such a case, the translator's decision will be
determined not by some elementary lexical equivalence between source and
target language but rather by the need to relay the appropriate structural
signal to users of the target text.

Above all, it is our contention that these – genre, discourse and text – are
the semiotic systems within which the expression of ideology is realized, and
that the investigation of ideology in translation is best handled within such
a framework.

3. Application: Ideology in translation

3.1 The data

The text sample reproduced in the Appendix appeared in the April 1990
edition of the *UNESCO Courier*, a monthly publication produced simultaneously in several different language versions. We may characterize the
institution, UNESCO, and its official organ, the *Courier*, as being dedicated
to the promotion of the cultures of the world, and to the dissemination of
knowledge and understanding about them. Following Kress (1985), we have
defined **genres** as conventionalized forms of texts appropriate to given types
of social occasion. In this sense, the social occasion is the international

dissemination of understanding, in the form of social history, of the peoples of Mexico. Unlike the case of Freud, discussed earlier, in which genre is modified in translation to meet different cultural conventions, source text (ST) and target text (TT) here belong to an identical generic specification: both have the same starting point, are aimed at similar international readers and have the same moderately didactic role. The channel of publication is the same: different language versions of the same periodical. Given this specification, we can expect that the primary rhetorical purposes of the article will be to expound (describe, narrate) but also to present a case and pass judgement (present argumentation and evaluation).

3.2 Lexical cohesion

The first and most obvious way in which ST and TT diverge from each other is at the level of individual lexical choice (see Appendix). In a translation which is far from a slavish rendition of ST form, lexical shifts are to be expected. But the manipulation here involves in some cases a radical shift of values. *Prolongados esfuerzos* (Prolonged efforts; ST 1) becomes in translation *obstinate determination* (TT 1); *enfrentamientos* (confrontations; ST 26) becomes *war* (TT 25) and *encuentros* (encounters; ST 32) becomes *clash of cultures* (TT 30). Even more significantly, *sabios* (wise men; ST 10) become *diviners* (TT 9). Whereas the meaning potential of *sabios* covers both Western (i.e. purely rational) and non-Western forms of wisdom, the use of *diviners* tends to exclude the form of wisdom which is currently valued in the West. A different perspective is also apparent in making *testimonios* (testimonies; ST 39) into *written records* (TT 41), *el hombre indígena* (indigenous man; ST 33) into *pre-Columbian civilization* (TT 31) and *antiguos mexicanos* (ancient Mexicans; ST44) into *Indians* (TT 45).

Yet something more systematic is at work in the realization of these two texts. The Spanish terms *esfuerzos* (efforts) and *memoria* (memory) are announced as themes in the opening sentence of the source text and form cohesive networks throughout. In the case of *memoria*, there is multiple recurrence (ST 2, 7, 9, 30, 43). Beaugrande and Dressier (1981:55) note that recurrence is "prominently used to assert and reaffirm one's viewpoint", and it is this discoursal value which is important here. *Memoria* is a term which takes on added meaning in societies where oral tradition is valued (although the Spanish term can also denote a written record or report, co-text here makes clear that 'memory' is the sense intended). It is clearly a keyword in the discourse; its recurrence is motivated by a rhetorical purpose which emerges in conjunction with other features we shall describe. *Esfuerzos* is echoed in co-referring items such as *búsqueda* (search), *luchar* (struggle), *quehacer* (task – with the added connotation of 'duty'), *creatividad* (creativity), to form what Halliday and Hasan call a chain of collocational cohesion – "the cohesion that results from the co-occurrence of lexical items that are

Table 1 Recurrence and collocational cohesion.

SOURCE TEXT	TARGET TEXT
memoria (memory; ST 2)	memory (TT 2)
memoria (ST 7)	history (TT 7)
memoria (ST 9)	knowledge of the past (TT 8)
memoria (ST 30)	memory (TT 27)
memoria (ST 43)	——
destino (destiny; ST 4)	destiny (TT 5)
destinos (ST 10)	the future (TT 11)
destino (STT 22)	——
destinos (ST 22)	——
esfuerzos (efforts; ST 1)	obstinate determination (TT 1)
búsqueda (search; ST 4)	the way in which they view (TT 4)
luchar contra (struggle against; ST 8)	to save . . . from (TT 7)
quehacer (task; ST 11)	desire (TT 14)
épocas de gran creatividad (ages of great creativity; ST 25)	bursts of creativity (TT 24)

in some way or other typically associated with one another" (1976:278). We can now make an initial comparison of source text versus target text at the level of networks of lexical cohesion (Table 1). It is immediately apparent that neither the multiple recurrence of *memoria*, nor the notion of 'destiny', nor the collocational chain of 'effort' has been adequately maintained. Moreover, the first signs of a fundamentally different discourse emerge. When memory becomes *history* (TT 7) and *knowledge of the past* (TT 8), the direct links between past and present are severed. Memory as such is down-played, and the active search for the past and the task of recording it turn into a passive *view* of the past and a *desire* to interpret it. *Creativity*, meanwhile, has been reduced from whole 'ages' to occasional *bursts*, and the neutral *hubo* (there were; ST 25) has correspondingly been transformed into *were punctuated by* (TT 24).

3.3 Discourse indicators

At this point, we must address a procedural matter. Translation criticism as an activity has been censured for concentrating on the written text as a product divorced from the circumstances of its production and reception, and for ignoring the translation process. The cross-textual comparison of individual lexical items in section 3.2 above may seem open to such censure. But our interest in these items resides in their value as signs, and in the clues they provide to the construction of a text-world by text users. It is in this semiotic dimension that divergences become significant, rather than at the level of discrepancies between individual lexical items. A further example may serve to illustrate this point. *Mas de veinte siglos* (more than twenty centuries; ST 14) is relayed in translation as *two thousand years* (TT 12).

146

Table 2 Discourse of emphatic appeal.

SOURCE TEXT	TARGET TEXT
miles de vestigios (thousands of remains; ST 13)	countless remains (TT 11)
más de veinte siglos (more than twenty centuries; ST 14)	two thousand years (TT 12)
los muchos pueblos (the many peoples; ST 23)	peoples (TT 22)
gran creatividad (great creativity; ST 26)	creativity (TT 24)
el más grande de los traumas (the greatest of traumas; ST44)	the traumatic fate (TT 44)

Referentially, twenty centuries and two thousand years are equivalent; in traditional forms of analysis, the difference of expression would be put down to (presumably unmotivated) stylistic variation. Yet there is evidence in the ST of a discourse of emphatic appeal in the use of hyperbolic expressions, as shown in Table 2. Equivalence of referential meaning between items in the source text and target text is much less important here than relaying discoursal indices that contribute to an overall discourse of epic narration in which history, memory and destiny are seen as subject to human will and effort.

3.4 Theme/rheme arrangement

It was mentioned above that 'effort' and 'memory' constitute the themes of the initial sentence of the source text. (In Functional Sentence Perspective, the theme constitutes the topic of a sentence while rheme is the name given to whatever constitutes a comment on the topic). A cursory glance at the developing text shows that these notions form a kind of hyper-theme that spans the themes of various sentences (see Table 3, in which the ST is represented in a literal English translation).

Thus, 'effort/memory/destiny' are the featured themes in parts of this discourse. In contrast, the target text at these points tends to put people(s) in theme position (see Table 4) and the dramatic *prever los destinos* (foresee the destinies; ST 10) becomes the prosaic *predictions of the future* (TT 10). But even within the thematic structure illustrated in Table 4, the choice of verb

Table 3 Hypertheme in source text.

THEME	RHEME
(1) (Ancient . . . efforts to preserve the memory)	(constitute the first great chapter . . .)
(8) (That memory)	(was indispensable)
(11) (Such a task)	(lives on in thousands of remains)
(22) (The destiny – or destinies)	(experienced propitious times and fatal times)

147

Table 4 Hypertheme in target text.

THEME	RHEME
(1) Mexicans	have always exhibited
(6) they	have been engaged
(22) The people, or rather peoples	met with mixed fortunes

in the rheme does not portray humans in a particularly pro-active role: they *exhibit* features and *meet with* their fate. Contrast too, for example, *interesarse por* (to take an active interest in; ST 7) with *have been engaged* (TT 6).

This theme/rheme arrangement is closely associated with the expression of discourse. Admittedly, word order and theme/rheme arrangement correspond to different textual norms in Spanish and in English, and one cannot be prescriptive about the translator's choices in this respect. Nevertheless, all of the textural devices of the source text noted so far combine in the expression of a discourse which relays an ideology: destiny as personal commitment rather than as passive observation. Our last category, text structure, provides further evidence of the discoursal shift in the translation.

3.5 Text structure

The dominant text-type focus of the source text is expository, although there is a substantial element of evaluation which gives rise, in the third paragraph, to an argumentative text structure. A concession is made, followed by a counter-argument. A formal – 'literal' – translation of the source text (ST 32–39; cf. TT 30–41) at this point might read as follows:

> About the greatest and most tragic encounters experienced by indigenous man [persons] would have to write such as the conquistador himself, Hernán Cortés in his *Letters of Account* and the soldier-chronicler, Bernal Díaz del Castillo in his *True History of New Spain*. But also the vanquished left their testimonies . . .

The effect of this source text structure is to downgrade the initial concession (the Spaniards were the official chroniclers of these events), relative to the counter-argument (**but** the indigenous people did write their own account); here, the second text element has a higher rhetorical status. In the target text, however, the counter-argument signalled by 'but' is missing:

> The vanquished peoples also left written records.

Moreover, the first element is upgraded by the addition of the term *pre-Columbian* (TT 31), making the arrival of a European the main historical milestone, and by a more detailed and at times laudatory rendering in *sent five remarkable letters [. . .] back to Spain between 1519 and 1526* (TT 33–35) and *who served under Cortés, fifty years after the event wrote . . .* (TT 37–38), which foregrounds the Spanish over the indigenous documentation – a clear rhetorical reversal in the achievement of a subtly different purpose.

The evidence for this claim might be judged insufficient: at first glance, there appears to be no overt concessive in the source text (equivalent to *Certainly . . . , Of course . . .* or *Although . . .*) and the item *pero* (but) might not, for all readers, carry the rhetorical weight I am attributing to it. Such a view, however, would overlook the modality of the verb form *habrían de escribir*, with its clear implied value of: 'it was natural that . . .' or: 'were bound to . . .'. Thus, the concessive is indeed present (though not expressed in the conventional adverbial manner of English) and the counter-argumentative structure is beyond doubt. Moreover, an identical structure occurs in a later portion of the text, not included in the excerpt reproduced in the Appendix. Here it is, rendered in my formal translation into English:

> To an extraordinary Franciscan monk, Bernardino de Sahagún . . . was owed the recovery of a great treasure of testimonies of the pre-Hispanic age. But there were also indigenous people who continued to write in their own language . . .

This section of the source text makes a strikingly similar point with its contrastive *but*, rhetorically subordinating the known Spanish accounts to the lesser known indigenous texts. In the translation, the adversative *but* has turned into a mere time-adverbial *meanwhile*, and the volume of writings suggested by *continued to write* gets lost in the simple *were writing*:

> An extraordinary man, the Spanish Franciscan Bernardino de Sahagún, . . . gathered invaluable, first-hand information on the pre-Columbian era. Meanwhile, indigenous chroniclers were writing in their own languages . . .

Overall, these divergent structures relay two different world-views or ideologies. Within a humanist discourse of people striving to forge their own destiny, and within an institutional framework (i.e. UNESCO) for the promotion of indigenous cultures, the rhetorical purpose of the source text structure is clear: in conceding that the Spanish Conquistadors were the official chroniclers of Mexican history, the text strongly counter-argues that there are indigenous voices, under-represented hitherto, which are equally worth listening to and which have preserved the precious legacy of 'memory' in their own written records. The text world constructed in the translation is radically different.

In sum, genre, discourse, and text are found to be mutually supporting entities within the producer's plan towards an overarching communicative goal. We can see how the sets of constraints imposed by genre, discourse and text are important variables in the translator's search for translational adequacy and how, as super-ordinate factors, they take precedence over incidental equivalences at the level of the referential meaning of individual lexical items.

4. A text-linguistic approach to descriptive translation studies

When I first discussed these two text samples with a group of Spanish linguists and English-language Hispanists, they were outraged at what they saw as a deliberate skewing by the translator of the intended meaning of the source text. Without access to the inner motivations and thought processes of the translator, we cannot state with any certainty what the intentions were. But I would suggest that there is no need to attribute the divergent discourse of the target text to any deliberate intention of the translator. Mediation, as "the extent to which one feeds one's current beliefs and goals" into processing a text (Beaugrande and Dressler 1981:182), may largely be an unconscious process. And, as noted earlier, an individual's discursive history will shape his or her perception and use of discoursal features. As James Paul Gee (1990:174) notes, text users "serve apprenticeships in social settings where people characteristically read, write, speak and listen in [certain] ways"; he continues: "thus I am at one and the same time an active subject (agent) in the Discourse and passively subjected to its authority" (*ibid.*:176).

In this sense, the discourse belongs to the user, who also belongs to it. If such an account of discourse is well-founded, then it would suffice to explain our two divergent text samples. The reception and production of texts have been mediated through variant discursive histories. The results reveal two distinct ideologies, only one of which is entirely consistent with the conventional norms of the institutional setting of the texts.

Our analysis has been far from exhaustive. A comparison of the titles of the two texts would, for example, reveal further corroborative evidence of the divergent discourses we have described. But our aim here has been to show that there are implications both for descriptive translation studies and for translator training. Empirical studies must seek not to contrast disembodied entities or isolated phrases from the source text and target text but to trace generic, discoursal and textual developments which reveal ideologies and highlight the mediating role of the translator. If training programmes consider these important dimensions of text production and reception, the discussion of translators' techniques and strategies can be greatly enriched.

Postscript

In the years since this article was published, various scholars have commented from differing perspectives on the case study related in it. Venuti

(1998:2–3) drew on it as the opening example in his *Scandals of Translation*, thus associating the case with his project for an "ethics of difference" (*ibid.*:82) in translation. Brotherston (2002:165–67) then took Venuti to task for claiming that the translation downgraded Mexican oral culture and thus implying that pre-Conquest Mexican history was essentially oral – in direct contradiction to what León Portilla was actually saying (cf. section 3 above). Brotherston then proceeded to demonstrate the importance of written texts to the ancient Mexicans and the challenges to our conception of translation thrown down by the multi-layered meanings offered by the iconic script of some key texts. Munday (2001:100; 2007:199) cites the case as an example of critical-linguistic approaches to the analysis of translation, opening up a discussion of the potential and limitations of such approaches. These studies open up substantial issues, which continue to occupy a central position in contemporary translation studies.

My own original aims were more modest. They were to show how the individual choices made by language users – and here, specifically, translators – on the surface of the text (**texture**) may provide evidence of underlying ideologies – in the sense of sets of the "taken-for-granted assumptions, beliefs and value systems which are shared collectively by social groups" (Simpson 1993:5). In this way, such categories as cohesion (or transitivity, or modality) are lifted out of the realm of technical linguistics to become the tools for the construction of a text world, intertextually echoing other text worlds, discourses and genres. My source and target texts were chosen for the way in which they each reflected patterned behaviour, networks of expression projecting two contrasting discourses.

The analysis could, of course, have been more comprehensive. The contrasting perspectives of source and target text producers are, for example, reflected in patterns of personal reference. Whereas the ST presents processes in a relatively impersonal fashion, the TT adopts a resolutely third-person form of reference: *Mexicans* (1), *their society* (3), *they view* (4), *their identity* (5), etc., thus positioning the author as if he were an outside observer rather than a member of the subject group. Conspicuous too is the absence from the translation of ST anaphora and junction: *Así* (thus; ST 5), *Esa memoria* (This memory; ST 8), *Tal quehacer* (Such a task; ST 11), *Así, por ejemplo* (Thus, for example; ST 16), *Entre otros* (Among others; ST 39) provide a form of linkage which, while it might be associated with Spanish rather than English style, nevertheless signals a continuity and dynamism in the source text account. Clearly, evidence in support of the argument advanced in the article is not lacking.

In the intervening years, there have been a number of other studies in a similar vein, drawing attention to the role of textural devices in projecting ideology via discourses. For example, Schäffner (2003) analyses a policy document, jointly published by the leader of the Labour Party in the United Kingdom and of the Social Democratic Party of Germany in English- and

German-language versions, a case of parallel text production. Adopting a critical discourse analysis approach, she relates textural decisions (lexical choice, metaphor) to contextual factors: the ideological positioning of both parties and the generally hostile reception of the text in Germany, thus providing an excellent example of politics at work in an intercultural environment (cf. also Meylaerts 2007). Bennett (2007) studies the ideological effects of the globalization of academic English, noting how microtextual features (nominalizations, passives, etc.) impose alien norms on academic discourses in other cultures. Kang (2007) shows how translators' decisions in the genre of news reporting serve to reconstruct North Korea between US and (South) Korean versions of texts. Munday (2002) compares English translations of an article by Gabriel García Márquez, finding that choices made in the representation of processes (transitivity) and of interpersonal meaning (attitude) appear to be compatible with the ideological positions of the channels in which the translations are published (the Cuban *Granma International*, *The New York Times*, *The Guardian*). This leads to the question of whether such shifts in translation (including omission of some items) might be deliberate moves on the part of the translator or publisher.

In a separate study of different data, however, Munday (2007) finds that ST institutional agendas are not necessarily inscribed in translation practice, citing cases where translators' decisions appear to run counter to the ideological outlook of the channel of publication. He concludes that translators tend to be "guided by intuition and previous linguistic experience of the two languages alone" (*ibid.*:204). This statement matches the evidence presented in the present article, in the sense that the translator appears to present a detached outsider's view of Mexico and its history rather than a discourse representative of the UNESCO ideology of promotion of indigenous cultures. Munday (*ibid.*) also uses Michael Hoey's concept of **lexical priming** (the way in which a word "becomes cumulatively loaded with the contexts and co-texts in which it is encountered" – Hoey 2005:5) to account for ways in which translators' language use depends at least in part on their previous socio-textual experience. This too is close to the conclusion drawn in the present article: that the reception and production of texts are mediated through variant discursive histories. The added significance lies in the fact that lexical priming can be empirically investigated through the techniques of corpus linguistics and therefore provides opportunities for more reliable supporting evidence in future work of this kind.

These studies and others not mentioned here considerably broaden our understanding of ways in which translators' decision making at the level of texture reflects higher-order concerns and influences. Among the many insightful notions that would be relevant to the analysis of the León Portilla translation are: institutional policies and recontextualisation (Kang 2007,

Schäffner 2003), the translator as gatekeeper (Bennett 2007), and thus as a means of reinforcing or resisting power structures (Cunico and Munday 2007). Further, Hatim (2001:131–32), drawing on Bruce (1994), suggests **interdiscursive mixing** (competing discourses, the hijacking of one discourse in the service of another, discursive subversion, and so on) as an over-arching category that subsumes many kinds of textural moves involved in the projection of ideology, including those related here.

It will be noted that this discussion of discourse in relation to ideology constantly moves between the personal (translators' choices) and the public (ambient discourses). Baker (2006) proposes narrative theory as an altern-ative account of these and similar phenomena in translation studies. In narrative theory a distinction is made between **ontological narratives** (narrat-ives of the self) and **public narratives**, as "stories elaborated by and circulating among social and institutional formations larger than the individual" (*ibid.*:33). Baker's account makes explicit the interaction between individual and collective perception and expression – an immensely useful insight for both translation and discourse studies, especially in situations where the individual voice and the public narrative conflict with each other.

These notions and others provide a much richer framework within which to conduct analyses of language and ideology in translation. In pursuing such studies, however, we shall have to confront some methodological prob-lems, raised by Stubbs (1997) amongst others, about the practice of critical discourse analysis (CDA). One is that CDA studies typically do not aim at comprehensive coverage of the data, instead merely selecting elements in texts which support the argument being put forward. The present study might be accused of this failing since there are, of course, some counter-examples in the texts which go against the general trend. Occasionally, for instance, the translator does represent the discourse of effort and engage-ment: *a continuous battle* (TT 6–7), *the memory lives on . . .* (TT 27–28). So are we just cherry-picking evidence to suit our case? The logical way to counter this criticism would be to provide a full, quantitative analysis of shifts (and non-shifts) in the translation. The results that would emerge from such a study, however, would tell us very little about what is going on – and might even prove misleading. For numbers of shifts do not represent significance of shifts. In the first three lines alone of ST and TT, it is very difficult to quantify the precise number of shifts (there are many); and some which would have to be counted (e.g. *comunidad* becoming *society*, *conservar* becoming *safeguard*) are hardly significant. This problem was recognized long ago by van Leuven-Zwart (1990:88) in her pioneering study of trans-lation shifts: the macro-structural impact of shifts depends not upon their quantity but upon their quality or significance. Qualitative assessment, including counter-examples as well as patterned behaviour, still seems to be the best way forward.

Another criticism of CDA is that one of its central claims – that discourses are both "socially shaped and socially constitutive" (Fairclough 1995:131; cf. Gee 1990, above) – is often asserted but has not as yet been empirically substantiated. How could the relation between cause and effect posited in this double process be tested? Specifically, how can we tell that the sets of decisions that make up the translated text have any particular cumulative effect? I have described elsewhere (Mason 2008) the beginnings of an attempt to investigate actual reader response to translated texts as a way of testing whether discoursal shifts have any effect on readers. It is, of course, a highly problematic undertaking – perhaps even a quixotic enterprise, as Hermans (1999:63–64) has suggested. Nevertheless, enquiry into the actual effects of translators' decision making on users of translations would add considerable support to the kinds of claims we wish to make about discourse and ideology in translation. If we wish to substantiate our beliefs about the role of translators in spreading or resisting the spread of narratives and discourses, it is to this area of enquiry that we should perhaps turn our attention.

References

Baker, Mona (2006) *Translation and Conflict. A Narrative Account*. London and New York: Routledge.

Beaugrande, Robert de and Wolfgang Dressler (1981) *Introduction to Text Linguistics*, London: Longman.

Bennett, Karen (2007) 'Epistemicide! The Tale of a Predatory Discourse', in Sonia Cunico and Jeremy Munday (eds), 151–169.

Bettelheim, Bruno (1983) *Freud and Man's Soul*, London: Chatto & Windus.

Crick, Joyce (1989) 'Misreading Freud', *Times Higher Education Supplement*, 15 September.

Brotherston, Gordon (2002) 'Tlaloc Roars. Native America, the West and Literary Translation', in Theo Hermans (ed), 165–179.

Bruce, D (1994) 'Translating the Commune: Cultural Politics and the Historical Specificity of the Anarchist Text', *Traduction, Terminologie, Rédaction* 1: 47–76.

Cunico, Sonia and Jeremy Munday (eds) *Translation and Ideology. Encounters and Clashes*, special issue of *The Translator* 13 (2).

Fairclough, Norman (1995) *Critical Discourse Analysis: the Critical Study of Language*. London: Longman.

Foucault, Michel (1971) *L'Ordre du discourse*, Paris: Gallimard.

Gee, James Paul (1990) *Social Linguistics and Literacies: Ideology in Discourses*, London: Falmer Press.

Halliday, Michael (1978) *Language as Social Semiotic*, London: Edward Arnold.

—— and Ruqaiya Hasan (1976) *Cohesion in English*, London: Longman.

Hatim, Basil (1991) 'The pragmatics of argumentation in Arabic: The rise and fall of a text type', *Text* 11 (2): 189–199.

—— (2001) *Teaching and Researching Translation*, London: Longman.

—— and Ian Mason (1990) *Discourse and the Translator*, London: Longman.

—— and Ian Mason (1991) 'Coping with ideology in professional translating', *Interface: Journal of Applied Linguistics* 6(1): 23–32.

Hermans, Theo (1999) *Translation in Systems. Descriptive and System-oriented Approaches Explained*, Manchester: St. Jerome Publishing.

—— (ed) (2002) *Crosscultural Transgressions. Research Models in Translation Studies II. Historical and Ideological Issues.* Manchester: St. Jerome Publishing.

Hoey, Michael (2005) *Lexical Priming: A New Theory of Words and Language*, London and New York: Routledge.

Kang, Ji-Hae (2007) 'Recontextualization of News Discourse: A Case Study of Translation of News Discourse on North Korea', in Sonia Cunico and Jeremy Munday (eds), 219–242.

Kress, Gunther (1985) *Linguistic Processes in Sociocultural Practice*, Victoria: Deakin University Press.

León Portilla, Miguel (1990a) 'Tiene la Historia un Destino?' *El Correo de la UNESCO*, April 1990, Paris: UNESCO.

—— (1990b) 'History or Destiny?' *The UNESCO Courier*, April 1990, Paris: UNESCO.

Leuven-Zwart, Kitty van (1990) 'Translation and Original; Similarities and Dissimilarities II', *Target* 2, 69–96.

Mason, Ian (2008) 'Translator Moves and Reader Response: the Impact of Discoursal Shifts in Translation' in Monika Klein-Kuhle and Michael Schwarzer (eds) *TranslationswissenschaftlichesKolloquium I.* Bern: Peter Lang, 2008.

Meylaerts, Reine (2007) '"La Belgique vivra-t-elle?": Language and Translation Ideological Debates in Belgium (1919–1940)', in Sonia Cunico and Jeremy Munday (eds), 297–319.

Munday, Jeremy (2001) *Introducing Translation Studies. Theories and Applications*, London and New York: Routledge.

—— (2002) 'Systems in Translation. A Systemic Model for Descriptive Translation Studies', in Theo Hermans (ed), 76–92.

—— (2007) 'Translation and Ideology: A Textual Approach', in Sonia Cunico and Jeremy Munday (eds), 195–217.

Newmark, Peter (1991) *About Translation*, Clevedon: Multilingual Matters.

Prince, Ellen (1981) 'Toward a taxonomy of given-new information', in Peter Cole (ed) *Radical Pragmatics*, New York: Academic Press, 223–255.

Reynolds, Siân (1991) 'Shadowland gospels', *Times Higher Education Supplement*, 29 November.

Schäffner, Christina (2003) 'Third Ways and New Centres. Ideological Unity or Difference?' in María Calzada Pérez (ed) *Apropos of Ideology. Translation Studies on Ideology – Ideologies in Translation Studies*, Manchester: St. Jerome Publishing, 23–41.

Simpson, Paul (1993) *Language, Ideology and Point of View*, London and New York: Routledge.

Stubbs, Michael (1997) 'Whorf's Children: Critical Comments on Critical Discourse Analysis', in Ann Ryan and Alison Wray (eds) *Evolving Models of Language. Papers from the Annual Meeting of the British Association for Applied Linguistics, Swansea 1996.* Clevedon: BAAL/Multilingual Matters, 100–116.

Venuti, Lawrence (1998) *The Scandals of Translation. Towards an Ethics of Difference*, London and New York: Routledge.

Appendix

¿Tiene la historia un destino?	History or Destiny?
Miguel León-Portilla	Miguel León-Portilla

1	Antiguos y prolongados esfuerzos por	Mexicans have always exhibited an obstinate
2	conservar la memoria de sucesos que afectaron	determination to safeguard the memory of the
3	a la comunidad integran el primer gran	major events that have marked their society and
4	capítulo de la búsqueda del ser y del destino	this has coloured the way in which they view
5	mexicanos. Así, ya en la época prehispánica	their identity and destiny. From pre-Columbian
6	se afirma una forma característica de	times they have been engaged in a continuous
7	interesarse por preservar la memoria de sí	battle to save their history from oblivion.
8	mismo y luchar contra el olvido. Esa memoria	Knowledge of the past was the foundation on
9	era indispensable a los viejos sacerdotes y	which their priests and diviners based their
10	sabios para prever los destinos en relación con	astronomical calculations and their predictions of
11	sus cálculos calendáricos. Tal quehacer de	the future. Countless archaeological remains
12	elaboración y registro de una historia divina y	from the two thousand years before the arrival of
13	humana perdura en miles de vestigios	the Spaniards in 1519 bear witness to the
14	arqueológicos que abarcan más de veinte siglos	Mexican desire to interpret and record the
15	antes de la llegada de los españoles en 1519.	history of gods and man. The stelae known as
16	Así, por ejemplo, las estelas de 'Los	danzantes ('dancers') at Monte Albán in the
17	Danzantes' en Monte Albán, Oaxaca, fechadas	Oaxaca valley, on which are inscribed a record
18	entre 600 y 300 a.C., constituyen en el Nuevo	of the passing days and years, place-names and
19	Mundo el más antiguo registro de aconteceres,	the names of kings and other notables,
20	con sus años y días, nombres de lugares, de	constitute the oldest known chronicle (600 to
21	reyes y señores.	300 BC) of the New World.
22	El destino - o los destinos - de los	The people, or rather peoples, who succeeded
23	muchos pueblos que han vivido y viven en	one another on Mexican soil met with mixed
24	tierras mexicanas tuvo tiempos propicios y	fortunes. Bursts of creativity were punctuated by
25	tiempos funestos. Hubo épocas de gran	times of crisis and war which even led to the
26	creatividad y otras de crisis y enfrentamientos,	abrupt disappearance of entire populations and
27	que llevaron a dramáticas desapariciones de	civilizations. The memory of these events lives
28	hombres y de formas de exisitir. Los mitos y	on in the thousands of inscriptions and the
29	leyendas, la tradición oral y el gran conjunto	legends of oral tradition.
30	de inscripciones perpetuaron la memoria de	The greatest and most tragic clash of cultures
31	tales aconteceres.	in pre-Columbian civilization was recorded by
32	Del más grande y trágico de los encuentros	some of those who took part in the conquest of
33	que experimentó el hombre indígena habrían	Mexico. Hernán Cortés himself sent five
34	de escribir personajes como el propio	remarkable letters (Cartas de relación) back to
35	conquistador Hernán Cortés en sus Cartas de	Spain between 1519 and 1526; and the soldier-
36	Relación y el soldado cronista Bernal Díaz del	chronicler Bernal Díaz del Castillo (c. 1492–
37	Castillo en su Historia verdadera de la Nueva	1580), who served under Cortés, fifty years after
38	España. Pero también los vencidos dejaron sus	the event wrote his Historia verdadera de la
39	testimonios. Entre otros, un viejo manuscrito	conquista de la Nueva España ('True History of
40	fechado en 1528, que se conserva ahora en la	the Conquest of New Spain'). The vanquished
41	Biblioteca Nacional de Par's, consigna en	peoples also left written records. A manuscript
42	lengua náhuatl (azteca) la memoria de lo que	dated 1528, now in the Bibliothèque Nationale in
43	fue para los antiguos mexicanos el más grande	Paris, recounts in Nahuatl, the language of the
44	de los traumas. (. . .)	Aztecs, the traumatic fate of the Indians. (. . .)

Reprinted from: *El Correo de la UNESCO*, April 1990	*The UNESCO Courier*, April 1990

156

47

ROSE BLANCHE IN TRANSLATION

Susan Stan

Source: *Children's Literature in Education* 35(1) (2004): 21–33.

This comparative study focuses on three editions of *Rose Blanche*, Roberto Innocenti's picturebook portrayal of a young girl who discovers a Nazi concentration camp on the outskirts of her German city. The original text, written in French by Christophe Gallaz to accompany Innocenti's illustrations, was translated into English and published in the United States; this text is compared with the British text, rewritten by Ian McEwan, and the German text, translated by Abraham Teuter. An examination of differences in the three texts demonstrates some of the ways in which cultural, aesthetic, national, ideological, pedagogical, and economic issues influence the translation of a children's book.

Rose Blanche, Roberto Innocenti's story of the girl who discovers a Nazi concentration camp on the outskirts of her German city, received a mixed reception when it was published in 1985. In the United States, reviewers wondered what to make of this marriage of mature content and picturebook art form. The book's publication raised questions along the line of this one: "How can one reconcile the need to protect young children from the constant onslaught of life's ugly realities with the need to share knowledge that may give meaning to the past and enable children to gain perceptions that can lessen the likelihood of recurrence of such trauma?" (Seidman, 1985).[1] A review of the British edition called the book "a total mistake," explaining that "every page is like a quotation with vast amounts of detail of huge resonance to adults and much mystery to a child" (Rosen, 1985). Another British reviewer saw the book as unique—"I can think of nothing with which to compare *Rose Blanche*"—and certainly suitable for children (Crouch, 1986). The American edition was given the 1986 Mildred Batchelder Award for best translation, and the book also won a prestigious Special Mention in the Graphic Prize at the international Bologna Book Fair that year.

More recent discussions of *Rose Blanche,* such as those by Israeli scholar Zohar Shavit (1999) and Canadian scholar Adrienne Kertzer (2002), have examined ways in which the text and pictures contribute to the historical narrative that writers of children's books have constructed about the Third Reich. Since its original appearance in 1985 in Switzerland, *Rose Blanche* has been translated and published in a dozen or more countries. The differences among some of these texts forms the focus of this article.

Publication history

Although the text of *Rose Blanche* was originally written in French by the Swiss writer Christophe Gallaz, the book itself originated with the Italian artist Roberto Innocenti. Early in the 1980s, Innocenti had the idea for the story of Rose Blanche and had created three paintings with the idea of making a book. Not only were the several Italian publishers to whom he presented the idea not interested, they told him outright that nobody would ever publish such a book (Delessert, 2002). The paintings sat in Innocenti's studio in Florence, Italy, until 1983, when Etienne Delessert and Rita Marshall walked in. They were working on a fairy-tale project for the American publisher Creative Education—she as art director and he as consultant—and were looking for illustrators. John Alcorn, one of the artists they approached, was unable to take the job and suggested Innocenti, whom he had come to know while living in Florence. Innocenti had little work at the time and had never illustrated a children's book, but, recalled Delessert,

> Rita and I loved what we saw that day, commissioned Roberto to illustrate *Cinderella*—he was able to complete the book in a very short amount of time for a 1983 publication—and we told him that we would try to find enough money to work on Rose Blanche for a year. I was at the time the editor of Tournesol, a Swiss company I had created years before and sold recently to Edipresse. I convinced Pierre Lamunière, head of Edipresse, to finance Innocenti's book.
>
> (2002)

Innocenti prepared a dummy with sketches to work out how he would tell the story, and Delessert assumed the role of his editor, "even rearranging some of the sequences with Roberto's approval" (Delessert, 2002). When Innocenti finished his paintings, he sent them to Delessert along with a few lines of text that explained what was happening in the pictures. Delessert

158

brought the pictures and the notes to author Christophe Gallaz to write the story. From the beginning, Innocenti had called the little girl Rose Blanche in honor of the resistance movement. Writing in French, Gallaz deliberately chose a spare style for the story. "I didn't want to be melodramatic, or moralizing, or too explicit," he explained. His mentions of winter and spring were purposeful, "both to celebrate life and to show that there's a seriousness about spring just as there is about fall and winter" (Gallaz, 2001).

Delessert and Marshall had told Creative Education about *Rose Blanche*, and Creative bought the American rights. With Gallaz's text in hand, Creative editor Ann Redpath looked for a translator and hired Martha Coventry. Although she cannot remember specific examples, Redpath remembers dissatisfaction with Coventry's translation and Delessert's strong resolve to keep the text faithful to the original. Richard Graglia, who had previously worked with Rita Marshall, was brought in to rewrite the translation. By contrast, the British publisher, Jonathan Cape, chose to have the story rewritten, and the new text includes contextual information as well as substantial editorializing. The title page of that edition reads, "text by Ian McEwan based on a story by Christophe Gallaz."

Because of its financial outlay, Edipresse (under the imprint 24 Heures) held the copyright to *Rose Blanche*, and in 1985, the book was printed as a coproduction with Creative Education and Editions Script, a Swiss publisher who bought the rights to the French edition. The Jonathan Cape edition, also published in 1985, was printed separately. Other editions, including those from German, Spanish, Scandinavian, and Chinese publishers, came out in subsequent years. The Creative Company, which publishes under the imprints Creative Editions and Creative Education, now controls the rights to *Rose Blanche*, having purchased the copyright from Edipresse in the early 1990s. Creative sold the French rights to Gallimard, which published the book in a miniature paperback form with supplementary material that makes it appropriate for use in an educational setting.

Rosa Weiss, the German edition, was translated by Abraham Teuter and published by Alibaba Verlag in 1986. It is a fairly direct translation of Gallaz's text, although it contains numerous small but significant changes, including both additions and deletions. *Rosa Blanca*, the Spanish edition, was translated by Maribel G. Martínez. Although the title page credits the idea and illustrations to Roberto Innocenti and the text to Christophe Gallaz, the German text appears to have been the basis for this translation, as the Spanish text contains certain elements added by the German translator and not present in the original edition.

Although the illustrations in all of the above-mentioned editions are identical, the texts are not. Using the Coventry/Graglia translation from the French and an English-language translation from the German by Gisela Moffit,[2] this article explores the differences between the texts of the Swiss, German, and British editions of *Rose Blanche* and assesses how changes made by the German and British publishers position the book within the context of children's literature in their own countries.

The original text

As mentioned in the previous account of Gallaz's approach to writing the story, the original French text is spare and underscores the allegorical nature of the illustrations. Rose Blanche herself symbolizes the German resistance movement, which was clearly intentional on Innocenti's part when he gave the girl in his paintings that name. Framing the story are the seasons of winter and spring, longstanding signifiers of death and rebirth. Winter arrives at the same time that the National Socialist Party gains power in Rose Blanche's town. Soldiers are coming and going, bringing death with them—a literal death for the Jews they transport, and a more figurative death for the German townspeople, who are engaged in their own form of hibernation and know-nothingness. In the pivotal spread where the little boy escapes from the truck, we see a woman with her back to the action; aside from the soldiers and the mayor; only Rose Blanche is a witness to the event. Even though, as the text reads, "everyone watched everyone else" (n.p.),[3] no one sees anything. By the time spring is about to burst forth, the German soldiers are in retreat from the Russian army. As Rose Blanche's story comes to a close, vegetation is burgeoning in the countryside and traces of the death camp have all but disappeared. With this framework, Innocenti gives his story a cyclical time structure rather than a linear one, placing it firmly in the idyllic mode.[4] He yokes very real, horrific subject matter with a mode synonymous with the innocence of childhood to heighten an already powerful effect.

Neither the camp nor the town is ever named, but the graffiti makes it clear that the setting is in Germany. In addressing the book's allegorical quality, David Russell posits that "Rose Blanche represents all German resistance movements, and her town is Everytown. The tale appears to cover the course of a single winter, but the winter seems symbolic of the Nazi rule in the wartime years and with the springtime comes the forces of liberation" (1996, p. 350).

The second striking characteristic of Gallaz's original text, beyond its allegorical nature, is the switch that occurs midstory from first person to third person. Rose Blanche gives her own account of the changes in her town and her discovery of the concentration camp—observations without elaboration because she has no context to explain what she is seeing. Then, as Rose Blanche begins systematically squirreling away food to carry to the prisoners, the narrating voice switches to third person. This switch has usually been explained as necessary because the story culminates in the death of Rose Blanche, but it has an additional rhetorical effect. Although the narrator, like Rose Blanche herself, sticks to description and action while avoiding explanation or opinion, the use of the third person both distances the reader from Rose Blanche and gives the reader more freedom to ascribe qualities to her, to imagine her thoughts and feelings during that long, hard winter. This third-person narrator is also omniscient and moves away from Rose Blanche's perspective to describe scenes in which she is not present.

Through her actions, Rose Blanche has separated herself from the rest of the citizens in the town, including her mother, and on the day when the townspeople are evacuating, she is not among them. Her end, in death, parallels the death of those people executed for their work in the White Rose resistance movement. As Rose Blanche ponders the empty space where the camp had been, she lays a flower on the barbed wire, almost as an offering. A close-up of this flower intertwined with the wire is used as the final image of the book, and it is impossible to carry out a close reading of the book without placing her in the role of martyr.

Innocenti conveys this separation from other citizens by his placement of Rose Blanche on the page. In the opening scene, Rose Blanche and her mother are pictured together in front of a crowd of soldiers and towns-people. From that point on, Rose Blanche is always pictured alone—off to the side, or foregrounded, separated by a window, hidden behind a wall. When she is observing the escape and recapture of the little boy, her position in the foreground and her bright clothing—in particular her red hair bow—attract the reader's eye, but she appears to be invisible to the soldiers. The only other time she is shown interacting with people is when she hands a piece of bread to another child through the barbed wire.

The entire narrative, from the ascendancy of the National Socialist Party to Rose Blanche's disappearance, is contained in Innocenti's series of paintings. His pictures are full of symbolism and visual allusions.[5] Gallaz saw Innocenti's illustrations as "subdued, both in the way they are drawn and in the colors" (Gallaz, 2001) and wanted to match this understated tone in his text. He chose to present a framework for the pictures rather than to construct a full-blown, detailed story set in Nazi Germany. A writer would be hard pressed to construct from these paintings a piece of sound historical fiction, as such a task would involve explaining the unexplainable. For the story to be realistic, the reader would have to be satisfied that Rose Blanche could elude detection by the soldiers pictured in the background when she first finds the clearing, or that her visits to pass food through the wire fence would not be noticed by SS guards, or that her mother would not be more persistent in finding out how a young girl could eat so much and still lose weight. Fables and allegories have no such restrictions.

The German text

Several changes are apparent when comparing the first page of the German translation by Abraham Teuter with Gallaz's original text. First of all, the

Opening page of American text	Opening page of German text
Translated from the French by Martha Coventry and Richard Graglia (Creative Education, 1985)	*Translated from the French by Abraham Teuter * (Alibaba Verlag, Frankfurt/Main, 1986)*
My name is Rose Blanche. I love in a small town in Germany with narrow streets, old fountains, and tall houses with pigeons on the roofs. One day the first truck arrived and many men left. They were dressed as soldiers. Winter was beginning.	Rosa Weiss lived in a small city in Germany. The city's streets were small: There were old fountains and tall houses, and on the rooftops sat doves. One day there came the first of many trucks and many men got in. They wore uniforms and waved. Mayor Schröder gave a long speech. Colored flags hung everywhere and the children waved.

Closing page of American text	Closing page of German text
Spring sang.	In the city, the children were busy with their mothers cleaning away the rubble. Mayor Schröder was far away.

Figure 1
*German-to-English translation by Gisela Moffit.

story is told entirely in the third person, rather than beginning in Rose Blanche's voice. Gone is the framing device of the seasons (Figure 1), and, therefore, gone too is the invitation to draw the parallel between Nazi rule and the long, bleak days of winter. Instead, details of Innocenti's illustration are described ("colored flags hung everywhere and the children waved"). The town mayor, who plays a pivotal role in the story, is singled out on the first page and given the name of Schröder.

The mayor appears in six of Innocenti's paintings but is only mentioned twice in Gallaz's text, both related to the incident of the boy's escape and recapture. In Teuter's translation, the mayor's name appears seven times, and in fact, the German story begins and ends with his presence. In the illustrations, he is portrayed as a petty bureaucrat and party member, Nazi watchdog and enforcer. In the first painting, he stands above the crowd, flanked by SS officers, embodying the party's position of power. The last time we see him, he has removed his red armband and is getting into an automobile (the sole one visible), ready to flee the city along with its other residents.

Mayor Schröder's increased presence in the text has at least two significant effects. First, it reduces the tendency to invest Rosa Weiss with symbolic meaning because she is no longer the only named character in the book; in fact, there are now three, since Rosa Weiss's mother is referred to as Frau Weiss. Second, by calling attention to Mayor Schröder in the text, Teuter ensures that he is separated from the rest of the German people, just as Rosa Weiss has been separated. Innocenti's illustrations support this notion, as the only bright spots of color on most pages are found in Rosa Weiss's red hair bow and Mayor Schröder's red armband, symbols of goodness and evil. Neither his actions nor hers are to be conflated with the general German populace.

This differentiation was, in fact, Abraham Teuter's purpose in calling attention to the role of the mayor in the text. Teuter is not only the translator but also the publisher of *Rosa Weiss*. He chose to translate the book himself because he had some definite ideas about the original text. He was conscious that he was translating a text about German history that was not created in Germany: "This is part of the Federal Republic's past, not Switzerland's," Teuter has explained, and to drive home that point he turned the mayor, who "out of all the people in the city is the one person who stays round and fat," into a symbolic figure (Schulte, 1986, p. 1652).

Another fundamental consideration concerning names is that of Rosa Weiss herself.[6] Rose Blanche is both the exact name of the resistance movement in the French language and a conceivable first name for a girl (e.g., Anne Marie or Mary Honor). The name Rosa Weiss combines a first name and a surname (her mother is Frau Weiss), and is close to but not the exact name of the German resistance movement, *die Weiße Rose*. Thus, the character of Rosa Weiss may call to mind *die Weiße Rose* but does not have the same strong allegorical overtones as Rose Blanche in the original text. Rosa Weiss is as much the main character in a story grounded in time and place as she is a symbol of German resistance.

Finally, a striking addition is found on the second-to-last spread of the German edition (Figure 2). The illustration on this double-page spread portrays the town in ruins, with Russian tanks rolling in and soldiers scattered about. No civilians are visible in the illustration, and yet the text reads, "With the soldiers in the foreign uniforms there came also people

American text	German text
Translated from the French by Martha Coventry and Richard Graglia (Creative Education, 1985)	Translated from the French by Abraham Teuter (Alibaba Verlag, Frankfurt/Main, 1986)
At that moment in town, some other soldiers arrived. Their trucks and their tanks were also noisy, and they smelled like diesel oil. But their uniforms were a different color. And they spoke a different language.	In the city, other soldiers had arrived. They also had trucks and tanks that made noise and stunk. With the soldiers in the foreign uniforms there came also people who, a few years before, had disappeared from the city. They were looking for their friends, often in vain.

Figure 2

163

who, a few years before, had disappeared from the city." Just prior to this point in the story, townspeople and soldiers alike have fled the town in anticipation of the arrival of Occupation forces. The implication, then, is that these returnees were Holocaust survivors, German Jews who either went into exile or survived the death camps.

One effect of this addition is to soften the impact of what Rosa Weiss saw behind the barbed wire by placing the emphasis on the survivors and minimizing the reality of the six million who did not survive. Whether or not this effect was intentional, the change supports the German historical narrative that Zohar Shavit's study of historical children's novels revealed: "a certain retelling of the national past which provides a source of national pride and a sound basis for the child's feeling of belonging" (1999, p. 92). Characteristic of this narrative is the tendency to foreground the trials and tribulations of the German people during this time and minimize the treatment of the Jews.

For Innocenti, a compelling force behind the book is his memory of two German soldiers whom his parents harbored during the war. In his introductory note on the jacket flap of the American edition, he writes:

> I was a little boy when the war passed in front of my door. One day, two very young German soldiers, wearing gray uniforms, came to our house and begged us to hide them. They probably weren't even 18 years old. They wanted to surrender to the English troops. And they kept repeating: "Stop the war." ... My father did not want to answer my questions, but I knew then that something terrible was happening. When the Allied troops arrived, the two German soldiers left with them.

Innocenti's casting of this tale—initially from Rose Blanche's point of view—already conforms to the pattern Shavit identifies, as it focuses, albeit metaphorically, on the German resistance movement. However, Teuter's insertion of new material into the text—wholly unsupported in Innocenti's illustrations—seems intended to mold the events into a more palatable outcome. The choice of the verb "had disappeared" (*verschwunden waren*) suggests the absence of blame or responsibility, as if the disappeared had left of their own free will.

Teuter's own explanation is completely different. Rather than to minimize the effect of the death camps, his intention was to remind adult readers about the situation of the German Jews. The mention of the people who return was, as he explains, "directed at the conscience of adults. For children it should remain inexplicable" (Schulte, 1986, p. 1654). That is, Teuter does not expect children to understand the reference, but he wants to make sure that adults recognize their continued responsibility for educating children about the events of World War II. Teuter's decision in this regard is an explicit example of the dual-address children's book (Wall, 1991).

American text	British text
Translated from the French by Martha Coventry and Richard Graglia (Creative Education, 1985)	*By Ian McEwan based on a story by Christophe Gallaz (Jonathan Cape, London 1985)*
My name is Rose Blanche.	When wars begin, people often cheer.
I live in a small town in Germany with narrow streets, old fountains, and tall houses with pigeons on the roofs.	The sadness comes later. The men from the town went off to fight for Germany. Rose Blanche and her mother joined the
One day the first truck arrived and many men left. They were dressed as soldiers. Winter was beginning.	crowds and waved them goodbye. A marching band played, everyone cheered, and the fat mayor made a boring speech.
	There were jokes and songs and old men shouted advice to the young soldiers. Rose Blanche was shivering with excitement. But her mother said it was cold. Winter was coming.

Figure 3

The British text

Rather than publish the same text as the Americans or a closely related text, the British publisher, Jonathan Cape, turned to Ian McEwan to write a new text based on the original. McEwan, a writer who has since become well known for his fiction for adults, begins with a general statement about war and then, like the German text, describes some of the activities portrayed in Innocenti's opening illustration (Figure 3). He uses a third-person narrator to tell the story and does not limit the point of view to Rose Blanche. Like Gallaz, however, McEwan uses the device of the winter and spring seasons to frame the events of the story.

Particularly interesting is the attribution of feeling to Rose Blanche: she was "shivering with excitement." This description, which in this passage serves to underscore the advent of winter, is the first of many such feelings and emotions injected into the narrative. The mayor is described as "immensely pleased with himself" when he corrals the escaping boy; a soldier is "furious"; the boy "burst into tears." Rose Blanche is "furious" and "so tired she felt like giving up." The townspeople are "no longer patient."

These descriptions are part of McEwan's overall approach to write the story as realistic fiction and bring the characters and situations to life. In those instances where child readers lack the necessary prior information to make sense of the elements in his story, McEwan supplies explanations. For example, one of Innocenti's paintings shows a line of people outside waiting for the bakery to open. Although the original text dwells on the military

165

tanks rolling down the cobblestone street, McEwan shifts the focus to the everyday living conditions of the townspeople. His text reads: "Rose Blanche often went shopping for her mother. There were long queues outside the shops, but no one grumbled. Everybody knew that food was needed for the soldiers who were always hungry." Not only has he explained the presence of the people in the illustration, but he has also included the reason for the food shortages. The emphasis here is on life during wartime, and the picture McEwan presents will be familiar to anyone who has either experienced or read about the same time period in Britain.

Similarly, in cases where readers might have reason to doubt the plausibility of the plot, McEwan inserts the missing details. The original text does not question how Rose Blanche might have been able to keep up with the truck that is transporting the boy. The British text circumvents the question: "She followed the lorry right through the town. She was a fast runner; she knew all the short cuts. Winding streets forced the lorry to go slow."

In its attempt to make Innocenti's story into realistic historical fiction, McEwan has reduced it from a text with multiple meanings to a history lesson. It was successful neither aesthetically nor critically for one British reviewer, who found it "a mish-mash of caricature, myth, fantasy and documentary" (Rosen, 1985). In commenting on a similar kind of retelling of *Emil and the Detectives,* Akiko Yamizaki (2002) brings up the issue of cultural context adaptation. To her, deviation from the original text shows not only a lack of respect for children but also for children's books and their authors, since faithfulness to the original text is a central issue in the translation of texts for adults.

Conclusion

One can never take for granted that a book in translation will be the same as the original edition, and of course the reading experience can never be duplicated, mediated as it is by the smell of the binding, the weight of the paper, the touch of the cover. Aside from the French school edition, all of the original hardcover editions of *Rose Blanche* that I have seen (Swiss, German, American, British, Italian, and Spanish) look alike from the outside, with only small variations in the cover finish, yet the views they offer of a little girl's wartime experience are not the same. As the examples given demonstrate, cultural, aesthetic, national, ideological, pedagogical, and economic issues are all at work in shaping these translations. The Italian saying *traduttóre, traditóre*—"to translate is to betray"—underscores the impossibility of capturing the whole of the original in a translation, but perhaps more to the point in a work for children, where fidelity is not always the main concern, is the Latin motto of the marketplace, *cavet emptor*—"let the buyer beware."

Notes

A preliminary version of this article was delivered at the ChLA 2002 conference in Wilkes-Barre, Pennsylvania.

1 An extensive discussion of the use of the picturebook form to introduce controversial subject matter can be found in Russell (1996). He focuses the discussion on *Rose Blanche, Hiroshima No Pika* by Toshi Maruki, and *Smoky Night* by Eve Bunting.

2 Several years ago, Dr. Gisela Moffit, professor of German in the Department of Foreign Languages and Literature at Central Michigan University, and I found we had a mutual interest in *Rose Blanche* and began our research together. Our directions are different, but I have benefited greatly from our collaboration and am indebted to her for the translation of the German text used for this article.

3 Because all editions of *Rose Blanche* are unpaginated, no page indications are included for subsequent citations from the texts.

4 For a discussion of markers of the idyllic mode, see Maria Nikolajeva's article, "Growing up: the dilemma of children's literature," in *Children's Literature as Communication*, ed. Roger D. Sell (2002), pp. 116–117, or her book-length study *From Mythic to Linear: Time in Children's Literature* (2000).

5 The picture on the left side of the third spread, showing the boy with his hands up, visually alludes to a well-known photograph taken by Juergen Stroop, an SS officer and functionary who documented the activities of the Nazis in Warsaw in memo and photographic form. These are reproduced in *The Stroop Report: The Jewish Quarter of Warsaw Is No More!* translated from the German and annotated by Sybil Milton (Pantheon, 1979). Zohar Shavit (1999) analyzes Innocenti's use of this photo and concludes that it detracts rather than adds credibility to the story.

6 Alice Lincoln Ward, faculty member of the Department of Foreign Languages and Literature at Central Michigan University, first offered many of the observations regarding the name Rosa Weiss found in this section.

References

Crouch, Marcus, "Review of *Rose Blanche*, by Christophe Gallaz," *Junior Bookshelf*, April 1986, 50, 62–63.

Delessert, Etienne, E-mail to Susan Stan. 10 June 2002.

Gallaz, Christophe, *Rose Blanche*. Neuchâtel, Switzerland: Editions Script, 1985.

Gallaz, Christophe, *Rose Blanche*. Translated by Martha Coventry and Richard Graglia. Mankato, MN: Creative Education, 1985.

Gallaz, Christophe, *Rose Blanche*. Translated by Abraham Teuter. Frankfurt/Main: Alibaba Verlag, 1986.

Gallaz, Christophe, *Rose Blanche*. Paris: Gallimard, 1990.

Gallaz, Christophe, E-mail to Alice Lincoln Ward. 23 March, 2001.

Kertzer, Adrienne, *My Mother's Voice: Children, Literature, and the Holocaust*. Peterborough, Ont: Broadview Press, 2002.

McEwan, Ian, *Rose Blanche*. London: Jonathan Cape, 1985.

Nikolajeva, Maria, "Growing up: the dilemma of children's literature," in *Children's Literature as Communication*, Roger D. Sell. Amsterdam/Philadelphia: John Benjamins, 2002.

Nikolajeva, Maria, *From Mythic to Linear: Time in Children's Literature*. Lanham, MD: Scarecrow Press, 2000.

Redpath, Ann, Conversation with Susan Stan. New York City, 17 May 2002.

Rosen, Michael, "Review of *Rose Blanche,*" *New Statesman,* 8 November 1985, 110, 25.

Russell, David L., "Hope among the ruins: Children, picture books, and violence," *Para*doxa,* 1996, 2, 347–356.

Schulte, Bergitte, "In dieser Drastik beispiellos," *Börsenblatt,* 1986, 43, 1652–1654.

Seidman, Eric, "Review of *Rose Blanche,*" *Science Books and Films,* 1985, 21, 64.

Shavit, Zohar, "The untold story: What German writers tell their children about the Third Reich and the Holocaust," *Canadian Children's Literature/Littérature Canadienne pour la Jeunesse,* 1999, 95, 90–119.

Stroop, Jürgen, *The Stroop Report: The Jewish Quarter of Warsaw Is No More!* Translated and annotated by Sybil Milton. New York: Pantheon, 1979.

Wall, Barbara, *The Narrator's Voice: The Dilemma of Children's Fiction.* New York: St. Martin's Press, 1991.

Yamizaki, Akiko, "Why change names? On the translation of children's books," *Children's Literature in Education,* 2002, 33, 53–62.

48

'DU HAST JAR KEENE AHNUNG'

African American English dubbed into German[1]

Robin Queen

Source: *Journal of Sociolinguistics* 8(4) (2004): 515–37.

This paper explores the translation of sociolinguistic variation by examining the ways that African American English (AAE) is dubbed into German. In discussing this ubiquitous yet poorly studied area of language use, I show that ideas about language as an index to social groupings are transferable to the degree that the ideas overlap in the cultures in question. In the case of German, if the character being dubbed is young, male and tied to the street cultures of the urban inner city, then AAE is dubbed using a form of German that has links to the urban youth cultures of north-central Germany. The transferability of sociolinguistic variation is important to issues related to cross-cultural communication and the ideologies that may play a role in the outcomes of that communication as well as to linguistic creativity and language style more generally.

Introduction

Among the wide-ranging set of styles found in American mainstream films, African American English (hereafter AAE) stands out. As a form of American English that stereotypically connotes characteristics such as toughness, lack of education and low socio-economic status, AAE has long been subject to close public attention and scrutiny, and many public debates about language in the United States center on AAE (cf. Lippi-Green 1997; Milroy 2000; Rickford and Rickford 2000). Certain features of AAE and their attendant social meanings are highly recognizable, salient and accessible to a broad and general American audience (Rickford and Rickford 2000).

This paper explores how the linguistic styles found in American mainstream films are dubbed into German with a particular emphasis on the dubbing of African American English. The goal of this exploration is an

169

understanding of the degree to which the social meanings associated with linguistic variation may be transferable cross-culturally. Although not necessarily an obvious choice for sociolinguistic research, dubbing presents a unique avenue for such an inquiry precisely because it focuses upon stylistic variation as a central problem and transparently provides a solution.

Style has played a central role in sociolinguistic inquiry since its inception and has been presented as the window to language change, to social indexicality and to semiotics more generally (Eckert and Rickford 2001). At its most basic, linguistic style can be understood as a distinctive and recognizable form of language use that involves meanings that are independent of the semantic content of the words. In order to be recognizable, styles must be built in large part around a consistent package of linguistic features and usage patterns (cf. Irvine 2001). At the same time, linguistic styles are dynamic, developing out of the ongoing interaction between real-time language use and beliefs about the place of language within the social world.

Once linguistic styles become widely recognized as distinctive and established, they may become useful for achieving artistic or creative effects because they are available to quickly index a certain type of person, activity or attribute (e.g. Coupland 2001). As Lippi-Green writes:

> In traditions passed down over hundreds of years from the stage and theater, film uses language variation and accent to draw character quickly, building on established preconceived notions associated with specific regional loyalties, ethnic, racial or economic alliances. This shortcut to characterization means that certain traits need not be laboriously demonstrated by means of a character's actions and an examination of motive. It also means that these characterizations are culture- and period-bound. In this films have much in common with fiction and as the representation of our cultures and ourselves [are] equally worthy of study.
>
> (Lippi-Green 1997: 81)

In other words, styles can be stylized. Coupland (2001: 199) notes that stylization 'suggests . . . an inbuilt self-critiquing function in style-choice' and emphasizes that this function illuminates the dialogic nature of stylistic variation. Although stylized linguistic variation is unlikely to correspond to real-world distributions, its use in the mass media indicates a conscious effort to perform social juxtapositions that are found in the everyday world of the audience. Rickford writes:

> It occurs to me, however, that some verbal (and non-verbal) performances – especially those that involve radio broadcasts, large audiences, and public occasions **are** more stylized than others. And that people in such situations are trying more consciously than

170

most of us may do in everyday life, to project personas of various types.

(Rickford 2001: 230)

It is precisely such projections that make the scripted mass media an inviting avenue of sociolingusitic investigation.

Despite considerable research into language in the mass media, much of the work that has concentrated on spoken language has centered on media venues that revolve around the broadcast of 'real' events rather than on broadcasts of more obviously scripted events. Thus, political debates (Mendoza-Denton 1995), talk shows (Carbaugh 1990), news (Cotter 1999), sports events (Lefkowitz 1995) and real-time sales shows (Bucholtz 1999), among others, have been analyzed for various sociolinguistic markers and usages. While it is the case that these kinds of presentations appear to approximate real-world language use in that they are more or less spontaneous and unscripted, there is no *a priori* reason to assume that scripted productions are of less sociolinguistic interest than are un-(or less) scripted productions. In fact, scripted productions may be more conducive than unscripted ones to the study of sociolinguistic indexicality because the stylized choices found in scripted productions are generally highly focused and easily manipulated indexes that can be (and are) taught to actors (see also Coupland 2001: 209).

The variability that is present in the mass media is stylized to the extent that it typically draws on styles that are largely pre-existent and thus more stereotypical than is variation in the primary social world. For instance, in the film *Fargo*, the stereotypical regional accent of North Dakota is highly stylized to represent links between this accent and particular social characteristics such as provincialism, honesty and friendliness. Similarly, the linguistic variation that distinguishes the North Dakotans as essentially good, hard-working and honest people from the New Yorkers as essentially criminal, shifty and dangerous taps directly into the perceptions of many Americans about those regional varieties (e.g. Preston 2000). In both cases, the primary semiotic power rests with the representation of links between linguistic form and social function that pre-exist their occurrence in the film. The representation of AAE in mainstream films and their dubbed counterparts similarly relies on indexes to socio-cultural life that pre-exist its incidence in film.

Data

The data for this study are drawn from a larger corpus of mainstream American films and their German dubbed counterparts. The selection of films to include in this larger corpus was *ad hoc* except that I sought a balance between four genres of mass market films: dramas, comedies, action films and children's animated films.[2] A number of the films in the corpus were selected because of my own familiarity with the fact that they involved interesting variability. The others were chosen via surveys of students, colleagues and friends about films they were familiar with that involved linguistic variability. Children's animated films showed very little variability when dubbed into German and thus were ultimately excluded. The final corpus included 32 films of which 15 were comedies, six were action films and 11 were dramas. These films appeared over the course of 17 years (1983–2000), were produced by different studios and dubbed in different studios. Thus, the patterns found are unlikely to be attributable to the norms of a single studio or dubbing house.

Films involving at least one character who used AAE were then sub-categorized into the corpus used for this study. The determination of such characters was based on the use of at least one of the following linguistic features (cf. Green 2003, and Rickford and Rickford 2000 for details concerning AAE grammar): /æks/; invariant 'be'; zero copula; word-final glottal stop; or the use of prosodic patterns often associated with AAE. These include: initial stress shifts; a relatively wide pitch range; level or falling tones in yes-no questions; a rising-falling contour that extends over a full phrase; and lengthened vowels (see Green 2003 for a general discussion of AAE prosody). These prosodic patterns were identified based on an impressionistic analysis and were used to capture AAE-speaking characters who did not exhibit the grammatical features noted above.

The justification for using this set of features to indicate AAE is that they are highly emblematic for speakers of American English and they can be assumed to implicate other features of AAE for the characters using them. Indeed, all the characters who were thus identified as AAE speakers used multiple features generally associated with AAE (again see Green 2003). The resulting corpus is detailed in Table 1 below. The majority of African American characters in all the films except *Clueless* exhibit linguistic features commonly associated with African American English.

This corpus provides a broad range of AAE usage that includes variation based on age, socio-economic class, region, gender and other sorts of affiliations, especially affiliations with a local, urban 'street' culture. Just as is true in real-world communities where AAE is used, the characters vary with respect to both the combinations of features they use and with respect to the frequency of use of any given variant. Since this study sought a general understanding of the treatment of AAE in dubbed films, the data from the original films were only minimally quantified and were done so primarily as a means of comparison between an original and its dubbed counterpart. Nonetheless, several interesting patterns emerged across the corpus, particularly in the representations of young, male characters associated with local, urban street culture. Before presenting those patterns in detail, I first turn to a brief discussion of dubbing in general, and in Germany specifically, in order to contextualize those patterns both historically and socio-culturally.

172

Table 1 Corpus of films.

Film	Year	Genre	Setting	Fewer than three African American characters	Majority African American casts
Boyz N the Hood	1991	Drama	Inner-city Los Angeles		X
Bring it On	2000	Comedy	Suburban and inner-city Los Angeles		
Clockers	1995	Drama	New York		X
Clueless	1995	Comedy	San Fernando Valley	X	
Coming to America	1988	Comedy	Queens, New York		X
Crazy in Alabama	1999	Comedy	Rural Alabama		
Falling Down	1993	Drama	Los Angeles	X	
Girl 6	1996	Drama	New York		X
Jungle Fever	1991	Drama	New York		
Mississippi Burning	1988	Drama	Rural Mississippi		
Primary Colors	1998	Drama	U.S., but especially southern U.S.		
Rush Hour	1998	Comedy	Los Angeles		
The Nutty Professor	1996	Comedy	Suburban Los Angelos		X
Trading Places	1983	Comedy	New York City		X

Film dubbing

Translation presents one of the most interesting and vexing issues for language study both because of the ubiquity of translation cross-culturally and because of the impossibility of a translation that is completely true to the original while also being realistic for the target audience. For instance, one of the central concerns of Berthele's (2000) study of multiple translations of *Huckleberry Finn* involves the means through which the regionally and socially specific dialect used by the African American character Jim is rendered into German. As Berthele shows, translators' choices have shifted over time with the earliest translations using a more or less L2 or pidgin-like model for portraying Jim's speech and more recent translations shifting to the portrayal of Jim's speech more in terms of a colloquial variety depicted primarily through non-standard spellings. Berthele argues that this shift coincides with a more general rise in anti-racist and anti-discriminatory discourses in Germany, thus demonstrating the socio-cultural and historical specificity of translation, particularly in terms of target cultural norms and expectations. Film translation must contend with the same specificity; however, it must also solve several problems that are unique to the medium itself.

There are three major types of film translation: *subtitling, voice-overs* and *dubbing*, each of which presents its own set of costs and benefits to the overall process of translation. Dubbing is perhaps the most target-oriented form of film translation because it is the only form of translation in which characters appear to be speaking the target language. As such, it is also the most expensive and time-consuming form of film translation. Since the vocal track is completely changed, dubbing presents a number of special concerns, including synchrony between the vocal channel and lip, jaw and tongue movement, and between the vocal channel and other physical gestures. Further, the stylistic and affective characteristics that are verbally cued in the original require much more careful attention than is the case for other forms of film translation.

The choice to subtitle or dub is tied to socio-cultural preference and historical practice. In Western Europe, dubbing has long been more common in larger countries in which a certain linguistic homogeneity is assumed (though, naturally, not practiced) and which therefore have large audiences that use the target language. Thus, Germany, Spain, Italy, Austria and France typically dub foreign-language films while Holland, Switzerland and the Scandinavian countries typically subtitle foreign-language films (Delabastita 1989; Dries 1995; Luyken 1991). Audiences generally prefer that type of film translation with which they are most familiar.

The German dubbing industry emerged during the 1920s and 1930s in tandem with the shift from silent films to films that included an audio track. However, German fears (particularly in the 1930s and 1940s) that French and English were corrupting the German language also fed a preference for dubbing (Bräutigam 2001: 9–10). Since the end of WWII, the number of imported films shown in Germany has steadily increased and currently 85 percent of the films shown in movie theaters are of non-German origin. Of those, 90 percent are dubbed. Between 70 and 80 percent of the films of non-German origin are American media products and most of the top-grossing films in any given year are American (Müntefering 2002).

Although there has not been a great deal of linguistic interest in either dubbing generally or German dubbing specifically, some studies do exist (Bräutigam 2001; Garncarz 1992; Herbst 1994; Pisek 1992; Pruys 1997; Whitman-Linsen 1992). These studies point out that dubbing practices tend to erase most linguistic variation, especially regional variation. This erasure is likely to be related to the recognition that there is no direct one-to-one mapping of regional variants since those variants commonly used in American originals bring with them wholly different social connotations than do regional varieties in the German context. As Bräutigam (2001: 33) writes:

Ähnliche Schwierigkeiten [wie bei Lippensynchronisierung] bereiten sprachliche Varietäten des Dialogs wie z. B. Dialekte. Deutsche Entsprechungen wirken meist ziemlich gesucht und unfreiwillig

174

komisch, so daß es besser ist, auf entsprechende Transponierungen zu verzichten, als im amerikanischen Film jemanden sächseln zu lassen.

'Other linguistic variation in the dialog can cause similar difficulties [as lip synchrony], for instance, dialects. German options usually seem forced and unwittingly funny so that it is generally better to forgo transfer than to have someone in an American film use Saxon.'

(Author's translation)

German dubbed films have their own sets of conventionalized features that Herbst (1994) has called *Synchronisierdeutsch* or 'dubbing German'. Of the many characteristics of this variety, two stand out for their prevalence: anglicisms and the lack of 'spoken-like' quality of much of the work (see Herbst 1994: 133–136 for a discussion of anglicisms and 167–171 for stylistic issues associated with *Synchronisierdeutsch*), This style presents a verbal text that may be perceived as odd by the German-speaking audience. However, since German-speaking audiences generally know that they are watching a dubbed film and thus expect it to differ from original German productions, the use of *Synchronisierdeutsch* does not appear to hinder a general under-standing of the film nor to stop audiences from attending such films, as box office sales attest. Further, the use of anglicisms in particular may help remind the audience that they are watching a dubbed film.[3]

The German context for dubbing AAE

AAE is often dubbed just like other varieties of American English as described above. However, in some specific contexts, for instance, in films set in urban contexts, a somewhat different style may be used. This style involves linguistic elements linked to general informality, *Jugendsprache* ('youth language'), and the urban working class, particularly as located in the northern and central regions of Germany, especially Berlin and the *Ruhrgebiet*, the West German center of heavy industry for much of the 20th century. The linguistic features of this dubbing style include: palatal rather than velar articulations of word-initial /g/, especially in the lexical items *gar*, *genau*, *gut* and *genug*; some vowel shifts, particularly /aɪ/ to /eː/; pronominal cliticization; final consonant deletion in clusters; frequent prosodic reductions, especially in inflectional morphology; and lexical items that index youth and informality.

Of the linguistic features of this style, the palatal realization of /g/ provides the primary index to the northern and central regions of Germany (see Barbour and Stevenson 1998; Schlobinski 1987). Although palatal /g/ is by no means the only or even the most prevalent characteristic of these varieties in the non-film world, its use in dubbed films with urban settings importantly implicates one region of Germany over others. Monophthongal [aɪ] is more specific to *Berlinisch*, although again it is neither the most canonical nor the most prevalent vowel associated with this variety.[4] From the dubbed data alone it is unclear why these two phonological features appear to the exclusion of others; however, since films present stylized rather than accurate characterizations of real-world variation, it is not surprising that dubbed variation does not follow real-world patterns.

Similar to real-world variation is the fact that these features, taken in tandem with the others mentioned above, implicate social characteristics other than region, particularly those associated with age, gender and social class. Although social class is differently imagined and realized in the German context than in the American one, the use of *Berlinisch* and other urban varieties is generally associated with the German industrial working class (Johnson 1995; Schlobinski 1987) and particularly with working-class males (however, see Johnson 1992). Indeed, the use of the features of the urban dubbing style is found exclusively among urban male characters, despite the fact that *Berlinisch* (and similar urban varieties) is quite hetero-geneous with usage patterns that crosscut most social demographics (Dittmar and Schlobinski 1993; Schönfeld and Schlobinski 1995).

The features other than palatal /g/ and monophongal /aɪ/ that are part of the urban dubbing style are not regionally specific and index the generally colloquial varieties of German known as *Umgangsprachen* and the youth-based register known as *Jugendsprache* (Androutsopoulos and Kallmeyer 2000; Androutsopoulos and Georgakopoulou 2003; Schlobinski 1995). While there is not space here to provide a detailed account of the relationships between dialects, registers, *Umgangsprachen* and standard German, the rela-tionships between these varieties and their location in social and geographic space has formed one of the critical components of research into German variation and change (e.g. Barbour and Stevenson 1998; selected papers in Mattheier 1997; Mattheier 1990). This research has shown a shift over time from dialects as primary markers of geographic differences such as rural/urban to dialects as markers of 'regionally and socially significant phenomena . . . that are not only horizontally distinguishable from other regional varieties but can also be seen as a type of variation that can be located and evaluated vertically along a local linguistic continuum' (Barbour and Stevenson 1998: 110).

As Barbour and Stevenson further note (1998: 149), it is especially in the metropolitan areas of northern and central Germany where varieties such as dialects, *Umgangsprachen*, registers and the standard are difficult to cat-egorically distinguish from one another. In these areas (as compared to the southern German-speaking regions), the traditional dialects have receded drastically. At the same time, the use of regionally-specific *Umgangsprachen* has increased and has even displaced the standard in many situations. As this shift has occurred, the ideological link between less-standard linguistic forms and the working class has largely been maintained, however (Barbour

176

and Stevenson 1998: 150). The use of the *Umgangsprache* among youths in these areas is especially prevalent and is accompanied by *Jugendsprache*-specific characteristics such as particles like *ey* and *man*, English lexical items and other register-based characteristics (see also Schlobinski 1995).[5] It is also increasingly influenced by the multilingualism found throughout Germany, but especially in large urban centers (Auer and Dirim 2004; Kallmeyer, Keim and Tandogan-Weidenhammer 2000).

The urban dubbing style and AAE

The ideologies concerning these varieties of German and their relationships to one another represent the backdrop against which the urban dubbing style may be interpreted. When used to dub AAE, this style helps align AAE speakers with speakers of German urban varieties and in so doing constitutes them ideologically along similar lines. In his discussion of a 1983 workshop on the literary translation of AAE, Berthele writes:

> ... the participating translators seemed to give a light preference to the choice of a colloquial, slangy German which can be located in the 'Ruhrgebiet', the important center of heavy industry in Germany ... This solution gives the German parallel to AAVE a clear proleterian overtone ...
>
> (Berthele 2000: 607)

Example 1, from the film *Boyz N the Hood*, shows the use of the urban dubbing style for dubbing AAE.[6] The excerpts are arranged by speaker turn, with the English original being followed by the German dub (in boldface), which is then followed by a back translation into English (in italics).

Example 1 from *Boyz N the Hood*

1. Doughboy: Orig. Yeah. I heard you be gettin that dopehead pussy.
   Dub **Klar. Wenn du jede Junkyvotze ficks.**
   Back trans. *Sure. If you fuck every junky cunt.*

   Orig. See me, I get more pussy than you get air
   Dub **Guck mich an. So oft wie ich ficke**
   Back trans. *Look at me. As often as I fuck*

   Orig. wich your wanna-be Mac Daddy.
   Dub **kriegst du dein: Möchte-gern Schwanz da gar nich hoch.**
   Back trans. *you don't get your would-like-to dick even up.*

2. Dooky: Orig. Wanna-be Mac, who de hell you callin wanna-be Mac Daddy?
   Dub **Wen meinste mit em möchte-gern Schwanz?**
   Back trans. *You do you mean with the would-like-to dick?*

3. Doughboy: Orig. You nigga. No pussy-gettin mother-fucker.
              Dub **Ja, dich nigga. Du bis doch en müder Wichser**.
              Back trans. *Yes, you nigger. You're a tired jerk-off.*

              Orig. Fuckin dem dopeheads. Stupid ass nigga.
              Dub **Du fickst da bloss ein paar Junkies, du schlapper Neger**.
              Back trans. *You're just fucking a couple of junkies, you lame Negro.*

4. Dookie: Orig. Look, you don know what I be gettin.
              Dub **Man, du hast jar keene Ahnung**.
              Back trans. *Man, you don't have any idea.*

              Orig. Don be fuckin no dopeheads.
              Dub **Ich fick doch keine Junkies**.
              Back trans. *I don't fuck any junkies.*

              Orig. I might let em suck my dick,
              Dub **Die durften mir höchstens ein: blasen, du**,
              Back trans. *At the most they're allowed to give me a blow job,*

              Orig. but I don't be fuckin em. Man, dey got AIDS an shit.
              Dub **mehr aber auch nich. die ha:m doch AIDS n so ne Scheiss**.
              Back trans. *but not anything else. They have AIDS and shit like that.*

5. Monster: Orig. Stupid mother fucker.
              Dub **Ach du bis en blöder Sack**.
              Back trans. *Oh, you're a stupid jerk.*

              Orig. Don't you know you can catch that shit
              Dub **Du kannst dir die Scheisse auch holen**
              Back trans. *You can also get that shit*

              Orig. from lettin em suck on your dick, too?
              Dub **wenn sie dir ein: blasen. Weiss du das etwa nich**?
              Back-trans. *when they give you a blow job. Don't you know that?*

6. Doughboy: Orig. Thank you.
              Dub **Jenau**.
              Back trans. *Exactly.*

This scene occurs between four young men playing cards at a picnic. All four are tied to an alternative street economy that includes controlled substances, guns, alcohol and petty crime. In addition to numerous visual cues to these characters' affiliation with street culture, their language also helps anchor them as participants in that culture. Several salient features of African American English appear, including: invariant 'be' ('be gettin'); palatal realization of /θ/ ('wich'); vocative 'nigga'; multiple negation ('don be fuckin no dopeheads'); and alveolar stop rather than interdental fricative realizations of initial /ð/ ('dey'). There are also markers of a more general informality, including numerous lexical items and alveolar rather than velar progressive verb morphology.

Something similar occurs in the German version; however, in this case, the primary linguistic marker of the street affiliation of the characters occurs with the use of an informal, youth-marked variety of German rather than with an ethnically marked variety. In terms of the grammatical markers, pronominal cliticization (*meinste* Eng. 'you mean'), final consonant deletion in word-final clusters (*nich* Eng. 'not'; *bis* Eng. 'are' [2nd sg.]), and frequent syllable reduction in inflectional morphology (*ham*: Eng. 'have'; *ein*: Eng. 'one') occur in the dubbed version. Additionally, the initial stop in the lexical items 'gar' (discourse particle) and 'genau' (Eng. 'exactly') is palatalized and the low back-high front dipthong shifts to a lengthened /e/ in one instance. These features, coupled with the general informality indicated by lexical items (e.g. *man, schlapp, Junkies, Schwanz, ficken*; Eng. 'man', 'slack', 'Druggies', 'dick', 'fuck'), help place these characters in a youth culture that is geographically located in a non-southern urban area of Germany and socially located outside of the middle class (see also Androutsopoulos and Kallmeyer 2000). The use of the urban dubbing style thus corroborates the information about the characters available to the audience from their physical appearance, gestures and activities.

This form of dubbing is often used quite creatively to provide equivalent information to the German audience as is provided to the American audience. For instance, in Example 2 below, the dubbed version is remarkably close to the original both in its sociolinguistic meaning and in its linguistic form:

Example 2 from *Clockers*

1. Rodney: Orig.   Erol tol me you talked to the homicide cop.
            Dub   **Erol hat mir erzälht, du hast mit den Bullen geredet**.
      Back trans.   *Erol told me you talked with the cops.*

            Orig.   How dat go?
            Dub   **Wie ist das gelaufen?**
      Back trans.   *How did it go?*

2. Strike: Orig.   [S aːaiʔ]
            Dub   **War n'Ordnung**.
      Back trans.   *Was O.K.*

3. Rodney: Orig.   [Aːaiʔ] or all right?
            Dub   **N'Ordnung oder in Ordnung?**
      Back trans.   *In order or in order?*

4. Strike: Orig.   It was [.] [aːaiʔ] [.] all right?
            Dub   **S war [.] n Ordnung [.] in Ordnung?**
      Back trans.   *It was in order. In order?*

As with Example 1, the original version of this excerpt involves linguistic markers of African American English, including final consonant deletion, alveolar rather than interdental release of /ð/, and the vocalization of liquids.

The excerpt focuses on the different meanings associated with variable pronunciations of 'alright'. The pronunciation first used by Strike in which the final stop has a glottal release and medial /l/ and /r/ are realized as elongation on the initial vowel indicates a general informality and flippancy. Rodney indicates the different meanings associated with different linguistic realizations by juxtaposing [aːaɪʔ] with the more formal (and standard) [alraɪt]. The more standard pronunciation highlights Rodney's concern that Strike does not recognize the importance and seriousness of his involvement with the police. Strike's answer in the final line of the excerpt creatively demonstrates his understanding of this difference by embedding [aːaɪʔ] as a stressed nominal complement within a larger clause. That clause is preceded by a pause and followed by an adverbial adjunct [alraɪt], the rising intonation of which (coupled with raised eyebrows, forward body movement and outstretched arms with a palms-up hand movement) marks the implication that he (Strike) has everything under control and that Rodney is worrying unnecessarily.

The German dubbed version is strikingly similar. Unlike Example 1, where multiple linguistic markers of informality appear in the German dub, in this example, the primary indicator of that type of German occurs in Strike's prosodic reduction of the phrase *in Ordnung* (literally 'in order', idiomatically 'alright' or 'O.K.') from [ɪn ʔɔrdnʊŋ] to [nɔ̯dʊŋ]. The prosodic reduction occurs in the elision of the preposition's vowel and the word-medial glottal stop, and in the lowering of the initial vowel of 'ordnung'. (This lowering is likely to be compensatory rather than specifically sociolinguistic in nature.) By maintaining the poetic structure of Strike's answer in the original, the dubbed version achieves a virtually identical effect.

Examples 1 and 2 show the use of the urban dubbing style as a means of translating African American English when it occurs among young, male characters who are socially located in the urban street. In the following example, also from the film *Clockers*, Strike meets his brother Victor in a bar and tries to entice him to commit a murder. Although Victor still lives in the housing project where Strike lives and works, he is not involved with the local street culture.

Example 3 from *Clockers*

1. Victor: Orig. I know somebody.
          Dub **Ich kenne jemanden**.
          Back trans. *I know someone.*

2. Strike: Orig. Who?
          Dub **Wen?**
          Back trans. *Who?*

3. Victor: Orig. My man.
          Dub **Irgendjemand**.
          Back trans. *Just someone.*

4. Strike: Orig. Well, who dat?
           Dub   **Wer isen das?**
           Back trans. *Well, who is it?*

5. Victor: Orig. Look, my man. A friend of a frien.
           Dub   **En Bekannter. Der Freund von em Freund.**
           Back trans. *An acquaintence. The friend of a friend.*

           Orig. He'll do the job.
           Dub   **Lass ihn das machen.**
           Back trans. *Let him do it.*

6. Strike: Orig. How much we talkin bout?
           Dub   **Wieviel willer dafür ham:?**
           Back trans. *How much does he want for it?*

7. Victor: Orig. Nothin so whas the deal?
           Dub   **Gar nichts. Er macht das so.**
           Back trans. *Nothing at all. He'll just do it.*

8. Strike: Orig. Nothin?
           Dub   **Jar nix?**
           Back trans. *Nothing at all?*

9. Victor: Orig. Listen, whatchu wan me ta do.
           Dub   **Sag mal, was erwartest du eigentlich von mir?**
           Back trans. *Listen, what do you expect from me?*

10. Strike: Orig. Nothin'man. A:ait. Just chill man a:ait.
           Dub   **Gar nix man. Alles klar? Reg dich ab, O.K.**
           Back trans. *Nothing at all, man. Everything O.K? Calm down, O.K.*

           Orig. Whassup wid my little mans, my nephews.
           Dub   **Wie gehts en mein Kumpeln, mein klein: Neffen.**
           Back trans. *How are my buddies, my little nephews.*

           Orig. How dey doin?
           Dub   **Was machen die so?**
           Back trans. *What are they doing?*

As in the previous examples, both Strike and Victor use multiple, salient features of African American English. In the dubbed version, only Strike is dubbed with the urban dubbing style. The only markers of informality in Victor's speech are the syllabically reduced articles in line 5; otherwise, his speech is completely standard. Strike, on the other hand, uses: pronominal cliticization (*willer*); frequent syllable reduction (*ham:, isen*); a velar affricate as the final consonants in 'nichts' 'nothing'; palatal rather than velar realization in 'gar' 'completely'; colloquial lexical items (*man, okay, Kumpeln*; Engl. 'man', 'O.K.', 'pal'); and relative pronouns rather than pronouns (*die* for *sie* [3rd pl.]). The differences in the dubbing choices help locate Strike as part of the local street culture while also differentiating him from Victor, who is not part of the local street culture.

Table 2 Frequency of multiple negation and the null copula in *Boyz N the Hood.*

	All characters	*Tre*	*Doughboy*
Multiple negation	78% (146/187)	65% (17/26)	82% (18/22)
Null copula	71% (385/402)	62% (51/82)	74% (35/47)

Quantifying the urban dubbing style

Although the urban dubbing style offers a means to project identities associated with German urban youth culture, its use remains relatively restricted and even characters who are dubbed using features of it use those features relatively infrequently. For instance, in the film *Boyz N the Hood*, two common characteristics of AAE show relatively high frequencies of occurrence, as seen in Table 2 above.

In this table, which is based on data from the last 60 minutes of the film, the frequency of multiple negation and the null copula are given for all characters and then for the characters Tre and Doughboy. In the film overall, the frequencies of the AAE variant of each strategy are relatively high, exceeding 70 percent in both cases. Tre and Doughboy differ from one another with respect to their overall orientation to local street culture, with Doughboy being tightly connected and Tre being somewhat more peripheral. Correspondingly, Doughboy shows a higher frequency in both multiple negation and the null copula than does Tre.

When the strategies identified as part of the urban dubbing style are examined for the final 60 minutes of the dubbed version of *Boyz N the Hood*, the overall rates of each are lower than those shown in Table 2 for the null copula and multiple negation in the originals.

Table 3 shows the frequencies for five of the six features noted above for the urban dubbing style. Lexical items associated with varieties of German other than the standard were not quantified. Table 3 is organized as follows:

Table 3 Frequency of characteristics of the urban dubbing style.

Strategy	*Frequency*
Consonant cluster reduction	48% (111/233)
Prosodic reduction of einen	42% (66/156)
Pronominal cliticization of nominative 2nd person pronoun	19% (21/108)
Monophthongal /aɪ/	16% (67/423)
Palatal /g/	17% (8/46)

- The ratio for /aɪ/ represents the occurrence of [eː] relative to all occurrences of /aɪ/
- The ratio for /g/ represents the occurrence of [j] relative to all occurrences of word-initial, pre-vocalic /g/
- The ratio for consonant clusters represents the number of clusters reduced to a single consonant (e.g. [nɪç] rather than [nɪçt]) for clusters in word-final position)
- For cliticization, only 2nd person pronominal cliticization was quantified because instances of other forms of cliticization were infrequent
- The only prosodic reductions that were quantified involved the following forms of the indirect article: *einen/einer/einem* and the phonologically similar forms of *kein, mein, sein,* and *dein.* As with cliticization, these forms provided the most consistent basis on which to quantify prosodic reductions because they are relatively frequent in the data even though they are not the only forms that undergo prosodic reduction in spoken German generally or in dubbed films specifically (cf. Barbour and Stevenson 1998).

As seen in Table 3, the non-standard variants of these forms occur less frequently that those quantified for AAE in the originals (e.g. in Table 2), with none of the non-standard variants occurring more than 50 percent of the time.[7] Further, there is an apparent distinction between consonant cluster reduction and prosodic reductions of 'ein' forms on the one hand and pronominal cliticization, monophthongal /aɪ/ and palatal /g/ on the other. The differences in these strategies are not necessarily surprising given that consonant cluster reduction and prosodic reductions are more generally tied to spoken German without strong connotations of non-standardness while the other three strategies are more linked to varieties that are regionally and socially specific, as discussed above.

The differences in the frequencies of these strategies are even more pronounced when the characters Tre and Doughboy are compared to one another, as seen in Table 4. As was the case in the originals, Tre and Doughboy show different frequencies of the strategies in question. Different

Table 4 Comparison of two characters' use of characteristics of the urban dubbing style.

Strategy	Tre	Doughboy
Consonant cluster reduction	32% (18/57)	52% (22/43)
Prosodic reduction of einen	36% (17/48)	55% (17/31)
Pronominal cliticization of nominative 2nd person pronoun	0% (0/23)	39% (7/18)
Monophthongal /aɪ/	0% (0/64)	18% (10/56)
Palatal /g/	0% (0/11)	33% (3/9)

from the originals, however, is the categorical distinction between the characters in the use of the three strategies more closely associated with varieties other than the standard.

Although Tre and Doughboy differ from one another in the frequencies with which they were dubbed with prosodic reductions of *ein* forms and reduced, word-final consonant clusters, the more drastic distinction can be seen in the production of the other three strategies associated with the urban dubbing style. In this instance, there is a categorical difference between the two speakers, with Tre using only those features more generally characteristic of spoken forms of German and Doughboy using those features in addition to the features that more strongly implicate a (northern) urban setting.

Thus, the gradient differentiation shown in the original (as represented by the null copula and multiple negation frequencies shown in Table 2) is replaced in the dubbed version by a more or less categorical division between a character who is strongly street-oriented and consequently dubbed using all the features of the urban style, and a character with weaker ties to the street, who is dubbed using only those characteristics of the urban dubbing style that are related to spoken German more generally. This difference is found throughout the corpus as indicated in Table 5 below, which shows those films in which all the features of the urban dubbing style occur in the far left column. Based on the evidence offered in Tables 3–5, the urban dubbing style can be distinguished from a more generally colloquial style based on the appearance of palatal /g/, monophthongal /aɪ/ and pronominal cliticization, which implicate the other features.

The urban dubbing style and characters who are not young, urban, African American males

Although most of the films in the corpus include female characters who use African American English, none of the dubbed versions uses linguistic variability to distinguish female speakers of AAE from non-speakers, including in the films that feature primarily female casts. *Bring It On*, a film set in Los Angeles, contrasts a white, suburban cheerleading squad with a black, inner-city cheerleading squad. The contrasts between them are underscored by linguistic contrasts in the original; however, those contrasts are erased completely in the dubbed version. Although it remains clear that these two squads are socially different from one another, the quick characterization afforded by different linguistic styles in the original version is lost, as are the individual differences between characters.

Similarly, in the films *Crazy in Alabama*, a film set during the Civil Rights era in Alabama, and *Mississippi Burning*, a film set during the Civil Rights era in Mississippi, characters are highly juxtaposed by race, a division that is sustained in part through their language use. In the dubbed versions, both the southern varieties of American English spoken by the white characters

Table 5 Distribution of north-central urban variety of German in films that include AAE-speaking characters in the original version.

Types of AAE-speaking characters in the original version	North-central, urban variety	More 'colloquial'	More 'standard'
Urban, male characters with strong ties to street culture	*Boyz N the Hood* *Coming to America* *Falling Down* *Trading Places* *Clockers* *Jungle Fever*		
Urban, male characters with weak ties to street culture		*Rush Hour* *Coming to America* *Trading Places* *The Nutty Professor* *Jungle Fever* *Clockers* *Girl 6* *Boyz N the Hood*	
Southern male characters			*Crazy in Alabama* *Mississippi Burning* *Primary Colors*
Suburban male characters			*Clueless* *The Nutty Professor**
Female characters			*Bring it On* *Girl 6* *Jungle Fever* *Clockers* *The Nutty Professor* *Crazy in Alabama* *Primary Colors* *Mississippi Burning* *Coming to America* *Boyz N the Hood*

* In *The Nutty Professor*, many, though by no means all, of the characters (male and female) are played by the same actor, Eddie Murphy.

and the southern varieties of African American English spoken by the black characters are erased. Although the visual effects, gestures and general plotline no doubt maintain a clear ethnic distinction for the German-speaking audience, the loss of linguistic distinctiveness in the dubbed version nonetheless shifts the social meanings of those distinctions.

Just as it is difficult to find comparable regional varieties for dubbing the regional variation that occurs in the originals, the same is true for ethnically marked varieties. While ethnicity plays a part in the socio-cultural life of Germany, its history and role are quite different than in the United

States. The closest similar index available to Germans today involves more recent migrant populations, particularly those from Turkey and other parts of the Mediterranean.[8] These populations share many of the character- istics of urban African American populations in the U.S. At the same time, however, the sociolinguistic indexes for these migrant populations primarily involve non-nativeness rather than ethnicity specifically. Hence the use of one of the varieties of German associated with these populations would significantly change the sociolinguistic meanings involved in the originals.

Instead, AAE is dubbed using a variety that has recognizable ties to German urban, working-class youth cultures. That class is being marked with this urban style is made particularly clear when films, which involve urban, working-class characters who are not African American English speakers, are examined. In those cases, the same variety of German is used as for urban African American English speakers.[9] For example, one of the films in the corpus, *Jungle Fever*, uses this style to index the urban working class gener- ally. The film involves an urban, African American middle or upper middle class and an urban, Italian American working class. In this case, most of the AAE-speaking characters are dubbed using standard German with none of the markers of the urban style while the Italian American characters are dubbed using a number of such features, as shown in Example 4:

Example 4 from *Jungle Fever*

1. Charlie: Orig. Paulie Carbon
   Dub **Paulie Carbone**
   Back trans. *Paulie Carbone*

2. Jimmy: Orig. hey, com'ere. Wassup?
   Dub **unser Mann was liegt an? Wie jeht's?**
   Back trans. *our man. What's going on? How are you?*

3. Charlie: Orig. Look, Paulie, uh we was wantin ta know
   Dub **Hör mal Paulie, wir wollten nur mal anfragen**
   Back trans. *Listen Paulie, we wanted to just ask*

   Orig. if you was fuckin our siste?
   Dub **ob du unser Schwester fickst.**
   Back trans. *if you are fucking our sister.*

4. Jimmy: Orig. You fuckin my sister Angie?
   Dub **Fickst du meine Schwester Angie?**
   Back trans. *Are you fucking my sister Angie?*

5. Paulie: Orig. What kina question is dat?
   Dub **Was ist denn das für eine Frage?**
   Back trans. *What kind of question is that?*

6. Jimmy: Orig. Da's a good question.
   Dub **Eine gute Frage.**
   Back trans. *A good question.*

186

7. Paulie: Orig.   It's a stupid question and I ain answerin it.
                 Dub   **Ich find sie blöd und werd nich darauf antworten.**
      Back trans.   *I think it's dumb and won't answer it.*

8. Charlie: Orig.   Look Paulie, if you're fuckin my sister,
                 Dub   **Hör zu Paulie, ich hoffe für dich,**
      Back trans.   *Listen Paulie, I hope for your sake,*

                 Orig.   ya bette not be,
                 Dub   **dussde sie nich fickst,**
      Back trans.   *that you aren't fucking her,*

                 Orig.   cause you'll get a fuckin beatin.
                 Dub   **denn kannste dich auf was gefass machen.**
      Back trans.   *because otherwise you can get ready for something.*

Although the variety of American English used in this example differs from AAE, the dubbing choices are quite similar to those made for AAE-speaking characters who are similarly involved in urban street culture. In the original version of the scene, which is set in Bensonhurst, New York, the Italian American characters are using a regionally identifiable, urban, working-class variety of American English. All three characters exhibit features of this variety, including: vowels characteristic of the region; categorically alveolar realizations of the progressive verb suffix ('wantin', 'answerin') and of the nominalizing suffix (-ng) ('beatin'); r-lessness ('siste', 'bette'); adjectival 'fuckin'; non-standard negation (ain't); stop realizations of /ð/ ('dat'); and non-standard realization of 'be' ('we was').

When dubbed into German, two of the characters use many of the same features noted for AAE in Examples 1–3. These include: a palatal realization of /g/ (*jeht's*); pronominal cliticization (*dassde, kannste*); final consonant deletion (*nich, gefas*); reduction of unstressed syllables (*unser* rather than *unsere*); and informal phrasal and lexical items (*ficken*). As was the case with dubbed AAE, characters who don't have a strong affiliation with local street culture are dubbed using only those features that are generally common in spoken German. Paulie represents a good example of this pattern.

Although not part of the corpus used for this study, several additional films show similar dubbing patterns for characters who are not speakers of African American English but who are involved in urban street culture. These include characters in the film *Good Will Hunting*, a film that focuses on young men from a working-class neighborhood of Boston and *Analyze This*, a comedy about organized crime among Italian Americans in New York. Similarly, the hired killers from New York who appear in the film *Fargo* also use some of the features of the urban style used to dub AAE. In each of these films, the use of the urban style helps highlight characteristics such as working-class status, street culture, urban, industrial settings and local rather than global affiliations. These characteristics are linguistically highlighted regardless of the variety of American English the character uses in the original version. In each case, the different ethnic links (African American, Italian American, Irish American) indexed in the originals are elided while the class-based indexes remain.

Conclusion

This project began as an exploration of the ways in which AAE is dubbed into German. I assumed a style-based framework and further assumed that for language to evoke any particular social meaning within the films, it needed to be linked in some way or another to pre-existing social variability. In the case of film dubbing, that linkage must be pre-existent in two different contexts, a requirement that strongly circumscribes its possibilities.

For the most part, stylistic variation is erased in dubbed films, particularly in cases of regional variation. The same is true for dubbing AAE except in those cases involving an AAE-speaking character who is young, male, urban and involved with street culture. In such cases, AAE is dubbed using a style with indexes to an urban youth culture that is geographically located in the northern and central parts of Germany and socially located in the German working class. The use of this urban style was demonstrated across the corpus as a whole and within individual films to distinguish characters from one another.

This study is of course limited to the analysis of a finished product and thus lacks information concerning the specific practices and decisions made by those involved in dubbing when faced with linguistic variation. It also has no way to comment on the reception and perceptions of the German-speaking audience as regards stylistic variation and its ties to social juxtapositions and distinctions. Further, the degree to which other types of stylistic variation, such as those tied to gender or to specific affective stances, are transferable remains to be explored.

While each of these additional areas likely provides an important piece to the overall puzzle of dubbing linguistic variation, this study nonetheless provides a new vantage point for the study of the stylized variation commonly found in the mass media and the connection of that to the more general exploration of linguistic variation. As such, it also highlights the creativity with which the mass media makes use of linguistic variation and points to the importance of wide-spread accessibility for the interpretation of that use. Finally, in demonstrating at least one method through which one culture interprets the linguistic variability of another, it draws attention to the place of linguistic style within more general processes of cross-cultural communication.

Notes

1 This research was supported by generous grants from the Undergraduate Research Opportunity Program, The Office of the Vice President for Research, and

the Center for Research on Learning and Teaching at the University of Michigan. I'd like to thank Rizwan Ahmad, Allan Bell, Nikolas Coupland, Vera Eremeeva, Kader Konuk, Lesley Milroy, Jennifer Ngugyen, Damani Partridge, Sai Samant, Erik Schleef, Lisa Del Torto, two anonymous reviewers and, as always, Susan Garrett for insightful comments on various versions of this paper. I'd also like to thank Benjamin Becker and Cristina Cocadiz for research assistance.

2 The genre classification of films is based on the classifications of the studios that produced the films: dramas consist of films that have a serious plot or character orientation; comedies consist of films that are light-hearted and intended to be humorous to the audience; and action films consist of films that focus primarily on action sequences rather than on plot or character development. Like all classification systems, the classification of films is not leak-proof and many films have multiple classifications, e.g. action-comedies, action-dramas, etc.

3 There is little evidence to suggest that anglicization indexes specifically English-language films because there is no evidence that films dubbed from languages other than English differ in terms of the use of these types of constructions. However, this remains an area for future research.

4 Schlobinski (1987: 149) provides the following implicational scale for different features of *Berlinisch*: monophthongal [aɪ] > monophthongal [aU]1 > stop realization of [s] syllable finally > palatal [g] > velar stop realization of [ç] > monophthongal [aU]2.

5 A full account of the characteristics and usage patterns of the *Jugendsprache* is beyond the scope of this paper. (For relevant papers and commentary, see Androutsopoulos and Georgakopoulou 2003; Schlobinski 1995.)

6 A note on transcription conventions: I have used standard orthography to indicate most of the characters' speech, but have used non-standard spellings to indicate those linguistic features that are tied to phonological or grammatical variation (e.g. non-standard spellings are not 'eye-dialect', or the use of non-standard spellings to represent standard differences in pronunciation and orthography, see Preston 1985). Rising intonation in interrogatives is marked with '?', falling intonation is marked with '.', and elongated vowels and consonants are marked with ':'; otherwise prosody remains unmarked.

7 The broad sociolinguistic variation in German dialects and *Umgangsprachen* in the use of the features constituting the urban dubbing style makes it difficult to compare the frequencies found in the dubbed films with those reported for real-world speakers, even when such quantitative data are available.

8 There is a literary tradition of using 'foreigner talk' or a pidginized version of German in contexts involving Native Americans and Africans as for instance in the works of Karl May. Thanks to an anonymous reviewer for pointing to Karl May's works as a basis of comparison.

9 One of the earliest examples of the use of a class-marked variety of German occurred with the dubbing of *My Fair Lady*, in which the character Eliza Doolittle is dubbed using *Berlinisch* (Bräutigam 2001).

References

Analyze This. 1999. Dir. Harold Ramis. Warner Brothers Pictures.

Androutsopoulos, Jannis and Alexandra Georgakopoulou. 2003. *Discourse Constructions of Youth Identities*. The Hague, The Netherlands: De Gruyter.

Androutsopoulos, Jannis and Werner Kallmeyer. 2000. Was geht'n? *Newz von der Szene. Sprachreport*: 2–8.

Auer, Peter and Inci Dirim. 2004. *Türkisch aus dem Munde der Anderen: Eine Studie über die Unschärfebeziehung zwischen Sprache und Ethnie.* Berlin: De Guyter.

Barbour, Stephen and Patrick Stevenson. 1998. *Variation im Deutschen. Soziolinguistische Perspektiven.* Berlin: Walter de Gruyter.

Berthele, Raphael. 2000. Translating African-American Vernacular English into German: The problem of 'Jim' in Mark Twain's *Huckleberry Finn. Journal of Sociolinguistics* 4: 588–613.

Boyz N the Hood. 1991. Dir. John Singleton. Columbia.

Bräutigam, Thomas. 2001. *Lexikon der Film- und Fernsehsynchronisation: Stars und Stimmn: Wer synchronisiert wen.* Berlin: Lexikon.

Bring It On. 2000. Dir. Peyton Reed. Universal Pictures.

Bucholtz, Mary. 1999. Purchasing power: The gender and class imaginary on the shopping channel. In Mary Bucholtz, A. C. Liang and Laurel A. Sutton (eds.) *Reinventing Identity: The Gendered Self in Discourse.* New York: Oxford University Press. 348–368.

Carbaugh, Donal. 1990. *Cultural Communication and Intercultural Contact.* Hillsdale, Illinois: Lawrence Erlbaum Associates.

Clockers. 1995. Dir. Spike Lee. Universal Pictures.

Clueless. 1995. Dir. Amy Heckering. Paramount Pictures.

Coming to America. 1988. Dir. John Landis. Paramount Pictures.

Cotter, Colleen. 1999. From folklore to 'News at 6': Maintaining and reframing identity through the media. In Mary Bucholtz, A. C. Liang and Laurel A. Sutton (eds.) *Reinventing Identity: The Gendered Self in Discourse.* New York: Oxford University Press. 369–387.

Coupland, Nikolas. 2001. Language, situation, and the relational self: Theorizing dialect-style sociolinguistics. In John Rickford and Penelope Eckert (eds.) *Style and Sociolinguistic Variation.* Cambridge, U.K.: Cambridge University Press. 185–210.

Crazy in Alabama. 1999. Dir. Antonio Banderas. Sony Pictures.

Delabastita, Dirk. 1989. Translation and mass-communication: Film and TV translation as evidence of cultural dynamics. *Babel* 35: 193–218.

Dittmar, Norbert and Peter Schlobinski. 1993. Stile und Polyphonie des Berlinischen. In Johannes Janota (ed.) *Kultureller Wandel und die Germanistik in der Bundesrepublik Deutschland.* Tübingen, Germany: Niemeyer. 118–128.

Dries, Josephine. 1995. *Dubbing and Subtitling: Guidelines for Production and Distribution.* Düsseldorf, Germany: The European Institute for the Media.

Eckert, Penelope and John Rickford (eds.). 2001. *Style and Sociolinguistic Variation.* Cambridge, U.K.: Cambridge University Press.

Falling Down. 1993. Dir. Joel Schumacher. Warner Brothers Pictures.

Fargo. 1996. Dir. Joel Coen. Gramercy Pictures.

Garncarz, Joseph. 1992. *Filmfassungen: Eine Theorie signifikanter Filmvariation* (volume 16: Studium zum Theater, Film und Fernsehen). Frankfurt, Germany: Peter Lang.

Girl 6. 1996. Dir. Spike Lee. 20th Century Fox.

Good Will Hunting. 1997. Dir. Gus Van Sant. Miramax Films.

Green, Lisa. 2003. *African American English: A Linguistic Introduction.* Cambridge, U.K.: Cambridge University Press.

Herbst, Thomas. 1994. *Linguistische Aspekte der Synchronisation von Fernsehen.* Tübingen, Germany: Max Niemeyer Verlag.

Irvine, Judith. 2001. Style as distinctiveness: The culture and ideology of linguistic differentiation. In Penelope Eckert and John Rickford (eds.) *Style and Sociolinguistic Variation*. Cambridge, U.K.: Cambridge University Press. 21–43.

Johnson, Sally. 1992. On the status of female informants in Peter Schlobinski's 'Stadtsprache Berlin' [1992]. *Linguistische Berichte* 140: 246–255.

Johnson, Sally. 1995. *Gender, Group Identity and Variation in the Berlin Urban Vernacular*. Frankfurt, Germany: Peter Lang.

Jungle Fever. 1991. Dir. Spike Lee. Universal Pictures.

Kallmeyer, Werner, Inden Keim and Deniz Tandogan-Weidenhammer. 2000. Deutsch-Türkisches: Sprache und kommunicativer Stil von Migranted. *Sprachreport*: 2–8.

Lefkowitz, Daniel. 1995. On the mediation of class, race and gender: Intonation on sports radio talk shows. In Miriam Meyerhoff (ed.) *(N)Waves and Means: A Selection of Papers from NWAVE 24*. Philadelphia, Pennsylvania: University of Pennsylvania Linguistics Dept. 135–145.

Lippi-Green, Rosina. 1997. *English with an Accent*. London: Routledge.

Luyken, Georg-Michael. 1991. *Overcoming Language Barriers in Television: Dubbing and Subtitling for the European Audience*. Düsseldorf, Germany: The European Institute for the Media.

Mattheier, Klaus J. 1990. Dialekt und Standardsprache. Über das Varietätensystem des Deutschen in der Bundesrepublik [1990]. *International Journal of the Sociology of Language* 83: 59–81.

Mattheier, Klaus (ed.). 1997. *Standarisierung und Destandardisierung europäischer Nationalsprachen*. Frankfurt, Germany: Peter Lang.

Mendoza-Denton, Norma. 1995. Pregnant pauses: Silence and authority in the Anita Hill–Clarence Thomas hearings. In Kira Hall and Mary Bucholtz (eds.) *Gender Articulated*. New York: Routledge. 51–66.

Milroy, Lesley. 2000. Britain and the United States: Two nations divided by the same language (and different language ideologies). *Journal of Linguistic Anthropology* 9: 56–89.

Mississippi Burning. 1988. Dir. Frank Parker. 20th Century Fox.

Müntefering, Matthias. 2002. Dubbing in Deutschland. *Language International* 14: 14–16.

The Nutty Professor. 1996. Dir. Tom Shadyac. Universal Pictures.

Pisek, Gerhard. 1992. *Die Grosse Ilusion: Probleme und Möglichkeiten der Filmsynchronisation*. Trier, Germany: Wissenschaftlicher Verlag.

Preston, Dennis. 1985. The li'l Abner syndrome: Written representations of speech. *American Speech* 60: 328–336.

Preston, Dennis. 2000. Some plain facts about Americans and their language. *American Speech* 75: 398–401.

Primary Colors. 1998. Dir. Mike Nichols. Universal Pictures.

Pruys, Guido Marc. 1997. *Die Rhetorik der Filmsynchronisation: Wie ausländische Spielfilme in Deutschland zensiert, verändert und gesehen werden*. Tübingen, Germany: Gunter Narr Verlag.

Rickford, John. 2001. Style and stylizing from the perspective of a non-autonomous sociolinguistics. In Penelope Eckert and John Rickford (eds.) *Style and Sociolinguistic Variation*. Cambridge, U.K.: Cambridge University Press. 220–234.

Rickford, John and Russell Rickford. 2000. *Spoken Soul: The Story of Black English*. New York: Wiley.

Rush Hour. 1998. Dir. Brett Ratner. New Line Cinema.

Schlobinski, Peter. 1987. *Stadtsprache Berlin. Eine soziolinguistische Untersuchung.* Berlin, Germany: Martin de Gruyter.

Schlobinski, Peter. 1995. Jugendsprachen: Speech styles of youth subcultures. In Patrick Stevenson (ed.) *The German Language in the Real World*. Oxford, U.K.: Oxford University Press. 317–340.

Schönfeld, Helmut and Peter Schlobinski. 1995. After the Wall: Social change and linguistic variation in Berlin. In Patrick Stevenson (ed.) *The German Language and the Real World*. Oxford, U.K.: Oxford University Press. 119–135.

Trading Places. 1983. Dir. John Landis. Paramount Pictures.

Whitman-Linsen, Candace. 1992. *Through the Dubbing Glass: The Synchronization of American Motion Pictures into German, French and Spanish*. Frankfurt, Germany: Peter Lang.

Part 11

THE VOICE OF AUTHORITY: INSTITUTIONAL SETTINGS AND ALLIANCES

49

THE REGISTRATION INTERVIEW

Restricting refugees' narrative performances

Marco Jacquemet

Source: Mike Baynham and Anna De Fina (eds) (2005) *Dislocations/Relocations: Narratives of Displacement*, Manchester: St Jerome Publishing, pp. 197–220.

"Refugees should stay home".
Italian Senator Umberto Bossi, leader of the Lega Nord,
an anti-immigrant political party.

Introduction

In 2000 the United Nations High Commission on Refugees' office in Tirana, Albania, held responsibility for granting refugee status to Kosovars seeking UN protection and aid. By then, almost a year after the Kosovo war had ended, it had become apparent that a large number of the people claiming to be refugees had never set foot in Kosovo and were in fact Albanian citizens. One of UNHCR's responses to these bogus claims was to alter the registration interview radically: would-be refugees were no longer allowed to tell their stories in free and unobstructed narratives but had to be thoroughly quizzed on their local knowledge of Kosovo (toponymy, local terms, and cultural labels). Using data gathered in the UNHCR Registration office in Tirana, this paper discusses the link between narratives and credibility, explores the problematic nature of turning the interview process into a judicial process, and assesses the sociopolitical and humanitarian consequences of restricting refugees' narrative performances.

Tirana, Albania[1]

Winter 2000. The southwestern Balkans were in a suspended state of calm, as if someone had pushed the pause button in a war video game. The legions of NATO officials and journalists who watched the war from the relative safety of Tirana had, for the most part, cleared out. To the north, NATO air power had succeeded in chasing Serbian forces out of Kosovo. This region of the Yugoslavian Federation, in which NATO had engaged its military power to protect the Albanian majority from Serbian 'ethnic cleansing', had become a somewhat autonomous zone under international protection. Though the border between Kosovo and Serbia remained sealed, communications and transport between Albania, Kosovo, Macedonia, and Montenegro had improved dramatically since the war's conclusion in July 1999.

Meanwhile, the swell of people passing through the United Nations High Commission for Refugees (UNHCR) Registration Office in Tirana to apply for refugee cards had subsided. Still, the appointment schedule was filled to capacity. Each morning five or six families patiently waited their turns. One by one, each family was invited into a small inner office to be interviewed by UNHCR staff who would determine the legitimacy of the applicants' asylum claims.

In the warmth of this office the asylum-seekers sat down next to an interpreter, across the table from a UNHCR officer. During the interview they heard the hum of computers in the background, as well as the noise of power generators in the backyard – the international community's audible affirmation of power and autonomy from a local government unable to deliver electricity. Outside the UNHCR office, Tirana was a mess. Because of the need for heating during the freezing Balkan winter, the energy supply was spread thin. Electricity was available just two to three hours a day. Since the former Communist regime chose electricity to be Albania's sole form of energy, this meant that one could do practically nothing outside those hours. People could not heat their homes, cook, run water to wash dishes or clothes (because pressure was maintained by electric pumps), take warm showers, watch television, or use other electronic appliances.

As a result it seemed that everybody in Albania wanted out. For a brief period during the Kosovo war, the invasion of Albania by NATO military personnel, international news organizations, and aid agencies had allowed Albanians a taste at home of the Western life they had previously only glimpsed on the TV screens or heard about from returning migrants. Anybody who could speak a foreign language was hired for $100 a day by foreign news media. Spare rooms could be rented to foreigners for $50 a day. Drivers were in constant demand. Money was finally flowing in a country where the average pension was $60 per month. However, by fall 1999 all of this was gone, leaving behind only a handful of agencies in need of Albanian workers. Even shadowy entrepreneurs trafficking in dope, humans, and weapons had moved their operations to Kosovo – by then the ultimate lawless zone.

Before the war, Albanians who could not leave by legal means were left with only one option: to take the *gommoni*, rubber speedboats that could bring them to Italy in two hours, but were also liable to lose their passengers overboard in the choppy Adriatic waves. Even once would-be migrants made it to Italy, they were often intercepted by the Italian police, interned in prison-like camps, and sent back at the earliest opportunity. But with the Kosovo War, Albanians found a new avenue: they could try to pass for Kosovar refugees. By the winter of 2000 a growing number of Albanians, locked out of rich countries by immigration restrictions, increasingly resorted to scoring an asylum card as the only legal means of achieving the right to migrate.

This was perhaps the most ironic development of the Kosovo crisis, and the most telling evidence of the quality of life in Albania. Among the asylum applicants in the UNHCR Registration Office on any given day there may have been a number of Albanian citizens desperately seeking to be recognized as Kosovar refugees. While most people designated as 'refugees' have had this label imposed upon them, Albanians sought it out and, when they attained it, saw it as a godsend. Besides a weekly allowance of food and cash for lodging, refugee status brought the right to medical treatment (in the most urgent cases, even air evacuation to a European Community hospital) and, most importantly, the chance to be resettled abroad in Western Europe, the United States, or Canada.

As a result, the UNHCR mission in Albania had evolved from providing legal documentation to refugees and mediating between refugees and humanitarian organizations, to investigating the asylum-seekers' claims to be Kosovar refugees. The priority of the Registration Office (for both staff and interpreters) became identifying bogus claims for this status filed by Albanian citizens. Every interview conducted by the office's staff and interpreters included careful screening of the identity of the asylum-seekers – a process that depended heavily on the interpreters' fluency in multiple Albanian dialects as well as in English.

In their interactions with asylum-seekers, caseworkers and interpreters made a point of never asking the would-be refugees to tell any stories of their ordeal. During the interview, they abandoned their curiosity for narratives in an effort to determine the asylum-seeker's objective link to Kosovo. In short, stories were denied a role in the determination of the refugees' status. Refugees perceived this denial both as a lack of trust on the part of the caseworkers and as a sign that their suffering did not count in this bureaucratic encounter. This in turn caused serious problems in refugees' perception of the asylum process and, more importantly, in their ability to utilize their encounter with relief workers as a therapeutic moment in the search for closure of a usually traumatic experience. As a result these interviews were experienced as confrontations rather than as exchanges based on trust, and some refugees found themselves resorting to angry posturings to vent their frustration with the bureaucratic handling of their case.

In documenting such a denial of narratives, this chapter first addresses the link between stories and credibility, then looks at the UNHCR's treatment of refugees' attempts to launch a narrative performance. Finally, it discusses how the denial of narratives was interpreted by refugees as a symptom of the relief organization's lack of 'humanity', resulting in an antagonistic stance that hindered any chance for an open and frank exchange, which led to serious consequences for the entire asylum process.

Narrative performances and credibility

The link between refugees' stories and their referential value is fraught with ambiguity and paradox. As Knudsen remarked in his contribution to *Mistrusting Refugees*, after the first interaction with the asylum process, refugees learn that a carefully crafted interview is a ticket for an easy certification process while a mismanaged one can cause delays, even application denials: "Any incongruity has serious consequences if judged to be a deliberate deception intended to advance one's position in the departure queue. Inconsistencies must, therefore, be minimized, not only in the personal data reported but also in the life history presented" (1995:22).

Refugees must manipulate their experience – inevitably messy, complicated and confusing – to provide a straight, simple narrative reality perceived to fit the requirements of the asylum process. The resulting narrative performances are scattered along a continuum between understatement and overstatement. Quite often, refugees tend to understate their experience. Val Daniel, in his research on Tamil refugees, pointed out the "unshareability and incommunicability of pain and terror" (1996:139): the telling of an act of torture or execution is believed to be too monstrous for words, the experience to be unlike any other, making it impossible to relate. Asked to explain their ordeal, refugees rely on stock narratives that couch that pain in acceptable scenarios that can be shared with people who have not experienced their unutterable suffering.

At the same time, we find many cases where these narratives are overstated. For instance, the British writer Caroline Moorehead, one of the country's most eloquent defenders of asylum rights, was reported in the *New Yorker* to be saddened by the fact that each refugee, knowing the odds against asylum – knowing that asylum itself involves a kind of triage – has to describe a past that is more horrific than the one his compatriot, and often his friend, has just recited to the person who will assess their cases (Kramer, 2003).

Either understated or overstated, refugees' stories run the risk of losing a measure of their truth, of their integrity, and thus of their credibility. This is partly due to the fact that these stories are not shared casually with friends, but are told to strangers in institutional settings invested with the infinitesimal techniques, tactics and devices through which authority, legitimacy, and dominance operate.

How should the international agencies in charge of refugees respond to this conundrum? Should they simply trust the refugees? Should a therapeutical concern for the healing power of narratives overwrite a bureaucratic concern for precise information and accurate facts? Or should they altogether cease listening to the refugees' stories?

In 2000 the UNHCR office in Tirana opted for the latter. Its decision not to rely on narratives reflected a common-sensical suspicion on the part of UN officers of the power of stories. To explain this suspicion we can point to three phenomena which constitute the inner workings of narrative performances: *persuasion, entextualization*, and *participation framework*. In other words, the motives at the basis of UN officers' refusal to collect stories stemmed from a resistance (more or less below the level of awareness) to the structural and rhetorical capabilities of narratives.

First, stories persuade by appealing to a human need for syntagmatic coherence. Stories string individual and separate facts into a compelling isotopic plot, able to increase the credibility not only of the entire narrative but also of single facts (Greimas, 1982). Defence attorneys, for instance, are known to encourage their clients to provide testimony in a narrative form, precisely to enhance their credibility (O'Barr, 1982; Jacquemet, 1996; Hirsch, 1998; Conley and O'Barr, 1998; Taslitz, 1999). By refraining from assessing refugee narratives, the UNHCR sought to establish 'objective' criteria for the assessment of each individual 'fact', evaluating each case by running through a checklist of facts instead of listening to the narrative development of a personal history.

Second, as Briggs argues in his study of conflict talk: "the art of connecting words to form narratives provides humans in a wide range of societies with powerful tools for creating and mediating conflict and in doing so, constituting social reality" (1988:272). Stories constitute social reality through the process of *entextualization*, that is: "the process of rendering discourse extractable, of making a stretch of linguistic production into a unit – a text – that can be lifted out of its interactional setting" (Bauman and Briggs, 1990:70). Through distinctive features of narration (framing devices, reported speech, metalinguistic statements) stories not only recreate and comment on prior events, but in the process allow a particular recollection of these events to become a text, transposable to a variety of different contexts. In institutional settings, this means that stories can be lifted from their interactional context to enter the public record, thereby acquiring legal force.

Finally, narrative performances such as storytelling allow participants to reframe and transform social relations. As Goodwin (1990) pointed out, stories operate on the *participation framework* of the people involved in the performance. In many cases, stories can dramatically alter the relationships among participants, making it possible for people to align themselves with particular narrators and be recruited into the storytelling performance to declare their position vis-à-vis the characters and events in the story. Storytelling thus has the capacity to transform power alliances among participants, to force them to take sides: stories are in fact addressed to everybody in reach, and these people become an active audience charged with the task of evaluating the story and declaring their disposition towards the matter under examination.

These three factors (persuasion based on isotopy, entextualization, and participation framework) would considerably reduce the power of an interviewer to control and unilaterally manage a verbal interaction. This is, in my opinion, the reason for the UNHCR's policy against allowing refugees to engage in open, unobstructed narratives. But how was this discouragement of stories achieved in the on-going flow of an institutional interview?

In the next section, I will look in detail at the interactional strategies and verbal tactics used between UNHCR agents and asylum-seekers in the aftermath of the Kosovo War. After introducing the socio-political context of these interactions, I will explore UNHCR's tactics for stopping stories by examining micro-sequences of institutional encounters during the asylum registration process.

The registration procedure

The registration process is one of the technologies of power set up by humanitarian relief agencies for managing mass displacements of people. Together with the refugee camp (see Malkki, 1995), the registration process establishes an ordered, replicable, and consistent operation that depends on smooth interactional routines to achieve its goal of surveillance, discipline, and control. In this way, the registration process may be considered a discourse practice. As we know from Foucault (see for instance his inaugural lecture at the Collège de France, 1981[1972]), discourse practices do not necessarily seek to depict the world: rather, they dictate the world by mobilizing tactics of social indexicality and strategies of social inequality advantageous to the dominant group(s) in charge of institutional decision-making.

The caseworkers

The UNHCR international staff in Tirana in 2000 came from all over the world – Spain, Uganda, Peru, Japan. Most of them were young, and were on their first or second UN mission, in many cases under temporary contracts renewable every six months. The majority had been hastily recruited for Kosovo emergency and had been quickly deployed to the field after minimal training (in most cases provided by individual nations and not by the UN).

Their duty during the registration process was to find a clear and substantial connection between the asylum-seeker and his/her purported Kosovar origin. They routinely spoke in English (the official language of this global organization) for internal communication, to direct their local staff (all fluent in English and usually another international language), and to communicate with the interpreters.

Their lack of cultural and linguistic awareness was at times quite pronounced. Behaving like post-colonial players, they seemed unable to grasp and understand the complexities of local interactions, and as a result relied heavily on their staff, and especially on the interpreters, for almost all their dealings with the refugees. This placed a heavy burden of responsibility on the local staff and again especially on the interpreters, who were left squarely in charge of the registration process.

The interpreters

The UNHCR interpreters, Kosovar refugees themselves, played a pivotal, though often unrecognized, role in managing the interaction between asylum applicants and the international community represented by the UNHCR. They were the most transidiomatic of speakers among Kosovar refugees. They were fluent in the Gheg variety of Albanian spoken in Kosovo, able to detect its differences from the Gheg spoken across the mountains in Northern Albania, conversant in Albania's standard language, and effective in an English-language environment. All were male and most came from an urban, college-educated milieu. They were recognized as 'community elders' by both refugees and the UNHCR, although in some cases they were still in their twenties.

At the peak of the registration drive during the Kosovo war, the UNHCR employed twelve interpreters, who were scattered all over Albania: near the checkpoints at the Kosovo border, in the refugee camps and in the temporary offices opened by the UNHCR in the main Albanian towns. At that time registration interviews were hastily conducted while the interviewees were waiting in line for food or shelter. The interviews lasted five minutes at the most – a short time indeed to determine whether someone really came from Kosovo, if s/he belonged to a Kosovar family, if s/he was a Kosovo Liberation Army member.

Once the emergency ended, all interviews were moved to the UNHCR headquarters in Tirana. Only the best of the interpreters were retained, and were given more time and responsibility for addressing asylum requests. Interpreters were also in charge of scheduling interviews and helping asylum-seekers fill out the many forms required prior to the interview.

These pre-interview screenings were somewhat problematic, since they inevitably biased the interpreters' assessment of the asylum-seekers. Instead of relying on hard evidence, in most cases interpreters' first impressions were heavily influenced by such communicative factors as accent, looks, or politeness. From the moment the asylum-seekers approached them to set up interviews, the interpreters turned into communicative detectives – they tuned their ears to accents, checked clothes and communicative behaviour, and observed women's gazes and postures. As a consequence, before the interview proper had even started, the interpreters in many cases had already made up their minds, often based on the conviction that they had detected the 'wrong' accent (i.e. a North Albanian accent when speaking Gheg) or other non-Kosovar clues. This bias was then carried over into the interview proper, with potentially life-changing consequences.

The interview

The interview itself was based on a well-oiled routine. The UN caseworker would ask short questions, through the interpreter, to determine an applicant's name, date of exit from Kosovo, prior contacts with relief organizations, and number and whereabouts of close relatives. Together, officer and interpreter would also check the authenticity of identity documents (if they had not been lost or destroyed at the border by Serb police). Then the UN officer would turn the entire proceeding over to the interpreter, who took the initiative in evaluating the applicant's claim of being Kosovar.

This relay was usually achieved by the caseworker (C) asking the interpreter (I) to ask the would-be refugee (R) a question about Kosovo's toponymy:

03108100 [2]

> R=young man
> C ↔ I
> 01 C so can you ask him some questions about this part of kosovo?
> I ↔ R
> 02 I pa thuma tash ndonjë fshat të rrethinës së malishevës aty?
>   (now, can you name any village of the malisheva area?)
> 03 R po (. .) është- belanica/ thuj mbas qysh i thone belza- baja-
>   (yes . . there is- belanica/ and after it I say belza- baja)
> 04   prejucaki- seniti- është:: (. .) si e ke emrin- është klecka një-
>   (preucaki- seniti- then:: . . what's its name . . . klecka, this is a-)
> 05   një lagje komplet në prizren- sa thashë unë- pese t'i thashe-
>   (a- large neighbourhood in prizren- how many I mentioned- five?)
> 06   (. .) pastaj vjen durgazi- vjen bllaca- vjen kemecia- asht-
>   (. . . then there's durgazi- then bllaca- then kamenica- that's it)
> C ↔ I
> 07 C yes he knows well that region.

The interpreter/questioner would initially limit himself to probing the applicant's knowledge of his/her alleged area of origin. Most people, such as the man above, would answer this query with a long list of toponyms. If an interpreter did not know the applicant's home town, he would compare the applicant's description with the sketches of villages and towns drawn by other refugees at the request of the UNHCR. Or he would ask about the nearest large town, the villages that one passes en route to that town, or the name of the most important mosque or bridge in the area. Here again, he would often consult maps drawn up exclusively to verify the answer's accuracy.

If, in the pre-interview screening, the interpreter's first impression of dealing with a compatriot had been positively reinforced by the applicant's responses, the interview was conducted in a relaxed mood. Sometimes the interpreter would preface questions about Kosovo with disclaimers about the need to follow 'procedure'; at other times he might even suggest the right answers. A smooth interview would, in this case, last only a few minutes.

On the other hand, if an interpreter suspected the accent, behaviour, or look of the asylum-seeker, then the interview quickly turned into a rigorous interrogation. Family members were separated and interviewed in succession. Knowledge of local geography and Kosovar practices were probed over and over again. Some people, unable to answer, blamed their ignorance on the isolation of their lives. Women, in particular, would claim never to have left their houses after their wedding days (a claim eagerly corroborated by their husbands, who proudly confessed that they were 'religious fanatics').

If people were unsure about toponyms, the interpreter would test knowledge of local farming and cooking terminology, or Yugoslavian bureaucratic practices. After the interpreter was satisfied, he would give the officer a synopsis, in English, of his questioning and the applicant's responses; sometimes he would give his assessment alone of the case (as in line 7 above).

The majority of the asylum-seekers were somewhat puzzled at having to describe their town or region to prove that they came from there, and sometimes did not comprehend the connection between this line of questioning and their asylum application.

03109100

R=young woman
C ↔ I
01   C   can you ask her some questions?
I ↔ R
02   I   yes- mirë si ashtu thotë- na thuni ca lagje të gjakovës-
(yes- well, how- so she says- name us some neighborhoods in giakova)
03   diçka për gjakovën
(some things about gjakova)

→ 04 R do të dij ça kam bërë atje?
       (does she want to know what I did there?)
→ 05 I JO. lagjet lagjet e gjakovës
       (NO- neighborhoods, neighborhoods of gjakova)
  06 R rrugët?
       (streets?)
  07 I rrugët- mëhallat- mund t'na i thush?
       (streets- city quarters- can you tell us?)
  08 R po
       (yes)

Most asylum-seekers, such as the university student interviewed above, thrown off by the topographic inquiries, instinctively sought to provide autobiographical narratives (line 4, where she asks whether they wanted to know some narrative details of her life in Gjakova). However, as we already mentioned, the UNHCR was not interested in narratives, and the interpreter was quick and forceful in rejecting the asylum-seeker's offer of personal stories (line 5). This active discouragement of narratives stood in striking contrast with asylum-seekers' expectations about the registration interview: that the entire process of becoming a refugee would entail the reconstruction of their past lives and the deliberate, exquisitely detailed telling of the story of their ordeal. In this case, the university student could only reply to the interpreter's questions with a meek "yes" (line 8) before producing a list of Giakova's streets.

Yet the power of syntagmatic coherence was often too great to resist and some applicants, even in recalling toponyms, managed to give detailed narrative descriptions of the area, walking the interpreter through the village streets: at the left is the mosque, the market is down on the right, home is just on the other side of the stream.

Preventing stories

Both caseworkers and interpreters put considerable effort into trying to prevent asylum-seekers from relating unobstructed narratives. The caseworkers' main concern was to restrict the interview through punctual and detailed questions with the goal of determining the asylum-seeker's link with Kosovo. This concern was readily apparent in one of the first encounters I observed, in which a young woman arrived at the office with an identity card (supposedly, but unverifiably hers – identity cards produced during the war did not have pictures) cut in two. She asked to have a new one issued to her. The caseworker, suspecting identity fraud, decided to interrogate the woman regarding the card. After asserting that it had been cut during a car accident, she tried to launch into a narrative that would provide some credibility to her claim of being a refugee:

02107100

R=young woman

(..)

I ↔ R

08   R   jo jo jo- kur kina ardhë në shqipëri- na kanë- kanë sjellë në
               (no no no- when we came to Albania we were pushed to
               Albania)

09   shqipëri serbët- na kanë- qit nëpër rrugë- nëpër mal kish pasë
               dhe
               (by the Serbs- they- drove us away- into the mountains-)

10   një minë- asht ra mixha jem baba-
               (a mine was there – my uncle and father stepped on it)

C ↔ I

11   I   she explain something during the war how they came here –
12   Albania
13   (..) and she said on the mine my father cut the leg-
14   C   yeah
15   I   and my uncle lost his life
16   C   and?
17   I   he were- he was died.
→ 18   C   and what's the relation with this card?

By bringing the young woman back to the issue of the card (line 18), the caseworker seeks to avoid the open-ended development of the narrative. At the same time, this move might be read as demonstrating callous disregard for the highly traumatic story being told by the woman. Note also the interpreter's freedom in relaying the events, where the statement "my uncle and father stepped on a mine" (line 10) is rendered as a wounded father (line 13) and a dead uncle (line 17).

While in the case above control of the interaction was mostly achieved by the caseworker, in most cases the task of stopping storytelling fell heavily to the interpreters who, because of their interactional role, represented the first line of defence against unobstructed narratives. The simplest way to prevent storytelling was achieved by implementing a strict question and answer format:

02107100

R=adult male

C ↔ R

01   C   but did you obtain a- uh passport in kosovo?

I ↔ R

02   I   po ju a keni marrë pasaportë në kosovë a keni marrë
               pasapor- =
               (did you obtain a passport in Kosovo a passport did you)

```
03   R   =janë djegë
             (they are burned)
C ↔ R
04   C   before the war
I ↔ R
05   I   PARA lufte/ para lufte para lufte a keni pasë ju pasaportë?
             (BEFORE the war, before the war did you have a passport?)
06   R   po po
             (yes yes)
07   I   po po apo jo?
             (yes, yes or no?)
08   R   po pasaportë-
             (yes passport)
09   I   keni pasë?
             (did you have one?)
10   R   kemi pasë e janë met andej ato hupë
             (we had them but we left them behind, they are lost)
I ↔ C
11   I   he repeat the same thing,
12       we lost the passport, we lost the documentation
```

Most of the time asylum-seekers tried to expand the question and answer format into a more conversational structure, which in most cases meant trying to launch a narrative explanation of their case. However, the ever-vigilant interpreters were quick to stop any attempt at storytelling in its tracks. As soon as an answer departed from the expected script and especially if it seemed to lead into a story, the interpreter promptly redirected the asylum-seeker to the solid ground of well-known toponyms:

01/28/00

```
R=man in his forties
C ↔ I
01   C   can you ask him some question about the region?
02   I   yes
I ↔ R
03       tash a mundet me thanë diçka për uh uh- rrethin e deçanit-
             (now can you say something about uh uh-deçan county-)
04       katundet rreth decanit a mund i thuni?
             (the villages around deçan can you name them for me?)
05   R   iznici-raxhaja-ralia-deri deri ( . . )
             (iznici-raxhaja-ralia-deri deri . . ) [pause]
06       në plavë e në guci e i kam shtëtit unë e =jam ken-=
             (up to plava and gusi I have been there because I went to-)
```

→ 07   I   = hajde =
                                                     (come on!)

08   thumi katundet e rrethit të deçanit
                   (name me the villages in deçan county)

In the case above, as soon as the asylum-seeker moves to launch a narrative (see the two story preface cues in line 6: 'because' and 'I went' mark the motive and deictical pronominalization for the story), the interpreter quickly overlaps (=), interrupts the other, and directs him to stick to the question. Metalinguistic awareness, ever present in any good interpreter's bag of tricks, is here so heightened that the interpreter recognizes story cues as soon as they emerge. He is thus able to pre-empt the actual launching of the story, thereby avoiding the more difficult task of stopping a narrator in the middle of his performance.

As Goodwin (1990) reminded us, stories have the power to engage participants in a speech event and impede early unilateral exit from the event. Particularly in the case of a one-on-one interaction, obligations imposed by the interactional order (such as those described in Goffman, 1974) make quite difficult for the listener to interrupt the storytelling without serious face loss for everybody involved. It is much easier to halt a story before its full emergence by resorting to metalinguistic directives (such as the "come on! name me the villages" in lines 7–8) that successfully restore control of the exchange to the interpreter.

Another tactic used to halt refugees' attempts to launch narratives was offered by the particular sequential organization of turn-taking set up by the need to interpret. Other researchers (Berk-Seligson, 1990; Davidson, 2000) have already pointed out the gate-keeping role played by interpreters. Rather than serving as a neutral conduit between case worker and asylum-seeker, the interpreter is an active participant in the exchange, maintaining parallel and related conversations with the other two participants, keeping each informed of the other's general drift. In the material under study here, this role is boosted by the interpreter's power to silence one of the other speakers (that is, the asylum-seeker) by simply ceasing to translate and selecting the caseworker as next speaker:

01/28/00

R=old man

I ↔ R

01   R   jo unë po t'thome se unë jam shëtit e jam kon atje- për-
               (no I am saying I have been around and I was there-for-)

02   më ka rasti që të ngrihem q'aty-
               (I had the chance to go up there-)

03   I   jo uh- të rrethit të deçanit katundet
               (no uh-{tell me about] deçan county, the villages)

04   R   t'i thashë- këvralla- elebi- s'jam marrë me atë punë unë veç-
         (I told you: këvralla, elebi- I didn't just walk around but-)
05   (xx) në postë jam =marrë me-
→   (once in the post office I dealt with-)
     I ↔ C
06   I   =he doesn't know.

In the case above, as soon as the asylum-seeker begins a story (line 5), the interpreter quickly overlaps and interrupts him by switching to English and directly addressing the caseworker, producing a realignment in the participation framework. Moreover, the interpreter does not limit himself to addressing the caseworker, but uses this opportunity to assess the communicative performance of the asylum-seeker (line 6). This behaviour on the part of the interpreter points to his role as 'interpreter-judge' (a label devised by Davidson in his study of interpreters in medical encounters, 2000): instead of serving as an advocate for interpreted asylum-seekers, the interpreter acts as an informational gatekeeper, assuring a smooth interactional routine while maintaining a role of prominence in the exchange. His interpreting competence allows him not only to control the flow of the interaction but also to pass judgement on the asylum-seeker being interviewed.

The next case, a stringent interrogation of a young woman claiming to have been attacked by Serbian soldiers, clearly shows the interpreter's personal involvement in determining the asylum-seeker's credibility. Here again, as soon as the asylum-seeker attempts to initiate a story involving Serbian policemen, the interpreter stops her by asking a fact-seeking question regarding their uniforms:

02107100
     R=young woman
     I ↔ R
     01   I   çfarë uniforme kanë pasë?
              (What was their uniform?)
     02   R   kur na-
              (when we-)
     03   I   çfarë ngjyre kanë pasë?
              (What color?)
     04   R   ngjyrë- unë kur jam ardhë vetëm për shqipni kam pa ma së
              shumti serb-
              (color- while coming to Albania I saw mostly Serbians-)
     05   ata ishin me ngjyrën- qashù ngjyrë ushtarake-
              (they had the color- a military color, like this)
     06   I   çfarë?
              (which?)

208

```
07   R   sikur ajo ngjyra [points to green sweater]
         (like that color)
08   I   kjo? [points to green sweater]
         (this one?)
09   R   e si ajo-
         (yes like that-)
I ↔ C
10   I   this kind of color [points to green sweater]
11       the uniform- uniform
12   C   uh uh- serbian force/
13   I   serbian police
14   C   uh uh
R ↔ I ↔ C
15   R   edhe me maska në kry-
         (and with masks on their heads)
16   I   and with some masks=
17   R   =ne na kanë vjedh- kur kemi ardhè këndej na kanë vjedhé=
         (they robbed us- when we came here they robbed us=)
18   I   =but is not true
```

After having forced the young woman to identify the colour of Serbian police uniforms (lines 1–9), the interpreter dismisses the case as a false claim (Serbian police uniforms, he knows, are black). He quickly loses interest in this case and ends up declining to translate the asylum-seeker's last turn (line 17), offering instead his assessment of the mendacity of the interviewee (line 18).

Against the procedure

Most of the asylum-seekers in Tirana resented the UNHCR procedure, finding it a demeaning and final trauma in their already traumatic adjustment to life as a refugee. They were particularly shocked by the implicit lack of trust underlying the registration interview. Moreover, the apparent callousness with which they were asked to recall toponyms of an area severely damaged by war made a deep impression on them. The refugees' perceptions of the lack of trust and callousness of the UN officers gave rise to the most common complaint about the interview process: its utter disregard for refugees as human beings.

This perceived lack of interest for refugees as human beings features prominently in the next case examined here, the clamorous and at times quite emotional outburst of a man in his forties, well-known in the UNHCR offices for his self-appointed role as protector of refugee rights. This 'procurator' (P), a 'certified' Kosovar refugee himself, had taken up the cause of an elderly couple denied refugee status because they failed to provide any factual information linking them to Kosovo. After having learned from the couple about the denial, he burst with them into the UN office demanding an explanation for the dismissal of their case:

31/01/00

I ↔ P

```
01  I   ashtu- sipas procedurës-
        (so- according to the procedure)
02  P   po sipas procedurës- PERSE- PERSE?-
        (according to procedure- WHY-WHY-)
03      DUHET ME DITE PERSE ARESYEN UNE
        (I HAVE TO KNOW THE REASON)
04      procedurën PO e LEXOJ- PO PSE?-
        (I READ THE procedure- BUT WHY?)
```

I ↔ C

```
05  C   ok-if he (xxx)
06  I   he say why-
07      I follow the procedure and at the end
08      they are not resulted to be kosovars- then why?- why?
09  C   because we cannot find their link with kosovo
```

I ↔ C ↔ P

```
10  I   sepse nuk mund të gjejmë lidhjen e tyre që kanë me kosovën/
        (because we can't find the link they have with kosovo/)
11  P   po more- po more- po kjo është e palogjikshme-
        (yes sir- yes sir- this is illogical)
12  I   it's- it's illogic- they are kosovars
13  P   po- po- kein logic hier- wie verstahen/
        (ok ok, there's no logic here, understand?)
14      keine logik
        (no logic)
15      (..)
16      po- keine logik-
        (right, no logic)
17      po kjo s'ka një logjikë mre burrë-
        (but this is illogical man)
18      qysh bohet- po këto nuk janë buburreca mor-
        (how can that be- they are not fleas-)
19      janë dy njerëz të thjesht- t'vjetër-
        (they are simple people, simple, old)
20  C   if they are (xxx)
21  P   bitte?
22  C   i think- we have already told you
23  I   ne iu thamë-
        (we told them)
```

210

24 C what we can tell you?

25 I çka mund t'ju themi?
       (what can we tell you?)

26 P mor në rregull- atëhere thuj që ne jemi të pakënaqur-
       (well all right- then tell her we are not satisfied-)

27   që kundërvenia juaj nuk ka logjikë
       (that her way of confronting [refugees] is illogical)

28 I we are not satisfactory

29 C yes

30 (..)

31 C but I have to work up here-

32 P përgjegjësinë- KUSH E MERR PËRGJEGJËSINË-
       (responsibility- WHO HAS THE RESPONSIBILITY?)

33 I ajo thotë kam punë të tjera thotë-
       (she says I have other work to do she says)

34 C so please go to OFR

35 P në rregull- thuj- thuj- ne nuk e meritojmë këtë mënyrë-
       (all right- tell her- tell her- we don't deserve this attitude)

36 I we are not deserving to be treated like this

37 P und I say you goodbye

[P storms out of the office]

The UNHCR caseworker's response to the procurator's outburst is typical of bureaucrats trying to shield their work from criticism: she appeals to a higher form of authority, in this case the 'procedure', (which the interpreter promptly translates, line 1) of establishing a link to Kosovo through detailed questions (line 9). By citing an abstract, impersonal principle, the caseworker is trying to dilute responsibility for her own decision (on the concept of responsibility in verbal exchanges, see Hill and Irvine, 1992).

This strategy is countered by the procurator's claim that the procedure is illogical (line 11, reinforced in his next turn by code-switching to very rudimentary German, 'keine logik') and does not allow for a humane treatment of the asylum-seeker (lines 18–19: "they are not fleas / they are simple, old people"). The appeal to necessary procedural steps is interpreted as evidence that the caseworker has an 'attitude problem' (line 35), and that she turns a request for help into an "illogical way of confronting [refugees]" (line 27). Any attempt at establishing rapport between caseworkers and asylum-seekers is clearly compromised.

The perceived disregard for the humanity of refugees is again displayed in the final case examined here, an interview with a Kosovar lawyer (one of the few educated individuals whom I observed undergoing the procedure). After having described (correctly) the toponymy of the area around Prishtina (Kosovo's main city), the lawyer objects vigorously to the UNHCR line of questioning:

03105100

1 ↔ R

01 R   kështu që ndihem shumë i ofendum
        (well, I feel very offended)

02 I   për çka?
        (what for?)

03 R   për pyetjet rreth prishtinës për fshatrat e ma tjerat-
        (for the questions about Prishtina and villages and so on)

04   kam marrë me qindra njerëz/
        (I sheltered many people in my house)

I ↔ C

05 I   and I- I feel that uh- my feelings is- is that

06   I am like offenced- offenced-

07 C   uh uh

08 I   from this- kind of questions

09 C   uh uh

10 I   you know- because you are not believing to my words

I ↔ C ↔ R

11 R   uh- më fal- jam ofendum-
        (excuse me but I'm offended)

12 I   yes he says I'm offenced

13 R   jam i vetmi avokat këtu që kam qenë (xxx)
        (I am the only lawyer here that has been xxx)

14 I   because I am a lawyer-

15 R   në kosovë- i vetmi avokat jam që jam i akuzum/
        (in kosovo- the only lawyer who's been accused)

16 I   and he:: was charged in kosovo

16 R   baza e akuzes është= se i kam =
        (the charge is I had)

17 C   =uh sorry sir=

18   I'm sorry sir but we have a procedure

19   we believe you but we follow procedure

20   (. .)

21 R   ska problem
        (well . . . no problem)

This exchange features not only the case worker's ready invocation of 'procedure' to avoid personal responsibility for her questions, but also the interpreter's awareness of the UNHCR office's underlying mistrust of asylum-seekers.

When the lawyer/refugee vents his displeasure with the interview and tries to recount his experience with political dissent before the war (line 4), the interpreter quickly identifies for the caseworker the basic issue behind the lawyer's displeasure: the lack of trust (line 10). While other refugees made this point explicitly, the issue of trust does not come to the foreground in the lawyer/refugee's complaint. He seems mainly interested in telling his story, rather than complaining about the lack of trust. Nevertheless, his second attempt to begin a narrative is cut short by the intervention of the caseworker, again with an appeal to the need 'to follow procedure' (line 19).

By appealing again to procedure, the caseworker tries to minimize responsibility for her own questions, and their underlying implication of mistrust. The issue, as implied by the caseworker, is not suspicion of the present interviewee, but a more formal principle of equal treatment for everybody which, as in any institutional setting, is guaranteed through universally applied procedural means.

It is interesting to note that both the caseworker's and the interpreter's responses prevent the refugee from telling his story of political dissent that started well before the war. Twice silenced, by the end this interviewee can only give up on his narrative, and after a pregnant pause (line 20), acknowledge the authority of the UNHCR office over the interview process.

Conclusion

Refugees should not be seen solely as a burden. Without underestimating the humanitarian and security issues related to the presence of large refugee populations, it must be recognized that refugees are not merely the beneficiaries of humanitarian aid. They can make positive contributions. Rather than marginalizing refugees, our challenge is to find ways of empowering them, so that they can contribute to our societies. We must ensure respect for the individual dignity and worth of each and every refugee.

(Ruud Lubbers, United Nations High Commissioner for Refugees, in a speech to the UNHCR headquarters in Geneva, December 12, 2001)

Why should we care that asylum-seekers in Albania were systematically denied the chance to tell their stories in the UNHCR registration procedure? After all, most people applying for refugee status have endured experiences far more traumatic than the interviews examined above.

The UNHCR in Tirana made it a practice to discourage the refugees from sharing narratives. But if it wanted to do so, it should have clearly spelled out its reasons to the interviewee, to allow them to make sense of the proceedings.

Storytelling is precisely one of the practices refugees have for making sense of their experience, by exploring traumatic events in front of an audience and hearing comforting responses. Refugees use storytelling to locate themselves in a specific space and time, countering on the symbolic plane the material dislocation they have had to endure. By denying asylum-seekers the opportunity to tell their stories, the UNHCR office may have succeeded in saving time on interviews and avoiding the persuasive force of narratives, but this policy carried hidden costs for both itself and the refugees: the agency lost credibility as an advocate for displaced people and the refugees lost the opportunity to use the interview as the first step in their road to recovery.

Through its 'procedure', the UNHCR may have caught some bogus applicants, but in so doing it may have seriously jeopardized its relationship with 'true' refugees. By abruptly launching a barrage of questions without proper framing, that is, without giving the interviewees any explanation about why they were being asked to recite Kosovar toponyms or why they were not allowed to engage in storytelling, the UNHCR turned a neutral conduit (the interview) into an absurdist (and at times antagonistic) exchange. With their future on the line, the refugees were subjected to judiciary techniques that made very little sense to them, except that they knew that a wrong answer could lead to a denial of their application.

The abrupt switch to factual questions very soon into the interview did more than just signal to all asylum-seekers that they were 'suspects' in the eyes of the UNHCR and that their stories were irrelevant: it disempowered them, turning them into automatons asked to recite toponymic lists. Moreover, deprived of a clear explanation of the proceedings, the refugees left the UNHCR office baffled and frustrated. In other words, by being reduced to automatons and kept in the dark about the UNHCR's rationale for handling these encounters, they were denied their agency.

If the UNHCR is sincerely concerned with "finding ways of empowering" the refugees and ensuring "respect for their dignity" (in the words of its High Commissioner quoted above), its officers need to do a better job of explaining their methods and procedures to people seeking their help. In Tirana such an explanation was never properly offered, and as a result the UNHCR came to be perceived by refugees as an institutional, insensitive body of bureaucrats, disinterested in their agency and their suffering.

Notes

1 The research for this chapter was conducted in Tirana, Albania, from December 1999 to June 2000 with the aid of a Wenner-Gren Travel Grant and a Sabbatical Leave Fellowship from Barnard College, New York. Final write-up was supported by a Summer Research Grant from the University of San Francisco. I would like to thank these institutions; my field assistants, Idlir Azizi and Ilirjana Stringa, for their help in transcribing, translating, and editing the transcripts; Roz Morris (Columbia U), Caz Philips (Barnard), Lesley Sharp (Barnard), Radhika Subramaniam (Connect/ArtsInternational), Paul Silverstein (Reed), Christopher Kamrath (USF), and Johnnie Johnson Hafernik (USF) for their comments, and Dawn Cunningham for her insights and editing.
2 The transcripts identify the date of the interview, the gender and age of the refugee, and the primary axis of conversation (caseworker-interpreter: C ↔ I, interpreter-refugee, I ↔ R, or multi-party C ↔ I ↔ R). The interpreters' English turns are left in their original form. I use the following transcription conventions:

=	latching turns
=/=	overlapping turns
CAPS 1	oudness
(text?)	difficult to hear
(xxx)	impossible to hear

References

Bauman, R. and C. Briggs (1990) 'Poetics and Performance as Critical Perspectives on Language and Social Life', *Annual Review of Anthropology*, 19:59–88.

Berk-Seligson, S. (1990) *The Bilingual Courtroom: Court Interpreters in the Judicial Process*, Chicago: University of Chicago Press.

Briggs, C. (1988) 'Disorderly Dialogues in Ritual Impositions of Order', *Anthropological Linguistics*, 30:3–4:448–91.

Conley, J. and W. O'Barr (1998) *Just Words: Law, Language, and Power*, Chicago: University of Chicago Press.

Daniel, V. (1996) *Charred Lullabies: Chapters in an Anthropology of Violence*, Princeton: Princeton University Press.

—— and J. Knudsen (eds.) (1995) *Mistrusting Refugees*, Berkeley: University of California Press.

Davidson, B. (2000) 'The Interpreter as Institutional Gatekeeper', *Journal of Sociolinguistics*, 4 (3):379–405.

Foucault, M. (1981) 'The Order of Discourse', in R. Young (ed.) *Untying the Text: A Post-Structuralist Reader* (pp. 108–138), London and New York: Routledge and Kegan.

Goffman, E. (1974) *Frame Analysis*, Cambridge, Mass: Harvard University Press.

Goodwin, M. J. (1990) *He-Said-She-Said: Talk as Social Organization Among Black Children*, Bloomington: Indiana University Press.

Greimas, A. J. (1982) *Semiotics and Language: An Analytical Dictionary*, Bloomington: Indiana University Press.

Hill, J. and J. Irvine (eds.) (1992) *Responsibility and Evidence in Oral Discourse*, Cambridge: Cambridge University Press.

Hirsch, S. (1998) *Pronouncing and Persevering: Gender and the Discourse of Disputing in an African Islamic Court*, Chicago: University of Chicago Press.

Jacquemet, M. (1996) *Credibility in Court: Communicative Practices in the Camorra's Trials*, Cambridge: Cambridge University Press.

Knudsen, J. (1995) 'When Trust is on Trial: Negotiating Refugees Narratives', in V. Daniel and J. Knudsen (eds.) *Mistrusting Refugees* (pp. 13–35) Berkeley: University of California Press.

Kramer, J. (2003) 'Refugee: An Afghan woman who fled tyranny on her own' *New Yorker*, January 20:64–73.

Malkki, L. (1995) 'Refugees and Exiles', *Annual Review of Anthropology*, 24:495–523.

O'Barr, W. (1982) *Linguistic Evidence: Language, Power, and Strategy in Courtroom*, New York: Academic Press.

Taslitz, A. (1999) *Rape and the Culture of the Courtroom*, New York: New York University Press.

50

THE INTERPRETER AS INSTITUTIONAL GATEKEEPER

The social-linguistic role of interpreters in Spanish–English medical discourse[1]

Brad Davidson

Source: *Journal of Sociolinguistics* 4(3) (2000): 379–405.

Increases in immigration have led to an enormous growth in the number of cross-linguistic medical encounters taking place throughout the United States. In this article the role of hospital-based interpreters in cross-linguistic, internal medicine 'medical interviews' is examined. The interpreter's actions are analyzed against the historical and institutional context within which she is working, and also with an eye to the institutional goals that frame the patient-physician discourse. Interpreters are found not to be acting as 'neutral' machines of semantic conversion, but are rather shown to be active participants in the process of diagnosis. Since this process hinges on the evaluation of social and medical relevance of patient contributions to the discourse, the interpreter can be seen as an additional institutional gatekeeper for the recent immigrants for whom she is interpreting. Cross-linguistic medical interviews may also be viewed as a form of cross-cultural interaction; in this light, the larger political ramifications of the interpreters' actions are explored.

'Interpreters are the most powerful people in a medical conversation.' *Head of Interpreting Services at a major private U.S. hospital, May 1999.*

1. Introduction

In this article, I examine the linguistic and social roles played by hospital-based interpreters in medical discourse. The need for interpreters has become a fact of contemporary medical practice; one study of 83 U.S. public and private hospitals found that 11 percent of all patients required the services of an interpreter (Ginsberg *et al.* 1995). Since Shuy (1976), a growing number of researchers has become interested in close linguistic analyses of medical discourse, but very little has been said to date about the linguistic and social role of the interpreter in cross-linguistic medical discourses. Yet these encounters are common, and it is the interpreter, the only conversational participant with the ability to follow both sides of the cross-linguistic discourse, who is uniquely positioned within these discourses, to control the flow of information necessary for the achievement of the participants' medical and social goals.

In addition, in an era of massive population movements, the increase in number and frequency of cross-linguistic medical encounters can also be viewed as an increase in an institutional form of cross-cultural encounter (Blackhall *et al.* 1995; Erzinger 1991; Marcos and Trujillo 1984; Martinez, Lenoe and Sternback de Medina 1985; Phillips *et al.* 1996; Thamkins 1995), with the interpreter acting as the point of negotiation and exchange between the social contexts inhabited by the physician and the patient (Davidson 1998, 1999; Kaufert and Koolage 1984). In this article, then, I explore the contextually and historically situated nature and role of the interpreter within these socio-medical interactions.

That there *is* a social component to hospital interpreting is itself a reasonably uncontroversial, but largely unstudied, hypothesis. Hospital administrators and physicians alike insist that it is both possible for, and the duty of, medical interpreters to interpret without adding or subtracting meaningfully from the content and intentions, and thus the effects, of utterances (to the degree to which she does do so, she is considered incompetent). The problem lies in that most, if not all, serious analyses of interpretation acknowledge that perfection in interpretation is unattainable. At the very least, differences in linguistic form lead, inevitably, to differences in meaning and reception, however small, and semantically 'identical' utterances in different languages vary greatly in their social and contextual evaluation by speakers (e.g. Bendix 1988; Cartellieri 1983). In addition, the time constraints placed on interpreters forces them, in the cases I observed, to do more than simply change the nuances of utterances: they edit, and in some cases delete wholesale, conversational offerings on a regular basis. There is considerable slippage, then, between how the tasks that hospital personnel set for interpreters are believed to work in practice, and the actual functions and linguistic actions that interpreters perform.

The question remains as to what are the patterned ways in which the interpreter influences the discourses she interprets through these small, and in some cases not-so-small, changes in linguistic form; what is the 'interpretive habit' of the socially positioned agents known as 'interpreters' in a typical medical encounter, and how do they conceive of their role in achieving conversational goals? Interpreters interpret *for a reason*, because there is some communicative or social goal that needs to be met; they do not simply wander upon two speakers shouting at each other in different languages and offer their services. From this point of view, the measure of the interpreter's success may not be an abstract count of how 'accurate' they are, but rather the degree to which she allows, through her actions, the speakers first to negotiate and then to achieve their goals for the speech event in question.

The mediated negotiation of conversational goals, however, is no trivial matter; such goals are determined, for each conversational participant, by historical contexts that frequently preclude any analysis of social equality between the primary speakers. Many researchers have already noted that even same-language medical discourse can be viewed as a form of inter-action between unequals, in which patients, as clients of the institution of the hospital clinic, find it difficult to establish a voice outside of the expected parameters of medical practice (Mishler 1984; Waitzkin 1991; West 1984; Wodak 1996). In the data examined in this article, the addition of a con-versational mediator (the interpreter) increases tremendously the patient's difficulty in making herself, or her agenda for the discourse, heard. The fact that the patients for whom these interpreters are speaking are recent immigrants, mostly from the Third World, highlights the fact that what interpreters are mediating in hospital discourse is not only the diagnosis and care of patients, but also a form of cross-cultural encounter between immigrants and agents of the institutions of the First World; it is these agents who both provide services to these immigrants while simultaneously educating them as to their role within the modern nation-state (cf. Gupta and Ferguson 1997).

2. Background

Historically, most analyses of interpretation (the conversion of utterances from one language into another) have been based on an oral model of *translation* (the conversion of written texts), which has meant that most analyses of interpretation have focused on *monologues*. Students of dis-course have rarely focused their attention squarely on interpretation itself, instead producing in passing a tacit model of discourse interpretation as a sequence of discrete linguistic conversions of isolated utterances. Inter-preters are seen as conduits, not conversational participants. For example, Hymes (1972), in his famous SPEAKING mnemonic, lists the interpreter's role as that of 'spokesman' or 'sender', but not as a 'source' or 'addresser'; similarly Goffman (1981) calls the interpreter an 'animator', or one who makes noises, but not an 'author' or 'principal', one to whom the meaning of utterances can be attributed (see also Clark 1992, 1996).

But in interpreting a monologue one does not need to worry about turn-sequence, the rights of hearers to become speakers, or even the level at which the primary speaker is being understood by the audience; mono-logues involve one-way transmission, and the audience is largely unable to respond or to act in setting the agenda for what will be discussed. However, the act of oral interpretation of *discourse* is very different (cf. Roy 1999); it must take into account all of these factors, but it is often reduced, in passing analyses, as the interpreter's obligation to be a perfect echo of the primary interlocutors.

2.1 The interpreter as conversational participant

Recently, however, students of language and discourse have turned their attention to the nature and, to some degree, consequences of the inter-preter's role as an historical agent. This has led to a number of works that examine the role of the interpreter or translator as linguistic and social intermediary (Bassnet and Trivedi 1999; von Flotow 1997; Hatim 1997; Hatim and Mason 1989; Rafael 1993; Snell-Hornsby 1988; Roy 1999; Venuti 1998; Wadensjö 1998). All of these works share the common analysis that interpreters or translators, far from 'merely' converting and conveying the words of others, are centrally employed in the work of mediating the achieve-ment of conversational or interactional goals, and that to a large degree responsibility for the achievement of these goals lies squarely with the inter-preter herself. Interpreters do not merely convey messages; they shape, and, in some very real sense, create those messages in the name of those for whom they speak. The context of the interpreted speech event itself has also received considerable attention, and the influences of the social and historical facts surrounding an interpreted speech event are seen to influence greatly the interpreter's choices and the resulting outcomes of the inter-action (cf. Rafael 1993).[2]

2.2 Institutions and the mediation of post-colonial discourses

One significant factor influencing the manner and effects of interpretation is the location of interpreted speech events within an historical-political time-line. With the exception of business or diplomatic interactions, the majority of interpreted discourses in the U.S. take place within the context of state-sponsored or -run institutions (the hospitals, schools, and judicial/legal system), between agents of those First World institutions and the Third World immigrants who require or are subjugated to the services provided. Institutional discourse is defined, in large part, by the fact that institution-ally defined goals and the institutionally reinforced habits for achieving them provide clear signposts for how communication should, and does, proceed, at least to those speakers familiar with the institution in question (Bourdieu 1977; Cicourel 1983; van Dijk 1993; Gupta and Ferguson 1997; Schegloff 1992; Wodak 1996; inter alia).

These institutional interactions thus stretch the notion of 'neutrality' in interpretation to the limit, as interpreters 'are *always* placed in this contested arena between being providers of a service and being agents of authority and control' (Candlin, in the introduction to Wadensjö (1998): xvii; italics in the original). Wadensjö (1998: 68–69) writes:

'As do all professionalized intermediaries, interpreters work at providing a particular *service*. Simultaneously, they – of necessity – exercise a certain *control*. Obviously there is a potential conflict between the service and the control aspects, which sometimes surfaces in dilemmas reported in the literature on institutional communication. It largely remains to be investigated how this conflict is handled in institutional interpreter-mediated talk, where the gatekeeping is, in effect, doubled.'

(italics in the original)

Institutional interpretation has, then, a potentially disruptive social component that cannot be ignored.

There have been several excellent studies of interpreted courtroom discourse, all of which have pointed to the legal habit of selecting, privileging and codifying certain utterances as 'facts' (Scheppele 1989) as being the dominant factor in determining how interpreters are allowed, and not allowed, to interpret (Berk-Seligson 1990; Edwards 1995; Hewitt 1995; Mikkelson 1998). In this article, I examine the 'interpretive habits' of hospital interpreters through a close analysis of their actions within the structured speech event known to physicians as the medical interview; these habits are influenced directly by both the medical habit of differential diagnosis and the institutional reality of chronic time shortages in contemporary clinical practice.

2.3 Medical discourse and medical interpretation

There have been numerous, detailed studies of physician-patient discourse, focusing primarily on the difficulties patients and physicians have in communicating effectively with each other (Ainsworth Vaughn 1994; Cicourel 1983; Frankel 1990; Hein and Wodak 1987; Mishler 1984; Robins and Wolf 1988; Sarangi and Stembrouk 1996; Waitzkin 1983, 1991; West 1984; West and Frankel 1991; Wodak 1996; inter alia). Most of these analyses center on one type of medical discourse, the named speech event 'medical interview'; this is a structured, practiced interaction between the physician and the patient, taught in medical schools, designed to quickly elicit the patient's complaint(s) so that they may be diagnosed and treated. Medical interviews are thus a type of verbal and physical investigation, a matching of unorganized experiences against familiar patterns and processes of human vulnerability to disease. The overt, elaborated goals of the medical interview are: 1) from the data provided, determine what, if anything, is wrong with the patient; 2) elaborate a plan of treatment for that ailment; and 3) convince the patient of the validity of the diagnosis so that treatment will be followed. However, the elicitation of medical 'facts', or from another point of view the creation of medical facts through medical practice, is heavily influenced by a social evaluation of the meaning and importance of whatever facts are thus uncovered or created (Foucault 1963; Waitzkin 1991); the practice of medicine, like the practice of interpreting, has a social dimension that cannot be ignored.

Diagnosis is, then, an interpretive process in which the patient's physical and verbal data is passed, by physicians, through a grid of medical meanings (biological *and* social) and re-analyzed, so that 'irrelevant' input from the patient may be excluded and the story of the disease constructed (Foucault 1963; Kleinman 1988; Mishler 1984). Indeed, this is the unmarked use of the word 'interpreting' in medical contexts; when I first told the physicians at the General Medical Clinic I would be conducting a study of interpreting, they universally assumed that I meant a study of the ways in which physical and verbal input are re-read as signs and symptoms of disease processes.

In fact, very little has been said about the concrete forms or effects of interpretation of medical discourse. There are exceptions to this trend (Bendix 1988; Erzinger 1991; Marcos and Trujillo 1984; Martinez, Lenoe and Sternback de Medina 1985; Weaver 1982), but the majority of literature written about medical interpretation has come from two camps: physicians who use interpreters (Baker *et al.* 1996; Baker, Hayes and Fortier 1998; David and Rhee 1998; Ebden *et al.* 1988; Putsch 1985; Vasquez and Javier 1991; Woloshin *et al.* 1995), and interpreters themselves (Haffner 1992; Juhel 1982; Kaufert and Koolage 1984). The physicians generally lament the difficulties of diagnosing patients, establishing a clinical relationship, or providing adequate care to patients when using an interpreter; the interpreters tend to focus on their role as 'linguistic ambassadors' for the patient, a stance in favor of overt 'advocacy' interpretation. Neither group, however, rests their arguments on analyses that explore exactly *how*, in discourse, interpreters advocate or obfuscate the conversational process.

It is not surprising that physicians have taken a recent interest in interpretation: it would be hard to imagine a physician in practice or training today who has not had to use an interpreter at least once to converse with a patient. At Riverview General Hospital, the large, public county hospital in Northern California where I conducted my research, the recent increase in interpretation is readily apparent in Table 1. While Riverview may be unusual in the degree to which multilingualism pervades everyday life, it is typical in the way that the number of patients who need interpreters has increased in the last two decades. It is also typical in that Spanish is both the most prevalent non-English language, and in that it will remain so for the foreseeable future (cf. Berk-Seligson 1990). For this reason, in addition

Table 1 Riverview General Hospital patient demographics, by year.

Year	# of patients seen	# of patients requesting interpreter	% of total patient population
1981	67,000	14,000	21
1993	133,000	53,000	40

Spanish-language visits in 1993: 34,000 (25% of *all* visits).

to the fact of my own bilingual abilities in English and Spanish, Spanish language visits were chosen as the subject of study.

2.4 Methods and data

In the Spring and Summer of 1996, I conducted fieldwork at Riverview General Hospital's General Medicine Clinic (GMC), the outpatient unit of the internal medicine division of the hospital. The patients there were undergoing treatment for a variety of long-term illnesses, ranging from chronic back pain to stroke rehabilitation to diabetes to congestive heart failure; their physicians were also the primary care physicians within the hospital hierarchy, meaning that patient referrals to other specialist physicians and clinics were orchestrated by these internists.

Data collection centered on the ways in which hospital-based interpreters were utilized within the clinic, how their presence during medical interviews helped to shape the course and content of those interviews, and how they mediated the potential clash of goals between the achievement of the overt institutional goals of diagnosis and treatment that are set by standard medical practice, and the not-necessarily identical goals held by the patients. I approached the study as a political, social, and linguistic enterprise, with an eye towards answering the following questions:

- What is the role of the interpreter within the goal-oriented, learned form of interaction known as the 'medical interview'?
- What is the 'interpretive habit', and how does one engage in the practice of interpreting?
- If interpreters are *not* neutral, do they challenge the authority of the 'physician-judge' (cf. Foucault 1979), and act as patient 'ambassadors' or 'advocates' (as Haffner 1992, Juhel 1982, and Kaufert and Koolage 1984 suggest); or do they reinforce the institutional authority of the physician and the health-care establishment, and should we create a model for the 'interpreter-judge'? (cf. Foucault 1979)

In order to answer these questions, I observed both the interpreted medical interview itself, and the institutional context that supported and gave meaning

222

to this speech event. Every physician and interpreter asked, and almost every patient, agreed to participate in the study, most of them enthusiastically. It was typical for patients, especially patients waiting for an interpreter to arrive, to tell me that they thought it was an excellent idea for someone to study how physicians talked to patients, largely because they thought it wasn't very well at all.

The interpreters who form the focus of this article were professional in the sense that they were paid employees of the hospital; none, however, had any formal degree in interpretation or translation, and in this they appeared to be quite typical of all of the hospital interpreters I have observed or spoken with in Northern California. The specifics of training are different from hospital to hospital in the San Francisco Bay Area, but in general they constitute nothing more than a period of time following an interpreter on her daily rounds, an assurance that the interpreter in question is actually bilingual in the relevant languages, and paperwork documenting that the interpreter is informed (somewhat) about issues of patient confidentiality. In this sense Riverview General was 'normal' – interpreters were neither trained extensively nor supported institutionally, and they performed their work in an ad-hoc vacuum of accountability; the hospital monitored if they were present at a certain number of physician-patient encounters, but expressed virtually no interest in determining what they actually *did* in these encounters.

The data reported on here come from observations of over one hundred patient visits, 50 of which were both observed and audiotaped. For those interactions that were taped, all participants were requested to fill out a questionnaire, and most were interviewed, at the end of the visit. The audiotaped encounters included visits with both hospital-based staff and family members acting as interpreters, and also monolingual interviews conducted all in English or all in Spanish with no interpreter. There was a total of 10 Spanish-English, professionally interpreted medical interviews taped. These 10 visits were matched with 10 English-English visits, as closely as possible, for similarity of patient, physician, and interpreter age, race, religion, and ethnicity, and for nature of the interaction (first time visit, routine check-up) and the patients' illnesses (diabetes, high blood pressure, etc.). The data presented here, then, represent an exhaustive accounting of the data collected on hospital-based interpreters specifically. The analyses of linguistic data below are drawn from the set of 20 fully transcribed medical interviews, and from the ethnographic and survey data collected on the clinic as a whole.

3. The interpreter in medical interviews

During the study at Riverview, one factor stood out as being overwhelmingly contextually salient: the scarcity of time in modern medical institutions. The amount of time patients spent waiting for their physician, the even longer amounts of time spent waiting for interpreters, and the brevity of the physician-patient-interpreter encounter, added to the time constraints on modern medical practice in general, seemed to be overriding factors in how interpreted medical interactions took place. In myriad ways, all patients were shown that, from the minute they entered the clinic until the minute they left, their time was not as valuable as that of the physician, or of any other member of the clinic (cf. Elliot 1999). Patients who used interpreters had this message delivered in even stronger terms. Often they were left alone in windowless examining rooms, sometimes for up to an hour, while they waited for the interpreter to arrive. In such cases the physicians would not wait, but rather would move on to the next patient.

3.1 The interpreter as co-interviewer

One common scenario for interpreted medical interviews at Riverview was, then, that the interpreter would arrive while the physician was busy elsewhere, and she would begin some form of interaction with the patient before the physician arrived. This had two effects. The first was that, from the physician's point of view, the process of elaborating a Chief Complaint (a named entity in medical practice, usually written in chart notes as the abbreviated 'CC') from the patient was (apparently) simplified; the interpreter might greet the physician at the door of the examining room with an announcement of whatever the patient had specified as his or her problem, as in Excerpt 1, where 69 lines of transcript have occurred before the physician enters the room. The second effect was, however, that the interpreter thus set the focus of the initiation of the interview, and would occasionally go so far as to conduct the initial portions of the interview herself:

Excerpt 1 (from Visit 30):[3]
(Dr enters the room)

70	Pt	Anda, a ver que dice el doctor.
		Well, let's see what the doctor says.
71	Dr	Hi:!
72		how are you doing?
73	Int	Doctor, I was looking for something to put over there because he
74		wants to show you his:
75	(1.5 seconds)	
76		foot but I didn't find something.
77	Dr	Oh.
78		Let's see:=
79	Int	=One of those (xx)s. or.
80	Dr	Maybe he: re, no:
81	Int	Maybe in the (xx). ((banging noises – searching for a stool))

82 (2 seconds)

83 Dr Wouldn't surprise me.

84 (6 seconds)

85 Int At least we are not (xx).

86   Levante(te?) un poquito la pierna. (louder than previous English)
Lift your foot a little bit.

87 Pt Sí, sí, señora.
Yes, yes, ma'am.

88   Ahora bien.
Okay now.

89   [x]

90 Int [¿Cuál] es el malo?
[Which] is the bad one?

91 Pt ¿Mande?
Excuse me?

92 Int ¿Cuál es el   [enfermo?]
Which is   [the 'sick' (bad) one?]

93 Pt   [Éste.]
[This one.]

94 Int A ver,
Let's see,

95   quitense el caletín y el [XXX]   por favor.
take off your sock and [XXX]   please.

96   [(loud banging noise)]

97 Pt Oh, no.

98 (2 seconds)

99 Int He says that, ah,

100   you explained to him the last time then ah, . . .

It is impossible, in this stretch of text, to construe what the interpreter is doing as 'merely' conveying information. She is essentially running the interview, not interpreting sequences of utterances. She asks the questions, and begins the physical exam; her only interaction with the doctor is a request to help her find a stool for the patient to elevate his foot, and at line 99 the beginning of a recapitulation to the physician of what was said in his absence. In taking charge of the interview, she is preventing a potential initial greeting phase between the physician and patient, and nowhere does she ask the patient, nor allow the physician to ask the patient, what exactly has brought him to the clinic today. Note that in line 70, the patient expresses an interest in hearing what his *physician* has to say about his problem, but it is the interpreter with whom he converses.

The interpreter has not, however, misunderstood the patient's earlier expressions of concern over his foot, which is, as becomes clear throughout the interview, his true Chief Complaint; nor does the physician seem concerned that the interpreter is conducting the preliminary physical exam. The only problem, then, is that the interpreter has sacrificed completely the notion that the physician and the patient are participating, at this moment, in a conversation *with each other*.

The patient and the physician appear to understand that the interpreter is not interpreting, in the strict sense, but rather maintaining parallel and related conversations that inform them, approximately, of the other's general verbal offerings. They frequently make it clear when they want the interpreter to actually interpret by telling her explicitly to do so. Excerpt 1 is taken up, below, a little further along in the interview:

Excerpt 1 (from Visit 30), continued:

195 Int He says he feels:
196   good except his foot,
197 (.5 seconds)
198   ah: =
199 Dr   =can I see his other foot?
200 Int A ver,
    Let's see,
201 Pt Dígale que,
    Tell him that,
202 Int Y, y it stops when, when,
203   it's worse, when he walks.
204 (3 seconds)
205 Pt Y yo, ya sí me siento bien.
    And I, now I feel good.
206 (2 seconds – Dr takes off Pt's sock and looks at other foot).
207   Ah, (que esos?) no los pongo, si no los (pide?).
    Ah, (that these?) I won't wear these, if he doesn't (ask?).
208 Int Oh my god, it's totally (xx) – (very softly, aside to Dr).
209 (1.5 seconds)
210 Pt Dígale que eso no me duele, eso es solo como una reventadita.
    Tell him that this doesn't hurt me, it's like a little eruption.
211 Int He says that one is nothing, and it's like a little,
212   (xx?)
213 (3 seconds)
214   ¿Pero se acuerda que así le empezó el otro?
    But do you remember that the other one started this way?
215 Pt Sí, así como está ése.
    Yes, just like this one is.
216   Que bien que Ud. se acuerde.
    How good that you remember.
217 Int I mentioned that remember then the other one start the same way.

218 Dr I know. ((e.g. that the other foot started the same way))
219 Int And he said, yeah, that's good that you remembered that.

The interpreter is still not following a model of strict sequential interpretation: the only straightforward sequence of utterance-interpretation happens in lines 210–212. Even a request for interpretation may not be granted. In lines 201 and 210, the patient expressly asks the interpreter to interpret his words by prefacing his statements with *dígale*, 'tell him', but the patient's subsequent offering after line 201, presumably the 'I feel good now' in line 205, is not interpreted. It is not only the patient who has his offerings left untranslated, however: line 199 from the physician is not put into words, either, although his request to 'see [the patient's] other foot' is fulfilled. Notice also that the interpreter, who knows the patient from past interactions, comments upon the state of the patient's foot as being the same way that the other foot started to have problems (line 214), a comment which elicits a response from the patient directed at her ('Ud.', line 216) and not the physician; only when this interaction, initiated by the interpreter herself, is completed does she recount what she has said to the physician.

The patient's problem is not minor: he is in danger of having his toes amputated as a result of complications from unmanaged diabetes. The physician knows this, the interpreter knows this; the one conversational participant who does not seem to grasp the severity of the problem is the patient himself, who at the end of the interview remains unconvinced by the physician's warnings that if his diet does not change he will lose, not only his toes, but eventually his feet as well. The patient manages to get a referral to the wound management clinic to have his feet cleaned, which was his initial goal; but if one of the institutional goals of a medical interview is to not only elaborate a diagnosis and plan of treatment, but also to convince the patient of the validity of the diagnosis and plan, this interview has failed in that the patient leaves completely unconvinced that his problems are as severe as the physician and interpreter tell him they are. It is not possible to say with certainty that this is the result of the interpreter's actions; what is clear, however, is that the patient's voice is significantly modified by having to speak through an interpreter, and that the interpreter is frequently speaking, not as an echo, but in her own voice.

3.2 Quantifiable patterns of interference in interpreted medical interviews

One could ask at this point, as did many of the physicians who took part in this study (acting perhaps as devil's advocates), what is the harm in the interpreter assisting the physician in conducting the medical interview, especially if time is short and it speeds the interview process along? The first response would be that nowhere is it stated that speed is the *primary* goal of a medical interview; these are institutional constraints, but they are universally decried as having a detrimental effect on the physician-patient experience. Time *is* scarce in hospitals today, however, and interpreters are conscious of their role as facilitator and editor; during one interaction (visit 11), after several minutes of conversation with the patient in the absence of the physician, the interpreter looked at me and said, 'you chose one that's hard to keep on track'. The patient had been providing a detailed history of the difficulty he had had at various clinics affiliated with Riverview General. The interpreter's statement made it clear that she felt this was extraneous information, and that it was her job to keep the patient on track, as measured against what *she* believed to be relevant information for a medical interview. It was not clear that the patient's narrative was, however, irrelevant; the 'Social History' relating to an illness is part of the routine medical interview, coded in patient charts under the heading 'SH'.

The consistent attempt to keep patients 'on track' led to a number of quantifiable phenomena in the discourse. Tables 2 and 3 show how patient-generated direct questions were dealt with in the two sets of interviews. For both sets of interviews, almost all of the direct questions asked were answered. However, for the patients using an interpreter over half (18/33) of all of the questions which were directed at the physician were answered by the interpreter, without the physician ever hearing the question. The significance of this pattern of short-circuiting question-and-answer sequences between patients and physicians is not only that patients are receiving answers from their interpreter and not their physician; it is also that physicians have no idea that their interpreted patients are asking questions at all, which increases the likelihood that these Hispanic patients will be seen as 'passive' (cf. Baker, Hayes and Fortier 1998; Erzinger 1991) and also

Table 2 Treatment of patient-generated direct questions in 10 same-language visits.

	# of questions from patient	Answered by physician	Not answered by physician
Total	55	53	2

Table 3 Treatment of patient-generated direct questions in 10 interpreted visits.

	# of questions from pt	Passed on to Dr	Not passed on to Dr	Answered by Dr	Answered by interp	Not answered
Total	33	15	18	12	17	4

prevents the physician from following up on difficult questions or questions that display a deep misunderstanding, on the part of the patient, as to what the diagnosis or plan of treatment are.

Another possible analysis for this treatment of direct questions is that these questions pose a threat to the physician's authority within the medical interview (Ainsworth-Vaughn 1994). In medical interviews it is the physician, and not the patient, who typically asks the questions (cf. Mishler 1984). We have already seen in Excerpt 1 that interpreters are themselves capable of producing spontaneous requests to patients, thus taking on the physician's right to ask questions; the interpreters' habit of *answering* questions might be viewed as a move to insulate the physician, and thus the institution of the clinic, from patient challenges to its authority. We will return to this issue in Section 3.3, below.

In a related vein, patients' physical complaints themselves, the *raison d'être* of the medical interview, are often lost in the conversational shuffle. Table 4 shows the number and content of identifiable patient complaints from two matched interviews, interviews 6 and 7. They have been chosen for detailed comparison because of the large number of similarities they share: both interviews took nearly the same time, and dealt with 'typical' patient complaints at the GMC – chronic discomforts that did not appear life-threatening and which were difficult to diagnose and subsequently treat. Both interviews took place on the same day, with the same physician, and the patients were roughly the same age. Both the English speaking patient in visit 7 and the Spanish speaking patient in visit 6 produced new complaints, in addition to a number of vaguely-defined and difficult to treat conditions that had been addressed in previous visits. The two visits were also representative in that, given roughly similar clinical scenarios, in comparison to the same-language

Table 4 Complaints addressed and diagnosed in visits 6 and 7.

	Diagnosis supplied	Treatment suggested
Complaints: visit 6, Spanish		
Vision (new)	No	No
Foot pain	No	No
Arm/hand pains	Yes	No
General pains	Yes	Yes
Mood	No	Yes
Complaints: visit 7, English		
Wrist pain (new)	No	Yes
Cough (allergy)	Yes	Yes
High blood pressure	Yes	Yes
Frequent urination (new)	Yes (possible diagnosis)	Yes
Prostate node (new)	Yes	Yes (urologic referral)

visit the interpreted visit was marked, as were nearly all of the observed interpreted visits, by severe communicative difficulties. These were of a type and to a degree that far surpassed the 'normal' communicative difficulties encountered by same-language patients and reported in research on physician-patient discourse.

The complaints offered by the English speaking patient were all addressed directly, in one form or another, and nearly all of them were diagnosed and treated; for the Spanish speaking patient, however, most of his complaints were left undiagnosed and untreated, most significantly the one complaint that he is most concerned with (see Excerpt 2, Section 3.3). This was due to one of three processes: to the physician not hearing the complaint because the interpreter didn't pass it along; to the physician hearing the complaint but not addressing it, leaving the interpreter with nothing to say to the patient; or to the physician hearing and addressing the complaint, but the interpreter not passing the physician's commentary on to the patient. The majority of the patient's complaints, in visit 6, were left without a concrete or even partial diagnosis or plan of treatment. Notice also that the final diagnosis for most of the Spanish speaking patient's complaints are 'general pains, which the physician sees as related to his "mood"'; his illnesses are considered psychosomatic, to a large degree, which is common for patients who speak Spanish (Erzinger 1991; Marcos and Trujillo 1984). The English speaking patient, a recovering intravenous drug abuser, was no less depressed, but his complaints of physical discomfort were taken seriously enough by the physician to have them addressed individually and concretely. One of the most negative effects of interpretation at Riverview, in fact, is the tendency for physicians to see patients who can't speak for themselves, as a result of the conversational difficulties, as 'cranks' or patients who complain of phantom problems (Davidson 1998). What is left to examine is the role played by the interpreter in interview 6, to determine what part she played in thwarting the elaborated goals of diagnosis and care delivery.

3.3 The loss of patient complaints

In Excerpt 2 we see portions of the interview in visit 6, which took place between a Spanish speaking male patient in his mid-40s, an English speaking, male, Anglo physician in his mid 30s, and a Spanish-dominant, professional female interpreter in her mid 40s (a different interpreter from that in Excerpt 1). This is not the first visit between the patient and the physician, who have known each other for three years; the interpreter, too, knew the patient, as this was the 'third or fourth' time she had interpreted for him. The excerpt begins after the patient and the physician had already had a chance to interact, briefly, an interaction that I observed; the patient had enough English to say his 'eyes hurt', but he could say no more than this, at which point the physician decided to call the interpreter (why, after a 3 year clinical relationship, the physician decided to call the interpreter *after* trying to converse with the patient, remains unclear). The patient had been left waiting in the examining room for over 45 minutes, as the physician moved on to his next patient rather than wait for the interpreter to show up.

The excerpt begins, then, with the physician and the interpreter (and myself) arriving in the exam room to see the patient, who has at this point been waiting alone in a windowless room. Notice that the interpreter is licensed, in the physician's first turn, *not* simply to interpret, but rather to explore 'what did [the patient] mean by this?' (line 23) when he said his 'eyes hurt'. From the very beginning of the interaction, she becomes responsible, then, for not only conveying information, but for first collecting it, in immediately usable fashion, in the name of the physician. The interpreter's subsequent actions should be judged in the light of this request from her institutional superior, the physician for whom she is interpreting, to actively clarify the patient's verbal output.

Notice also that, from the beginning, we hear the physician, patient, and interpreter struggling to construct a coherent account of the patient's Chief (or at least initial) Complaint about his eyes, but that they fail to establish anything more than that the patient's eyes have a problem relating to 'burning', 'tearing', and cloudiness or a possible complete loss of vision. The interaction was perhaps even more muddled than the transcript shows; when the interpreter struggles to convey exactly what the patient has said, it is because what he is saying is not entirely clear, a fact which is not commented upon by either the physician or the interpreter. The problem of definition, central to medical diagnosis, is never resolved:

Excerpt 2 (from visit 6):

15	Dr	Mr. X was telling me – no, come sit *here*.
16		We have all these chairs, no there's two chairs.
17		Grab a seat.
18		Ok,
19	Int	mm-hm.
20	Dr	So: he was telling me tha: t
21		he was having problems no: w, he said, with his vision.
22		He said sometimes he can't see at all.
23		What did he mean by this?
24	Int	Mm-hmm.
25		Dice el doctor que está teniendo problemas con la vista
		The doctor says that you are having problems with your vision
26		que unas veces
		that some times
27		no puede VER?
		you can't SEE?

28 Pt   Ah, sí, sí, xx en la: la vista, se me,
          Ah, yes, yes, xx in the:, the vision,
29   empieza a salir agua
          water starts to come out
30   aunque estoy en xxx
          even though I am in xxx
31   y-y: como que tengo chile allí
          and-and like I have chili there
32 Int Eyes get teary,
33   and, burning, feels like,
34   hot chili.
35 Dr   Hot chili. But it's not that his eyes go black
36   it's that his eyes ar: e.
37 Int Pero no es que la vista se le
          But it is not that your vision
38   se le ponga totalmente oscura, negra.
          goes completely 'obscure' (opaque), black.
39 Pt   Bueno: =
          Well: =
40 Int   =Es simplemente que le arden los ojos.
                     =It's simply that your eyes burn.
41 Pt   A veces se me pone, se me va la vista.
          Sometimes it gets, sometimes my vision goes.
42   Cuando pasa esto se me va la vista.
          When this happens my vision goes.
43 Int Se le va la vista =
          Your vision goes=
44 Pt   =Sí
                           =Yes
45 Int ah:, ¿que muy oscuro?
          ah:, what very dark?
46 Pt   Muy oscuro.
          Very dark.

One aspect of this transcript fragment seems immediately apparent, which is that this opening phase of the interview, which phase typically concerns the elicitation and elaboration of the patient's complaint, neither clarifies nor furthers the physician's understanding of what, exactly, is wrong with the patient's eyes. To this point in the transcript, very little has been established beyond the fact that the patient's eyes hurt him, they may go dark, and they burn. The doctor has entered, in his attempt to clarify the patient's complaint, what the colonial missionary Father Murillo, cited in Rafael, referred to as '"a labyrinth without a clue" . . . beset with digressions and non-sequiturs' (Rafael 1993: 133); while Rafael is referring to the difficulty

232

in hearing cross-linguistic confessions from native Tagalogs in the colonial Philippines, the phrase could easily apply to the physician's attempts at clarification and definition of the patient's problem with his eyes.

The confusion that is evident in the transcript was equally evident in the actual interview; the physician was visibly upset that he could not get a clear picture from the patient of what was wrong, and the patient was also visibly upset that he was asked the 'same' question over and over. Clark (1992, 1996) describes the 'achievement' of a contribution to a discourse as the moment when both parties understand what has been said, and believe that the other also understands; at this point in the excerpt, nothing substantial that would aid in diagnosis has been achieved in the medical interview.

It should be noted here also that the interpreter's changes to the dialogue are not entirely related to problems inherent in the act of linguistic conversion itself. Her insertion in line 40, for example, of the evaluative adverb *simplemente*, 'simply', to modify the question about the patient's eyes burning, is a judgment that is hers and hers alone. The physician, by his negative question, implies this relative scale of severity (burning eyes are less serious than loss of vision), but it is the interpreter who puts this implication into concrete form. In addition, her follow-up question to the patient at the end of the fragment, in line 45, represents a small but significant departure from the notion that the interpreter conveys all and only what was said; she is asking the patient to clarify, to her, what he is saying, before she attempts to pass this information along to the physician. In the end, lines 47–83 do not serve to pin down the complaint, and the physician finally moves on. In lines 84–85, below, he turns from the problem of definition of symptoms to the question of duration of these (still vaguely defined) symptoms, asking, 'Ok, so, how often does this happen?'

To this point in the encounter the patient can infer from the interpreter's offerings that both he and the physician understand that he is concerned about his eyes, and that the physician now shares this concern. But when the patient reports that his eyes burn and get teary, the question that is addressed to him in reply to this report is the negative, 'but it is not the case that you lose your vision' (lines 37–38). What may be inferred, by the patient, from this question is that the physician has taken the patient's reported symptoms, not as a positive affirmation of illness, but rather as a negative affirmation of a more serious illness. The patient then states that he *does* lose vision when his eyes tear and water, although he then modifies that, after being led by the interpreter (line 45), to agree that, instead of losing sight, his vision goes 'very dark'.

I do not wish, here, to overstate the analyses of what the conversational participants are attempting to achieve with their turns-at-talk; it is not possible to say, with absolute certainty, the goals of the different conversational offerings that each participant proffers. Epistemic and emotional states are not available for definite analyses, and it is impossible to fully catalogue the intended effect of utterances. It is possible to claim, with some very high degree of certainty, that the interview in Excerpt 2 has very quickly become bogged down in an attempt, on the part of the physician, to determine what exactly the nature of the Chief Complaint is, centering, not on a differential diagnosis, but on the establishment of an agreed upon set of symptoms that the patient is reporting. With this in mind, it is noteworthy that the physician chooses to move on in the interview at all, from defining the complaint to finding out about the temporal markers of diagnosis, that is, frequency, intensity, and duration of the (as yet undefined) symptoms (lines 84–85, below).

The next transcript fragment from visit 6 shows how the question of the patient's eyes is resolved within the interview. Here the interpreter's role as co-diagnostician comes to the fore: the physician asks for a further clarification of time-of-onset of the complaint, to which the patient answers in an indirect, but entirely relevant, fashion. The interpreter, however, ignores the patient's offerings in lines 105–111, and instead re-tracks him to give a strictly temporal answer to the physician's initial question:

Excerpt 2, continued:

84	Dr	Ok, so,
85		And how often does this happen?
86	Int	Uh, ¿cuánto le sucede esto?
		Uh, how often does this happen to you?
87	Pt	Pues, uh:,
		Well, uh:,
88		unas dos veces yo creo al mes,
		about two times I think a month,
89		me sucede.
		it happens to me.
90	Int	two times
91		[a month.]
92	Pt	[más o menos]
		[more or less]
93	Int	[more or less.]
94	Dr	[Twice a month.] For how long?
95	Int	¿Por cuánto tiempo le [(xxx)]?
		For how long does it [(xxx)] (to you)?
96	Pt	[me dura como:]
		[it lasts (me) like:]
97		(1 second)
98		a veces me dura casi media hora.
		Sometimes it lasts almost a half hour.
99	Int	Sometimes he takes, ah, i-it lasts
100		uh-h, half an HOUR when it happens

101 Dr Ok, right
102   So::
103   And how long has it been going on for?
104 Int ¿Y por cuánto tiempo le ha venido sucederle esto?
          And for how long has this been happening to you?
105 Pt Pues, yo traté de decirle al doctor de
          Well, I tried to tell the doctor
106   de hace más,
          more than,
107   cuatro cinco visitas para atrás
          four five visits ago
108 Int mm- [hm]
109 Pt   [que] ya me estaba sucediendo.
              [that] it was already happening to me.
110   Pero:,
          But,
111   Que no sé si él me entendía o no.
          I don't know if he understood me or not.
112 Int Pero, ¿hace,
          But, since,
113   ha-hace cuándo que le comenzó a,
          Si-since when did this start,
114   a suceder esto?
          to happen to you?
115 Pt Mas o menos como un año, yo creo.
          More or less about a year, I think.
116 Int About a year.
117 Dr Ok. (9 second pause)
118   And it goes away by itself?
119 Int Ah:
120   y, it.
121   Así como le viene esta molestia,
          And as this discomfort comes to you,
122   se le quita sola.
          it goes away by itself?
123 Pt Me quita, sí.
          It goes away (from me), yes.
124 Int Yes, it goes away by itself.

Lines 101–116 are critical to this analysis. After a string of successful closed questions (lines 85–100), the physician asks for how long the patient has been suffering these (uncertain) symptoms (lines 101–103), and the interpreter relays this question (line 104). But the answer, from the patient, is not a direct one: instead he replies that he has been trying to tell the physician for quite some time that his eyes are bothering him, but that he is unsure if the physician has heard (and by implication understood) him or not (lines 105–111).

The reply is indirect, but relevant. The patient is not simply replying to the question, but is rather addressing himself to the inferable basis of the question; this is that a commonly-held and agreed upon medical fact has not been established, despite the patient's repeated attempts to establish it over time. The patient does not believe that the physician has assimilated his complaint into the medical record, and the patient has every reason to suspect this is the case given the nature of the physician's question in line 103. The patient does not know if a crucial piece of information has been accepted by the physician, and suspects, correctly, that it has not, because he has never had a reply, in this or prior visits, that would make it possible for him to infer that this is the case. The interpreter's subsequent action, which is an attempt to re-focus the dialogue on the immediate semantic basis of the physician's original question (lines 109–114), is met with a reply of 'one year' (line 115).

The interpreter's verbal actions in lines 104–116 are critical. Having been asked to initially determine 'what the patient meant' by his complaint about his eyes, the interpreter has moved on to determining the relevance of an utterance to the process of diagnosis at hand: the physician has asked a question, presumably in anticipation of a strict temporal reply, and the patient answers with a more complicated, albeit entirely relevant, answer about the nature of the question itself. The interpreter here evaluates the patient's response and dismisses it as irrelevant ('but . . .', line 112) to the initial closed question, denying its entry into the discourse. The interpreter is acting as pre-filter for patients' utterances, screening them for relevance to the physician's questions: as noted earlier, however, converting data by passing it through a grid of medical meanings is the central component of the process of diagnosis itself. In addition, it is entirely possible that the interpreter here is not merely screening the patient's answer for relevance, but that she is deleting it wholesale, to protect the physician and the institution of the hospital from the critique that the patient's complaint has been repeatedly ignored.

This maneuver effectively obliterates the chance that in this visit, as in prior visits, the patient will be able to establish the medical fact that, not only do his eyes bother him, but that he has been attempting to report this problem for quite some time. With respect to patient complaints in general, the physicians who took part in this study often spoke about the importance of determining, not only the exact complaint, but why the complaint has become significant or urgent enough to be brought up by the patient *now*. The fact that the report has been made repeatedly, over time, is important, because it supplies the physician with the information that this complaint is neither trivial nor recent. The physician, however, does not question the interpreter with regards to what the patient has said in lines 106–111; he hears a coherent reply to a closed question, and moves on.

Far from being a valid CC, the report of burning eyes now becomes a somewhat trivial complaint, for how bad could it be if a year has passed and only now the patient is bringing the symptom to the physician's attention? The physician's subsequent question, in line 118, adds credence to the analysis that, because the physician receives a strictly temporal reply via the interpreter, he no longer takes the patient's complaint seriously: the question, 'it goes away by itself?', may be read, in a medical context, as the question, 'is this ailment self limiting (e.g. self-correcting), and do I need to seriously address it?' Self-limiting ailments, such as colds (which go away in a few days regardless of the medical care delivered or withheld) are generally considered non-issues by medical practitioners, because there is nothing that can be done, medically, to fix them. When the reply comes back that yes, the symptom cures itself (line 124), the physician quickly works, over the next 50 lines of transcript, to move the interview past the report. When the physician hears, finally, that perhaps the patient's need of glasses may in the future give permanent relief, he resets the interview with an open question, still in search of a valid CC upon which to focus:

Excerpt 2, continued:
179 Dr Oh, good.
180 (8 seconds).
181   And:,
182   Is there any, other,
183   main thing that is bothering him today?
184   I know there's a lot of problems,
185   but if there was only one
186   other thing he was gonna tell me about today, what would he choose?

Notice that the question in lines 182–186 can be read as serving several functions: the first, of course, is to re-set the interview, so that a 'valid' Chief Complaint may be identified and addressed. Another, however, is that the physician here is himself trying to keep the patient on track, by asking him to pre-evaluate, on his own, what is most medically important. One final message which might be read into this question is that the physician may be serving notice to the patient that he has wasted a certain amount of time with his complaint about his eyes, and that there is now time for only one more of his complaints to be addressed before the physician will close out the interview. The problem is that the patient's problem with his eyes is, in fact, a valid Chief Complaint. The interpreter's pre-evaluation and de-facto editing of the patient's contributions to the interview result, in this case, not in keeping that patient 'on track', but rather in un-tracking the

achievement of the institutional goals (diagnosis and treatment) of the interview itself.

4. Conclusions and discussion

In this article I have outlined the role of interpreters in one form of medical
discourse, the internal medicine 'medical interview'. The linguistic data, both
quantitative and qualitative, points strongly away from a conclusion that interpreters are acting as 'advocates' or 'ambassadors' for interpreted patients,
but are rather acting, at least in part, as informational gatekeepers who keep
the interview 'on track' and the physician on schedule. While the interpreters do in fact convey much of what is said, they also interpret selectively,
and appear to do so in a patterned (non-random) fashion. There is no
evidence in the data presented here (nor in the larger data set) of interpreters
putting forth the patient's agenda vigorously, as is claimed by Haffner (1992)
and others. This is not the inevitable role that interpreters must take in
hospital discourses, however, and the reasons they act in this way at Riverview
is largely a result of their position within the hospital hierarchy.

The practice of medical interpreting is not highly valued within the hospital
clinic; when I began my study, I was told by a sympathetic physician that
he had also been interested in studying interpreters, but had been told by a
hospital administrator not to do 'any studies that tell me I need to hire more
interpreters; we can't afford the ones we have now'. There were only seven full-
time Spanish-English interpreters at Riverview General Hospital, not nearly
enough to take care of the 33,000 patients who needed Spanish interpretation,
even given the large number of bilingual physicians and family-member
interpreters utilized in individual clinics. The training given to these interpreters was scant; the requirements for becoming an interpreter at Riverview
were a good grasp of both English and Spanish, and the ability to translate
50 medical terms on a test with complete accuracy. There was no training in
discourse processes, and the training for how medical interactions worked was
on-the-job. Physicians, for their part, received absolutely no training in how
to use interpreters, beyond being told how to call them to come interpret.

The clinic staff were also consistently wrong in their predictions of who
would need an interpreter, and more often than not would be forced to call
an interpreter for an unscheduled interpretation, rather than scheduling in
advance. Consequently, the interpreters were always running behind, post-
poning scheduled interpretations and answering pages through the day that
added to a large list of patients who needed their services. In addition,
during my study over 100 nurses were fired at the hospital, at the same time
that the physicians themselves were being asked to see more and more
patients in a shorter and shorter time period.

These time pressures all gave rise to competing mandates for the interpreters. Institutionally, they are officially required to act as an 'instrument',

saying all and only what has been said; in practice, however, they are encouraged to keep the interview short, and to keep patients 'on track'. In competition, it was almost always the latter requirement that won out, and interpreters frequently engaged in furthering the physician's perceived agenda for the discourse. This happened, not only because of time pressures, but because hospital based interpreters are, in the end, members of the hospital community where they work and interact daily; they are institutional insiders, and ally themselves as such.

The larger ramifications of the interpreter's role in medical discourses are also significant. Of the power of institutional encounters to define citizens' relations with the state itself, Foucault writes (1979: 304):

> We are in the society of the teacher-judge, the doctor-judge, the educator-judge, the "social-worker"-judge; it is on them that the universal reign of the normative is based . . .

All that is needed to make this quote perfectly relevant to the analysis at hand is to add the words 'the society of the interpreter-judge', for it is interpreters with whom and through whom recent immigrants interact with institutions of the state.

Interpreters are not, and cannot be, 'neutral' machines of linguistic conversion, both because they are faced with the reality that linguistic systems are not 'the same' in how they convey information contextually, and also because they are themselves social agents and participants (albeit special ones) in the discourse. It is possible for them to interpret evenly, however, and it is *not* the case that professional, hospital based interpreters need to work as an extra gatekeeping layer through which patients must pass in order to receive medical care. One could argue, as I would, that the interpreters' wholesale alignment with the institution of Riverview General Hospital (which is, not coincidentally, their employer) is both unethical and a truly poor form of interpretive practice.

As stated earlier, however, it is the context of communication that is fundamental in defining how the interpreter will carry out her role, and how she should be judged in that role; given that the physicians' command was, first and foremost, to keep the interview short, interpreters at Riverview may in fact be doing a good job at a bad task. The real issue is that they are doing a job that is different, in daily practice, from the job they are typically assumed to be doing. This means that they are not trained, nor licensed within the institution (i.e. they cannot write referrals or prescriptions, and may not make notes in the patient's permanent record), to do the things they are in fact doing (collection and analysis of data; establishing a 'therapeutic rapport' with the patient); nor are they given any form of institutional support for the true nature of the work that they do. The construction of the interpreter as a simple instrument of semantic conveyance is only possible when those who hire and use interpreters imagine that it is possible for interpretation to be the task of merely echoing content faithfully. It is this conceptualization of the interpreter's work that renders her daily practice of acting as co-diagnostician invisible, which in turn engenders a vacuum of responsibility, both within the discourse and with respect to the delivery of health care to non-English speaking patients in general. This slippage, between what interpreters are asked, officially, to do, and what they are really doing in daily practice, allows the practice to continue unmonitored and unevaluated; the invisible nature of the interpreter's role as co-diagnostician is the effect, rather than the interpreter's incompetence being the cause, of the broad dissatisfaction physicians and patients at Riverview express towards medical interpreting in general.

Notes

1 The research for this article was conducted with the aid of a Doctoral Fellowship from the Department of Linguistics at Stanford University; part of the preparation for this manuscript took place with the aid of a Postdoctoral Fellowship at the Stanford University Center for Biomedical Ethics, funded by the Robert Wood Johnson Foundation's 'Last Acts' Campaign. I would like to thank Stuart Tannock, Elizabeth Traugott, John R. Rickford, Penelope Eckert, Elizabeth Armstrong Davidson, and the members of the Sociolunch group at Stanford University for their insights. All faults are entirely my own.
2 In this view, one might call interpretation the pre-eminently contextual linguistic act, or at least the most consciously contextual of linguistic behaviors.
3 Transcription Conventions:

[ ]	overlapping turns
=	simultaneous beginning of one speaker's turn/end of another's turn (latching)
:	lengthening
CAPS	loud
Italics	translation of Spanish
(text?)	difficult to hear
(noise)	description of non-verbal noise
(xx)	impossible to hear; each x is one syllable, if syllables can be discerned
((text))	description of physical actions, or meta-commentary on discourse

References

Ainsworth Vaughn, Nancy. 1994. Is that a rhetorical question? Ambiguity and power in medical discourse. *Journal of Linguistic Anthropology* 4: 194–214.
Baker, David W., Ruth M. Parker, Mark V. Williams, Wendy C. Coates and Kathryn Pitkin. 1996. Use and effectiveness of interpreters in an emergency room department. *Journal of the American Medical Association* 275: 783–788.
Baker, David W., Risa Hayes and Julia Puebla Fortier. 1998. Interpreter use and satisfaction with interpersonal aspects of care for Spanish-speaking patients. *Medical Care* 36: 1461–1470.

Bassnett, Susan and Harish Trivedi. 1999. *Post-colonial Translation: Theory and Practice*. London and New York: Routledge.

Bendix, Edward H. 1988. Metaphorical and literal interpretation: Cross-cultural communication in medical settings. *CUNYForum* 13: 1–16.

Berk-Seligson, Susan. 1990. *The Bilingual Courtroom: Court Interpreters in the Judicial Process*. Chicago and London: The University of Chicago Press.

Blackball, Leslie J., Sheila T. Murphy, Geyla Frank, Vicki Michel and Stanley Azen. 1995. Ethnicity and attitudes toward patient autonomy. *Journal of the American Medical Association* 274: 825.

Bourdieu, Pierre. 1977. The economics of linguistic exchanges. *Social Science and Information* 16: 645–668.

Cartellieri, Claus. 1983. The inescapable dilemma: Quality and/or quantity in interpreting. *Babel* 29: 209–213.

Cicourel, Aaron V. 1983. Language and the structure of belief in medical communication. In Sue Fisher and Alexandra Todd (eds.) *The Social Organization of Doctor-Patient Communication*. Washington, D.C.: Center for Applied Linguistics. 221–240.

Clark, Herbert H. 1992. *Arenas of Language Use*. Chicago: University of Chicago Press/Center for the Study of Language and Information.

Clark, Herbert H. 1996. *Using Language*. Cambridge: Cambridge University Press.

David, Rand A. and Michelle Rhee. 1998. The impact of language as a barrier to effective health care in an underserved urban hispanic community. *The Mount Sinai Journal of Medicine* 65: 393–397.

Davidson, Brad. 1998. Interpreting medical discourse: A study of cross-linguistic communication in the hospital clinic. PhD Dissertation. Department of Linguistics, Stanford University.

Davidson, Brad. 1999. Dialogue in cross-linguistic medical interviews: The interpretation of interpretive discourse. Proceedings from the Sixth Annual Symposium on Language and Society, Austin.

Diaz-Duque, Ozzie. 1989. Communication barriers in medical settings: Hispanics in the United States. *International Journal of the Sociology of Language* 79: 93–102.

van Dijk, Teun A. 1993. Principles of critical discourse analysis. *Discourse and Society* 4: 249–285.

Ebden, Phillip, Arvind Bhatt, Oliver J. Carey and Brian Harrison. 1988. The bilingual consultation. *The Lancet* 1988: 347.

Edwards, Alicia Betsey. 1995. *The Practice of Court Interpreting*. Amsterdam: John Benjamins Publishing Company.

Elliot, Carl. 1999. *A Philosophical Disease: Bioethics, Culture, and Identity*. New York: Routledge.

Erzinger, Sharry. 1991. Communication between Spanish-speaking patients and their doctors in medical encounters. *Culture, Medicine, and Psychiatry* 15: 91–110.

Flotow, Luise von. 1997. *Translation and Gender: Translating in the 'Era of Feminism'*. Ottowa: University of Ottowa Press.

Foucault, Michel. 1963 (1973). *The Birth of the Clinic: An Archaeology of Medical Perception*. New York: Vintage Books.

Foucault, Michel. 1979. *The History of Sexuality, Vol. 1*. London: Allen Lane.

Frankel, Richard. 1990. Talking in interviews: A dispreference for patient-initiated questions in physician-patient encounters. In George Psathas (ed.) *Interaction Competence*. Lanham, Maryland: University Press of America, Inc. 231–262.

Ginsberg, C., V. Martin, Dennis Andrulis, Yoku Shaw-Taylor and C. McGregor. 1995. *Interpretation and Translation Services in Health Care: A Survey of U.S. Public and Private Teaching Hospitals.* Washington, D.C.: National Public Health and Hospital Institute.

Goffman, Erving. 1981. Footing. In Erving Goffman (ed.) *Forms of Talk.* Philadelphia: University of Pennsylvania Press. 124–159.

Gupta, Akhil and James Ferguson (eds.). 1997. *Culture Power Place: Explorations in Critical Anthropology.* Durham: Duke University Press.

Haffner, Linda. 1992. Translation is not enough: Interpreting in a medical setting. In Cross Cultural Medicine – A Decade Later [Special Issue]. *The Western Journal of Medicine* 157: 255–259.

Hatim, Basil. 1997. *Communication across Cultures: Translation Theory and Contrastive Text Linguistics.* Exeter: University of Exeter Press.

Hatim, Basil and Ian Mason. 1989. *Discourse and the Translator.* London: Longman.

Hein, Norbert and Ruth Wodak. 1987. Medical interviews in internal medicine: Some results of an empirical investigation. *Text* 7: 37–65.

Hewitt, William E. 1995. *Court Interpretation.* Williamsburg, Virginia: National Center for State Courts.

Hymes, Dell. 1972. Models of the interaction of language and social life. In John J. Gumperz and Dell Hymes (eds.) *Directions in Sociolinguistics: The Ethnography of Communication.* New York: Holt, Rinehart and Winston, Inc. 35–71.

Juhel, Denis. 1982. *Bilinguisme et traduction au Canada: role sociolinguistique du traducteur.* Quebec: International Center for Research on Bilingualism.

Kaufert, Joseph M. and William W. Koolage. 1984. Role conflict among 'culture brokers': The experience of native Canadian medical interpreters. *Social Science and Medicine* 18: 283–286.

Kleinman, Arthur. 1988. *The Illness Narratives: Suffering, Healing, and the Human Condition.* Harper Collins: Basic Books.

Marcos, Luis R. and Manuel Trujillo. 1984. Culture, language, and communicative behavior: The psychiatric examination of Spanish-Americans. In Richard P. Durán (ed.) *Latino Language and Communicative Behavior.* New Jersey: Ablex Publishing Co. 187–194.

Martinez, Deborah, Elizabeth A. Lenoe and Jennifer Sternback de Medina. 1985. Language as a barrier to health care. In Lucia Elias-Olivares (ed.) *Spanish Language Use and Public Life in the United States.* Berlin: Walter de Gruyter and Co. 153–164.

Mikkelson, Holly. 1998. Towards a redefinition of the role of the court interpreter. *Interpreting* 3: 21–45.

Mishler, Elliot G. 1984. *The Discourse of Medicine: Dialectics of Medical Interviews.* New Jersey: Ablex Publishing Company.

Phillips, Russel S., Mary Beth Hamel, Joan M. Teno, Paul Bellamy, Steven K. Broste, Robert M. Califf, Humberto Vidaillet, Roger B. Davis, Lawrence H. Muhlbaier, Alfred F. Conners, Joanne Lynne and Lee Goldman. 1996. Race, resource use, and survival in seriously ill hospitalized adults. *Journal of General Internal Medicine* 11: 387–396.

Putsch, Robert W. III. 1985. Cross cultural communication: The special case of interpreters in health care. *Journal of the American Medical Association* 254: 3344–3348.

242

Rafael, Vicente. 1993. *Contracting Colonialism: Translation and Christian Conversion in Tagalog Society under Early Spanish Rule*. Durham and London: Duke University Press.

Robins, Lynne S. and Frederic M. Wolf. 1988. Confrontation and politeness strategies in physician-patient interactions. *Social Science Medicine* 27: 217–221.

Roy, Cynthia. 1999. *Interpreting as a Discourse Process (Oxford Studies in Sociolinguistics)*. New York: Oxford University Press.

Sarangi, Srikant and Stefaan Stembrouk. 1996. *Language, Bureaucracy, and Social Control*. London and New York: Longman.

Schegloff, Emanuel. 1992. On talk and its institutional occasions. In Paul Drew and John Heritage (eds.) *Talk at Work: Interaction in Institutional Settings*. Cambridge: Cambridge University Press. 101–136.

Scheppele, Kim Lane. 1989. Telling stories. *Michigan Law Review* 87: 2073–2098.

Shuy, Roger. 1976. The medical interview: Problems in communication. *Primary Care* 3: 365–386.

Snell-Hornby, Mary. 1988. *Translation Studies: An Integrated Approach*. Philadelphia: John Benjamins Publishing Company.

Solis, Julia M., Gary Marks, Melinda Garcia and David Shelton. 1990. Acculturation, access to care, and use of preventive services by Hispanics: Findings from HHANES 1982–1984. *American Journal of Public Health*, Volume 80 Supplement: 11–19.

Thamkins, Theresa. 1995. Culture influences patients' desire to hear unfavorable diagnosis. *Asian Medical News*: October 1995.

Vasquez, Carmen and Rafael A. Javier. 1991. The problem with interpreters: Communicating with Spanish-speaking patients. *Hospital and Community Psychiatry* 42: 163–165.

Venuti, Lawrence. 1998. *The Scandals of Translation: Towards an Ethics of Difference*. London and New York: Routledge.

Wadensjö, Cecilia. 1998. *Interpreting as Interaction* (Language in social life series). London and New York: Longman.

Waitzkin, Howard. 1983. *The Second Sickness: Contradictions of Capitalist Health Care*. New York and London: The Free Press.

Waitzkin, Howard. 1991. *The Politics of Medical Encounters: How Patients and Doctors Deal with Social Problems*. New Haven and London: Yale University Press.

Weaver, Charlotte Ann. 1982. Role evolution of language translators in a major medical center. PhD Dissertation: University of California at San Francisco.

West, Candace. 1984. *Routine Complications: Troubles with Talk between Doctors and Patients*. Bloomington: Indiana University Press.

West, Candace and Richard Frankel. 1991. Miscommunication in medicine. In Nikolas Coupland, Howard Giles and John Wiemann (eds.) *"Miscommunication" and Problematic Talk*. Newbury Park: Sage. 166–194.

Wodak, Ruth. 1996. *Disorders of Discourse*. London and New York: Longman.

Woloshin, Steven, Nina A. Bickell, Lisa M. Schwartz, Francesca Gany and Gilbert Welch. 1995. Language barriers in medicine in the Unites States. *Journal of the American Medical Association* 273: 724–728.

51

TOWARD UNDERSTANDING PRACTICES OF MEDICAL INTERPRETING

Interpreters' involvement in history taking

Galina B. Bolden

Source: *Discourse Studies* 2(4) (2000): 387–419.

Abstract

This article examines the role of medical interpreters in structuring interaction between physicians and their patients. Through a detailed analysis of interpreters' involvement in the history-taking part of medical consultations, it is demonstrated that their participation in this activity is organized by their understanding of its goals rather than by the task of translation alone. Specifically, the different ways in which interpreters participate in history taking display their orientation to obtaining from the patient and conveying to the doctor medically relevant information about the patient's symptoms – and doing so as effectively as possible. Medical interpreters are found to share the physicians' normative orientation to obtaining objectively formulated information about relevant biomedical aspects of patients' conditions. Thus, far from being passive participants in the interaction, interpreters will often pursue issues they believe to be diagnostically relevant, just as they may choose to reject patients' information offerings if they contain subjective accounts of their socio-psychological concerns.

Introduction

This work examines the role of medical interpreters in structuring interaction between health care providers and their patients. It aims to dismantle the traditional image of interpreters as 'non-participants' whose involvement in interaction is limited to transforming messages from one language

244

into another. Through a detailed analysis of interpreters' participation in actual medical consultations, I will demonstrate that interpreters' actions are primarily structured by their understanding of the ongoing activity and only secondarily by the task of translation.

The relevance of this type of work in the current geopolitical situation cannot be overemphasized. The growing trend in migration throughout the world has increased the number of linguistic minorities who are not proficient in their new country's majority language. According to the 1990 US census, approximately 6.1 percent of the population have limited English proficiency. In states like Hawaii, New York, New Mexico, and Texas, this number exceeds 10 percent, and in California 16 percent. Nearly 14 percent of Europeans speak a language other than the official language of the country they live in (European Bureau for Lesser-Used Languages). It has also been estimated that in urbanized Western Europe a third of the population under the age of 35 will have an immigration background (Broeder and Extra, 1999). The 1996 Australian census revealed that 11 percent of the population considered themselves to have a limited proficiency in English.

The growing number of linguistic minorities has contributed to a wider recognition of the need to provide adequate linguistic services (and, in particular, medical interpreting services) to those who do not speak the majority language. In the United States, linguistic rights of the minorities have been protected by Title VI of the Civil Rights Act of 1964, which prohibits linguistic (and other) discrimination in federally funded programs. In addition, several states have enforced specific language access laws that require health care facilities to ensure communication with patients of limited English proficiency. In California, for example, the Dymally–Alatorre Bilingual Services Act imposes direct obligations on state and local agencies to provide appropriate translation services.

Despite the growing need for medical interpreting and the recognition of its importance, very little is currently known about the role interpreters play in the interaction between medical practitioners and their patients. Among the few studies into medical interpreting, the majority have been based on interview, observation, or survey data (for example, Baker et al., 1996; Brooks, 1992; Giacomelli, 1997; Hatton, 1992; Hatton and Webb, 1993; Hornberger et al., 1996; Hornberger et al., 1997). While this sort of research is valuable in obtaining a general understanding of interpreters' work and the ways in which health care institutions deal with linguistic minority patients, these studies can provide little insight into what happens during real life medical encounters conducted through an interpreter.

In order to understand how interpreters affect the ongoing interaction, researchers need to conduct detailed analyses of recorded consultations. To date, few studies have attempted to do this. Among the most notable are Downing's (1991) and Athorp and Downing's (1996) studies of health care interpreting in the United States and Wadensjö's (1992; 1998) research in Sweden.[1] A brief review of this work will help situate the current project vis-a-vis the findings attained by prior research.

Most work has underscored the problems that arise in using interpreters and attempted to explain interpreters' performance. For example, Bruce Downing (1991) demonstrates that the unskilled bilinguals often used as interpreters in hospitals and doctor's offices may actually impede communication between the doctor and the patient. In the interaction analyzed in Downing's paper the inter-prefer was found to ignore or mistranslate the utterances he either fails to understand or lacks the vocabulary to translate adequately; to provide his own responses to questions; to fail to interpret and to distort the messages in the process of interpretation. The study shows that the interpreter's low linguistic proficiency and his lack of understanding of the interpreter's role make it difficult, if not impossible, for the doctor and the patient to communicate with each other.

A study carried out by Catherine Athorp and Bruce Downing (1996) also found that non-professional interpreters have a negative impact on doctor–patient interaction. The investigators conducted a comparative analysis of monolingual and bilingual medical interviews that contrasted 'monolingual' (doctor and patients speak the same language), 'bilingual helper' (bilingual nurse acts as an interpreter), and 'interpreted' (professional interpreter is used) modes of communication. The study found that in the 'bilingual helper mode', the bilingual nurse often assumes a caregiver role, which results in reducing the number of direct doctor–patient interactions and patient-initiated turns (compared to the 'monolingual mode'). However, in the 'interpreted mode' (with a professional interpreter), the distribution of turns between the speakers is comparable to that in the 'monolingual mode', and the interpreter's utterances are, for the most part, translations of the doctor's or the patient's words. Thus, Athorp and Downing's work suggests that using professionally trained interpreters (as opposed to bilingual hospital staff) has a positive effect on communication between medical providers and patients when they lack a common language.

Downing's (1991) and Athorp and Downing's (1996) studies have focused on evaluating interpreters' performance by looking at how closely interpreters' contributions match the words of the other participants. A somewhat different definition of 'good' interpreting has emerged from the work of Cecilia Wadensjo (1998), who took a closer look at the situations in which interpreters are forced to step outside the strict interpreting role. Her book, *Interpreting as Interaction* (1992; 1998), reports the results of her Sweden-based study of interpreter-mediated interactions in medical and police settings. Adopting an interactive approach to 'dialogue interpreting', the author distinguishes between the interpreter's 'normative role', which presupposes a close translation of everything that is being said by each party, and the 'typical role' which the interpreter can adopt in order to coordinate the conversation (and, in particular, to resolve or prevent a communicative problem). Wadensjö argues that the two roles do not necessarily have negative consequences for the interaction. In fact, dialogue interpreters are often expected to use both of these roles in their work.

To summarize, all interaction-oriented studies on medical interpreting have emphasized the crucial role that interpreters play in managing communication between doctors and their patients. Researchers have found that inadequate linguistic proficiency or conflicting professional notes imposed on the interpreter can impede interaction between doctors and their patients. Additionally, in their attempt to describe the different ways in which interpreters participate in the interaction, investigators have noted the different options available to interpreters in organizing their participation. In the first place, interpreters can try to provide a close rendition of each utterance; secondly, they can choose to take on a more active role by regulating the flow of the interaction. However, aside from Wadensjö's (1998) work on resolving interactional difficulties, the issue of how interpreters' moment-by-moment behavior fits into the activity currently in progress has largely been neglected. Instead, researchers have opted for a more global analysis of interpreters' involvement that does not distinguish between the different activities that constitute medical encounters and the different requirements they impose on the participants. Without taking into consideration the specific activities in which interpreters engage, however, it is impossible to understand what guides interpreters' actions at any particular time.

This article is an attempt to fill this gap in our understanding of interpreting practices by means of a close analysis of actual interpreter-mediated consultations. The article will examine one activity that commonly takes place during medical consultations: taking the patient's medical history. Through an analysis of several consultations, I will investigate how an interpreter's understanding of the ongoing activity and the most appropriate ways of participating in it structure his actions, and in what ways these understandings affect interaction between medical providers and their patients.

What is interpreting?

The view of interpreting that underlies the discussion in this article contrasts with the traditional perception of interpreting as simply a means of conveying verbal messages between people who do not share a common language. A popularly held metaphor used to describe interpreters' work is that of a 'voice box' or a 'translating machine'. According to this view, each utterance in language A is transformed by the interpreter into an equivalent utterance in language B. Then, in dialogic situations, a response in language B is converted into an equivalent utterance in language A, and so forth. Thus, the interpreter's contributions to the interaction are limited to translations (in the next turn) of the previous speaker's utterance.

The analysis presented in this article will demonstrate that this view of interpreter-mediated interaction is extremely simplistic and does not account for the wide range of phenomena found in real life communication. I will argue that interpreting should be understood more broadly, as an activity in its own right, coordinated with and embedded within an ongoing set of actions. In fact, what interpreters do or say is only partially, and sometimes hardly at all, limited to translating other people's talk. Instead, interpreters' actions manifest a choice between several alternatives available to them at any particular time within the frame of the ongoing activity. These alternatives, ranging from being a 'translating machine' to having an independent interactional position, embody interpreters' moment-by-moment decisions about what role will be the most appropriate in a particular interactional environment.

Thus, interpreters, as full-fledged social actors, have different options in organizing their participation in the unfolding activity. Structurally, their choices may result in two distinct types of interaction (see Figure 1 for a graphical representation). First, the interaction may take the shape of a single conversation between the two principal parties (in the case of a medical consultation, the doctor and the patient). In this situation, the interpreter *directly interprets* what has been said in the previous turn by one of the participants. The doctor and the patient primarily address each other rather than the interpreter. Second, the interaction may take the shape of two interweaving but separate conversations. In this case, the interpreter

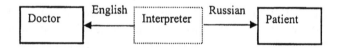

(a) 'Directly interpreted' interaction

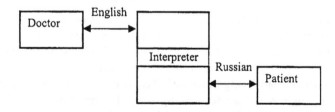

(b) 'Mediated' interaction

Figure 1 Types of doctor/interpreter/patient interaction.

acts as an independent participant in each interaction, *mediating* the conversation instead of directly translating what has been said. As a result, rather than communicating directly with each other, the doctor and the patient interact mainly with the interpreter.[2]

Note that the first type of interaction emerges, for example, when the interpreter chooses to embrace the role of a 'translating machine'. This mode of interaction does not, however, mean that the interpreter's contributions are necessarily limited to 'neutral' translations of other parties' talk. Even when the interaction is organized in this way, the interpreter's turns display his orientation to the objectives of the specific activity taking place at the time.

This article will be concerned with ways in which interpreters' actions are structured by the roles they adopt within the interaction and how these roles fit into the overall organization of the activity. We will see that in the medical encounters examined here, the interpreter's involvement in the activity of history taking is organized by his understanding of what this activity needs to achieve. Specifically, the interpreter's involvement in this part of the consultation displays his orientation to obtaining from the patient and conveying to the doctor medically relevant information about the patient's symptoms – and doing it as effectively as possible. In this article, I will detail how this orientation to the goals of the activity organizes the interpreter's actions.

Data

The data for this article come from a corpus of video- and audio-recorded interpreter-mediated consultations between English-speaking doctors and Russian-speaking patients. The two interviews analyzed here were audio-recorded at a large urban hospital in the Midwestern part of the USA. At the time of the recording, the interpreter participating in these interviews was an on-staff interpreter at the hospital. He was highly proficient in both languages and had had some professional interpreting training. The participants in each of the consultations knew each other from prior visits. In both interviews, the patients' main medical concern was the chest pain and the symptoms related to it. Information about the participants is summarized in Table 1.

The interpreter's participation in history taking

A prototypical medical consultation consists of the following major phases (see Byrne and Long, 1976; Waitzkin, 1991):

- the opening (when a relationship between the doctor and the patient is established);

249

Table 1 Summary information about the participants in analyzed consultations.

	Interpreter	*Medical Providers*	*Patients*
Consultation 1	native Russian-speaker; male; around 25	physician; male; around 40	Russian immigrant: male; around 65
Consultation 2		*Doctor 1*: same as above; *Doctor 2*: cardiologist; male; around 45; invited by Doctor 1 for a consultation	Russian immigrant; female; around 70

- presentation of the problem (the patient presents the reason for the visit);
- history taking and physical examination (the doctor questions the patient about his or her condition and conducts a physical examination);
- the diagnosis (the doctor presents the diagnosis);
- the treatment (the doctor and the patient discuss treatment); and
- the closing (the consultation is terminated).

During the history-taking stage of the consultation (which is our focus here), the doctor conducts a verbal interview in order to obtain information about the patient's symptoms (the process often referred to as 'differential diagnosis'). The physician's goal is to collect information that would make it possible for her to diagnose the problem and to prescribe appropriate treatment (see, for example, Bates *et al.*, 1995; Billings and Stoeckle, 1989; Greenberger and Hinthorn, 1993; Heath, 1986; Robinson, 1999; Seidel *et al.*, 1995; Swartz, 1998; Zoppi, 1997).

The history-taking part of consultations normally consists of sequences of doctor-initiated questions pertaining to various aspects of the patient's condition (Frankel, 1990). If the interpreter adapts the role of a 'translating machine' and restricts his or her participation to providing close translations of previous turns, doctor-initiated questioning sequences during the history-taking phase will be organized in the following way (see Figure 2):

- the doctor asks a question (in English);
- the interpreter translates the question (into Russian) for the patient;
- the patient provides an answer (in Russian);
- the interpreter then translates the answer (into English) for the doctor.

I have found, however, that in my data the questioning sequences are organized quite differently (see Figure 3). A doctor-initiated question in English launches a questioning sequence in Russian. The first question in

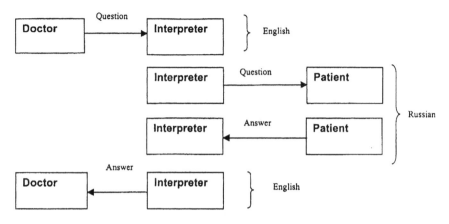

Figure 2 A possible organization of doctor-initiated question and answer sequences.

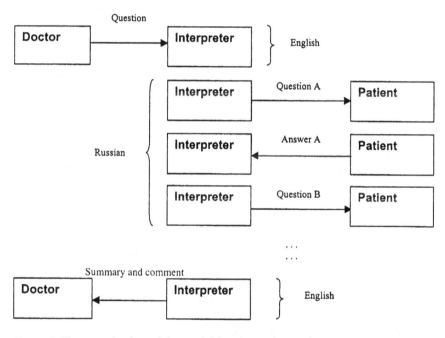

Figure 3 The organization of doctor-initiated question and answer sequences.

the Russian-language sequence (Question A) is usually a translation of the doctor's initial question. After the patient provides an answer to this question (Answer A), the interpreter poses another question (Question B). After the patient answers that question, the interpreter may continue asking additional questions. The sequence comes to a close when the interpreter provides a summary translation of the patient's replies, sometimes followed by a comment in which the interpreter remarks on the course of the discussion, the patient's state, etc.

Questioning sequences of this sort occur regularly in interpreter-mediated consultations, and in my view their occurrence is not accidental. Rather, they manifest the interpreter's systematic orientation to the particular activity the participants are engaged in. Moreover, I will argue that the interpreter's questions and summary translations are designed in such a way as to further the activity of the history-taking interview.

Medical contingencies for diagnosis and treatment

The verbal examination of the patient is conducted in order to diagnose the patient's medical problem and to prescribe appropriate treatment. In other words, at this stage of the consultation the doctor is oriented to collecting information about a set of issues related to a particular medical condition. The specific problems raised by the doctor will, of course, vary depending on the particulars of the situation (for example, the patient's symptoms, the doctor's prior knowledge of the patient, and the patient's medical history). However, it is possible to compile a list of issues that are likely to be brought up during the course of the verbal examination. An analysis of several consultations with patients who have a history of chest pain has shown that doctors orient toward the following set of contingencies for diagnosis and treatment:

- a symptom's presence, frequency, duration, and development over time (i.e. whether the condition is getting worse or better);
- a symptom's description (for example, whether the pain is dull or sharp);
- causality (i.e. what seems to cause the occurrence of the symptom); and
- the presence of other related symptoms.

If the symptom has been treated before, the doctor may inquire about

- the effects of the current treatment, and
- the presence of any side-effects associated with the treatment.

If the symptom has *not* been previously treated, the doctor may ask about

- the patient's own remedies.

These contingencies for diagnosis and treatment specify a domain of relevance (see, for example, Mishler, 1984) – a set of issues that not only the doctor but also (as I will show) the interpreter consider important and worth attending to. This set of medical contingencies also designates certain topics as irrelevant, and thus excludable from the discussion. In other words, the goals of the history taking, as a particular kind of an activity system, specify the topics participants can and cannot legitimately address.

Presentation of medical information

The goals of the history-taking interview not only specify the domain of relevance but also the ways in which diagnostically-relevant information is talked about. Several researchers have found that physicians (at least those working in the western medical tradition) display a preference for objective and decontextualized presentations of information over personalized descriptions (see, for example, Drew and Heritage, 1992; Frankel, 1990; Korsch and Negrete, 1972; Meehan, 1981; Mishler, 1984; Roter and Hall, 1992; Ten Have, 1991; Waitzkin, 1985). Mishler (1984), for example, developed a concept of the 'voice of medicine' which, in contrast to the 'voice of the lifeworld', 'reflects a "technical" interest and expresses a "scientific attitude"' (p. 104). Commonly adopted by medical professionals, the 'voice of medicine' is characterized by its focus on decontextualized descriptions of reality in terms of its objective features. Physicians may prefer this form of presentation due to the fact that decontextualized, objective symptom descriptions fit into the traditional biomedical model of disease. Having been trained within such a model, physicians might be expected to be most efficient in diagnosing a medical problem presented in such a traditional 'scientific' manner.

The 'voice of medicine' does not simply formulate reality in a wide variety of objective terms, but only in those terms that are specifically relevant to the unfolding activity. Thus, the activity of history taking with its goal to diagnose a particular medical condition makes relevant a specific coding scheme (Goodwin, 1994) that delimits ways in which symptoms are described. For example, in medical interviews, pain is routinely talked about as being 'sharp' or 'dull' the onset of pain as being 'sudden' or 'gradual', etc. In other words, the 'voice of medicine' should not be loosely equated with the voice of science, but seen as being continuously adapted to the contingencies of a specific activity.

The question which arises is whether medical interpreters share physicians' normative orientation to obtaining objectively formulated information about a patient's medical condition. If they do, interpreters may be expected to systematically reject patients' information offerings if they contain subjective, contextually grounded accounts of their 'lifeworld' concerns presented in terms that lie outside a particular coding scheme. In the following sections, I will describe how one interpreter's understanding of the activity of history taking shapes the way in which he interacts (a) with the patient (i.e. the sorts of questions he asks and how he reacts to the patient's contributions), and (b) with the doctor (i.e. what sort of information the interpreter conveys to the doctor). These two sides of the interpreter's

253

involvement in history taking will be first exemplified in an analysis of one questioning sequence and then described more systematically in the later sections.

An analysis of one questioning sequence

If the interpreter shares the doctor's orientation towards addressing the contingencies for diagnosis and treatment, we can expect to find that inter-preter-initiated questions will elicit information directly related to this set of contingencies. Thus, after translating the doctor's question concerning a particular symptom, the interpreter may selectively attend to and topicalize those aspects of the patient's response that are directly related to medical contingencies, at the same time ignoring issues that he deems to be irrelev-ant. In addition, the design of the interpreter's questions may display his orientation to obtaining depersonalized descriptions of the symptoms rather than accounts grounded in the patient's life experiences.

This is exactly what happens in the segment of interaction presented in Excerpt 1. The transcript follows conventions developed by Jefferson (see, for example, Sacks *et al.*, 1974). Letter D stands for the doctor, I for the interpreter, and P for the patient. Utterances in italics are idiomatic trans-lations from Russian.

Excerpt 1 (Consultation 1)

```
1    D    Ah::: ar- (0.5) are you ah (0.8)
2         h-having a problem with uh chest pain?

3         (0.5)

4    I    Болит-ли сердце у  вас,
          hurts-QM³ heart with you
          Do you have a chest pain,

5         (4.0)

6    P    °Ну как  сказать, кто  его знает. Оно (1.5)°
          well how to + say who it   knows it
          °Well how should I put it, who knows. It (1.5)°

7         ИНОГДА БЫВАЕТ ДА:.
          sometime  happens   yes
          SOMETIMES IT DOES HAPPEN.

8         (0.4)

9    I    Раз в недело:, раз  в  две недели:,
          once a week     once in two weeks
          Once a week, Once every two weeks,
```

10 P <Нет бывает тогда такое смотря: от- (.) от
       no happens then such depending on on
       <No this thing happens then depending on- (.) on

11   обстано:вки (0.5) жи:зненной.
       circumstance   of + life
       the ci:rcumstances (0.5) of li:fe.

12 I <Ну в- в данный момент ваша жизненная
       well in in given moment your life
       <Well at- at this particular moment do your life

13   обстановка вызывает у вас боль раз в неделю или-
       circumstance causes   with you pain once a week or-
       circumstances cause you pain once a week or-

14   или чаше.
       or more + often
       or more often.

15 P Бывает и   чаше
       happens and more + often
       Sometimes more often

16 I Бывает и   чаше
       happens and more + often
       Sometimes more often

17 I Once or twice a week maybe: (0.6) a:nd

The sequence is initiated by the doctor's inquiry concerning the presence of a particular symptom (chest pain): 'Ah::: ar- (0.5) are you ah (0.8) h-having a problem with uh chest pain?' (lines 1–2). The inquiry gets translated in line 4. The translation, while preserving the format of the doctor's turn,[4] is somewhat more constricting than the initial question. Thus, the doctor's question not only invites the patient to confirm the presence of the chest pain, but also to describe in what ways the patient's experiences constitute a problem. By contrast, the interpreter's question simply invites confirmation of the presence of the chest pain. (A conforming answer to the interpreter's question would consist of *yes* or *no* (Raymond, 1998). However, this question is designed for, and, thus, 'prefers'[5] a *yes* response.) This change in the scope of the question seems to be achieved by replacing the doctor's reference to 'a problem' with the chest pain by the interpreter's inquiry into the presence of the chest pain specifically:

4 I Болит-ли сердце у   вас,
      hurts-QM heart   with you
      Do you have a chest pain

The patient seems to have trouble with the format of the interpreter's inquiry. Instead of simply confirming that he does indeed have a chest pain, the patient (after a long pause in line 5 which is indicative of the upcoming 'dispreferred' character of the answer[6]) first states that he is unable to answer the question:

6   P   °Ну как сказать, кто его знает. Оно° (1.5)°
           well how to + say who it   knows it
           °*Well how should I put it, who knows. It (1.5)*°

Note that the reference to the heart ('it')[7] the second turn-constructional unit (Sacks *et al.*, 1974) indicates that the patient might be on his way to offer an alternative description of what is wrong with his heart.[8] However, he abandons this turn-constructional unit (TCU), and offers a qualified affirmative response instead:

7   ИНОГДА БЫВАЕТ ДА:.
      sometime   happens   yes
      SOMETIMES IT DOES HAPPEN.[9]

The qualification ('sometimes') brings up the issue of the frequency of the chest pain. This, of course, is one of the medical contingencies for diagnosis and it gets topicalized in the immediately following discussion between the interpreter and the patient.

It is necessary to emphasize that the patient's response (lines 6–7), even if hedged, can serve as a valid and clear answer to the doctor's question (lines 1–2). It can, therefore, be translated back to the doctor without any further discussion. Given physicians' orientations during this part of medical encounters to obtaining information about medical contingencies and given that one such contingency has been brought up by the patient, the doctor would be likely to ask the patient to explain how often the chest pain occurs. The interpreter, however, does not translate the patient's response at this point, but, instead puts forward his own question about the frequency of the chest pain, thus preempting what was the doctor's most likely next question. The interpreter's actions at this juncture of the consultation thus demonstrate that, being familiar with how such sequences normally proceed, he is oriented to achieving the goals of the history-taking interview in a most efficient manner.

The interpreter's question (*'Once a week, Once every two weeks'*, in line 9) displays his orientation to collecting information about issues that may be diagnostically relevant (such as the frequency of the symptom). In addition, the question displays the interpreter's analysis of certain types of information as being more appropriate within the framework of a medical interview. Thus, the turn offers two examples of acceptable descriptions of the frequency of the chest pain. Both are objective, situation-independent measures of frequency. Thus, the design of the interpreter's question embodies his preference for more precise, quantifiable symptom descriptions. In addition, the list format of the question is designed to obtain a short, unelaborated answer.

The patient's response (in lines 10–11) however, does not contain a description of the frequency of the chest pain that is compatible with the format suggested in the interpreter's question. In fact, the patient seems to reject not just the two alternatives but the entire thrust of the interpreter's question. This rejection is evident in the turn-initial placement of an undelayed and unmitigated negation marker 'no' followed by an alternative symptom description:

10 P <Нет бывает тогда такое смотря: от- (.) от
       no   happens then   such depending on   on
       <*No this thing happens then depending on- (.) on*

11   обстано:вки (0.5) жи:зненной.
       circumstance   of + life
       the ci:rcumstances (0.5) of li:fe.

After the initial negation marker, the patient reformulates his chest pain as being causally related to his life circumstances, and thereby variable. Note that the variability of the symptom sharply contrasts with the underlying assumption of regularity in the interpreter's preceding question (in line 9). The interpreter's next question is designed to de-emphasize the variable character of the pain, insisting on an objective measure of frequency:

12 I <Ну в- в данный момент ваша жизненная
       well in in given   moment your life
       <*Well at- at this particular moment do your life*

13   обстановка вызывает у   вас боль раз в неделю или-
       circumstance causes   with you pain once a week   or-
       circumstances cause you pain once a week or-

14   или   чаше.
       or more + often
       or more often.

By starting the turn with 'well', the interpreter characterizes the patient's previous response as being in some way problematic.[10] He, then, proceeds to fix the time at 'this particular moment', thus eliminating the relevance of variability as a factor in pain description. Moreover, by questioning the frequency of the pain rather than the life circumstances that might cause it, the interpreter prevents the topicalization of the relationship between pain and life circumstances. Thus, the interpreter's question, while clearly built upon the patient's prior response, has the effect of eliminating from the discussion the two aspects of the chest pain that the patient has brought up (i.e. its variability and dependency on life circumstances). The question also re-formulates the two alternatives for characterizing the frequency of pain. The new alternatives (lines 13–14) are less specific than the original ones offered in line 9 ('once every two weeks' in line 9 versus 'more often' in line 14) and suggest that the pain may occur more frequently (cf. 'once every two weeks' in line 9 versus 'once a week or more often' in lines 13–14). The patient now picks one of the alternatives (the less specific and the more frequent one), adding again a reference to the pain's variable character ('sometimes'): *'sometimes more often'* (line 15). This response is accepted by the interpreter and translated for the doctor: 'Once or twice a week maybe: (0.6) a:nd' (in line 17).

Interestingly, the translation replaces the variable aspect of the pain insisted upon by the patient (e.g. 'sometimes' in line 15) with a marker of uncertainty ('maybe' in line 17). After providing the summary translation, the interpreter does not wait for the doctor to pose another question but instead initiates a questioning sequence designed to obtain more information about the patient's heart problem. Specifically, the interpreter's questions address the issue of causality – one of the medical contingencies relevant for diagnosis and treatment of chest pain:

Excerpt 2 (continued from Excerpt 1)

18 I А зт- зто вот- зто в'   относится к стре:ссу да?
       and th- this EMP this EMP refers   to stress   yes
       And th- this thing- this is related to stress right?

19 P Да
       Yes

20 I Не к физической нагрузке,
       not to physical   load
       Not to physical work,

21   (0.7)

22 P Ну физической нагрузки у   меня нету.
       well physical   load   with me   absent
       Well I don't have any physical work

23   <Я: пробывал даже заниматься:,
       I   tried   even exercise
       I: even tried to exerci:se,

24 I И   сердце не в- не начинает болеть когда вы
        and heart not v not begins   hurt   when you
        And the heart d- doesn't begin to hurt when you

25   [спортом занимаетесь?
        [sports   do
        [*exercise?*

26 P [(Вос-)восстанавливать нормал[ьное =
        [res- restore   normal
        [*(Res-) To restore nor [mal =*

27 I   [*Uh huh*

28 P = дыхание или что-нибудь. <У меня есть [( )
        breath   or   something   I   have
        = breathing or something. <I have   [*( )*

29 I   [Но сердце
                                but heart
                               [*But you don't*

30   не болит у   вас когда вы в'т   занимаетесь спортом да?
        not hurt   with you when you EMP do   sport   yes
        have the heart pain when you exercise right?

31   (.)

32   Или когда вы ходите по улице.
        or   when you walk on street
        or when you walk outside.

33   (1.0)

34 P Бывает да
        happens yes
        Sometimes yes

35 I Бывает болит.
        happens hurt
        Sometimes there is pain

36 P Да.
        Yes.

37 I Ah:::m: (0.5) sometimes the chest pain is stress

38   related sometimes it's exertion related_

The interpreter's question in line 18 appears to be related to the patient's reference to 'life circumstances' in lines 10–11:

18 I A   зт- зто вот- зто в'   относится к стре:ссу да?
         and th- this EMP this EMP refers   to stress   yes
         And th- this thing- this is related to stress right?

The question's contingency on prior talk seems to be marked by the Russian conjunction 'a', which can be translated as either 'and' or 'but', depending on context.[11] Interestingly, the patient's initial reference to 'life circumstances' as a factor in the chest pain is here replaced with 'stress' – a medicalized version of what the patient might have meant by 'life circumstances'. Notably, the interpreter's question is a *yes/no* question in the form of an assertion followed by a tag ('right?') (Sacks *et al.*, 1974). This question format (as opposed to more open-ended questions) limits the patient's opportunities for elaboration. In addition, 'assertion + tag' questions in Russian carry a strong preference for conforming responses.[12] Thus the interpreter's question is designed to get a brief confirmation that a relationship between the stress and the chest pain exists, and not to get a description of such a relationship.

After getting the confirmation in line 19 (note the undelayed, brief character of the patient response), the interpreter proceeds to specify other factors that might be related to the chest pain:

20 I Не к физической нагрузке,
       not to physical   load
       Not to physical work,

This question, designed as an increment to the prior turn (Sacks *et al.*, 1974), has an effect of moving the discussion even further away from the patient's psychosocial concerns (alluded to in the patient's reference to 'life circumstances'). The question is negatively framed with the negative polarity item 'не' (not) and, thus, designed to prefer a minimal negative response (Boyd and Heritage, forthcoming). By posing his question in this way, the interpreter shows his orientation to obtaining diagnostically relevant information from the patient in the fastest possible way.

The patient's answer, however, disaligns with the question's preference. Instead of confirming the absence of a relationship between the chest pain and the physical work, the patient topicalizes physical work as an aspect of his social circumstances:

22 P Ну физической нагрузки у   меня нету.
       well physical   load   with me   absent
       Well I don't have any physical work

23   <Я: пробывал даже заниматься:,
         I   tried   even exercise
         I: even tried to exerci:se,

The patient first indicates that the presupposition of the interpreter's question in line 20 (that the patient does physical work) is incorrect. The lack of physical work is formulated by the patient as a problem requiring a remedy (see line 23). The patient, however, is not given an opportunity to elaborate on this, since the interpreter's next question ьн is designed to shift the focus of the discussion from the patient's concerns back to the relationship between the physical work and the chest pain:

```
24  I    И   сердце не  в- не  начинает болеть когда вы
         and heart   not v  not begins    hurt     when you
         And the heart d- doesn't begin to hurt when you

25       [спортом занимаетесь?
         sports      do
         [exercise?
```

Note that the interpreter's question is prefixed with 'и', which appears to function similarly to the 'and' prefix in English questions. Relying on English language material, Heritage and Sorjonen (1994) demonstrated that *and*-prefixing may be used strategically 'to warrant a forward topical movement or shift in a possibly problematic environment' when, for example, the question is 'initiated in the context of an answer that is "non-minimal" and unexpected' (p. 21). In such cases, *and*-prefixed questions implicate agenda as an account for the topic shift and for closing off troubles talk. This is similar to what seems to be happening here. The 'and' prefix on the interpreter's question allows the interpreter to close off and to move away from a discussion of the problem presented in the patient's previous response. Without overtly rejecting the patient's answer, the interpreter reinvokes the continuing relevance of his line of questioning (and specifically, his question in line 20) for the ongoing activity of the history taking. Note also that the interpreter's question in lines 24–5 is a negatively formulated yes/no question that (similarly to line 20) prefers a brief confirming response.

Instead of responding to the interpreter's question in lines 24–5, the patient attempts to elaborate on his initial response in lines 22–3. Note particularly that lines 26 and 28 are designed as an increment to the patient's prior turn and that they sequentially delete (Lerner, 1987) the interpreter's prior question in lines 24–5. However, the patient's elaboration attempts are interrupted by the interpreter who pursues his own line of questioning:

```
26  P   [(Вос-)восстанавливать нормал[ьное =
        res-   restore              normal
        [ (Res-)  To restore   nor[mal =

27  I                                [Uh huh
```

28 P = дых<u>а</u>ние или что-нибудь. <У меня есть [( )
       breath   or   something   I   have
    = *br<u>ea</u>thing or something.<I have*   [( )

29 I   [Но с<u>е</u>рдце
                                                   but heart
                                                   [*But you don't*

30 не болит у   вас когда вы в'т   занимаетесь спортом да?
    not hurt   with you when you EMP do   sport   yes
    have the h<u>ea</u>rt pain when you exercise right?

31 (.)

32 Или когда вы   ходите по улице.
    or   when you walk   on street
    or when you walk outside.

The interpreter's question in lines 29–30, done as a virtual repeat of his prior question in lines 24–5, is now prefixed with a 'но' ('but'). Unlike the subtler 'and' in line 24, this contrastive conjunction rejects the appropriateness or the relevance of the patient's prior utterance. As a result of the interpreter's action, the patient's utterance in lines 26 and 28 is sequentially deleted (Lerner, 1987; Schegloff, 1987). In addition, the interpreter's question (lines 29–30) is a negatively formulated assertion followed by a tag. This question design, once again, prefers a brief confirming response from the patient. When none is forthcoming (see the brief silence in line 31), the interpreter adds an increment (line 32) in pursuit of a response from the patient, which he offers only after a substantial silence (line 33). The patient's disaligning response (*'sometimes yes'* in line 34) is, thus, clearly done in a dispreferred manner.

After reconfirming the patient's answer (lines 35–6), the interpreter provides a summary translation for the doctor (lines 37–8). The translation ('Ah:::m: (0.5) sometimes the chest pain is str<u>e</u>ss related sometimes it's ex<u>e</u>rtion related_') presents information in very medical terms (e.g. 'exertion' replaces physical work', 'exercise', and 'walking'). Notably, it also omits any reference to other concerns mentioned by the patient: for example, the lack of physical work, the fact that he exercises in order to remedy that, etc. Thus, the interpreter's translation demonstrates his orientation to providing the doctor with the information related to medical contingencies for diagnosis and treatment, and presenting that information in a scientific, objective fashion.

To summarize, the analysis of this questioning sequence has shown that the interpreter's involvement in this interaction is structured by his orientation to obtaining information directly related to the goals of history taking (i.e. information he believes to be diagnostically relevant). In addition, the interpreter's actions embody his orientation to achieving these goals in the fastest and most efficient way. On the one hand, the interpreter is found to question the patient himself and then present the doctor with summary translations containing only medically relevant information offered in a form that would allow for an easy diagnostic decision. On the other hand, the interpreter's questions to the patient are repeatedly designed in such a way as to obtain brief confirming responses. Thus, the questions are overwhelmingly yes/no questions formatted to display a strong preference for aligning answers.

Relevance of medical contingencies for diagnosis and treatment to the organization of questioning sequences

This section will provide further evidence for the claim that medical contingencies for diagnosis and treatment play an important role in shaping both the interpreter's questions and the content of the summary translations given to the doctor. Two brief examples will illustrate the pervasive influence they exert over the interpreter's participation in the history-taking part of the consultations.

In the following excerpt (Excerpt 3), the doctor's question about the patient's familiarity with a medication prompts the interpreter to pose a series of related questions about the medication (marked with arrows on the transcript):

Excerpt 3 (Consultation 2)

1   D2   Does she know what Nitroglycerin is?

2   I   А вы зна-
           you kno-
           You kno-

3   I   <<u>Ye</u>ah I'm sure she does.

4 → I   А:: вы не   принимаете нитроглицерин?
           ah you not take   nitroglycerin
           Ah:: you don't take Nitroglycerin?

5   (0.8)

6   p   Не-з, он же   мне не   выписал.
           no- he   EMP me   not prescribed
           No-o, he didn't prescribe it.

7   Мне н<u>а</u>до нитроглиц[e-
           me   need nitroglyce-
           I n<u>ee</u>d Nitroglyc[e

8   I   [Нитроглицерин вам нужен, да?
                    nitroglycerin   you need   right
                    [*You need Nitroglycerin right?*

9   P   Да [:
          Yes [:

10 →   I   [А когда вы принимаете он помогаег вам д[а?
                 and when you take   it helps   you right
                [*And when you take it it helps you r[ight?*

11   P   [да
                                              [*Yes*

12   (0.4)

13   I   When she ta[kes it,   [ah:

14   P   [Зажимает го[:лову но: помогает.
                          squeezes   head   but helps
                          [*It squeezes my he[a:d but it helps.*

15   I   Uh::: she gets som- uh (0.2)
16   a lit'l:e (.) uh:: headpressure headache,
17   but it does help.

After the doctor poses his question (line 1), the interpreter starts to translate the question (line 2), but abandons his translation halfway through,
choosing instead to answer the question himself (line 3). The interpreter
then proceeds to question the patient about her use of this medication
(line 4):

2   I   А вы зна-
          you kno-
          You kno-

3   I   <Yeah I'm sure she does.

4 → I   А: : вы не принимаете нитроглицерин?
          ah   you not take   nitroglycerin
          Ah:: you don't take Nitroglycerin?

The interpreter's actions in lines 2–4 demonstrate that he treats the doctor's
question (in line 1) as a preliminary to an inquiry about the patient's use
of the medication (Schegloff, 1988). Such treatment of the question clearly
shows the interpreter's orientation to the medical activity projected by the
doctor's question. Specifically, the interpreter's actions display his understanding that questions during a history-taking interview are posed to obtain
information relevant to the diagnosis and treatment, and not simply to
inquire into the patient's familiarity with various medications. Note that the
question the interpreter poses is a question about one such contingency
(prior treatment of the problem).

After ascertaining that the patient needs this medication (lines 7–9), the interpreter inquires into another medical contingency – the medication's effects (line 11). After receiving a one-word affirmative response to his question, the interpreter starts to report the treatment effects to the doctor (line 13):

13 I When she ta[kes it, [ah:

14 P   [Зажимает го[:лову но: помогает.
         squeezes head but helps
         [*It squeezes my he[a:d but it helps.*

15 I Uh::: she gets som- uh (0.2)
16   a lit'1:e (.) uh:: headpressure headache,
17   but it does help.

The summary translation is interrupted by the patient who mentions some side-effects she experiences from the medication (line 14). The interpreter then includes the issue of side-effects (another medical contingency) in his continuing report to the doctor (lines 15–16).

The next excerpt (Excerpt 4) provides further illustration of the role of medical contingencies in organizing the interpreter's questioning of the patient. Here, the sequence is initiated by the doctor's question concerning the effects of a particular symptom on the patient's regular activities (line 1).

Excerpt 4 (Consultation 2)

1 D2 No:w-can she: y'think sh-c'n she wa:lk up some s-stai:rs
     or things like tha[t

2 I   [По лестнице можете подниматься?
          on stairs you+can climb
          [*Can you climb some stairs?*

((several lines omitted))

16 I <So on the second s- uh floor: (.)
17   she needs to make three sto:ps.

18   (0.5)

19 D2 (Becau:se there)

20   (0.2)

21 I Из-за   чего вы останавлиаетесь?
   because + of what you stop
   Why do you stop?

22   (0.8)

23   P   Ну с<u>е</u>рдце не дает.
            well heart   not allow
            Well my heart doesn't let me.

24   (1.2)

25 → I   Отд<u>ы:</u>шка   или боль в сердце.
            shortness + of + breath or pain in heart
            Shortness of br<u>ea</u>th or heart pain.

26 → I   Или <u>о</u>[ба.
            or   both
            Or   b<u>o</u>[th.

27   P   [Б<u>о</u>ль.
                    [*P<u>ai</u>n.*

28   (0.5)

29   P   Бо[ль.
            Pa[in.

30   I   [Б<u>о</u>ль в седце. <Отдышки   нет, да?
                 pain   in heart   shortness + of + breath no   right
                 [*Heartpain. No shortness of breath, right?*

31   (0.8)

32   I   Pain.

33   (0.5)

34   I   Not- not adispia, just- pain.

In the first part of this questioning sequence (omitted from the transcript above), the interpreter poses a series of questions to specify how climbing up the stairs affects the patient. After the interpreter reports the results of this discussion to the doctor (lines 16–17), the inquiry about the patient's symptoms is reopened (by the doctor, if the hearing of line 19 is correct). After the patient provides a response to the question about the reason for her physical difficulty (line 23), the interpreter reformulates the question in line 21 to obtain a more precise description of the patient's symptoms (lines 25–6). The design of the interpreter's question is fitted to the ongoing activity of history-taking in that it uses a particular set of medical distinctions necessary for diagnosing the patient's specific medical problem:

25 → I   Отд<u>ы:</u>шка   или боль в сердце.
            shortness+of+breath or   pain in heart
            Shortness of br<u>ea</u>th or heart pain.

26 → I   Или <u>о</u> [ба.
             or   both
             Or   b<u>o</u> [th.

27   P   [Б<u>о</u>ль.
                    [*P<u>ai</u>n.*

After confirming the patient's response, the interpreter summarizes his findings about the patient's symptom to the doctor:

32   I   Pain.
33   (0.5)
34   I   Not- not adispia, just- pain.

Thus, in this case, the interpreter's questions display an orientation to obtaining information about the causal relationship between the patient's symptoms and her everyday activities.

To summarize, the analysis of several excerpts from the history-taking stage has demonstrated that patient-directed questions initiated by the interpreter are not random. Rather, they address a set of medical contingencies for diagnosis and treatment related to the symptom raised in the doctor's initial question. In addition, the interpreter's reports to the doctor include the information related to the contingencies and leave out those of the patient's remarks which are not relevant to them (see a later section for more discussion).

Relevance of the 'voice of medicine' to the organization of questioning sequences: sequencing of questions

As already mentioned, many of the interpreter's questions are designed in such a way as to elicit decontextualized, objective information about the patient's condition. This section will examine how the interpreter sequences questions in such a way as to further delimit the patient's responses.

A brief look at one segment of interaction will show that the interpreter may start with an open-ended question and change it to a more close-ended question in his pursuit of a specific response from the patient. This is what happens in Excerpt 5:

Excerpt 5 (Consultation 2)

21 → I   Из-за   <u>чего</u> вы останавлиаетесь?
             because+of what you stop
             <u>*Why*</u> *do you stop?*

22   (0.8)

23   P   Ну се́рдце не дает.
         well heart   not allow
         Well my he̱art doesn't let me.

24   (1.2)

25 → I   Отды̲:шка   или боль в сердце.
         shortness+of+breath or   pain in heart
         Shortness of bre̱ath or heart pain.

26 → I   Или о̲[ба.
         or   both
         Or bo̲[th.

27   P   [Боль.
              [*Pa̱in.*

28   (0.5)

29   P   Бо[ль.
         Pa[*in.*

30 → I   [Бо̲ль в сердце. <Отлышки   нет, да?
         pain in heart   shortness + of + breath no   right
         [*Heartpain. No shortness of breath, right?*

31   (0.8)

32   I   Pain.

33   (0.5)

34   I   Not- not adispia, just- pain.

Here the interpreter first poses a restricted *wh*-question (line 12), followed by a question in a list form (lines 25–6) and then a *yes/no* tag question (line 30). While the *uh*-question leaves the range of appropriate responses relatively open, the question formatted as a list presents several instances from a class of suitable answers. This sequencing of questions allows the interpreter to first specify (lines 25–6) and then confirm (line 30) the patient's response. Sequencing of questions is thus another piece of evidence for the interpreter's orientation towards obtaining clearly formulated and definitive responses from the patient.

To summarize, we have seen that the interpreter's involvement in the history-taking part of the consultations is shaped by his orientation to the 'voice of medicine'. Specifically, the norms of the 'voice of medicine' (such as a preference for decontextualized objective symptom descriptions) find their realization in how the interpreter's questions are sequenced.

Summary translations: what does the doctor hear?

Interpreter-mediated interactions are unique sites for a study of particip- ants' orientations, alignments, and understandings because they commonly provide room for the participants to voice their stances. Thus, interpreters have structurally-established places where their understandings of the ongo- ing actions and activities are articulated. In the case of the history-taking interviews described in this article, such places are summary translations provided to the doctor at the end of each questioning sequence (see Figure 3). An examination of what these summaries contain (as well as what they systematically miss) can give an important insight into what the interpreter believes to be relevant and important for the ongoing activity, and what he considers to be unimportant or irrelevant.

We have so far observed that the interpreter's involvement in history- taking interviews seems to be shaped by his orientation to obtaining informa- tion related to medical contingencies for diagnosis and treatment and, specifically, information formulated in the 'voice of medicine'. Given this fact, we may expect that issues considered by the interpreter to be irrelev- ant for diagnostic decisions, especially those formulated as subjective, contextually-grounded experiences, will be excluded from summary trans- lations offered to the doctor. At the same time, issues related to medical contingencies which are formulated in the 'voice of medicine' will be included in summary translations. A brief analysis of summary translations offered after several questioning sequences will demonstrate that this is, in fact, the case.

Here is a summary translation offered by the interpreter after the ques- tioning sequence discussed earlier as Excerpt 4:

Excerpt 6 (Consultation 2)

```
32   I   Pain.
33       (0.5)
34   I   Not- not adispia, just- pain.
```

We can see that the translation is telegraphic in form and that it presents information obtained from the patient in medical terms ('audispia') that are unlikely to be in the patient's vocabulary.

The following example is another illustration of the interpreter's orienta- tion towards obtaining description of symptoms presented in the 'voice of medicine':

Excerpt 7 (Consultation 2)

```
1    D1   How- how o:ften do you have the (0.2)
2         chest pain over here?
```

3 I как ч<u>а</u>сто у   вас боль (.) зд<u>е</u>сь (0.2)
       how often with you pain here
       How often do you have pain (.) here (.2)

4 I в гру- в л<u>е</u>вой стороне.
       in che- in left   side
       in the che- on the left side

5 P часто.
       Often.

6   (2.2)

7   Ну: во::т з:- Особенно перемена пог<u>о</u>ды, (0.8)
       well EMP uh especially change   of + weather
       We:ll uh::- Especially a change in w<u>ea</u>ther, (0.8)

8   и   я тогда лежу: пла:стом.
       and I then   lie   flat
       and then I lie fla:t on my ba:ck.

9 I Фа<u>и</u>на, вуз ч<u>а</u>сто сколько   как часто зто быва:ет.
       Faina ?   often how + many how often this happens
       Fa<u>i</u>na (?) <u>o</u>ften how often does it ha:ppen.

10   Зто раз в нед<u>е</u>лю, три ча- тр<u>и</u> раза
       this once a week   three of- three times
       Once a w<u>ee</u>k, three of- thr<u>ee</u> times

11   в неде[лю, каждый день,
       a week   every   day
       a wee[k, every day,

12 P   [( )

13 P И   тр<u>и</u> раза, и: п<u>я</u>ть раз, и: к<u>а</u>к когда.
       and three times and five times and how when
       And thr<u>ee</u> times, a:nd f<u>i</u>ve times, a:nd it dep<u>e</u>nds.

14   (1.0)

15 → I Pretty much every day.
16 →   (1.0)
17 → I °The way I understand.°

During the discussion, the patient mentions that her condition is related to outside factors, such as changes in weather, which make her chest pain particularly bad (lines 7–8). This correlation between the patient's condition and the weather is left out of the interpreter's translation. Among the possible reasons for this might be the fact that such a correlation comes

270

from the realm of folk theories of illness, and that it presents the pain as a contingent – and thus, subjective and somewhat uncontrollable – matter. Both of these factors come from outside the typical 'voice of medicine' accounts, so it is not surprising that the patient's observation gets excluded from the summary translation.

Note also that the interpreter's summary translation contains a commentary on the patient's answers ('°The way I understand.°' in line 17). This commentary embodies a complete departure from the traditional interpreting role that limits the interpreter's involvement to presenting somebody else's words in another language. Here the interpreter clearly shows his own analysis, in his own words, of his interaction with the patient.

A final example comes from a segment in which the interpreter elicits from the patient a particular description of the chest pain:

Excerpt 8 (Consultation 1)

1 D What- what kind of pain is it.
      <Is it a sha:rp pain, or du:ll pain,

2 I Могли бы'ли вы описать зту боль.
      could COND you describe this pain
      Could you describe this pain.

3   (0.4)

4 I зто (.) тупая боль, (0.5) острая, (1.0) или давление.
      this dull pain sharp or pressure
      Is this a dull pain, (0.5) a sharp one, (1.0) or the pressure.

5   (1.2)

6 P Ну какая боль, Просто вот у меня бывают случаи
      well what pain simply EMP with me happen occasions
      да:,
      yes
      Well what kind of pain, Simply there are occasions ri:ght,

7   (0.8) °если я вот я пробывал заниматься,°
            if I EMP I tried to + exercise
      (0.8) °if I tried to exercise,°

8   (0.8) з::: мне кажется что::
            ah me seems that
      (0.8) ah::: it seems to me tha::t

9   (1.5) ну: остано:вится сердце.
            well will + stop heart
      (1.5) we:ll my heart is going to sto:p.

10   (0.5)

11   P   Мне надо (1.3) двигаться сюда туда чтоб'
           me   need   move   here there to
           I have to (1.3) move back and forth to

12   I   <То есть Это не боль, (.) рто просто чувство
           that is   this not pain   this simply feeling
           <That is it's not a pain? (.) This is just the feeling

13   что сердпе   [>остановится,<
           that heart   will + stop
           that your heart [>is going to stop<

((several lines omitted))

25   P   Ну (1.0) Зто не то   чтоб постоянно,
           well   this not that that constantly
           Well (1.0) this is not like constantly,

26   <переодически бывает б:оль такая что >я говорю<
           periodically   happens pain such that I say
           <periodically there is such p:ain that >I mean<

27   я не могу (.) кажется оно встанет
           I not can   seems   it   will+ stop
           I can't (.) it seems like it's gonna stop

28   и Зто самое <м:не надо (0.4) д:ви:гаться
           and this such me   need   to + move
           and I kind of have to (0.4) m:o:ve

29   я не могу вот [(тут)
           I not can EMP here
           I can't just   [( )

30   I   [Но (.) вы не   можете сказать
                             but   you not can   say
                             [But (.) can't you say if

31   острая она или тупая.
           sharp it   or dull
           it's sharp or dull.

32   (0.5)

33   I   Острая Зто сильная боль и   резк' как-будто ножем,
           sharp   this strong   pain and harsh as if   by + knife
           Sharp means a lot of pain and acute as if with a knife,

32   а   тупая она больше как давит.
           and dull   it   more   like presses
           and dull means it's more like pressure.

33   P   Н:ет не резкая.
           no   not sharp
           N:o not sharp.

34   I   Не резк[ая.
           not sharp
           Not sha[rp

35   P   [Нет не резкая [(нет).
                   no   not sharp no
                   [No not sharp   [(no)

36 → I   [So it's more uv a dull pain a:nd
37 →   he has a hard time ah: describing it,
38 →   (0.8)
39 → I Ah:: at the same time (0.2) uh:: (0.4) he- (.) he-
40 →   it fee:ls like ah: the heart is going to stop.

During the discussion between the interpreter and the patient, the patient brings up several issues that are related to his medical condition. For example, in lines 6–9, and then later in lines 25–9 (Excerpt 8), the patient mentions that he tries to exercise to alleviate his symptoms. This issue, while potentially relevant to the diagnosis and treatment, is excluded from the interpreter's summary translation to the doctor, possibly because on both occasions it is brought up as part of a narrative description that presents the patient's medical condition in an experiential, subjective format. To be noted also is the interpreter's comment ('he has a hard time ah: describing it' in line 37) that similarly to the previous excerpt, presents the interpreter's own analysis of his interaction with the patient.

On the basis of the analysis in this section, it is possible to conclude that the interpreter displays a preference for objective, decontextualized representations of symptoms. In fact, patients' narrative, contextualized, subjective accounts, especially those presenting the causally contingent nature of the symptoms, are rejected and, sometimes, sanctioned by the interpreter. For example, the interpreter is found to suppress patients' lay explanations of illness which correlate occurrences of physical symptoms to weather conditions. In other words, the interpreter's summary translations are given in the 'voice of medicine'. At the same time, the interpreter dismisses patients' contributions offered in the 'voice of lifeworld' and does not include them in the summary translations (Mishler, 1984: 114).

The effects for the doctor of the exclusion of the patient's voice from the translation are, of course, hard to overestimate. Since interpreters have no (or very little) medical education, they are not qualified to make medical decisions about what is and what is not relevant for the diagnosis and treatment of the patient's condition. Thus, the observed conflict between the two 'voices' – the 'voice of medicine' and the 'voice of the lifeworld' – is not simply a theoretical issue. In fact, it may result in the exclusion of the patients' perspective from the medical interaction, and, in some cases, in the misrepresentation of medically relevant facts.[13]

Conclusion

The analysis of the interpreter's involvement in the activity of history taking has shown that the interpreter's actions are organized vis-a-vis the goals of this activity. Thus, first, interpreter-initiated questions directed to the patient are found to address a set of medical contingencies for diagnosis and treatment related to the symptom brought up in the doctor's initial question. In other words, the interpreter's questions pursue issues that are diagnostically relevant. Second, these questions display the interpreter's orientation to obtaining objective, decontextualized representations of information – information that could be used more easily in diagnosing the patient's condition. Third, the questions are designed and sequenced in such a way as to expedite the task of collecting relevant information from the patient. We have seen that in pursuit of appropriate patient responses, the interpreter poses questions that are progressively more close-ended, thus placing more limits on what the patient can appropriately do in response. Additionally, many of the interpreter's questions are negatively formulated *yes/no* questions that prefer minimal responses from the patient and, thus, attempt to limit patients' possibilities for presenting elaborate accounts of their concerns.

The interpreter's orientation to achieving the goals of the history-taking interview in a most efficient manner is also evident in summary translations offered to the doctor. Usually, in summarizing his conversation with the patient, the interpreter only conveys information related to the medical contingencies, and leaves out information presented by the patient if it is unrelated to that set of contingencies. Additionally, patients' narrative, experiential, subjective accounts are rejected and excluded from summary translations.

These findings have two important implications – one social and one analytical. We have seen that during history-taking interviews interpreters may adopt what Elliot Mishler (1984) calls the 'voice of medicine'. In other words, inter-prefers' turns can be designed in such a way as to display their exclusive orientation towards obtaining and conveying information that is relevant within the medical epistemological framework. Such involvement on the part of the interpreter decreases or even eliminates patients' chances of literally getting 'heard' by their doctors. Given interpreters' lack of medical expertise, their interventions may have negative consequences on the quality of medical care received by patients who lack linguistic skills in the majority language.

This problem raises the issue of importance of conducting an interactionally-sophisticated analysis of actual interpreting practices. The article has demonstrated that interpreting is a complex activity that cannot be understood as the straight forward rendering of other people's talk in another language. Interpreters' actions are shaped not only by other people's talk, but also by their own independent analysis of the ongoing activity and the specific requirements it poses for the participants. Clearly, further research on interpreting is needed to elucidate details on how different activity systems organize the interpreter's participation in the interaction. However, it is already apparent that in order to provide an adequate account of the practice of medical interpreting – an account that would give an accurate representation of what actually happens in doctors' offices – we need to analyze interpreting as a situated, locally organized activity embedded in a particular setting.

Acknowledgements

I am indebted to John Heritage for numerous invaluable discussions we have had about this paper and for his encouragement throughout my work on the project. I would also like to thank Chuck Goodwin for many fascinating insights that have greatly informed the argument developed here and Jeff Robinson for his extensive comments on an earlier version of the paper.

Notes

1 Wadensjö (1992) reviews a number of other studies on medical interpreting.
2 A similar distinction is made by Knapp-Potthoff and Knapp (1986) and Wadensjö (1992).
3 QM stands for 'question marker'.
4 Note that in Russian verbs are not marked for progressive vs. habitual aspect. Therefore, the interpreter's words in line 4 can be translated as either 'Do you have a chest pain?' or 'Are you having a chest pain?' Note also that the appropriate Russian term for 'chest pain' is, literally, 'heart pain'. Therefore, the interpreter's translation of the doctor's 'chest pain' as 'heart pain' is quite accurate.
5 See, for example Pomerantz (1984) and Schegloff and Sacks (1973).
6 See, for example, Pomerantz (1984) and Sacks (1987).
7 The fact that 'it' refers to the heart is fully transparent in Russian. The pronoun is co-referential with 'it' in the previous TCU which, in turn, is co-referential with 'heart' in line 4 (the pronouns and the noun are marked for the same neuter gender).
8 This, again, is clearer in Russian than it is in the English translation. When a problem with a body part is described, the body part in question appears in the

subject position of the sentence (in the nominative case), followed by a predicate formulating what the problem is. For example: 'The heart/the throat/the leg . . . hurts/aches/ . . .'

9 Note that the patient uses an impersonal verb form in Russian with no overt subject noun phrase that can be translated into English as 'it happens'. So the pronouns 'it' in lines 6 and 7 are *not* co-referential.

10 To my knowledge, the interactional functions of the 'ну' particle in Russian have not been investigated. I have noticed that when it prefixes second pair parts (such as responses to questions), 'ну' seems to function similarly to English 'well'. When prefixing questions, however, 'ну' seems to imply problematicity or rejection of the preceding turn.

11 This conjunction is, thus, different from the English 'and', in several ways. For example, *a*-prefixed questions do not seem to have the interactional functions of the *and*-prefixed questions in English described in Heritage and Sorjonen (1994). The interactional properties of this conjunction have not been investigated, however (for a functional account, see, for example Grenoble, 1998; Yokoyama, 1981).

12 In Russian, *yes/no* questions can be formulated in three principal ways: (a) by adding the question marker 'ли' (usually after the verb); (b) as an assertion with questioning intonation; and (c) as an assertion with a tag. The three alternatives are not equal in terms of preference organization. It can be suggested that the three formats are ranked in the following way:

(a) Questions with the question marker are the most neutral. For example:
Болит-ли у   вас серце?
hurts-QM with you heart?
Do you have chest pain?

(b) Assertions with questioning intonation prefer a conforming response. For example:
У   вас серце болит?
with you heart hurts
You have chest pain?

(c) Assertions with a tag strongly prefer a conforming response. For example:
У   вас серце болит, да?
with you heart hurts   right
You have chest pain, don't you/right?

These observations are, however, subject to further research.

13 For a discussion of the exclusion of patients' perspective and the consequences of such exclusion on medical care, see, for example, Barsky (1981), Fisher (1991), Larsson, Säljö and Aronson (1987), Lipkin *et al.* (1995), McWhinney (1981, 1989), Sankar (1986), and Todd (1984, 1989).

References

Civil Rights Act of 1964, §601, 78 Stat 252.

Athorp, C. and Downing, B. T. (1996) 'Modes of Doctor–Patient Communication: How Interpreter Roles Influence Discourse', paper presented at the 1996 Annual Conference of the American Association for Applied Linguistics, Chicago, March.

Australian Bureau of Statistics (1997) *1996 Census of Population and Housing: Basic Community Profile.* Canberra: Australia.

Baker, D. W., Parker, R. M., Williams, M. V., Coates, W. C. and Pitkin, K. (1996) 'Use and Effectiveness of Interpreters in an Emergency Department', *JAMA* 275(10): 783–8.

Barsky, A. J. (1981) 'Hidden Reasons Some Patients Visit Doctors', *Annals of Internal Medicine* 94: 492–8.

Bates, B., Bickley, L. S. and Hoekelman, R. A. (1995) *Physical Examination and History Taking* (6th ed.). Philadelphia: J.B. Lippincott.

Billings, J. A. and Stoeckle, J. D. (1989) *The Clinical Encounter: A Guide to the Medical Interview and Case Presentation.* Chicago: Year Book Medical Publishers.

Boyd, E. and Heritage, J. (forthcoming) 'Analyzing History-Taking in Primary Care: Questioning and Responding during Verbal Examination', in J. Heritage and D. W. Maynard (eds) *Practising Medicine: Structure and Process in Primary Care Encounters.* Cambridge: Cambridge University Press.

Broeder, P. and Extra, G. (1999) *Language, Ethnicity and Education: Case Studies on Immigrant Minority Groups and Immigrant Minority Languages.* Philadelphia, PA: Multilingual Matters.

Brooks, T. R. (1992) 'Pitfalls in Communication with Hispanic and African-American Patients: Do Translators Help or Harm?', *Journal of the National Medical Association* 84(11): 941–7.

Byrne, P. S. and Long, B. E. L. (1976) *Doctors Talking to Patients: A Study of the Verbal Behaviour of General Practitioners Consulting in their Surgeries.* London: Her Majesty's Stationery Office.

Downing, B. T. (1991, December) 'Professional Interpretation: Ensuring Access of Refugee and Immigrant Patients', paper presented at the National Conference on the Health and Mental Health of Soviet Refugees, Chicago.

Drew, P. and Heritage, J. (1992) 'Analyzing talk at work: an introduction', in P. Drew and J. Heritage (eds) *Talk at Work: Interaction in Institutional Settings*, pp. 1–65. New York: Cambridge University Press.

Fisher, S. (1991) 'A Discourse of the Social: Medical Talk/Power Talk/Oppositional Talk?', *Discourse and Society* 2(2): 157–82.

Frankel, R. M. (1990) 'Talking in Interviews: A Dispreference for Patient-initiated Questions in Physician–Patient Encounters', in G. Psathas (ed.) *Interaction Competence*, pp. 231–62. Washington, DC: University Press of America.

Giacomelli, J. (1997) A Review of Health Interpreter Services in a Rural Community: A Total Quality Management Approach', *Australian Journal of Rural Health* 5(3): 158–64.

Goodwin, C. (1994) 'Professional Vision', *American Anthropologist* 96(3): 606–33.

Greenberger, N. J. and Hinthorn, D. R. (1993) *History Taking and Physical Examination: Essentials and Clinical Correlates.* St Louis, MO: Mosby Year Book.

Grenoble, L. A. (1998) *Deixis and Information Packaging in Russian Discourse.* Philadelphia: John Benjamins.

Hatton, D. C. (1992) 'Information Transmission in Bilingual, Bicultural Contexts', *Journal of Community Health Nursing* 9(1): 53–9.

Hatton, D. C. and Webb, T. (1993) 'Information Transmission in Bilingual, Bicultural Contexts: A Field Study of Community Health Nurses and Interpreters', *Journal of Community Health Nursing* 10(3): 137–47.

Heath, C. (1986) *Body Movement and Speech in Medical Interaction.* New York: Cambridge University Press.

Heritage, J. and Sorjonen, M.-L. (1994) 'Constituting and Maintaining Activities Across Sequences: *and*-prefacing as a Feature of Question Design', *Language in Society* 23(1): 1–29.

Hornberger, J. C., Gibson, C. D. J., Wood, W., Dequeldre, C., Corso, I., Palla, B. and Bloch, D. A. (1996) 'Eliminating Language Barriers for Non-English-Speaking Patients', *Medical Care* 34(8): 845–56.

Hornberger, J. C., Itakura, H. and Wilson, S. R. (1997) 'Bridging Language and Cultural Barriers Between Physicians and Patients', *Public Health Reports* 112(5): 410–17.

Knapp-Potthoff, A. and Knapp, K. (1986) 'Interweaving Two Discourses: The Difficult Task of the Non-professional Interpreter', in J. House and S. Blum-Kulka (eds) *Interlingual and Intercultural Communication: Discourse and Cognition in Translation and Second Language Acquisition Studies*, pp. 151–68. New York: Mouton.

Korsch, B. M. and Negrete, V. F. (1972) 'Doctor–Patient Communication', *Scientific American* 227: 66–74.

Larsson, U. S., Säljö, R. and Aronson, K. (1987) 'Patient–Doctor Communication on Smoking and Drinking: Lifestyle in Medical Consultations', *Social Science and Medicine* 25(10): 1129–37.

Lerner, G. H. (1987) 'Collaborative Turn Sequences: Sentence Construction and Social Action', unpublished PhD thesis, University of California at Irvine.

Lipkin, M. Jr, Frankel, R. M., Beckman, H. B., Charon, R. and Fein, O. (1995) 'Performing the Interview', in M. Lipkin Jr, S. M. Putman, and A. Lazare (eds) *The Medical Interview: Clinical Care, Education and Research*, pp. 65–82. New York: Springer-Verlag.

McWhinney, I. (1981) *An Introduction to Family Medicine*. New York: Oxford University Press.

McWhinney, I. (1989) 'The Need for a Transformed Clinical Method', in M. Stewart and D. T. Roter (eds) *Communicating with Medical Patients*. Newbury Park, CA: Sage.

Meehan, A. J. (1981) 'Some Conversational Features of the Use of Medical Terms by Doctors and Patients', in P. Atkinson and C. Heath (eds) *Medical Work: Realities and Routines*, pp. 107–27. Aldershot: Gower.

Mishler, E. G. (1984) *The Discourse of Medicine: Dialectics of Medical Interviews*. Norwood, NJ: Ablex.

Pomerantz, A. (1984) 'Agreeing and Disagreeing with Assessments: Some Features of Preferred/Dispreferred Turn Shapes', in J. M. Atkinson and J. Heritage (eds) *Structures of Social Action: Studies in Conversation Analysis*, pp. 57–101. New York: Cambridge University Press.

Raymond, G. (1998) *A Preference for Conforming Answers?* Unpublished PhD proposal, Department of Sociology, UCLA.

Robinson, J. D. (1999) 'The Organization of Action and Activity in General Practice, Doctor–patient Consultations'. Unpublished PhD thesis, University of California, Los Angeles.

Roter, D. T. and Hall, J. H. (1992) *Doctors Talking with Patients/Patients Talking with Doctors: Improving Communication in Medical Visits*. Westport, CT: Auburn House.

Sacks, H. (1987) 'On the Preferences for Agreement and Contiguity in Sequences in Conversation', in G. Button and J. R. E. Lee (eds) *Talk and Social Organization*, pp. 54–69. Philadelphia: Multilingual Matters.

Sacks, H., Schegloff, E. A. and Jefferson, G. (1974) 'A Simplest Systematics for the Organization of Turn-taking for Conversation', *Language* 50: 696–735.

Sankar, A. (1986) 'Out of the Clinic into the Home: Control and Patient–doctor Communication', *Social Science and Medicine* 22(9): 973–82.

Schegloff, E. A. (1987) 'Analyzing Single Episodes of Interaction: An Exercise in Conversation Analysis', *Social Psychology Quarterly* 50(2): 101–14.

Schegloff, E. A. (1988) 'Presequences and Indirection: Applying Speech Act Theory to Ordinary Conversation', *Journal of Pragmatics* 12: 55–62.

Schegloff, E. A. and Sacks, H. (1973) 'Opening up Closings', *Semiotica* 8(4): 289–327.

Seidel, H. M., Ball, J. W., Dains, J. E. and Benedict, G. W. (1995) *Mosbys Guide to Physical Examination* (3rd ed.). St Louis, MO: Mosby Year Book.

Swartz, M. H. (1998) *Textbook of Physical Diagnosis: History and Examination* (3rd ed.). Philadelphia: W.B. Saunders.

Ten Have, P. (1991) 'Talk and Institution: A Reconsideration of the "Asymmetry" of Doctor–Patient Interaction', in D. Boden and D. H. Zimmerman (eds) *Talk and Social Structure*, pp. 138–63. Cambridge: Polity Press.

Todd, A. D. (1984) 'The Prescription of Contraception: Negotiating Between Doctors and Patients', *Discourse Processes* 7: 171–200.

Todd, A. D. (1989) *Intimate Adversaries: Cultural Conflicts Between Doctors and Women Patients*. Philadelphia: University of Pennsylvania Press.

US Bureau of the Census (1993) *Statistical Abstract of the US 1990 Census* (113th edn). Washington, DC: US Bureau of the Census.

Wadensjö, C. (1992) *Interpreting as interaction: On Dialogue-interpreting in Immigration Hearings and Medical Encounters*. Linköping, Sweden: Linköping University.

Wadensjö, C. (1998) *Interpreting as Interaction*. New York: Longman.

Waitzkin, H. (1985) 'Information Giving in Medical Care', *Journal of Health and Social Behavior* 26(2): 81–101.

Waitzkin, H. (1991) *The Politics of Medical Encounters: How Patients and Doctors Deal with Social Problems*. New Haven, CT: Yale University Press.

Yokoyama, O. T. (1981) 'On Sentence Coordination in Russian: A Functional Approach', in *Papers from the 17th Regional Meeting*, pp. 431–438. Chicago: Chicago Linguistic Society.

Zoppi, K. A. (1997) 'Interviewing as Clinical Conversation', in M. B. Mengel and S. A. Fields (eds) *Introduction to Clinical Skills: A Patient-centered Textbook*, pp. 41–55. New York: Plenum Medical Book Company.

Part 12

VOICE, POSITIONALITY, SUBJECTIVITY

52

THE TRANSLATOR'S VOICE IN TRANSLATED NARRATIVE

Theo Hermans

Source: *Target* 8(1) (1996): 23–48.

Abstract

When we read translated narrative, the original Narrator's voice is not the only which comes to us. The Translator's discursive presence in the translated text becomes discernible in certain cases, e.g. when the pragmatic displacement resulting from translation requires paratextual intervention for the benefit of the Implied Reader of the translated text; when self-reflexive references to the medium of communication itself are involved; when 'contextual overdetermination' leaves no other option. The ways in which the Translator's discursive presence manifests itself are demonstrated on the basis of different translations of the Dutch novel *Max Havelaar* (1860).

1.

When Boris Yeltsin speaks through an Interpreter, do we really want to hear the Interpreter's voice? We listen, surely, because we want to know what Yeltsin has to say. To the extent that we are conscious of hearing the Interpreter's voice, it is as no more than a minor distraction. We regard — or better: we are prepared, we have been conditioned to regard — the Interpreter's voice as a carrier without a substance of its own, a virtually transparent vehicle. Anything that takes away from this transparency is unwelcome 'noise' in the information-theoretical sense of the term.

At the same time we know perfectly well that, unless we understand Russian, the Interpreter's voice is all we have. It is all we have access to, all we can make sense of on this side of the language barrier. Even when on radio or television, for example, we can still hear Yeltsin's Russian in the background, we do not understand those words and so we shut them out, realizing they are being broadcast alongside the interpretation only to authenticate the Interpreter's re-enunciation. We are not unduly bothered about not having direct access to Yeltsin's language because we know we can trust the Interpreter's professionalism. We trust that the Interpreter's words are an accurate and truthful copy or reproduction of Yeltsin's words. This trust, underpinned as it is by a number of professional and institutional guarantees, allows us to accept, or to project, the Interpreter's discourse as matching Yeltsin's, as constituting the equivalent of it, as coinciding with it, as being, to all intents and purposes, identical with it.

Of course, as soon as we stop to reflect on the various a-symmetrical interlingual and intercultural processes taking place in the operation, we realize we are entertaining an illusion. The translation never coincides with its source, it is not identical or equivalent in any formal or straightforward sense, and it remains to be seen how the notion of the one discourse 'matching' the other is to be filled in. But the illusion is there, and necessarily there. It is part and parcel of what we, in our culture, have come to understand by 'translation'. It fits, that is, our ideology of translation, which is backed up by a vast amount of translation theory and history and by all manner of institutionalized agreements governing relations between primary and secondary texts, up to and including such things as intellectual ownership, copyright laws, authorized translations, legally certified copies, professional codes of conduct, etc. Translation, in this context, is delegated speech, and the delegate has no executive powers.

The illusion, then, the necessary illusion, is one of transparency and coincidence as exponents of equivalence. As the Interpreter's voice falls in with, coincides with and in so doing — paradoxically — disappears behind Yeltsin's voice, the physical experience of hearing two distinct voices speaking more or less simultaneously is suppressed, or sublimated, and in practice we consider the two voices to be wholly consonant. Even as we listen to the one voice we are able to follow, we negate its presence because we recognize its substantial and institutionally endorsed conformity to the primary enunciation, which, we accept, has integrity, authority, and therefore primacy. We conclude that 'Yeltsin has said so and so'. Because it has no substance of its own, the re-enunciation in the other language assumes the quality of direct quotation.[1]

2.

Although interpreting, as a rule, involves the simultaneous physical presence of two individuals and two voices in the same space, there are good grounds for arguing that very much the same factors, and the same illusion of transparency and coincidence, are at work in written translation, and in translated fiction. Perhaps the illusion is even stronger here.

Consider for a moment a certified translation of a degree certificate. The stamp issued by a third party declaring the translation to be a 'true copy' of the original reminds the user that this is a translation: the stamp marks the distance between original and translation (usually also identifying the sworn translator by name), but at the same time as formalizing their differential status it asserts that the copy is 'as good as' the original. Next, consider a translation, say, of a safety regulation in a large international concern, which first issues the new regulation in the head office and then has it translated into a number of languages for use in its subsidiary plants. In each country this version subsequently becomes one regulation among several, and the translators' interventions, including their proper names, are completely erased. Whether the translators are the firm's own employees or the job was contracted out to a translation agency, all concerned have every reason to take it for granted that the translation constitutes a truthful copy of the original. Translators, after all, like interpreters, speak in someone else's name and thus they are expected to subscribe to what Brian Harris has called the 'true interpreter' norm, or the 'honest spokesperson' norm, which "requires that people who speak on behalf of others . . . re-express the original speakers' ideas and the manner of expressing them as accurately as possible and without significant omissions, and not mix them up with their own ideas and expressions" (Harris 1990: 118). The translator is expected to observe total discretion.

Although nowadays many works of translated fiction routinely carry the translator's name and in this respect resemble the 'certified copy', in the way they are read they are mostly closer to the second case just mentioned. While reading translated fiction, readers are normally meant to forget that what they are reading is a translation. The translator withdraws wholly behind the narrating voice. So whose voice comes to us when we read a translated novel? Common usage is indicative. We tend to say that we are reading Dostoyevsky, for example, even when we are reading not Russian but English or French or Spanish words. This blotting out, this 'erasure' of the translator's intervention is paradoxical. In contrast to simultaneous or especially consecutive interpreting, with two speakers sharing a given physical space, when we read translated fiction we have only the translated text in front of us. The primary voice, the authoritative originary voice, is in fact absent. And yet we casually state it is the only one that presents itself to us. And in practice we do so largely, perhaps wholly, on the strength of the hierarchy implied by the order (and, more often than not, the size) of the names on the title page:

NOVEL by Writer X
Translated by Translator Y

The question arises: is the illusion of 'I am reading Dostoyevsky' all there is to it? Does the translator, the manual labour done, disappear without textual trace, speaking entirely 'under erasure'? Can translators usurp the original voice and in the same move evacuate their own enunciatory space? Exactly whose voice comes to us when we read translated discourse?

The question can be examined from a variety of angles, including an ideological one. In what follows it is treated first and foremost as a narratological issue, asking about the voice that produces the discourse that we read, and therefore asking about the discursive centre from which the text issues. Let us remind ourselves of the standard representation of narrative communication:[2]

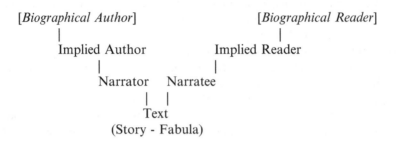

This scheme represents the normal situation, without reference to translation. What we read is a discourse produced by a Narrator. In translated fiction, who exactly articulates the translated discourse? It is the same Narrator as in the source text? Does this then mean that the translator, as Biographical Translator, is like the Biographical Author: another name on the title page, indicating an entity located firmly outside the narrative discourse?

As it is, narratology does not distinguish between original and translated fiction. The main narratological models currently available (Booth, Stanzel, Genette, Rimmon-Kenan, Bal, Chatman. Prince) are designed to apply to narrative texts in general, irrespective of whether they are original or translated. In what follows I will argue that these models overlook a presence in the narrative text that cannot be fully suppressed.[3] Translated narrative discourse, it will be claimed, always implies more than one voice in the text, more than one discursive presence. It may be that in many narratives this 'other' voice never clearly manifests itself, but it should nevertheless be postulated, on the strength of those cases where it is manifestly present and discernible. And it is only, I submit, the ideology of translation, the illusion of transparency and coincidence, the illusion of the one voice, that blinds us to the presence of this other voice.

3.

The claim, then, is that translated narrative discourse always contains a 'second' voice, to which I will refer as the Translator's voice, as an index of the Translator's discursive presence. The voice may be more or less overtly present. It may remain entirely hidden behind that of the Narrator, rendering it impossible to detect in the translated text. It is most directly and forcefully present when it breaks through the surface of the text speaking for itself, in its own name, for example in a paratextual Translator's Note employing an autoreferential first person identifying the speaking subject.[4] And then there are shades and degrees in between.

As far as I can make out, the 'other' voice in translated narrative texts is likely to manifest itself primarily in three kinds of cases. They all involve what may be termed 'performative self-contradiction' in that the Translator's self-denial runs into obvious, textually traceable contradictions. In each case there is a certain pressure on the Translator to come out of the shadows and directly intervene in a text which the reader had been led to believe spoke with only one voice. They are

(1) cases where the text's orientation towards an Implied Reader and hence its ability to function as a medium of communication is directly at issue;
(2) cases of self-reflexiveness and self-referentiality involving the medium of communication itself;
(3) certain cases of what, for want of a better term, I will refer to as 'contextual overdetermination'.

In each case the degree of visibility of the Translator's presence depends on the translation strategy that has been adopted, and on the consistency with which it has been carried through. Since each of the three cases listed, and certainly cases (1) and (2), involve a kind of communicative short-circuiting, a fissure within the discourse which draws attention to the linguistic and pragmatic dislocation that comes with translation, the resulting incongruity in the translated text needs to be accounted for in one way or another. Some translation strategies will effectively paper over the cracks and leave the reader unaware of the other voice. My interest here is in those instances where the translated text itself shows visible traces of a discursive presence other than the ostensible Narrator. Before illustrating the case with reference to a particular translation, a further word about the first two cases mentioned above; the third will be elucidated later, with reference to a concrete example.

As for (1): Unlike interpreting, where speaker and interpreter more or less simultaneously address a physically present if linguistically mixed audience, written translations normally address an audience which is not only linguistically but also temporally and/or geographically removed from that addressed by the source text. To the extent that a Reader is implied by and implicated in the overall 'intent' (Chatman) and orchestration of narrative fiction, translated narrative fiction addresses an Implied Reader different from that of the source text, since the discourse operates in a new pragmatic context. All texts are culturally embedded and require a frame of reference which is shared between sender and receiver to be able to function as vehicles for communication. The various forms of displacement that result from translation (Folkart 1991: 347ff. speaks of a 'décalage traductionnel') threaten this shared frame of reference. It is therefore not surprising to find that it is precisely with respect to the cultural embedding of texts, e.g. in the form of historical or topical references and allusions, that the Translator's Voice often directly and openly intrudes into the discourse to provide information deemed necessary to safeguard adequate communication with the new audience. As a rule, translations, and certainly modern translations of canonical literary fiction, stop short of reorienting the discourse so radically that the orientation to the original Implied Reader disappears altogether. The translated text can therefore be said to address a dual audience, and thus to have a 'secondary' Implied Reader superimposed on the original one. This can lead to hybrid situations in which the discourse offers manifestly redundant or inadequate information, or appears attuned to one type of Reader here and another there, showing the Translator's presence in and through the discordances.

As for (2): 'self-reflexiveness' and 'self-referentiality' are used here as rather broad terms covering various instances which have been discussed as exemplifying untranslatability by. among others. Jacques Derrida. Obvious cases are texts which affirm their being written in a particular language, or which exploit the economy of their idiom through polysemy, wordplay and similar devices. We are dealing, then, with instances in which language collapses upon itself, as it were, or, as Derrida would have it. 're-marks' itself. It is of course possible that the translated text solves the problems so discreetly that no trace of a 'second voice' is left behind. But sometimes translations run into contradictions and incongruities which challenge the reader's willing suspension of disbelief: or the translated text may call on the explicit intervention of a Translator's Voice through the use of brackets or of notes, and they then remind the reader of this other presence continually stalking a purportedly univocal discourse.

Examples of linguistic self-referentiality are not hard to find, and they are not restricted to narrative texts. In translations of many of Derrida's essays meta-linguistic notes or comments are added by translators in their attempts to cope with the French puns. Nowhere is this more in evidence than in 'Survivre: Journal de bord', where the lower band of the page, the 'journal de bord', openly challenges the translator to render the French puns ('pas de méthode', 'point de méthode', the series 'écrit, récit, série', etc.); again and again the English translation has recourse to square brackets in an effort to keep up, overtly displaying the translated nature of the text by showing the translator's hand (see e.g. Derrida 1991: 256ff.).

Derrida's discussion, elsewhere,[5] of a rather different instance of language affirming itself concerns the final chapter of Descartes' *Discours de la Méthode*, where in the French original the author declares that his book is written in French and not in Latin. The Latin translation omits this embarrassing sentence, to avoid the self-contradiction of a statement in Latin declaring it is not in Latin but in French. Derrida regards this as a case of institutional and statutory untranslatability, which is a perfectly valid observation. For the reader of the Latin version, however, the omission is not detectable and therefore does not reveal the translator's presence in the translated text as such. In translations into languages other than Latin, where the sentence *is* translated, the self-contradiction may be less glaring, but it is still obvious enough. When the English version has: "And if I write in French . . . rather than in Latin . . . it is because . . ." (Descartes 1968: 91), the anomaly of reading an English text which declares, in English, that it is actually in French creates a credibility gap which readers can overcome only by reminding themselves that this is, of course, a translation. But in so doing those readers also realize that the voice producing the statement cannot possibly belong to Descartes, or to Descartes alone. There is, clearly, another voice at play, duplicating and mimicking the first one. but with a timbre of its own. Derrida himself exploits the paradox in his 1984 address "Ulysse gramophone", which opens with the sentence: "Oui, oui, vous m'entendez bien, ce sont des mots francais", and leads to an inevitable if self-conscious self-contradiction in the English translation: "*Oui, oui*, you are receiving me, these are French words" (Derrida 1992: 256).

4.

In the following pages I will illustrate these points in more detail, with reference to several translations of a single book, the Dutch novel *Max Havelaar* by Multatuli, first published in 1860. With its complex narrative structure *Max Havelaar* provides instances not only of cultural embedding and linguistic self-referentiality, but also of 'contextual overdetermination', all of them, to varying degrees, bringing the Translator's voice to the textual surface. I will refer to two English translations, by W. Siebenhaar (1927) and Roy Edwards (1967, re-issued as a Penguin Classic 1987); and to the French and the Spanish translations by Mme Roland Garros (1968) and Francisco Carrasquer (1975), respectively. There are other translations, including older renderings into English and French as well as versions into German and other languages, but the four considered here will do for the purposes of the present exposition. The Dutch text referred to is the stand-ard scholarly 'historical-critical' edition (1992), which is based on the novel's fifth and last edition (1881) to appear during the author's lifetime.[6]

The Biographical Author of *Max Havelaar* is Eduard Douwes Dekker (1820–1887), who wrote under the pseudonym Multatuli. The novel was dedicated to Everdine Huberte van Wijnbergen.[7] In its barest essence the book tells the story of Max Havelaar, a Dutch civil servant in the colonial administration in the Dutch East Indies in the 1850s. Witnessing the exploitation of the local population by the native elite, he protests in vain to his immediate superior. When he ignores the administrative hierarchy and brings a charge against the local ruler he is relieved of his post and resigns in disgust.

The novel's unusual richness, however, springs at least in part from its narrative structure and its use of different narrators. The opening chapters employ the homodiegetic narrator Batavus Droogstoppel, an Amsterdam coffee broker and the epitome of Dutch petit-bourgeois values and hypocrisy. One day Droogstoppel runs into a former schoolmate, the destitute Sjaalman, who leaves him a bundle of documents which Droogstoppel reckons he can use for a book on the coffee trade. However, he delegates the writing to a young German trainee in his firm, the romantic Stern who, assisted by Droogstoppel's son Frits and probably helped by Sjaalman himself, writes an altogether different book, which is being composed as we read. Stern thus becomes the narrator of the dramatic story of Max Havelaar and his wife Tine in the East Indies. As the novel continues. Droogstoppel occasionally breaks into Stern's discourse to voice his disapproval of the way Stern is handling his material. In the Havelaar episodes, meanwhile, the Stern-Narrator dishes up other stories as well as documents purporting to authenticate Havelaar's conflict with his superiors. The novel's concluding pages contain the main surprise, as another first-person Narrator identifying himself as Multatuli suddenly takes over from Stern, dismisses Droogstoppel. and addresses the Dutch King with an impassioned plea to stop the oppression of the natives in the East Indies.

The different narrative levels in *Max Havelaar* may be represented schematically as follows:

DROOGSTOPPEL (in Amsterdam)
= *I-Narrator$_1$*
'you' addressee = the Dutch reader
→ Droogstoppel delegates narration to
        STERN (in Amsterdam)
        = *I-Narrator$_2$*
        'you' addressee = the Dutch reader
        → story of **Max Havelaar**, wife Tine etc.
        (in Dutch East Indies)
Final pages: 'I, MULTATULI' takes over as Narrator from Stern and Droogstoppel
= *I-Narrator$_3$*
'you' addressee = the Dutch King

As it happens, there is in *Max Havelaar* an instance similar to the Descartes case mentioned above. In the Dutch text Max Havelaar quotes a poem in French which he says he wrote himself and which is also reproduced in French (*MH*: 127). As Havelaar is Dutch, the poem serves as a signal to the reader, suggesting Havelaar's literary talent and linguistic abilities, favourably contrasting him with the dreary Droogstoppel Figure. The French translation, unable to translate the French poem into itself, merely quotes it (Garros: 186). But it adds a Translator's Note: "En français dans le texte (N.d.T.)".[8] The reason for rupturing the discourse and intervening by means of a paratextual note is clear enough: the surplus value signalled in the original by the use of a different language risks being lost on the French reader. The note itself, however, with or without its curious ambiguity ("dans le texte" is obviously redundant if it means the French text, so it must refer to the Dutch original), reminds its readers that this is a translated text — and at the same time alerts them to the presence of an altogether different voice, breaking through the narrative voice ostensibly established by the discourse. In contrast, a poetic dialogue in German also reported by the Narrator as having been penned by Havelaar (*MH*: 157–160) is left, unannotated, in German in the French translation (Garros: 225–228), revealing not a glimpse of the Translator's presence — except in the dissonance between a Note identifying the language of a French poem in a French text and remaining silent on how to read a poem in a foreign language.

5.

Before going on to consider examples of different ways in which, and degrees to which, the Translator's presence makes itself felt in translations of *Max Havelaar*, it may be useful to point out that they all concern instances where the presence of an enunciating subject other than the Narrator becomes discernible *in the translated text itself*. This means we are *not* looking at cases where only the comparison with the source text will show the intervention of a (biographical) translator, however revealing these manipulations, additions or omissions may be from an ideological or other such point of view. In the Havelaar narrative, for example, the Narrator at one point describes the layout of Havelaar's house in the Indies. In the Dutch, and in the French translation, this is done by means of numbers: imagine a rectangle divided into twenty-one compartments, three across, seven down, etc. (*MH*: 136; Garros: 198). In both the Spanish and the English versions diagrams are added as visual illustrations, without paratextual comment (Carrasquer: 190; Edwards: 224). Since the Spanish and English texts themselves provide no discernible trace of a linguistic subject other than the Narrator as the source of the diagrams, and consequently the intervention by (presumably) the biographical translator can be detected only through a comparison with the source text, such instances are not relevant to the argument being pursued here.

Hence, although the cases highlighted below mostly issue from source text cruxes, they do not focus on the retrospective comparison between translation and original. Rather, as different translations opt for different solutions, some bring the Translator's discursive presence clearly into view while others do not, or to a lesser extent. In each case the assumption is that, given the dominant conception of transparent translation in modern fiction, the reader's awareness of reading a translation lies dormant, leaving intact the notion that (with the exception of embedded narrative and character speech) there is only one Narrator speaking at any one time. As long as there are no markers in the text suggesting another voice, all is well. The following instances, however, concern places where another presence insinuates or parachutes itself into the text, breaking the univocal frame and jolting the reader into an awareness of the text's plurivocal nature.

5.1

A couple of examples will suffice to illustrate the rather obvious case of cultural references which, as a result of the displacement brought about by translation, threaten to be left in a vacuum and prompt the Translator to rupture the narrative frame by means of paratextual Notes.

In Chapter 9 of *Max Havelaar*, in a passage marking a sudden transition from Stern as Narrator (of the Havelaar story) to Droogstoppel as Narrator (of his own story), reference is made to Abraham Blankaart, a fictional character from the Dutch novel *Sara Burgerhart* (1782) by Betje Wolff and Aagje Deken. The name is first dropped in the Stern narrative, and taken up by Droogstoppel. That its recognition requires a Dutch cultural frame of reference is evident from Droogstoppel's comment that his own son Frits has obviously been lending young Stern a hand, for, as he says, "this Abraham Blankaart is much too Dutch for a German" (*MH*: 95). Ironically, in a note added by Multatuli himself to the fourth edition (1875) and retained in subsequent editions (Multatuli 1992, IT: xxxvii), he wondered how many of his own generation still recognized the literary allusion (*MH:* 263), suggesting that even within a specific cultural continuum shared frames of reference are time-bound phenomena.

Both English translations and the Spanish version at this point break into the text to insert a Translator's Note explaining the reference (Siebenhaar: 122–123; Edwards: 134–135; Carrasquer: 155–156).[9] The French translation retains the name, without an explanatory note; a second occurrence of the name, in the next paragraph, has been omitted (Garros: 142–143). This seems consistent, and at first sight does not allow the reader a view of the Translator's discursive presence. But before this passage other instances have occurred where Translator's Notes, identified as such, explained linguistic or cultural issues arising from the source text (Garros: 36, 38, 58, 60, 87, 108, . . .). It is precisely the inconsistency in the provision of paratextual information designed to safeguard the shared frame of reference which creates a disparity at the discursive level: the helpful voice which came to the French reader's rescue on other occasions remains inexplicably silent here. The deliberate silence of the voice, withholding information which is expected, signals the presence of a discursive subject different from either of the two homodiegetic Narrators whose words we read. As we are reading a translation, this 'differential voice' can only be the Translator's.[10]

A similar inference can be made, incidentally, with respect to the proper names in several of the translations. *Max Havelaar* is set in a particular place and time: the Netherlands and the Dutch East Indies in the 1850s. The proper names of the Dutch characters are recognizably Dutch. Some, like Havelaar, Bastiaans, Busselinck, Verbrugge, are proper names in the conventional sense; others are more Dickensian, motivated names, holding out an invitation to the reader to activate their latent semantic load. Roy Edwards' English translation copies most of the names intact, including e.g. the suggestive 'Droogstoppel' (paratextually annotated as meaning 'Drystubble', 'Dryasdust', which is the way the name was rendered in the two previous English translations). With a name like 'Slimering' (Dutch: 'Slymering'), luck is on the Translator's side, as minimal adaptation preserves the satirical intent without revealing the Translator's presence. But the pompous preacher Wawelaar appears in the text as 'Parson Blatherer', creating a sudden incongruity within the pattern of proper names which stretches the reader's willingness to suspend disbelief: an obviously Dutch character, in a Dutch setting, with so transparent and apposite an English name, yet without explanation" Given the otherwise consistent discourse of the Narrators delivering the story, the source of the disparity must surely be attributed to another discursive presence.

5.2

The name of the character Sjaalman in *Max Havelaar* is a special case. This is not a proper name at all, as Droogstoppel. the Narrator at this point, declines to tell us the person's real name (which the reader will infer later). It is first introduced as a descriptive term ("the man with the shawl, or scarf"), then contracted into 'de Sjaalman' ("the Shawl-man"), and Droogstoppel subsequently decides to continue to call the man 'Sjaalman' as if that were his name. The first occurrence of the designation is accompanied by Droogstoppel's metalinguistic comment to the effect that his son Frits prefers the English word 'shawl' to Droogstoppel's good old Dutch 'sjaal'. It is the first in a series of linguistic quibbles through which Droogstoppel characterizes himself as a pedant:

> In-plaats van een behoorlyken winterjas, hing hem een soort van sjaal over den schouder — Frits zegt: '*shawl*', maar dit doe ik niet — alsof hy zoo van de reis kwam.
>
> (*MH*: 10)

The translations render the passage as follows:

Instead of a suitable winter coat, he had a kind of shawl hanging over his shoulder — Frits says 'Châle': he is learning French, but I keep to our good old language — as if he had just come from a journey.

(Siebenhaar: 12–13)

Instead of a decent winter coal he had a sort of scarf dangling over his shoulder — we call it a *sjaal* in Dutch, so Frits has to call it a 'shawl', which isn't even right, just to show off his English — as if he — the scarf-man, I mean — was just back from being on the road.

(Edwards: 27)

Aunque en lugar de llevar gabán, como habría sido lo propio, colgaba de sus hombros una especie de bufanda or largo chal — Frits dice pañuelo de cuello, pero yo no paso por ahí — como si acabara de llegar de algún viaje.

(Carrasquer: 22)

Au lieu d'un pardessus convenable, une sorte de châle couvrait ses épaules, comme s'il rentrait de voyage.

(Garros: 36)

Neither Garros (on this page) nor Carrasquer upset the reading process, and hence the fictional universe, as neither text leaves the language the reader is engaged in. Garros omits Frits' use of a foreign term, and Carrasquer employs an intralingual variant. As Sjaalman's descriptive designation turns into a proper name, the Spanish version continues with 'Chalman'. At that stage the French translation runs into a linguistic problem: since "homme au châle" will not double up as a proper name in French, the transition from designation to name cannot take place within the terms first set out for it. The problem is solved by cutting into the text's linguistic homogeneity: the next occurrence has: "Un jour, le Sjaalman que j'avais devant moi était avec nous" and the novel term 'Sjaalman', more than halfway between designation ('*le* Sjaalman') and proper name ('Sjaalman' capitalized), is elucidated in a Translator's Note: "Littéralement: homme au châle (*N.d.T.*)" (Garros: 38). But the linguistic transgression, the Note and the fact that the reference is to the source language of a translation, break the narrative frame. The agent responsible for this discursive act cannot be the Narrator.

Siebenhaar solves the 'sjaal/shawl' problem by substituting 'shawl/châle', English/French for Dutch/English, culturally not dissimilar as a pair, and so the reader's awareness that in fact Droogstoppel is Dutch and speaks Dutch, remains largely dormant (not wholly, as the reader knows that Droogstoppel's 'our good old languae' is Dutch, not English). Edwards' triad 'scarf/sjaal/ shawl' does remind the reader of Droogstoppel's native language — and more than that, since Dutch is not only the language of Droogstoppel as

294

character and (homodiegetic) narrator, but also, inescapably, the source language of the translation as a whole. The occurrence, in the translated text, of a metalinguistic statement bearing coincidentally on both the fictional world (Droogstoppel as a fictional character) and its framing context (a novel translated from the Dutch) highlights a paradox. As readers, we accept the convention, which also operates e.g. in historical fiction or in narratives set in foreign lands, that we read words in one language while we know that the fictional characters, to the extent that they resemble lifelike individuals existing in identifiable locations, must have spoken a different language. In this crux in the English *Max Havelaar* the metalinguistic reference draws attention to that convention itself. This is no doubt partly because it involves the source language of the whole work, as the Translator's paratextual Notes remind us time and again. A further reason is that the 'sjaal/shawl' issue is only one of a series of similar instances of linguistic point-scoring between Droogstoppel and his son, some of which are presented within the terms of the English language while others draw on Dutch. These disparities within the discourse itself prevent the conventional suspension of disbelief and bring into focus the linguistic as well as pragmatic displacement consequent upon the act of translation.

The following passage provides additional illustration. This is Droogstoppel again, taking on Frits on a point of language:

> ... en dat ook de suikerraffinadeurs — Frits zegt: *raffineurs*, maar ik schryf *nadeurs*. Dit doen de Rosemeyers ook, en die *doen* in suiker. Ik weet wel dat men zegt: *geraffineerde* schelm, en niet: *geraffinadeerde* schelm ...
>
> (*MH*: 29)

> ... and that also the sugar-*raffinadeurs* — Frits says refiners, but I write *raffinadeurs*; this the Rosemeyers do also, and they *are* sugar people; I know, one speaks of a *refined* scoundrel, and not a *raffinadeur* scoundrel ...
>
> (Siebenhaar: 36)

> ... and that the sugar refiners, *raffinadeurs* as we say in Dutch — Frits says *raffineurs* but I say *raffinadeurs*; the Rosemeyers do too, and they're *in* sugar. I know one talks about a *geraffineerd* scoundrel, and not a *geraffinadeerd* scoundrel ...
>
> (Edwards: 54)

> ... y que también los refinadores (Frits dice 'refineros', pero yo hago como los demás, incluídos los Rosemeyer, y eso que trabajan en el ramo del azúcar; ya sé que se dice un carterista 'refino' y no refinado, ...
>
> (Carrasquer: 53)

... et que les raffineurs de sucre et les marchands d'indigo dussent y joindre les leurs.

(Garros: 61)

The Spanish translation again solves the linguistic problem within its own linguistic terms and the French version has suppressed it altogether; neither allows a glimpse of the Translator's discursive presence. Both English versions go beyond their own language. The Siebenhaar translation has Droogstoppel using a non-existent English word (the *OED* does not list 'raffinadeur') coupled with Frits' 'refiners'. Apart from the psychological inconsistency in Droogstoppel as a character/narrator who normally insists on solid Dutch values and is here found using a term which the English reader might conceivably (if erroneously) take to be French, there is little to suggest another voice speaking alongside the Narrator's.

In the Edwards version Droogstoppel specifically refers to Dutch as his own language, bringing in three terms: 'refiners', *'raffinadeurs'* and *'raffineurs'*. Curiously, Droogstoppel's discourse here short-circuits itself, as he writes, in English, 'sugar refiners', only to declare in the same breath, "but I say *raffinadeurs"*, a Dutch word. The issue of whether scoundrels are *'geraffineerd'* or *'geraffinadeerd'* will not only be lost on the English reader (both forms contain Dutch morphemes), but will draw further attention to Dutch as the real language of Droogstoppel's fictional world — and as the language of a book which, when the fictional narrative is shattered in the final pages, closes with a direct address by a Dutchman (see below) to the Dutch King. This pulls very closely together the different levels of language which are involved: the language of the fictional characters and narrators, the language of Multatuli's address to the King, and the source language of the translation. What is striking, however, is not so much the paradoxical nature of this situation — convention keeps that under control — but the linguistic anomaly in Droogstoppel's own usage. That anomaly points to a different discursive *locus*, not reducible to Droogstoppel's speech act.

5.3

Max Havelaar is a complex novel not only because of its different narrative levels, but also because it plays, ingeniously and decisively, on the distinction between fiction and non-fiction. A crucial aspect of this is the way in which the narrative levels are linked. Some of these links are immediately obvious, others are established piecemeal, through association, inference, and a number of subtle shifts and hints.[11] In this way it gradually becomes clear to the reader that Max Havelaar, who only appears as a character in Stern's narrative, is in fact the same person as the Sjaalman who later (but, as we read, in the opening chapters) runs into Droogstoppel in Amsterdam and leaves him the documents from which Stern constructs the Havelaar story. Stern also copies the correspondence detailing Havelaar's conflict with his superiors. However, when in the book's final pages Multatuli himself takes over, he radically changes the perspective, emphasizing the factual truth underlying the fictionalized Havelaar story (including the factual truth of the correspondence) and declaring the novel form to have been a mere ploy, since the book is really a tract written in self-justification. Together with a number of other indications (detailed in Sötemann 1972: 67–69, 276–280) this leads to the inescapable conclusion that Havelaar, Sjaalman and Multatuli are all the same individual, thus linking the most deeply embedded narrative level, the Havelaar story, with the framing discourse and the name on the cover and title page.

In the narrative, Havelaar's wife is never called anything but Tine, although she has a handkerchief with the letter E in the coiner, her grandfather is a 'Baron van W.', and we learn her initials: E.H.V.W. In the Droogstoppel narrative Sjaal man's wife is never mentioned by name, but there are certain parallels with Tine. The book's dedication to 'E.H.v.W.' (manuscript and first three editions) and, from the fourth edition onwards, to 'Everdine Huberte Baronnesse van Wynbergen" (*MH*: 1), leaves little doubt that the person in question is the wife of — well, of a pseudonym? 'Multatuli' is evidently a pen-name (Latin: 'multa tuli"), which the bearer himself translates in the text: 'I, Multatuli, who have borne much' ("ik, Multatuli, 'die veel gedragen heb'", *MH*: 235) just as it is said several times of Havelaar that he had suffered much. No. Tine/Everdine is evidently the wife of Eduard Douwes Dekker, inventor of Multatuli.[12] The chain of identification thus stretches beyond the pseudonym to the Biographical Author, exploding the fictional frame and revealing the book as autobiography, since Dekker = Multatuli = Sjaalman = Havelaar, and the Author = Narrator = Character (Genette 1991: 83).

It is also possible, of course, to read the claim to factual truth in the novel as being made within the limits of the fictional world presented by the narrative. The buck then stops with Multatuli rather than with Eduard Douwes Dekker. In that case the dedication is presumably also part of the fictional universe, and Everdine/E.H.v.W. is then indeed the wife of Multatuli. But this does not affect the identification of Havelaar's wife with Multatuli's dedicatee.

Now, at the novel's deepest narrative level, the story of Max Havelaar, we are at one point presented with a conversation between Havelaar, his wife Tine and some Dutch friends; they discuss the fact that Mrs Slotering, a native woman who is the widow of Havelaar's predecessor and lives in the same compound as the Havelaars, prefers to keep to herself. Tine remarks she can very well understand Mrs Slotering's keenness to run her own household (we learn the real reason later), and asks her husband:

"Weet je nog hoe je myn naam vertaald hebt?"

to which Havelaar replies:

"*E.H.V.W.: eigen haard veel waard*". (*MH*: 121)

In the translations the exchange is rendered as follows:

"Do you remember how you once translated my initials?"
"E.H.V.W. *Eigen haard veel waard.*"

Translator's Note: Own hearth great worth (One's own hearth is worth a good deal) (Siebenhaar: 159)

"Do you remember how you once translated my initials: E.H. v. W.?"
"Yes. *Eigen haard veel waard.*"

Translator's Note: "Literally 'one's own hearth is worth much'. Cf. 'There's no place like home'" (Edwards: 170)

"¿Te acuerdas de cómo interpretaste mis iniciales como si fueran siglas de una máxima: E.H.V.W.?"
"— Ya lo creo: 'Eigen Haard, Veel Waard."

Translator's Note: "Literalmente: 'El propio es el hogar que mucho vale', pero aquí se refiere a que vale mucho lo que uno hace y la casa propia gana si la administra y cuida la misma dueña. Las iniciales corresponden a: *E*verdina *H*uberta *v*an *W*ijnbergen". (Carrasquer: 199)

[Omitted] (Garros: 179)

The extent to which the initials are 'contextually overdetermined' will be clear by now. Both the immediate pragmatic context of the conversation and the complex chain of identification linking the fictional character Tine with the book's dedicatee bear directly on the passage. This severely reduces the Biographical Translator's room for manoeuvre, as the task consists of combining the initials (ultimately, those of a historical person, and therefore not open to manipulation) with an appropriate four-word proverb in which each word begins with a certain letter. Even the Spanish translation, which on other occasions coped with metalinguistic statements within the terms of Spanish, is at a loss here. The French version omits the exchange, sacrificing one of the strongest links in the identification chain, which in turn directly affects the book's status as representing fact or fiction (irrespective of whether the claim to factual truth is seen as being made within the fictional world only).

In so doing, however, the translated French text as it stands shows no trace of the Translator's discursive presence in this particular instance. In the Siebenhaar, Edwards and Carrasquer versions a sudden abyss opens up, even if we disregard the Translator's Note. As in some of the other examples listed above, the translated discourse operates under the convention that although Havelaar and company are Dutch-speakers, we read their words, and the presentation of their actions, in English or Spanish. This convention routinely spans the credibility gap by putting in place a suspension bridge, the willing suspension of disbelief. This convention collapses here. Since the Havelaar circle in this scene, as in most other scenes in the book, is monolingual, the sudden shift from English or Spanish to Dutch and back again creates a severe discursive anomaly, a crevice. Oddly enough, the Narrator appears not to register the anomaly: the voice leaps out of and back into its language of narration as if it were speaking independently of its linguistic medium. It is the other voice, the one which co-produces the text, the Translator's, which picks up on the disparity and provides an explanation in the form of a paratextual Note.

The Note in each case also translates the untranslatable. In the source text, Tine's question regarding Havelaar's having once 'translated' ('vertaald') her initials into a proverb rather than a proper name, prompts an intralingual response: the initials transposed into a proverb. In the English and Spanish versions, we get what we expect of translation, an interlingual shift. But instead of transforming the unfamiliar into the familiar, the shift (from English/Spanish to Dutch in the text) only produces an incomprehensible string ("eigen haard veel waard"), the opposite of translation. Since the discourse itself does not remark on this incongruity, the assumption must be that this is Dutch, Havelaar's 'real' language, which we knew was there but were meant to gloss over — but also, coincidentally, the 'original' language of the book as a whole. The Translator's Note confirms this by translating the Dutch proverb (though not the initials, for that transposition, barring a linguistic fluke, can only take place in Dutch) and showing the intractability of the problem. In invoking, explicitly or not, the book's dedication and thus going beyond the immediate Havelaar scene, the Note brings the translated nature of the entire discourse into the picture, self-referentially and self-reflexively. The combination, then, of the non-translation of the initials, the reversion to Dutch and the deferred translation of the Dutch proverb defines the discursive position of the Translator's voice.

6.

The discussion in the preceding paragraphs was designed to show the presence of the Translator's voice, as a discursive presence, in translations of *Max Havelaar.* If the points made have any validity, it is worth considering some broader and more general claims. Indeed, while we may have been concerned with the detail of one particular novel, and a particularly complex one at that, the issue would appear to be of some wider theoretical import.

6.1

What the discussion of *Max Havelaar* in translation will have shown is that the Translator's voice is always present as co-producer of the discourse. The Translator's voice may remain hidden behind the voice(s) of the Narrator(s) for long stretches. In some narratives it many never become clearly discernible at all, and in those cases we have to fall back on positing an Implied Translator as the source of the translated text's invention and intent. However, the inference from the *Havelaar* case must be that it is not only reasonable but necessary to postulate the presence of the Translator's discursive presence in translated fiction, because it is possible to cite specific cases which clearly bring that 'other' voice to the surface, e.g. in instances where its intervention is seen to cater for the needs of the Target Text reader (as a consequence of the cultural and pragmatic embedding of texts and the displacement resulting from translation), or in cases where the discourse short-circuits itself through linguistic self-referentiality or contextual over-determination.

Hence even in those instances where the Translator's discursive presence is not directly traceable, it is a presence that must be posited, just as we must also posit a Target-Culture Implied Reader superimposed on the Source-Culture Implied Reader. It also follows that, if a theoretical model of narrative communication is to be comprehensive, it must create room for instances like those highlighted here.

This makes untenable the model of translated narrative which simply assumes that every enunciation has a source (every text implies the presence of a voice producing it) and that the translator's presence does not interfere with that discursive situation, being located outside it as the reporting voice which repeats, verbatim, the words spoken by the first voice. That model, simplified, looks like this:

(text)
[I say: (text)]
{I translate: [I say: (text)]}

What is needed, rather, is a model of translated narrative which accounts for the way in which the Translator's voice insinuates itself into the discourse and adjusts to the displacement which translation brings about. The model, that is, needs to incorporate the Translator as constantly co-producing the discourse, shadowing, mimicking and, as it were, counterfeiting the Narrator's words, but occasionally — caught in the text's disparities and interstices: and paratextually — emerging into the open as a separate discursive presence. In Giuliana Schiavi's essay (in this issue) the theoretical case for an Implied Translator is argued and an alternative model proposed. In practice, many translated narratives indeed do not allow us to go further than the terms of that model, because what has been called here the Translator's voice or the Translator's discursive presence in the text is wholly assimilated into the Narrator's voice. It is only in specific cases that the 'other' voice becomes dissociated from the one it mimics.

6.2

The further question arises: Why do current approaches to narrative have this blind spot when it comes to the Translator's voice? Why do *we*, as readers, prefer to ignore this 'other' discursive presence?

The reason, it seems to me. lies in the cultural and therefore also the ideological construct which is translation. This takes us straight back to the dominant concept of translation in our culture: translation as transparency and duplicate, as not only consonant but coincident and hence to all intents and purposes identical with its source text; the view of translation as reproduction, in which the translation is meant to reproduce the original, the whole original and nothing but the original; the image of a translation being 'as good as' its original, except in regard of status. A translation is a 'good' or a 'proper' or a 'real' translation, we tend to say, if there are no loose ends, no foreign bodies; it should not contain anything that might affect the integrity of the original. Translators are good translators if and when they have become transparent, invisible, when they have spirited themselves away. Only a Translator who speaks 'under erasure' can be trusted not to violate the original. The loyal absence of the one guarantees the primacy and aura of the other.

This hierarchy governing the relation between original and translation is nothing new. Historically it has been construed in a number of ways, mostly around oppositions such as those between creative versus derivative work, primary versus secondary, art versus craft, authority versus obedience, freedom versus constraint, speaking in one's own name versus speaking for someone else. In each pair it is translation which is circumscribed, hemmed in, controlled, subordinated. And in case we think these are after all natural and necessary hierarchies, it may be useful to remind ourselves of the fact that in our culture the male/female distinction, too, has been constructed in terms of very similar oppositions of creative versus reproductive, original versus derivative, active versus passive, dominant versus subservient.

Deep down, of course, we know — as soon as we stop to think about it — that the oppositions in which we have placed translation are cultural and ideological constructs. But they still structure our way of thinking about these issues, because they are ingrained in our culture and in our mental habits and projections. To abandon them, and to abandon the control mechanisms which they keep in place, would be to upset established hierarchies, to deny the primacy and inviolability of the original, to stress the intertextual transformative streak in all writing, to assert the plurivocality of discourse.

And to let in plural voices means destabilizing and decentring the speaking subject, and creates the prospect of a runaway inflation of voices and meanings.[13]

Translation therefore needs to be controlled, to be kept under the lid. because it is recognized as an activity that continually risks producing this kind of proliferation and dissemination. Translation *is* controlled through the ideology of transparency, identity, reproduction, the translator's absence from the translated text. This allows us to suppress the loose ends, the hybridity of translation: we pretend they do not exist — or at least that they ought not to exist, so as not to endanger the notion of univocal speech, the single voice issuing from an identifiable source. And so we say that we read Dostoyevsky, that we hear Yeltsin: we do not *want* to hear the Translator's voice. However, as this essay has tried to demonstrate, that discursive presence is there — not only in exceptional circumstances in unusually complex books, but always. For in the final analysis it is impossible not to ask how far the plurivocal nature of translation extends. A translation as a rule addresses an audience different from that addressed by the original. If this adjustment calls for the recognition of a Target-Culture Implied Reader, for positing an Implied Translator and for the possibility of discerning the Translator's discursive presence in certain cases and under certain circumstances, then there is nothing to prevent extending this principle from translated narrative to translated texts in general. Translation is irreducible: it always leaves loose ends, is always hybrid, plural, and different.

Notes

1 The notion of translation as re-enunciation, and its relation to quotation and reported speech, is taken from Barbara Folkart (1991).
2 Different theorists use different terms for the various elements in the diagram. The triad 'text', 'story' and 'fabula' is from Mieke Bal (1985). I follow Rimmon-Kenan (1983), Chatman (1978, 1990) and others in assuming an Implied Author and an Implied Reader, despite Genette's reservations (1983).
3 This makes the present essay complementary to Giuliana Schiavi's "There is Always a Teller in a Tale" (in this issue), which argues the case for positing an Implied Translator in the translated text. My focus is on those instances where another discursive presence, another voice, becomes discernible in the text itself. Both essays posit an Implied Reader specific to the translated text.
4 In (he case of a paratextual note there is a difference between a Translator's Note and other possible Notes. In the context of narrative fiction Notes would normally be attributed to a Narrator, and signal the intervention of a different Narrator or a switch to a different narrative mode (as in, say, John Fowles' *The French Lieutenant's Woman*). In principle, Translator's Notes could be presented in exactly the same way and be indistinguishable from other Notes (i.e. be detectable only through comparison with the original). However, in our translational

culture the translator's professional ethos and other institutional rules and conventions forbid this option: Translator's Notes are normally identified as such. This gives them a different status, which raises a theoretical problem. The main point, however, is the observation that Translator's Notes break through the narrative discourse in a way different from other Notes; the voice which produces the Translator's Notes is clearly a different voice, with an identity of its own.

5 In *Ulysse gramophone* (1987) and in *Du droit à la philosophie* (1990); see Segers 1994.

6 I will henceforth refer to the Dutch text (volume 1 of the 1992 edition) as *MH*. The translations will be referred to by the name of the translator (Siebenhaar, Edwards, Carrasquer, Garros) immediately followed by the page number.

7 In the fifth edition (1881) the dedication is "To the revered memory of Everdine Huberte. Baroness van Wijnbergen, loyal wife, heroic, loving mother, noble woman" (Dutch: *MH:* 1). The manuscript (printed edition: Multatuli 1949) bears only the dedicatee's initials: "To E.H.v.W." (Dutch: Multatuli 1949: 1). The importance of the dedication will become clear later.

8 'N.d.T.' stands for 'Note du Traducteur', i.e. Translator's Note. Interestingly, the abbreviation makes it clear that the producer of the Note is the translator as a textual presence, a voice, not to be confused with the Biographical Translator. How else to explain the use of the masculine (generic?) 'Traducteur' when it was Mme Roland Garros who translated the book?

9 In view of what was said in Note 4 above, this obviously raises the question of how Multatuli's Notes (from the 1875 edition on) relate to Translator's Notes. Both are paratextual, and as such interrupt the narrative flow. Since 'Multatuli' is both a Narrator in the text and the name on the cover and title page of the book (which, as we shall see, plays on the distinction between fiction and non-fiction), and since the introduction lo the Notes (*MH*: 239–246) clearly indicates that he is their provider, the linguistic subject of these Notes is beyond doubt. They appear as a kind of editorial intervention, associated with the name on the cover and title page rather with the 'I, Multatuli' who enters as a Narrator in the book's final pages. This is partly because Multatuli-as-Narrator does not appear until the very end, and partly because many of the comments go well beyond the novel's narrative world, e.g. in commenting on the editor of the first edition of 1860.

10 The term 'differential voice' is Barbara Folkart's, who in the section in question develops an argument similar to mine: ". . . le ré-énonciateur ne se manifestera dans l'énoncé qu'il produit que sous forme de déviances, tant pragmatiques et référentielles que sémiologiques". She goes on to speak of "un ensemble hétéroclite de déviances (dont la saisie requiert une analyse plus ou moins poussée, du moins une confrontation avec le texte de départ . . .)" (Folkart 1991: 394–395). As I hope to have shown, the Translator's 'differential voice' can be seized in the translated text itself, without confronting it with the source text.

11 The following discussion, like all such discussions, is indebted lo Sötemann 1972, the classic and detailed study of the structure of *Max Havelaar*. Since Sötemann's study refers to the printed edition of the manuscript (Multatuli 1949) it does not address issues like those raised in Note 9 regarding the 'editorial' status of the Notes in the 1875 and subsequent editions.

12 Everdine van Wijnbergen died on 13 September 1874, hence the extended dedication in the fourth edition, which came out in October 1875 (Multatuli 1992, II:538). Although in the manuscript and the first three editions of *Max Havelaar* the initials E.H.v.W. do not explicitly identify the dedicatee as the author's

wife, the conclusion seems inescapable, as indeed Sötemann (1972: 23, 275ff.) has shown.

13 This is an idea which Karin Littau developed in several seminars and conference papers, with reference to Foucault, Barthes and Derrida. See Littau 1993.

References

Bal, Mieke. 1985. *Narratology: Introduction to the Theory of Narrative*, tr. Christine van Boheemen. Toronto: University of Toronto Press.

Chatman, Seymour. 1978. *Story and Discourse: Narrative Structure in Fiction and Film*. Ithaca-London: Cornell University Press.

Chatman, Seymour. 1990. *Coming to Terms: The Rhetoric of Narrative in Fiction and Film*. Ithaca-London: Cornell University Press.

Derrida, Jacques. 1991. *Between the Blinds: A Derrida Reader*, ed. Peggy Kamuf. New York etc.: Harvester Wheatsheaf.

Derrida, Jacques. 1992. *Acts of Literature*, ed. Derek Attridge. New York-London: Routledge.

Descartes, René. 1968. *Discourse on Method and the Meditations*, tr. F. E. Sutcliffe. Harmondsworth: Penguin.

Folkart, Barbara. 1991. *Le conflit des énonciations: Traduction et discours rapporté*. Candiac: Les Éditions Balzac.

Genette, Gérard. 1972. "Discours du récit". Gérard Genette. *Figures III*. Paris: Seuil, 1972. 65–281.

Genette, Gérard. 1982. *Palimpsestes: La littérature au second degré*. Paris: Seuil.

Genette, Gérard. 1983. *Nouveau discours du récit*. Paris: Seuil.

Genette, Gérard. 1991. *Fiction et diction*. Paris: Seuil.

Harris, Brian. 1990. "Norms in Interpretation". *Target* 2:1. 115–119.

Hermans, Theo. 1988. "On Translating Proper Names, with Reference to *De Witte* and *Max Havelaar*". *Modern Dutch Studies: Essays in Honour of Peter King*, ed. M. Wintle. London: Athlone, 1988. 11–24.

Littau, Karin. 1993. "Intertextuality and Translation: *The Waste Land* in French and German". *Translation — the Vital Link*, ed. Catriona Picken. London: Chamelon Press, 1993. 63–69.

Multatuli. 1927. *Max Havelaar or the Coffee Sales of the Netherlands Trading Company*, tr. W. Siebenhaar, intro. D. H. Lawrence. New York.

Multatuli. 1949. *Max Havelaar of de koffij-veilingen der Nederlandsche Handel-maatschappij*, ed. G. Stuiveling. Amsterdam: Van Oorschot.

Multatuli. 1968. *Max Havelaar*, tr. Mme Roland Garros. Paris: Editions universitaires.

Multatuli. 1975. *Max Havelaar o las subastas de café de la Compañía Comercial Holandesa*, tr. Francisco Carrasquer. Barcelona: Frontera.

Multatuli. 1987. *Max Havelaar or the Coffee Auctions of the Dutch Trading Company*, tr. Roy Edwards. Harmondsworth: Penguin.

Multaruli. 1992. *Max Havelaar of de koffiveilingen der Nederlandsche Handel-maatschappy* (2 vols.), ed. A. Kets-Vree. Assen-Maastricht: Van Gorcum.

Pym, Anthony. 1992. *Translation and Text Transfer: An Essay on the Principles of Intercultural Communication*. Frankfurt am Main etc.: Peter Lang.

Rimmon-Kenan, Shlomith. 1983. *Narrative Fiction: Contemporary Poetics*. London-New York: Methuen.

Schiavi, Giuliana. 1996. "There Is Always a Teller in a Tale". *Target* 8: 1. 1–21.

Segers, Winibert. 1994. "Derrida's onvertaalbaarheidsweb". *Bouwen aan Babel: Zes opstellen over onvertaalbaarheid*, ed. Raymond van den Broeck. Antwerpen-Harmelen: Fantom, 1994. 89–100.

Sötemann, A. L. 1973. *De structuur van de 'Max Havelaar'*. Groningen: Wolters-Noordhoff.

53

NATIONAL SOVEREIGNTY
VERSUS UNIVERSAL RIGHTS

Interpreting justice in a global context

Moira Inghilleri

Source: *Social Semiotics* 17(2) (2007): 195–212.

Interpreters/translators serve to both codify and clarify the cultural and linguistic boundaries used to symbolise and prop up nationalist agendas within the political asylum system. This paper examines the nationalist agenda operating within the immigration systems of receiving countries like the United Kingdom, drawing on contemporary political philosophical theory in which both universalist and nationalist discourses have come under increasing scrutiny. It discusses well-established dichotomies such as insider/outsider, national/universal, open/closed borders and the ways in which these explicitly or implicitly continue to inform and support the legitimation of exclusionary policies with regard to asylum seekers. It argues that scholarly appeals to a more internationalised discourse of human rights have not challenged these fundamental dichotomies in the case of refugees or asylum seekers. Instead, it notes a tension between public discourses that are oriented toward mutual understanding, "democratic iterations" and those "authorised discourses" in which pre-established power relations are maintained. The paper considers the role of interpreters/translators in helping to sustain or contest this tension in their place within the "politics of belonging" that informs immigration policies and practice.

Global relations create and attempt to sustain hybrid economic, social and political networks that inevitably involve some form of ongoing linguistic or cultural "translation" to ensure their function. There is a wealth of literature on the subject of globalisation from a range of disciplinary perspectives (e.g. political philosophy, international relations and migration studies), each of which directly or indirectly considers the effects of global mobility on local, national and transnational constructions of identity and belonging. Interestingly, however, there is little or no recognition in this literature of the role of translators or interpreters in global processes of communication. Indeed, within familiar discourses of global relations, concepts like hybridity, transnationalism or deterritoriality are treated largely as un-self-conscious conditions or consequences of globalisation. While there is much attention to questions regarding the effects of these conditions on, for example, the role of the nation-state and the re-construction of national or postnational identities, there is less mention of the communicative processes involved in such transformations.

Within translation studies, global processes of communication are at the centre of analysis of cultural and linguistic textual representations. Studies within the "culturalist" paradigm, foregrounding concepts such as hybridity and *métissage* derived from post-colonial, postmodern and/or multicultural discourses, have revealed how historical and existing inequalities at the national, regional and global level contribute to the suppression and emancipation of cultural and linguistic realities. Although these studies have tended to take the literary text as their starting point—and to view nations and national identities in fairly static terms (Robinson 1997)—there is increasing interest within this paradigm in the specific conditions of globalisation under which translated texts are produced, circulated and read (Gentzler and Tymoczko 2002; Cronin 2003) and in the translator's agency with respect to contact and changes to the global order (Buzelin 2005). A recognition of the global nature of translation activity has also been central to polysystems and descriptive translation studies (Even-Zohar 1978; Toury 1995). Systems approaches, while maintaining a stronger focus on the binary nature of the source-target linguistic/cultural interface, crucially locate processes and products of translation beyond the translator and the text and within complex configurations of macro-social and historical contexts.

Interpreting research on micro-contexts of utterances and the ways in which power and identity and "communication rights" are played out between officials, interpreters and their clients, has also revealed some of the complexities of the "contact zone" of interpreted interactions (Mason 1999; Hale 2004; Bot 2005). The types of contexts that have been analysed in interpreting research (e.g. legal, educational, health and social services) are crucial public spaces for the attainment of social and legal rights. They constitute the actual microcosms of the "transnational" spaces that are conceptualised in the abstract in philosophical and political discourses of globalisation and imagined and deconstructed in hybrid post-colonial literary texts. Where refugees, immigrants or guest workers—among the key agents of globalisation—are involved, inter-cultural, inter-lingual communication becomes a central part of the process in which global relations of power are played out.

The asylum interpreting process involves an array of contexts in which interpreters are involved. This carries from the initial port of entry interview through the development of narratives taking place within the solicitors' offices, through the Home Office interviews, and ultimately, and different again, in the appeals courts. No one of these moments can be isolated as the critical one. Outcomes are the product of activity across this process and therefore any analysis that focuses on one of these domains alone will be likely to be deficient. The process is therefore an arc of activity across which we must look.

What happens at the surface level of interaction is more often than not a micro-drama through which a larger social and political reality is acted out in a refracted form. Accounts of courtroom or immigration hearing interactions have recourse only to speculations concerning motivations or interpretations of intended meaning, providing little sure foundation other than interpretive plausibility, much as literary criticism does. While in interpreting research this has done much to reveal the complexity of the interpreter's role, under these conditions it is very easy to miss fundamental social and political realities. Through understanding and awareness of the whole arc of activity, the chances of distorting perspectives are diminished.

This paper explores the interface in interpreted encounters in the political asylum process between the notion of a "fixed" national identity/subject and that of a more globally defined, multicultural, de-territoriatised one. The right to asylum is simultaneously a national issue and an international issue.

It is thus a crucial context in which some of the key issues surrounding globalisation are enacted (e.g. national sovereignty, the construction of individual/collective identities and rights, and the question of territorial and symbolic borders). The paper will focus on the contribution of the wider historical and political context in constructing asylum seekers as outsiders and limiting the extent of their transnational "right to belong". It will then consider the extent to which the "communicative rights" granted to or claimed by interpreters and translators within interpreted interactions reflect the "politics of belonging" that informs current immigration policies and practice.

Formation of the nation-state

The organisation of the world into distinct and autonomous states has been the central organising principle in the West since the mid-seventeenth century when territorial boundaries supplanted religious ones (Donnelly 2003). Since its formation, the modern state has principally functioned in juridical terms—as an "entity in which the people are bound together, even defined, by their common participation in and subordination to (democratic public) law" (Donnelly 2003, 64).

Significantly, the modern state was defined in relation to and as a response to questions of international order and responsibility. Thus, the relationship between the notion of a global society and the sovereignty of nation-states—and its moral and political consequences—is not a new one.

It is generally accepted that this relationship takes on political, but more importantly, symbolic importance in Europe from the time of the Peace of Westphalia in 1648:

> After Westphalia the language of international justification gradually shifted, away from Christian unity and toward international diversity based on a secular society of sovereign states that acknowledged common practices and principles of international law.
>
> (Jackson 2005, 82)

The origins of the modern state are thus rooted in a vision of political society that is at once internationalist, based on "natural law"—which holds that all humans are equal members of the community of humankind—and nationalist, based on "positive law"—which holds that individuals have the right to form political associations in the form of independent states (Jackson 2005, 127–8). Under positive law, relations with other sovereign states are viewed as voluntary and contingent, and a private matter for individual states alone (Held 2002, 4).

Since the inception of the notion of state sovereignty, efforts have been made to recognise and/or reconcile the inherent tension between moral universality and national political autonomy with respect to human rights. In the realm of political philosophy, Hobbes, for example, writing in 1651, viewed the international world as a "state of nature" with no normative bonds or ties between states (Jackson 2005, 110). Hobbes likened this to a perpetual "state of war" in which "all men are equal in body, ambitions, and reason and there is no common power to restrain them" (Doyle 1997, 114). Nations were compelled to protect themselves from this anarchic state of affairs by operating according to their own self-interests, protecting their liberal principles and practices from the illiberal laws of nature (Cole 2000, 165–6). Kant would later attempt to reconcile this view through an appeal to a cosmopolitan world society united in solidarity over fundamental human rights. Kant was more optimistic about the possibility of an internationally based "state of peace" based on a pacific union of liberal democratic states, which would gradually be extended as non-liberal states disappeared (Doyle 1997, 257). In his essay *Perpetual Peace*, Kant argued for a set of common values and principles, shared by individuals as well as states, based on a universal law of right rooted in human reason, in "nature" itself (Kant 1957, 31–2). Kant's idea of a cosmopolitan law involved agreement on "conditions of universal hospitality" defined as follows:

Hospitality is the right of a stranger not to be treated as an enemy when he arrives in the land of another. One may refuse to receive him when this can be done without causing his destruction; but, so long as he peacefully occupies his place, one may not treat him with hostility. It is not the right to be a permanent visitor one may demand. A special beneficent agreement would be needed in order to give an outsider a right to become a fellow inhabitant for a certain length of time. It is only a right of temporary sojourn, a right to associate, which all men have. They have it by virtue of their common possession of the surface of the earth, where, as a globe, they cannot infinitely disperse and hence must finally tolerate the presence of each other.

(Kant 1957, 20–1)

In establishing the idea—at the time of its formation—that the modern democratic state draws its very legitimacy from conformity to universal human rights rooted in human reason, moral and political responsibilities became inextricably linked.

Globalisation, the nation-state and the management of migration

The relationship between a sovereign state's moral-legal requirement to offer temporary sojourn to "strangers" and the right of the state to control the type and extent of their stay continues to inform twenty-first-century refugee and asylum policies. Despite the development of international human rights agencies, conventions and the positive collective humanitarian actions of states in times of global crisis, the will of the sovereign state continues to serve as the ultimate arbiter over who is judged a worthy stranger.

The relationship between state sovereignty and cosmopolitan law has come under increased scrutiny in the context of more recent transformations of the global economy. While there is little debate over the fact of the global interconnectedness of modern nation-states, there is disagreement over whether "globalisation" is a positive phenomenon leading to the erosion of the independent political authority claimed in the name of sovereignty (see Held *et al.* 1999). Whatever one's position in contemporary debates over this issue, the issue of migration has emerged as central to questions of mobility and membership in the present global order. Migration practices and policies have become an explicit focus of interest for politicians, social scientists and philosophers alike. Migration-related questions concerning, for example, the nature of citizenship, the right of nation-states to act in their own self-interest, and the obligations of the "international community" toward migrants, forced or otherwise, are in evidence in political and academic debates at both an intranational level and an inter-national level.

Such questions address the very essence of what it means to "belong" in a global society. Although migration is acknowledged to be an inevitable consequence of the establishment of global economic networks, it is frequently portrayed by governments and perceived by members of the public as a potential threat to the internal economic or cultural order and stability of a sovereign nation (Statham 2003), often creating divisions between members of the same society. As Jordan and Düvell note:

> [Immigration] mobilizes resentment of those made insecure by their vulnerability to a global competition; it taps into rivalries between excluded groups; it links the fate of immobile and impoverished ethnic minority communities with the threat of mobile and resourceful newcomers, seen as further subverting the protection of citizenship. It allows the politics of nationalism and "race" to be rekindled and exposes the fragility of liberal democratic institutions.
>
> (2003, 62)

Although the national media frequently portray social and economic conflicts as primarily an outcome of tensions between citizens/insiders and migrants/outsiders, divisions among different types of migrant groups can be equally corrosive to an individual's or a group's sense of belonging. Such divisions may originate in or become perpetuated by the immigration policies and practices of receiving countries. Whatever the historical precedents, the motivations for current migration to and between countries have tended to be falsely portrayed, particularly in the developed world, in either economic or political terms. The persistence of this either/or interpretation of the causes of migration is evident in the pejorative categorisation of the "bogus" asylum seeker in cases where an asylum claim is believed to be based on "economic" rather than political reasons. This charge is highly problematic given that, at the present time, the United Kingdom and the European Union are positively encouraging the managed recruitment of highly-skilled and unskilled workers from outside the Union (Jordan and Düvell 2003, 68). Several points can be made in this regard. First, most asylum seekers are themselves "highly-skilled and unskilled workers" who are willing and able to contribute to the economic and social life of the receiving country. Secondly, it is increasingly difficult to make a distinction between "refugee" and "economic migrants" (Crisp 2003, 81) as most individuals and groups seeking asylum migrate as a result of a combination of factors deriving from the consequences of civil war, ethnic conflicts, and other forms of social and political violence. Thirdly, in the past, during times of economic boom, policies toward all immigrants, including asylum seekers, have been more accommodating (Joly 1996). In the current climate, despite the fact that applicants for entry may share similar social and economic characteristics, receiving countries operate discriminatory policies in order to control overall numbers:

> ... the crisis arises not from world migration movements but from the lack of a political rationale for integrating them; for reconciling them with other humanitarian demands for protection, or ethical principles of distribution, and for the internal rules of membership of liberal democratic states. Furthermore the diversity and complexity of migration processes in an integrated world economy challenges policy makers to frame consistent rules and apply them fairly to a whole range of different kinds of migrants.
>
> (Jordan and Düvell 2003, 69)

The migration "crisis", attributed to the rising numbers of people seeking asylum world-wide since the 1980s, has justified stricter controls at the borders of receiving countries. But while there has been a significant overall increase in migration since that time, the overwhelming majority of displaced persons still either remain in their countries of origin or seek refuge in neighbouring countries. Despite this reality, globalisation has played a role in the increased migration to Western Europe and North America. Since the end of the Cold War, many of the world's principal refugee populations have come from countries that have not had a significant role in global economic expansion and are therefore of little geo-political significance to the West. As a consequence, the West has tended to turn its back on any long-term economic commitment in the form of refugee assistance programmes, for example. Neighbouring states in the developing world have been increasingly reluctant and unwilling to accept sole moral or financial responsibility for the political conflicts in their regions (Crisp 2003, 78). In addition, unlike the situation during the Cold War, many asylum claimants currently come from countries with whom Western Europe and North America share or seek to develop close political and/or economic ties or are considered of strategic importance in the "global war on terror". Receiving countries have thus attempted to strike the right balance with their immigration policies—attempting to operate effectively, economically, politically and morally, as global partners while at the same time protecting their own national interests and those of their citizens.

Migration and the politics of belonging

Contemporary debates originating from western liberal democracies over migration, citizenship and belonging have predominated in countries with well-established histories of migration. In the United States and Canada the debate tends to centre around the issue of assimilation, comparing the styles and patterns of cultural and economic assimilation of European and East

Asian immigration from the late nineteenth century and early twentieth century to post-1960s immigration originating largely from the developing world (Portes 1997; Alba and Nee 2003; Reitz 2003). In western Europe, debates are focused on the continued impact of colonialism on contemporary migration patterns and practices and on the current and future status of guest workers and their families imported to countries such as Germany, Switzerland, The Netherlands and France during the period of industrialisation following the Second World War (Joppke 1998; Geddes and Favell 1999). Underlying these debates is an interest in the extent to which immigrant groups, past and present, contribute to a sense of a "national collectivity" and an increased recognition of the role played by their maintenance of "transnational" ties and allegiances. For some, this implies a diminished importance for traditional forms of nationhood and citizenship (Soysal 1994; Jacobson 1996). Others, however, emphasise the renewed relevance of the liberal democratic state as a crucial public site for constructive dialogue between national and transnational affiliations (Schuck 1998; Benhabib 2004).

The issue of asylum occupies a distinct position within these debates as refugees and asylum seekers normally are perceived primarily in terms of their potential to be returned or contained. In this way, questions of long-term citizenship rights or assimilatory potential are secondary, although significant, factors in determinations of admission. With the implementation in recent decades of far stricter interpretations of the 1951 Geneva Convention's criteria for what constitutes a refugee, most asylum seekers fail to obtain formal refugee status. Instead, because of individual states' adherence to the principle of non-refoulment,[1] those claimants who are not deported outright, returned after a negative determination or held indefinitely in the category of asylum seeker are permitted to remain with some form of temporary status until such time conditions in their country are considered safe. However, without the formal status of "Convention refugee"—which in most countries has usually led to the rights and benefits of permanent residence—both the quality of rights and conditions of settlement often remain vague or undetermined. Indeed, some non-governmental organisations have argued that governments have deliberately categorised refugees in this way in order to avoid the commitments involved in the Convention status (Joly 1996, 11; see also Joly 2002). By conferring temporary refugee status without any legal commitment to extend this to permanent residence or opting to hold applicants in reception/detention centres for the duration of the application process, nation-states visibly mark asylum seekers as outsiders whatever the eventual outcome of their claim. In doing so, states demonstrate an increasing ambivalence to the idea of universal hospitality and global inter-connectedness.

In addition to the political and economic influences involved in the management of migration, a strong justification for increasing border control has also been the protection of national cultures and identities. The political philosopher, Michael Walzer, for example, has argued that:

> The distinctiveness of cultures and groups depends on closure and without it, cannot be conceived as a stable feature of human life. If this distinctiveness is a value, as most people (though some of them are global pluralists and others are local loyalists) seem to believe, then closure must be permitted somewhere. At some level of political organisation, something like the sovereign state must take shape and claim the authority to make its own admissions policy, to control and sometimes restrain the flow of immigrants.
>
> (1983, 39)

Such a view suggests a relationship between the control of migration and the maintenance of cultural cohesion in the context of a sovereign state. Implied here are two distinct sites of "closure"—one that exists between diverse members of the same nation, and another that distinguishes members of a nation from would-be or non-members. Walzer has argued that, despite their differences, members of a national culture mutually construct a *political* culture and identity. In a liberal democracy, this gives them the right to exercise their self-determination, including the right to limit or restrict membership to others. Such restrictions are applied both to internal members (e.g. permanent residents, guest workers, third-country nationals) and to external non-members.

In the case of refugees and asylum seekers, the question of "closure" is closely linked to territorial boundaries. A nation-state exercises its legal right to refuse entry through deportation, stricter border controls, and reception/ detention centres that contain and effectively cordon off asylum seekers from the rest of the public. Provision of foreign economic and development aid itself has a twofold purpose, to fulfil a humanitarian duty of assistance and to discourage migration to donor countries.

Political asylum, universal human rights and the "trans-national"

Given the continuation of the significance of the nation-state with respect to the international politics of human rights, it is worth considering the impact and relevance of claims about the increased role of universal human rights and "transnational belonging" to refugee populations across the globe.

Some suggest that patterns of migration associated with globalisation have done much to erode images of permanent resettlement and assimilation with regard to the movements of peoples (Carens 2000; Papastergiadis 2000). Papastergiadis has argued that the "conditions of hospitality" for migrants should reflect this changing nature and should take into account

314

the historical reality of flexible borders and the increasingly "complex networks of responsibility that link a person to the past and to the future" (2000, 57). Similarly, Soysal claims that transnational norms and the discourse of human rights have begun to erode the boundaries of nation-states, suggesting the advent of a postnational model of membership and citizenship with respect to migrants:

> In the postnational model, universal personhood replaces nationhood—and universal human rights replace national rights. The rights and claims of individuals are legitimated in ideologies grounded in a transnational community, through international codes, conventions and laws on human rights, independent of their citizenship in a nation-state. Hence, the individual transcends the citizen. This is the most elemental way that the postnational model differs from the national one. Universal personhood as the basis of membership comes across most clearly in the case of political refugees, whose status in the host country rests exclusively on an appeal to human rights.
>
> (Soysal 1994, 142)

Soysal's claim that the idea of the nation persists mostly as an "intense metaphor" (1994, 162) is not predicated on the erosion of the nation-state *qua* state; rather, she argues that the persistence of legal and illegal migration into Europe, for example, indicates a weakening in the state's ability to successfully curtail entry. She locates this weakening in "ideologies grounded in a transnational community" and supported by human rights legislation such as the 1948 Universal Declaration of Human Rights and the 1950 European Human Rights Convention.

While these authors make insightful points regarding contemporary migration in the context of globalisation, much of their argument relates more pertinently to migrant groups or national minorities who are already inside the boundaries of the nation-state and who have or ought to have rights to move back and forth legally between territories. As discussed above, however, the movement of refugees and asylum seekers remains more restricted and arguably more dangerous. While it is true that states have begun to attend more to internationally recognised human rights (Forsythe 2000; Donnelly 2003), it is also true that in terms of foreign policy agendas human rights issues are not "even close to the top" (Donnelly 2003, 172). Moreover, despite their increasingly influential role in monitoring, education, relief operations and developing human rights norms, global human rights regimes such as the United Nations High Commission for Refugees, the UN Human Rights Committee and the UN Commission on Human Rights have limited international decision-making powers (Donnelly 2003, 138). Recently Louis Gentile, a UN High Commission for Refugees Protection

Officer, has argued that the notion of significant progress in protecting human rights is a myth:

> The human rights problem today is not about establishing principles but about practice, and it is in analysing the human rights situation on the ground, in judging progress in the practical application and respect for human rights principles, that this myth begins to disintegrate.
>
> (Gentile 2002, 40–1)

Thus, while expansive conceptions of human rights and transnational norms may be in evidence, the continuation of national policies of exclusion has not significantly altered the rights of refugee and asylum seekers. On the contrary, in the current climate, these rights have become increasingly suspended with humanitarian considerations or concerns for "universal personhood" the lowest priority for receiving countries.

The political philosopher, Seyla Benhabib, has attempted to fuse the idea of "transnational belonging" with that of a territorially based democratic political culture—of nationhood with personhood. She argues for a constructive inclusive dialogue between the established and the excluded inhabitants of a nation-state that does not depend on prior shared understandings based in ethnocultural commonalities or on permanent territorial allegiances. She suggests that although the precise interpretation of human rights must be considered in light of the "concrete historical traditions and practices of a given society", claims to the validity of such interpretation must be "context-transcending" (Benhabib 2004, 123); that is, the exercise of political agency must be considered valid not due to a shared national identity and culture, but to a belief in and commitment to moral cosmopolitanism.

Benhabib envisions a type of transnational dialogue, accomplished through what she terms, "democratic iterations", borrowing the notion of iteration from Derrida for whom it suggests the indeterminacy of meaning from one context to another; that is, that in the repetition of a linguistic utterance, the "performative force" of the utterance breaks from prior established contexts of socially established meanings. Benhabib takes up this idea, arguing that diverse linguistic, cultural or religious practices, for example, can and must be taken up in a political context of debate that does not require as a precondition the type of closure (and the fixed, shared meaning this notion implies) referred to above:

> By democratic iterations I mean complex processes of public argument, deliberation and exchange through which universalist rights claims and principles are contested and contextualised, invoked and revoked, posited and positioned, throughout legal and political

institutions, as well as in the associations of civil society. These can take place in the "strong" public bodies of legislatures, the judiciary, and the executive, as well as in the informal and "weak" publics of civil society associations and the media.

(Benhabib 2004, 179)

Benhabib's concern is to establish the minimal discursive norms and the fair and equal procedures necessary for reaching compromise and agreement between conversational partners in multicultural societies. Importantly, she wishes to do so without collapsing the distinction between moral and cultural discourses. That is, she wishes to acknowledge the possibility of a context-independent universalist moral language that can coexist with the complexities of and potential overlaps in the moral, ethical and evaluative discursive frameworks within which different cultural/national groups conduct their lives (Benhabib 2002, 40–2).

The notion of a democratic iteration offers the possibility of the emergence and re-emergence of meaning—and thus social knowledge—that is not weighed down and over determined by prior contexts or positions. It suggests that the capacity of the force of an utterance to assume new contexts—which Derrida suggests emanates in language itself—creates the necessary and sufficient conditions for the emancipatory potential of partners in cross-cultural contexts of communication to create new meanings that will themselves remain unfixed to any one context. Benhabib is interested in the potential of the decontextualised, dis-closed utterance to challenge existing forms of legitimacy. At the same time, however, she acknowledges that whether an individual or group is judged worthy of equal treatment and respect as conversational partners—their right to recognition—will ultimately determine the type and extent of their participation in public deliberations (2002, 56).

Bourdieu takes up this last point in his critique of the idea that social transformation can emerge out of linguistically constituted moral or cultural validity claims. Bourdieu insists that the efficacy of speech derives not from language but from the institutional conditions of its production and reception:

It is clear that all the efforts to find, in the specifically linguistic logic of different forms of argumentation, rhetoric and style, the source of their symbolic efficacy are destined to fail as long as they do not establish the relationship between the properties of discourses, the properties of the person who pronounces them and the properties of the institution which authorises him to pronounce them.

(Bourdieu 1991, 111)

Central to Bourdieu's claim regarding the intractable authority that language derives from social relations of power is the belief that this authority is maintained through the collaboration of those it governs through the functioning of the habitus—the social mechanism capable of producing this complicity based on misrecognition. For Bourdieu, language cannot perform a break with context—and the power of language cannot be invoked linguistically, authority comes to language from the outside (1991, 109); hence the impossibility of the emergence of "discursive gaps" that might challenge socially pre-established grounds of legitimate meanings. For Bourdieu, where an individual or group's language has no prior authorisation, it cannot participate equally in the type of transnational "democratic iterations" and the production of new forms of legitimacy envisioned above. For Bourdieu, this would require substantially more than a break with context, it would necessitate a break with the social conventions and modalities of practice that are inscribed in language and embodied or enacted through the habitus.

The interpreted encounter: transnational iteration or authorised discourse?

Acts of interpreting and translation are instantiations of language attempting to function in a context in which it has no prior authorisation. In the case of most public service contexts, including the political asylum context, interpreters and translators actively participate in negotiating the prior social conventions of usage that serve to constrain but also engage their clients as conversational partners. As active agents in the "transnational" spaces to which Benhabib and others refer, they contribute both consciously and unconsciously to the interplay or tension between the force of "democratic iterations" and that of "authorised language" as they help or are hindered in the negotiation of linguistic and cultural meanings between the established and excluded inhabitants of a nation-state.

In the political asylum system these negotiations take place in a climate in which the continuation of national policies of exclusion significantly restricts the right of refugees and asylum seekers to be heard. As discussed above, nationhood, not universal personhood, remains the reference point for claimants' rights of entry, significantly limiting the conditions for the emergence of a discourse of "transnational belonging" or moral cosmopolitanism. In interpreted asylum events, the force of linguistic utterances —for both claimants and the state—remains located firmly in the context of national cultures and identities. Yet at the same time, translation and interpreting play a central role in the development of expansive conceptions of human rights and transnational norms, which in turn effect the extent of an applicant's right to participate in a constructive inclusive dialogue within the asylum system. It is thus a crucial context in which to develop a more stable and shared understanding of the interpreter's role. The "communication rights" granted to or withheld from interpreters as well as those claimed and enacted by interpreters themselves are central to this development.

Despite established codes of practice and an increased awareness of the interpreter role, there is still much uncertainty and inconsistency among all participants in the political asylum adjudication system—adjudicators, solicitors, interpreters, Home Office representatives and claimants alike— regarding the exact nature of this role in interpreted encounters. Different approaches to training also contribute to these uncertainties. The conflicting perceptions and expectations of and by interpreters are an outcome of a further set of uncertainties over the "objective" nature of asylum adjudication on the one hand, and communicative practices on the other. The asylum process is the roughest of rough games. Beneath some of the interactional surface each participant in an official hearing can be in bad faith. Discussions within the solicitor's office between an asylum seeker, a legal representative and an interpreter involve the joint production of a narrative that will achieve the objective of winning the right to remain in the United Kingdom. The underlying motive of the Home Office's counter-narrative against a claimant's credibility is to return the applicant to his/her country of origin or an alternative "safe" country. The particular discursive moves of any or all of the participants in evidence in interpreted interactions are directly informed by both the local communicative and global political processes described above.

The interpreters involved in this process do not come from nowhere. They too are socially and politically situated. They are therefore operating at the grinding edge of macro-political realities. Given that asylum cases are won or lost based on the competing "ontological" narratives of applicants and "public" narratives of the receiving countries (Baker 2006, 4; see also Barsky 1996; Blommaert 2001; Jacquemet 2005; Maryns 2006), both sides have a stake in believing in and seeking to ensure that their case for or against persecution is relayed as comprehensively and "objectively" as possible.

In some instances, it is the *objective* norms of interpreting themselves that are believed to work for or against this aim, as the following examples suggest. In Example 1, in response to my question, the adjudicator describes as "unfortunate" but nevertheless "appropriate" the rule that interpreter and expert roles must be clearly distinguished from one another despite her own instincts against this distinction in the particular hearing described.

Example 1
M: If there were any queries about a political fact or a cultural fact or a social fact, a practice of some kind that takes place or doesn't take place, would you be comfortable with an interpreter making any clarification along these lines?

A: Terribly tempting, and I had the other day a Nepalese with a Gurkha, with a wise looking, to me a retired Colonel from the Gurkha Regiment I would have thought, who was doing some work as an interpreter and I was simply dying to ask him because I felt that from this man we could have got some balanced view that we would not have had from the so-called expert reports, but no it's not appropriate. No, it's not their job. If they're clued up about their country then they ought to be putting themselves forward as experts, so unfortunately, no.

In Example 2, however, this same adjudicator acknowledges as "silly" the bureaucratic consequences of another rule that interpreters (if willing and able) cannot do sight translations of short documents because they are written and not oral forms of communication.

Example 2
But sometimes, it's just silly, because you're faced with the prospect of adjourning something otherwise, because a letter had just come in, and it's nobody's fault, it seems that it's just come in and there's twenty words to be interpreted, well if nobody minds and the interpreter will read it out for me, that's fine.

At other times, it is the interpreter's *subjectivity*, based on political or national allegiances that is felt to have an effect on a case. In Example 3, an interpreter coordinator working in a major UK detention centre describes to me the difficulty of being aware of interpreters' actual or possible manipulation of claimants' stories. In the case he describes, the interpreter, a native of the Czech Republic, is interpreting for a Roma Gypsy. In Example 4, this same difficulty emerges for another interpreter coordinator over the issue of recruitment.

Example 3
IC: I've known of a situation where the client has turned round to the legal rep and has tried to say I don't want this person tomorrow because, you know, I don't trust him and we were told by the Home Office interpreter that our interpreter had said "Look, you know, that's not true, what you're claiming it's not like that in the Czech Republic", and, you know, there are problems, that's why we tend to use tried and tested people.

M: Yes, the client would feel the interpreter was misrepresenting him.

IC: Yes, it's like telling a story and missing out details. They leave out dates, they could leave out names and places. And it has happened, it goes on, and you pick it up the next day when you're in there and you've got a different interpreter sitting next to you and you feel that your client is saying something different to what the client said yesterday, and at the end of it you say to your client "you told me this yesterday" and then he says "no I said this", and you've got to make that judgement whether it's your client or whether it was the interpreter and most times the adviser will be able to make an assessment. And then you say "look fine you told me this yesterday, but I need to make representation, which one do you want me to go with"? Because then if you go against what they've said in the Home Office interview you've got to justify it really well because it raises that credibility thing again.

Example 4
I can remember I was recruiting Turkish interpreters around Christmas time and there was one who was really good and I thought, oh yes, maybe we could take her on. I was having trouble finding the right person actually, Turkish, and getting a bit exasperated. And then one of the caseworkers here sort of filled me in and said, don't take her on, her husband's in the PKK [a Kurdish independence party] and they're really extreme. So it's like aaah. So if they're very well known in the community for one reason or another then, you know, again you've got to have the clients' trust of uppermost concern.

In Example 5 and Example 6, two solicitors express their concern about different forms of cooptation of interpreters into the asylum system itself.

Example 5
The Home Office interpreters quite often get sucked into the Home Office system, so they are a part of the Home Office machinery, they've got a vested interest in weeding out the ones to be refused, and they're part of that culture because they're all behind locked doors and they all come in at the same time and so I think that's an additional pressure in terms of the Home Office interpreting which you don't get in court.

Example 6
By [names a London Underground Station] you'll see a sign that says [names an interpreter, X]. [X] brings them to law firms. They will turn up at such and such a time outside such and such a tube station and the interpreter will pick up clients and take them to firm X. What on earth goes on in his office I shudder to think. Are cases being concocted? There's stuff that goes on.

Interpreters are also divided, sometimes within themselves, over the issue of boundary maintenance in interpreted interactions. In Example 7, an interpreter coordinator and trainer refers to this difficulty for interpreters in general.

321

Example 7
It can be very difficult for interpreters to be interpreting in situations which might be very similar to the ones they themselves have come through. And I know how difficult interpreters find it sometimes well (a) to remain impartial, which they have to be able to do obviously, but (b) not to get emotionally sort of caught up with it, even if they manage to remain impartial in the actual interview. But actually how it leaves them feeling, it's a big issue.

Example 8 illustrates this difficulty. The interpreter, himself a torture victim, discusses interpreting for applicants whom he feels, based on his own experiences of torture, tell lies about theirs in order to conform to the official established criteria for establishing persecution and thus strengthen their chances to be granted asylum.

Example 8
I have witnessed liars get granted asylum and genuine refugees be refused. I have been tortured so I know what torture is. When I hear people say they have been tortured for 5 to 10 minutes with electric shock I know they are lying as it only takes 1 or 2 minutes to make an impact. I know what the pain of torture feels like. When you are hung in chains, for example, you sweat, lots of people never mention this, I think they are lying . . .

For this interpreter, however, there is no question of challenging these accounts; in his view, both the "liars" and the "genuine refugees" are equally victims. As he says about the "liars", "you gotta do what you gotta do". It is an interesting example of how personal experience, national and political allegiances and impartiality come to intersect in particular ways in interpreted events.

In this instance, the maintenance of impartiality, an interpreting norm perceived as a reflection/guarantor of objectivity, is firmly grounded in the subjectivity of the interpreter and his view of the asylum system as an institution in which facts can be manipulated on both sides in order to win.

Despite the evidence in the above examples of a range of "communicative rights" claimed by or withheld from interpreters, given the present constitution of the interpreting profession as a "zone of uncertainty" (Inghilleri 2005), the status of interpreters' knowledge remains largely vulnerable to exercises of power outside of their control, more authorised discourse, less democratic iteration. Nevertheless, as these examples make clear, in the arc of activity across the asylum system, interpreters are pivotal players in the emergence of a global society, not in some over-idealised linguistic or cultural conduit role but as participants in discourse. They enable the system to function by ensuring both the flow of communication and of applicants.

In this role, they may codify, clarify or challenge the cultural and linguistic boundaries used to symbolise national and political agendas. They are excluded and empowered, traitors and truth tellers, nationalists and internationalists, embodying the paradoxes of transnational discourses of belonging, out of which both conflict and consensus emerge.

Note

1 The principle of non-refoulment is one provision of the 1951 Convention that remains strictly implemented by signatory states. Under this provision, governments are prohibited from returning refugees "in any manner whatsoever to the frontiers of territories where his life or freedom would be threatened on account of his race, religion, nationality, membership of a particular social group or political opinion" (Joly 1996, 8).

References

Alba, R., and Nee, V. 2003. *Remaking the American mainstream: Assimilation and contemporary immigration.* Cambridge, MA: Harvard University Press.

Baker, M. 2006. *Translation and conflict: A narrative account.* London & New York: Routledge.

Barsky, R. F. 1996. The interpreter as intercultural agent in convention refugee hearings. *The Translator* 1: 45–64.

Benhabib, S. 2004. *The rights of others: Aliens, residents and citizens.* Cambridge: Cambridge University Press.

——. 2002. *The claims of culture.* Princeton, N.J.: Princeton University Press.

Blommaert, J. 2001. Investigating narrative inequality: African asylum seekers' stories in Belgium. *Discourse and Society* 12(4): 413–49.

Bot, H. 2005. *Dialogue interpreting in mental health.* Amsterdam: Rodopi.

Bourdieu, P. 1991. *Language and symbolic power. Translated by Gino Raymond and Matthew Adamson.* Cambridge: Polity Press.

Buzelin, H. 2005. Translation studies, ethnography and the production of knowledge. In *In Translation: Reflections, refractions, transformations*, edited by Paul St-Pierre and Prufella C. Kar. pp. 25–41. New Delhi: Pencraft International.

Carens, J. H. 2000. *Culture, citizenship and community.* Oxford: Oxford University Press.

Cole, P. 2000. *Philosophies of exclusion: Liberal political theory and immigration.* Edinburgh: Edinburgh University Press.

Crisp, J. 2003. Refugees and the global politics of asylum. In *The politics of migration*, edited by Sarah Spencer. pp. 75–87. Oxford: Blackwell Publishing.

Cronin, M. 2003. *Translation and globalisation.* London: Routledge.

Donnelly, J. 2003. *Universal human rights in theory and practice* 2nd ed. Ithaca, N.Y.: Cornell University Press.

Doyle, M. W. 1997. *Ways of war and peace: Realism, liberalism and socialism.* New York: Norton.

Even-Zohar, I. 1978. The position of translated literature within the literary polysystem. In *Literature and translation: New perspectives in literary studies*, edited by

James Holmes, Jose Lambert, and Raymond Van den Broeck. pp. 117–27. Leuven: Acco.

Forsythe, D. P. 2000. *Human rights in international relations.* Cambridge: Cambridge University Press.

Geddes, A., and Favell, A., eds. 1999. *The politics of belonging: Migrants and minorities in contemporary Europe.* Aldershot: Ashgate.

Gentile, L. 2002. New asylum regimes or a world without asylum? The myth of international protection. In *Global changes in asylum regimes*, edited by Danièle Joly, pp. 38–47. Houndmills, Basingstoke: Palgrave Macmillan.

Gentzler, E., and Tymoczko, M., eds. 2002. *Translation and power.* Amherst, Mass.: University of Massachusetts Press.

Hale, S. 2004. *The discourse of court interpreting: Discourse practices of the law, the witness and the interpreter.* Amsterdam: John Benjamins.

Held, D. 2002. Law of states, law of peoples. *Legal Theory* 8: 1–44.

Held, D., McGrew, A., Goldblatt, D., and Perraton., J. 1999. *Global transformations.* Cambridge: Polity Press.

Inghilleri, M. 2005. Mediating zones of uncertainty: Interpreter agency, the interpreting habitus and political asylum adjudication. *The Translator* 11(1): 69–85.

Jackson, R. 2005. *Classical modern thought on international relations: From anarchy to cosmopolis.* Houndmills, Basingstoke: Palgrave Macmillan.

Jacobson, D. 1996. *Rights across borders: Immigration and the decline of citizenship.* Baltimore, Md.: John Hopkins University Press.

Jacquemet, M. 2005. The registration interview: Restricting refugees' narrative performances. In *Dislocations/relocations: Narratives of displacement*, edited by Mike Baynham and Anna De Fina. Manchester: St Jerome Publishing.

Joly, D. 1996. *Haven or Hell? Asylum policies and refugees in Europe.* Houndmills, Basingstoke: MacMillan Press Ltd.

——. ed. 2002. *Global changes in asylum regimes.* Houndmills, Basingstoke: Palgrave Macmillan.

Joppke, C. 1998. *Challenge to the nation state: Immigration in Western Europe and the United States.* Oxford: Oxford University Press.

Jordan, B., and Düvell, F. 2003. *Migration: The boundaries of equality and justice.* Cambridge: Polity Press.

Kant, I. 1957. *Perpetual peace*, edited by Lewis White Beck. New York: The Bobbs-Merrill Company, Inc. First published 1795.

Maryns, K. 2006. *The asylum speaker: Language in the Belgian asylum procedure.* Manchester: St Jerome Publishing.

Mason, I., ed. 1999. *Dialogue interpreting Special issue. The Translator* 5(2).

Papastergiadis, N. 2000. *The turbulence of migration.* Cambridge: Polity Press.

Portes, A. 1997. Immigration theory for a new century: Some problems and opportunities. *International Migration Review* 31(4): 799–825.

Reitz, J. G. 2003. Immigration and Canadian nation-building in the transition to a knowledge economy. In *Controlling immigration: a global perspective*, edited by Wayne A. Cornelius, Peter L. Martin, James F. Hollifield, and Takeyuki Tsuda. 2nd ed. pp. 97–133. Stanford, Calif.: Stanford University Press.

Robinson, D. 1997. *Translation and empire.* Manchester: St Jerome Publishing.

Schuck, P. H. 1998. *Citizens, strangers and in-betweens.* Boulder, Col.: Westview Press.

Soysal, Y. N. 1994. *Limits of citizenship: Migrants and postnational membership in Europe.* Chicago, Ill.: University of Chicago Press.

Statham, P. 2003. Understanding anti-asylum rhetoric: Restrictive politics or racist publics? In *The politics of migration*, edited by Sarah Spencer. pp. 163–77. Oxford: Blackwell Publishing.

Toury, G. 1995. *Descriptive translation studies and beyond.* Amsterdam: John Benjamins.

Walzer, M. 1983. *Spheres of justice: A defence of pluralism and equality.* New York: Basic Books.

54

THE SUBJECT OF TRANSLATION/
THE SUBJECT IN TRANSIT

Naoki Sakai

Source: Extract from Introduction to Naoki Sakai (1997) *Translation and Subjectivity: On "Japan" and Cultural Nationalism*, Minneapolis and London: University of Minnesota Press, pp. 8–17.

A tentative distinction between heterolingual and homolingual addresses is thus called for in order to mark a difference in the attitude of the addresser to the addressee, which in fact derives from two conflicting modes of alterity. The homolingual address assumes the normalcy of reciprocal and transparent communication in a homogeneous medium so that the idea of translation does not make sense unless a positively heterogeneous medium is involved. In contrast, the heterolingual address does not abide by the normalcy of reciprocal and transparent communication, but instead assumes that every utterance can fail to communicate because heterogeneity is inherent in any medium, linguistic or otherwise. Every translation calls for a counter-translation, and in this sort of address it is clearly evident that within the framework of communication, translation must be endless. Thus, in the heterolingual address, the addressee must translate any delivery, whether in speech or writing, in order for that delivery to actually be received. Also in the heterolingual address, addressing in enunciation is not supposed to coincide with eventual communication, so that it is demanded of the addressee to *act* to incept or receive what is offered by the addresser. This is to say, what is addressed to the addressee is not automatically delivered precisely because of the disparity between addressing and communicating, of a disparity that also expresses the essential *distance* not only of the addressee from the addresser but also of the addressee or addresser from himself or herself. In the heterolingual address, therefore, the act of inception or reception occurs as the act of translation, and translation takes place at every listening or reading. Whereas translation is necessary only between the interior of a homogeneous medium and its outside in the case of the homolingual address, it is upheld in the heterolingual address that, in principle, translation occurs whenever the addressee accepts a delivery from the addresser.

Thus differentiated, the two addresses respectively suggest the two alternative attitudes with regard to the otherness of the addressee. Although you would presume that the addressee who is incapable of comprehending your delivery should appear marked and anticipated as such to you when you adopt the attitude of the homolingual address, such a precaution or anterior knowledge is not guaranteed in the attitude of the heterolingual address. In the latter attitude, you would probably have to address yourself to the addressee, no matter whether the addressee is singular or plural, without assuming that the addressee would necessarily and automatically comprehend what you were about to say: you would, of course, wish the addressee to comprehend what you say—for, without this wish, the act of addressing would not constitute itself—but you would not take it for granted. In this respect, you are always confronted, so to speak, with foreigners in your enunciation when your attitude is that of the heterolingual address. Precisely because you wish to communicate with her, him, or them, so the first, and perhaps most fundamental, determination of your addressee is that of the one who might not comprehend your language, that is, of the foreigner. The idea of a nonaggregate community of foreigners is unintelligible unless we are able to conceive of a community where we relate to ourselves through the attitude of the heterolingual address.

Precisely because of her positionality, the translator has to enunciate for an essentially mixed and linguistically heterogeneous audience. In order to function as a translator, she must listen, read, speak, or write in the multiplicity of languages, so that the representation of translation as a transfer from one language to another is possible only as long as the translator acts as a heterolingual agent and addresses herself from a position of linguistic multiplicity: she necessarily occupies a position in which multiple languages are implicated within one another.[10] The translator who is present to both the writer and the readers regulates communicative transactions, but her mediation must be erased in the representation of translation according to which the message issued by the writer in one language is transferred into an equivalent message in another language, which is then received by the readers. In these cases as well, the writer addresses the readers with the presumption of a homolingual communion. The assumption that one can make oneself understood without perceptible hindrance, as long as one belongs in the same linguistic community, survives intact here. Translation is believed to be necessary because incommensurability exists not necessarily between the addresser and the addressee but essentially between one linguistic community and another.

It is well known that Roman Jakobson classified translation into three classes: "1) Intralingual translation or *rewording* is an interpretation of verbal signs by means of other signs of the same language. 2) Interlingual translation or *translation proper* is an interpretation of verbal signs by means of some other language. 3) Intersemiotic translation or *transmutation* is an interpretation of verbal signs by means of signs of nonverbal sign systems."[11]

I do not think that the propriety of Jakobson's "translation proper" can be maintained outside the attitude of the homolingual address. And we would have to call into question the supposed discernibility of interlingual from intralingual translation, of translation between separate languages from rewording within the same language unity, as soon as we adopt the attitude of the heterolingual address. In other words, viewed from the position of the translator, neither the unitary unity of a language nor the plurality of language unities can be taken for granted. Moreover, not only the professionally assigned translator, but the rest of us as well, would have to be responsible for the task of the translator. At the same time, we would be obliged to call into question other discursive positivities similar to the unity of a particular ethnic or national language, such as the unities of ethnic and national cultures, when we take the attitude of the heterolingual address. So far I have talked as if those unities, English, Japanese, and other language unities, and the name "translator" itself were self-evident, but as soon as we are in the heterolingual address, we will find that these putative unities and names have to be put in brackets.

In addition, how could we possibly define what Jakobson calls intersemiotic transmutation, when we cannot easily separate verbal signs from nonverbal signs in such texts as the *calligraphic* one. Is a calligraphic text verbal or nonverbal? Is it a text to see or a text to read? Is it possible to translate a calligraphic text? If it is, in what sense is it so? What are the conditions under which the verbal is immediately equated to the linguistic? A series of questions like these will gradually suggest to us that there could be discursive formations in which the propriety of "translation proper" can hardly be taken for granted. Today, no matter whether you reside around the Pacific Basin or along the Atlantic, the idea of translation is almost always self-evident and very few would insist otherwise. However, by imposing on ourselves the attitude of the heterolingual address, we are able to call into question that self-evidence, and thereby explore those ethicopolitical assumptions and habituated regimes that serve to sustain this position.

Let me point to two sites where the problematic of translation seems to manifest itself most intensely, so as to delimit that self-evidence and mark its historicity. The first concerns itself with subjectivity, and the second with schematism in translation.

The subject of translation/the subject in transit

Can the translator make a promise in translation? Can she then be responsible for what she says while translating? The answer must always be double as long as the name "translator" signifies neither a professional specialty nor a social status but instead designates an agent or a human being who is engaged in the act of translation. Yes, the translator can make a promise, but always on behalf of somebody else. In that respect, no, she "herself" cannot really make a promise. Likewise, the translator must be responsible for her translation, for every word of it, but she cannot be held responsible for what is pledged in what she says. For she is not allowed to say what she means in what she says in translation; she is supposed to say what she says without meaning. At the same time that the translator must be absolutely responsible for what she says, her task begins with her pledge to say what the original addresser means to say. Her responsibility consists in her commitment to withdraw her wish to express herself from what she says even though she has to seek and interpret what the addresser means in the first place. Therefore the translator is also the interpreter.

A cursory reflection like this on the relations between the original addresser and his translator, or the translator and her addressee, amply illustrates the extremely ambiguous and unstable positionality the translator has to occupy with regard to the original addresser and the addressee. The translator listens to or reads what the original addresser enunciates. In this respect, there is no doubt that she is an addressee. But it is not supposed that the addresser speaks or writes to her. The addressee for the enunciation of the addresser must not be located at the site where the translator is, so that the addressee is always located elsewhere in translation. The translator is both an addressee and not an addressee at the same time. This is to say that, even though the translator is spoken or written to, she cannot be addressed as "you" by the addresser. Or, if she can be addressed as "you," then the putative audience for whom the translator interprets cannot be the direct addressee in the enunciation of the addresser; that audience will be redesignated as a third party, as "them." A similar disjunction can be observed in the translational enunciation of the translator. The translator speaks or writes to the audience, so in this respect she is undoubtedly an addresser. But, supposedly it is not the translator who in translation is speaking or writing for the addressee. "I" uttered by the translator does not designate the translator herself but the original addresser as the subject of the original enunciation. And if by "I" the translator indicates the subject of the secondary and translational enunciation, she will then have to designate the original addresser as "he" or "she."

Let me reformulate this pronominal disjunction slightly differently. It is always possible for what is translated to be conveyed as a quotation, either in direct or indirect mode. Suppose the original addresser says "Kyô wa ii tenki da." Then a translation of what the original addresser says can, for example, be accommodated as a subordinate clause in the statement of either "He/she (= the original addresser) said, 'It is fine today,'" or "He/she said that it was fine that day." Yet, when explicitly formatted as a subordinate clause, a translational utterance as a whole is rendered as the translator's—that is, the utterance would present itself as being addressed to the audience not by the original addresser but by the translator. In order to avoid the dislocation of the original addresser, the translator chooses to drop the phrase indicating the subject of the enunciation, and just say: "It is fine today." In translational utterance, however, we cannot assume that the translator can immediately make manifest her rapport to the subject of the enunciation by restating this utterance in the following manner: "I say 'It is fine today'" or "I say that it is fine today." Rather, it must be restated as follows: "I say 'he said "It is fine today"'" or "I say that he said that it was fine that day." In translational enunciation, every utterance must be able to be accompanied by the designation through a double framing "I say, 'the addresser says, ". . . ."'" In this respect, the translator must speak in a forked tongue, and her enunciation must necessarily be one of mimicry. Furthermore, the translator renders conspicuous the operation of framing in the process of the constitution of subjectivity in enunciation.[12]

In the enunciation of translation, the subject of the enunciation and the subject of the enunciated are not expected to coincide with one another. The translator's desire must be at least displaced, if not entirely dissipated, in translational enunciation. Thus, the translator cannot be designated either as "I" or as "you" straightforwardly: she disrupts the attempt to appropriate the relation of the addresser and the addressee into the *personal* relation of first person vis-à-vis second person. To follow the determination of a "person" as espoused by Émile Benveniste—that is, that only those directly addressing and addressed in what he calls "discourse" as distinct from "story" or "history" can be called persons, and that those who are referred to or talked about in the capacity of "he," "she," or "they" in "story" or "history" cannot be "persons"[13]—the addresser, the translator, and the addressee cannot be persons simultaneously; the translator cannot be either the first or second or even third "person" undisruptively. Although the translator can be so in Foucauldian "discourse"—whose formulation I understand to be explicitly antipersonalist—she can only have a transitory and temporary position in the personalist notion of "discourse" such as Benveniste's. Thanks to this formulation of "discourse" in which every enunciative position is depersonalized from the outset, we dispense with the hermeneutic problematics of the horizon of understanding. Ineluctably, translation introduces a disjunctive instability into the putatively *personal* relations among the agents of speech, writing, listening, and reading. In respect to personal relationality as well as to the addresser/addressee structure, the translator must be internally split and multiple, and devoid of a stable positionality. At best, she can be *a subject in transit*, first because the translator cannot be an "individual" in the sense of *individuum* in order to perform translation, and second because she is a *singular* that marks an elusive point of discontinuity in the social, whereas translation is the practice of creating continuity at that singular point of discontinuity. Translation is an instance of *continuity in discontinuity*[14] and a poietic social practice that institutes a relation at the site of incommensurability. This is why the aspect of discontinuity inherent in translation would be completely repressed if we were to determine translation to be a form of communication. And this is what I have referred to as the *oscillation or indeterminacy of personality in translation.*

Thus, by considering the position of the translator, we are introduced into the problematic of subjectivity in an illuminating manner. The internal split within the translator, which reflects in a certain way the split between the addresser—or the addressee, and furthermore the split within the addresser and the addressee themselves[15]—and the translator demonstrates the way in which the subject constitutes itself. In a sense, this internal split within the translator is homologous to what is referred to as the fractured I, the temporality of "I speak," which necessarily introduces an irreparable distance between the speaking I and the I that is signified, between the subject of the enunciation and the subject of the enunciated. Yet, in the case of translation, the oscillation or indeterminacy of the personality of the translator marks the instability of the we as the subject rather than the I. Particularly in the regime of homolingual address, the translator is supposed to assume the role of the arbitrator not only between the addresser and the addressee but also between the linguistic communities of the addresser and the addressee. Thus, translation ceases to be a *repetition* and is rendered representable. And, in the regime of homolingual address, translation as repetition is often exhaustibly replaced by the representation of translation.

Let me elaborate on the process in which translation is displaced by its representation, and the constitution of collective subjectivity such as national and ethnic subjectivity in the representation of translation. Through the labor of the translator, the incommensurability as difference that calls for the service of the translator in the first place is negotiated and worked on. In other words, the work of translation is a practice by which the initial discontinuity between the addresser and the addressee is made continuous and recognizable. In this respect, translation is just like other social practices that render the points of discontinuity in social formation continuous.[16] Only retrospectively and after translation, therefore, can we recognize the initial incommensurability as a gap, crevice, or border between fully constituted entities, spheres, or domains.[17] But, when represented as a gap, crevice or border, it is no longer incommensurate. As I discuss in chapter 4, incommensurability or difference is more like "feeling" that is prior to the explanation of how incommensurability is given rise to and cannot be determined as a represented difference (or species difference in the arborescent schemata of the species and the genus) between two subjects or entities.[18] What makes it possible to represent the initial difference as an already determined difference between one language unity and another is the work of translation itself. This is why we always have to remind ourselves that the untranslatable, or what can never be appropriated by the economy of translational communication, cannot exist prior to the enunciation of translation. It is translation that gives birth to the untranslatable. Thus, the untranslatable is as much a testimony to the sociality of the translator, whose figure exposes the presence of a nonaggregate community between the addresser and the addressee, as to the translatable itself. However, the essential sociality of the untranslatable is ignored in the homolingual address, and with the repression of this insight, the homolingual address ends up equating translation to communication.

By erasing the temporality of translation with which the *oscillation or indeterminacy of personality in translation* is closely associated and which can be thought in an analogy to the aporetic temporality of "I think," we displace translation with the representation of translation. Only in the representation of translation can we construe the process of translation as a transfer of some message from "this" side to "that" side, as a dialogue between one person and another, between one group and another, as if dialogue should necessarily take place according to the model of communication Thus the representation of translation also enables the representation of ethnic or national subjects, and, in spite of the presence of the translator who is always in between, translation, no longer as difference or repetition but as representation, is made to discriminatorily posit one language unity against another (and one "cultural" unity against another). In this sense, the representation of translation transforms *difference in repetition* into *species difference* (diaphora) between two specific identities, and helps constitute the putative unities of national languages, and thereby reinscribes the initial difference and incommensurability as a specific, that is, commensurate and conceptual, difference between two particular languages within the continuity of the generality of Language.[19] As a result of this displacement, translation is represented as a form of communication between two fully formed, different but *comparable*, language communities.

Following Kantian schematism, I have called the discursive apparatus that makes it possible to represent translation "the schema of cofiguration." As the practice of translation remains radically heterogeneous to the representation of translation, translation need not be represented as a communication between two clearly delineated linguistic communities. There should be many different ways to apprehend translation in which the subjectivity of a community does not necessarily constitute itself in terms of language unity or the homogeneous sphere of ethnic or national culture. The particular representation of translation in which translation is understood to be communication between two particular languages is, no doubt, a historical construct. And it is this particular representation of translation that gave rise to the possibility of figuring out the unity of ethnic or national language together with another language unity. Indeed, this is one of the reasons for which I have claimed that the Japanese language was born, or stillborn, in the eighteenth century among a very small portion of literary people, when the schema of cofiguration came into being. This is to say that the schema of cofiguration is a means by which a national community represents itself to itself, thereby constituting itself as a subject. But it seemed to me that this autoconstitution of the national subject would not proceed unitarily; on the contrary, it would constitute itself only by making visible the figure of an other with which it engages in a translational relationship. Hence, the figure of the Japanese language was given rise to cofiguratively, only when some Japanese intellectuals began to determine the predominant inscriptive styles of the times as pertaining to the figure of the specifically Chinese, or as being contaminated by the Chinese language. It is important to note that, through the representation of translation, the two unities are represented as two equivalents resembling one another. Precisely because they are represented in equivalence and resemblance, however, it is possible to determine them as conceptually different. The relationship of the two terms in equivalence and resemblance gives rise to a possibility of extracting an infinite number of distinctions between the two. Just as in the cofiguration of "the West and the Rest" in which the West represents itself, thereby constituting itself cofiguratively by representing the exemplary figure of the Rest, conceptual difference allows for the evaluative determination of the one term as superior over the other. This is how the desire for "Japanese language" was invoked through the schema of cofiguration in the regime of translation.

Finally, I must deal with one formative principle without which the national subject would fail to gather together a wide variety of conceptual differences around the unitary figure of an ethnos or nation; for, even processed through the schema of cofiguration, the regime of translation could multiply conceptual differences in many disparate registers. In particular there is no guarantee that Jakobson's intralingual translations can be organized with the interlingual translation or *translation proper* as the overall guiding rule of translation. Conceptual differences can be posited between one style and another—*Kanbun* or literary Chinese and *Sôrôbun* or a distinct epistolary style mixing the syntax of literary Chinese and *Kana* characters, for example, in the case of Tokugawa Japan—one regional dialect and another, so-called ideographic and phonetic inscriptive systems, and so on. These differences can be marked between genres, but what characterizes the emergence of the national language is that generic differences that can be represented cofiguratively in the regime of translation are all subsumed under the generality of the national language; these genres have to be perceived as the species within the genus of the Japanese language. This time, although our terminology may be confusing since the term "genre" itself derives from the genus, the generic difference must be allocated at the level of the species while the unity of national language transcends the species and is conceived of as an overarching genus. What Jakobson implies by the differentiation between intralingual and interlingual translations is nothing but the hierarchization of these translational registers. It goes without saying that this differentiation itself is a historical construct. I believe that, in historical contexts prior to the eighteenth century in the geographic regions designated as Japan today, we cannot assume such a generic taxonomy, and that the lack of historicity would only sanction the continuous regimes of National History and National Literature. At the same time, we now can understand why the regime of translation with the schema of cofiguration plays such an important role in the formation of the Japanese as a national subject.

By now it should be evident that, given my analysis of the regime of translation and the homolingual address, culturalism in which Japanese culture and nation are obstinately reified and essentialized is, as a matter of fact, not particular to Japanese journalism and academia at all. Culturalism that endorses nationalism in terms of national language and ethnic culture is as persistently endemic in Japanese Studies in the United States, Europe, and elsewhere as in Japan today. For, as I will show in some of the following chapters, behind Westerners' as well as Japanese insistence on Japanese cultural uniqueness looms an equally obstinate essentialization of the West.

East Asian names throughout this book, except those of Asians who are resident outside East Asia, are written in the East Asian order—surname first—after the style Asian Studies specialists have adopted in their studies in English.

Notes

10 With regard to the limits of the theories of translation, Jacques Derrida poses the following questions: "Let us note one of the limits of the theories of translation. They treat passages from one language to another too much and do not adequately consider the possibility for languages to be implicated into more than two [à plus de deux] in one text. How do you translate a text written in plural languages at the same time? How do you 'render' the effect of plurality? And if we translate by plural languages at the same time, will we call it translation?" ("Des tours de Babel," in *Psyché* [Paris: Galilée, 1987], pp. 207–8, emphasis in the original).

11 Roman Jakobson, "On Linguistic Aspects of Translation," in *Selected Writings*, vol. 2 (The Hague and Paris: Mouton, 1971), p. 261. As I have argued, there is no reason why translation must be understood to be interlingual translation (Sakai, *Voices of the Past*, pp. 211–39). To use Jakobson's terminology, the distinction between intralingual and interlingual translations cannot be sustained unless the economy of transmutation is captured in a specific regime of intersemiotic (or intertextual) correlation, that is, in a regime I call phonocentrism. Where there is no phonocentrism, intralingual and interlingual translations can hardly be distinguished.

12 For discussion of framing and subjectivity, see Sakai, *Voices of the Post*, pp. 113–207.

13 Émile Benveniste, *Problems in General Linguistics*, trans. Mary Elizabeth Meek (Coral Gables: University of Florida Press, 1971), p. 224.

14 This phrase with an apparent resonance with modern mathematics is from Nishida Kitarô (1870–1945). In conceptualizing social praxis and self-awareness (*jikaku*), Nishida appealed to the mathematical formulation of discontinuity. Following the tradition of modern philosophy since Leibniz and Kant, he conceived of the formation of the practical subject after the model of differential calculus but at the singular point of discontinuity. Therefore, for Nishida, as his later formulation clearly shows, the constitution of the subject in ethical action is also the poiesis or making of the social formation. "Hirenzoku no renzoku" (or continuity of discontinuity) thus suggests the possibility of conceptualizing the constitution of the subject at the site of the incommensurate in the social. See "*Genjitsu no sekai no ronri-teki kôzô*" or "the logical structure of the real world" (1934), in *Nishida Kitarô Zenshû*, vol. 7 (Tokyo: Iwanami Shoten, 1965) pp. 217–304, and "*Sekai no jiko dôitsu to renzoku*" or "the self-identity of the world and continuity" (1935), in ibid., vol. 8, pp. 7–106.

15 The split cannot be contained only in the cases of translation, for, as Briankle Chang suggests, the putative unities of the addresser and the addressee can hardly be sustained because the addresser himself is split and multiple, as is figuratively illustrated by the Plato-Socrates doublet in Derrida's "Envoi" in *The Post Card* (pp. 1–256). With regard to communication in general, Chang argues, "Because both delivery and signing are haunted by the same structural threat of the message's nonarrival or adestination, the paradox of the signature also invades communication. Communication occurs only insofar as the delivery of the message *may* fail; that is, communication takes place only to the extent that there is a separation between the sender and receiver, and this separation, this distance, this *spacing*, creates the possibility for the message *not* to arrive" (Briankle G. Chang, *Deconstructing Communication* [Minneapolis: University of Minnesota Press, 1996], p. 216).

16 Putting forth a different conception of continuity in discontinuity, Tanabe Hajime, who like his mentor Nishida based his argument on insights from modern mathematics, insisted that social formation in general is infinitely divisible and that a society cannot be conceived of as a homogeneous and harmonious unity. On the contrary, a society always contains an infinite number of societies, and every society consists of discontinuities and conflicts. What unites a society into one is not naturally given. Even an ethnic society, he argued, is not a given unity. Whether racial, ethnic, or national, no identity is naturally given and every identity has to be socially constructed through the dialectic process of negativity. See "*Shakai sonzai no ronri*" or "the logic of social beings," in *Tanabe Hajime Zenshû*, vol. 6 (Tokyo: Chikuma Shobo, 1963), pp. 51–168, and "*Shu no ronri to sekai zushiki*" or "the logic of the species and the schema 'world,'" in ibid., pp. 299–397.

It is important to keep in mind that Nishida and Tanabe both offered philosophical formulas by which to undermine the validity of ethnic nationalism and to legitimate the unity of the Japanese Empire against the implicit threat of anticolonial ethnic separatism. I am most critical of the philosophical discourses of Nishida Kitarô and Tanabe Hajime, two champions of what is usually referred to as the Kyoto School of Philosophy. But my critique of their philosophical formation is not premised on an assumption that their philosophy was primarily concerned with the justification of Japanese ethnic and cultural nationalism. On the contrary, I characterize theirs primarily as a universalistic philosophy of an imperial nationalism, and only secondarily as an ethnic nationalism in the sense that every universalism that does not denounce imperialism is inherently ethnocentric.

17 For example, Willard V. O. Quine's hypothesis of the radical translation, from which all the help of the interpreter is excluded, suffers from this retrospectivism. If there is no help of the interpreter, is it possible to recognize "a language of a hitherto untouched people"? See Willard V. O. Quine, *Word and Object* (Cambridge: MIT Press, 1960), pp. 26–80.

18 For a more detailed discussion about "feeling" and difference, see chapter 4, note 7. And for the poetic aspect of "feeling," see Gilles Deleuze, *Difference and Repetition*, trans. Paul Patton (New York: Columbia University Press, 1994), pp. 291ff.

19 Here let me draw attention to the notions of representation, concept, difference without concept, and conceptual difference, according to Gilles Deleuze. "The relation of a concept to its object under this double aspect, in the form that it assumes in this memory and this self-consciousness, is called representation" (ibid., p. 11). ". . . every determination is conceptual in the last instance, or actually belongs to the comprehension of a concept" (ibid., p. 12). "In so far as it serves as a determination, a predicate must remain fixed in the concept while becoming something else in the thing (animal becomes something other in man and in horse; humanity something other in Peter and in Paul). This is why the comprehension of the concept is infinite; having become other in the thing, the predicate is like the object of another predicate in the concept. But this is also why each determination remains general or defines a resemblance, to the extent that it remains fixed in the concept and applicable by right to an infinity of things" (ibid.). "Thus, the principle of difference understood as difference in the concept does not oppose but, on the contrary, allows the greatest space possible for the apprehension of resemblances. Even from the point of view of conundrums, the question "What difference is there?" may always be transformed into: "What resemblance is there?" But above all, in classification, the determination of species implies and supposes a continual evaluation of resemblances" (ibid.). "Repetition thus appears as difference without a concept, repetition which escapes indefinitely continued conceptual difference" (ibid., p. 13).

55

TRANSLATION IN WARTIME

Vicente L. Rafael

Source: *Public Culture* 19(2) (2007): 239–46.

Addressing a gathering of university presidents attending a conference at the State Department on January 5, 2006, President George W. Bush spoke about the country's dire need for translators to shore up national security. He promised to spend $114 million to expand the teaching of so-called critical languages such as Arabic, Farsi, Chinese, and so forth, at the university as well as K–12 levels as part of a new federal program called the National Security Language Initiative. He illustrated the importance of learning such languages with the following analogy: "In order to convince people we care about them, we've got to understand their culture and show them we care about their culture. You know, when somebody comes to me and speaks Texan, I know they appreciate Texas culture."[1]

Bush initially links translation, entailing the learning of a foreign language and culture, with "care" and "appreciation." If I were to learn "Texan," for example, I would be showing my capacity to defer to his idiom, suppressing my first language in favor of a second, foreign tongue. My deference would be evidence of my ability to recognize and respect his difference and, more generally, to know the difference that the other makes in any speech act. Such knowing is, of course, anything but disinterested, especially when it involves those who have some sort of "Texan" or some other American idiom as their native language. Such becomes evident in the rest of Bush's remarks: "When somebody takes time to figure out how to speak Arabic, it means they're interested in somebody else's culture. . . . We need intelligence officers who when somebody says something in Arabic or Farsi or Urdu, know what they're talking about." Here, "somebody" who "takes the time to figure out how to speak Arabic" is one who shows "interest" rather than "appreciation" in "somebody's culture." There is a curious doubling of the word "somebody" in this passage. The first is one who "takes time" to learn the other's language—Arabic, Farsi, or Urdu—while the second is one who, we might assume, is a native speaker of such languages. The first acts to know what the second is "talking about," while the second simply talks. Unlike the "somebody" who sets aside his or her first language in order to speak "Texan," and so show appreciation for Texans, this other somebody, for example, "intelligence officers," learns Arabic or Farsi because he or she is interested only in the content of the other's speech, listening for that "something" that could be anything, but might also be just the thing from which "we," as non-Arabic and non-Farsi speakers, need to be protected. In this case, translation occurs not in order to welcome and care for the other but precisely to ensure us that the other stays where it belongs.

Learning to translate thus entails two distinct but related movements. On the one hand, one is required to recognize the singularity of each idiom, for example, Texan or Arabic, that makes one distinct from and irreducible to the other. It is for this very reason that speaking the other's language necessarily means deferring to it, giving it primacy, and thereby keeping one's own out of mind. On the other hand, by promising the transportability and substitutability of one language for another, translation raises the possibility of mastering the language of the other, hearing in it some things that the other him- or herself did not mean or did not intend to be heard. We see, then, how translation looks two ways. It opens up a passage to the other in all its otherness, drawing near what at the same time will always remain far. Faithful to the original, it thus allows for the appreciation of and care for the foreigner whose very foreignness becomes an element of oneself. Translating the other's language, one is transformed, becoming other than oneself. However, translation is also a medium for hearing as well as overhearing what others say even if they did not mean to say it. It is in this sense a kind of instrument of surveillance with which to track and magnify the alienness of alien speech, decoding dangers, containing threats, and planning for interventions. Rather than dwell in the hospitality of the other, translation in this latter sense is unfaithful to the original, seeking to put the other in its putative place, apart from the self.

Bush's view on the learning of foreign languages, however crudely phrased, reflects a certain idea about translation that has a long history. Since the Spanish conquest and religious conversion of the native peoples of the New World and the Pacific, various projects of translation have always accompanied, enabled, and at certain moments disabled the spread of empire.[2] As with the Spanish empire, so with the United States: in both, translation has played the key role of what we might think of as an essential supplement. How so?

Demarcating as it seeks to the draw the other near, translation has always had at least a double aspect. First, translation historically has served as an instrument of domination under colonial rule. Speaking the other's language means replacing one's first with a second idiom, investing the second with the primacy that outstrips the first. In a colonial context, the second language, that of the foreign occupier, is usually instituted as the official one, subsuming all other vernaculars. To speak authoritatively and to address state authorities, one must be able to speak up, using this second language in place of one's native speech. Indeed, knowledge of the colonizer's language has often endowed speakers with considerable privileges. By insisting on the inequality of languages, translation tends to promote linguistic hierarchy. Within the context of Western imperialisms and their associated orientalisms, we see how this linguistic hierarchy also generates social hierarchies between those—usually missionaries, colonial officials, and educated elites—who are able to move back and forth between an official and a vernacular, and those—peasants, workers, women, children, the insane, and so on—whose knowledge is restricted to their own. Idealizing the colonizer's speech, empire employs translation as a means for appropriating and reorganizing native languages and their speakers in view of an overarching official language. Translation bound to empire thus imbues a second, foreign language with a social power surpassing any of the local idioms.

There is, however, another aspect to translation that has the potential to lead away from imperial rule. For translation not only erects hierarchy; it can also overcome its distinctions. It does so by establishing connections and contacts across linguistic, social, and geographical divides.[3] As such, translation functions as a telecommunicative medium offering the promise of communication at great distances and the prospect of bridging what had seemed unbridgeable. Such a promise makes conceivable all sorts of affiliations, collaborations, and even friendships between and among colonizers and colonized, even as it raises the possibility for misunderstanding, misrecognition, and conflict. Translation as a technic of promising novel connections can promote the formation of new publics attuned to other modes of publicity that often exceed the borders of the imperial public sphere. Indeed, it is arguably this mediating capacity that makes translation not only a necessary device for linking rulers to ruled—like teletechnologies of all sorts, translation also possesses a certain capacity to reshape the terms of hegemony. We can think of translation, then, as something other than an instrument of imperial power. As the agency of mediation, it is itself a kind of power productive of other modalities of empowerment that comes with crossing and double-crossing differences, linguistic as well as social.

But is there a third possibility? Harnessed into a mere instrument of imperial hegemony or other sorts of power premised on the promise of communication, translation is productive of order and meaning, whether on the register of domination or resistance. Is there a way, though, that translation can also be nonproductive? Can the task of translating result in neither order nor meaning but in an ongoing suspension of both? What happens when translation arrives at its limit, overtaken by the return of that which remains untranslatable?

I'd like to explore this third possibility—of translation giving rise to the untranslatable—by returning to the geopolitical context of George Bush's remarks above, the current U.S. occupation of Iraq. Since the start of the war, a number of news accounts have appeared about the place, at once indispensable and troubling, of Arabic-speaking translators, both Iraqi nationals and Arab American immigrants. From such accounts, it is difficult to infer the social positions of such translators, and as we shall see, it is precisely the indeterminacy of such positions that translation during war makes evident.

Translators are also called interpreters, which is why among the U.S. soldiers they are popularly referred to as "terps." Unlike the Americans they work for, interpreters are forced to hide their identities. They often cover their faces with ski masks and sunglasses as they venture outside the military bases and adopt American pseudonyms such as "Eric" or "Sally" so as to protect themselves from being singled out for insurgent attacks. At the same time, their identity within the U.S. military remains unsettled and unsettling inasmuch as their presence generates both relief and suspicion among soldiers. Some interpreters earn the military's trust and gratitude, and a handful of the Iraqi nationals are granted asylum to move to the United States. Others who are killed, especially among the very small number of women, are treated with tender regard, often memorialized by U.S. soldiers as "one of us."[4]

Still, doubts linger amid reports of some interpreters sending information to the insurgents. As one U.S. soldier puts it, "These guys [i.e., interpreters] have guts to do what they do. And we'd be nowhere without them. We'd be lost. . . . But . . . you always have this fear that they might be leaking op-sec [operational security] stuff. You want to trust them but you're still reserved."[5] Given the inability of most American soldiers to speak Arabic, interpreters, as one report puts it, provide "the public face of the U.S. occupation."[6] Essential in conducting military operations, they nonetheless are thought to threaten them by leaking information. They mediate the vast gulf that separates soldiers from people, often defusing conflict by being able to decipher, for example, documents that to Americans may look like plans for smuggling weapons but turn out to be in fact no more than sewing pattern.[7] In this way, they are "the military's lifeline in communicating with regular Iraqis," as the spokesman for the American Translators Association says.[8] Yet, despite their essential function in fighting insurgents, they are also feared as potential insurgents themselves. Translators allow Americans to communicate with Iraqis and for this reason are integrated into the ranks, given uniforms and salaries. But their loyalty is always suspect. Interpreters are the only ones searched within the base, especially after every meal, and are forbidden to carry cell phones and cameras, send e-mail, play video games, and as of this writing, even swim in the pool.[9] They are subjected to incessant racial insults ("raghead," "Taliban," and "hajji" being the most common) and physical harassment at the same time that they are forced to go out of base with neither weapons nor armor to protect themselves.[10] Just

340

by being who they are, translators thus find themselves stirring interest and sending out messages beyond what they had originally intended. Without meaning to, they generate meanings outside of their control. In this way, they come across as alien presences that seem to defy assimilation even as they are deemed indispensable to the assimilation of aliens. They are "foreign in a domestic sense" as much as they are domestic in a sense that remains enduringly foreign.[11]

It is precisely because they are of such great value to the U.S. forces that translators are targeted by insurgents and reviled by most Iraqis. They are accused of being mercenaries, collaborating with the United States to kill other Iraqis, so they face the constant threat of being kidnapped and killed themselves. One Iraqi interpreter with the pseudonym "Roger" says, "If you look at our situation it's really risky and kind of horrible. . . . Outside the wire, everybody looks at us like we are back-stabbers, like we betrayed our country and our religion, and then inside the wire they look at us like we might be terrorists."[12] Interpreters thus come to literalize that old adage *traduttore, traditore*, at times with tragic results. Recent reports, for example, put the number of slain interpreters at more than two hundred since the start of the war.[13] Moving between languages and societies, translators are also exiled from both. They are neither native nor foreign, but both at the same time. Their uncanny identity triggers recurring crisis among all sides. It is as if their capacity for mediation endows them with a power to disturb and destabilize far out of proportion to their socially ascribed and officially sanctioned positions. But it is a power that also constitutes their profound vulnerability.

These and many other stories about interpreters give us a sense that within the context of the U.S. occupation of Iraq, translation works only too well. That is, it produces effects and relations that are difficult if not impossible to curb. Faced with the translator, both Americans and Iraqis are gripped with the radical uncertainty about the interpreter's loyalty and identity. Translators come across as simultaneously faithful and unfaithful or, more precisely, faithful to their task by being unfaithful to their origins (and on those rare occasions that bear out the fears of the U.S. soldiers, doing the reverse). Rather than promote understanding and hospitality, the work of translation seems to spawn misgivings and misrecognition. In dealing with an interpreter, one is addressed in one's own language— Arabic or English—by an other who also has access to an idiom and culture alien because unavailable to one. Faced with the need to depend on such an other, one responds with ever intensifying suspicions. Such suspicions repeatedly trigger racial insults, often escalating into violence and, in some cases, murder, thereby stoking even more suspicions. Iraqis see in the translator one of their own used against them, a double agent who bears their native language now loaded like a weapon with alien demands. For the U.S. soldier, the indispensability of interpreters is also the source of the latter's duplicity, making them potential insurgents. "Terps" appear as enemies disguised as friends whose linguistic virtuosity masks their real selves and their true intentions.

The task of the translator is thus mired in a series of intractable and irresolvable contradictions. It begins with the fact that translation itself is a highly volatile act. As the displacement, replacement, transfer, and transformation of the original into another language, translation is incapable of fixing meanings across languages. Rather, as with the story of Babel, it consists precisely in the proliferation and confusion of possible meanings and therefore in the impossibility of arriving at a single one. For this reason, it repeatedly brings into crisis the locus of address, the interpretation of signs, the agency of mediation, and the ethics of speech. Hence the impossibility of fully controlling, much less recuperating, its operations and effects. The treachery and treason inherent in translation are the insistent counterpoints to its promise of telecommunication and the just exchange of meaning. In the body of the interpreter, translation reaches its limits. "Terps," as the uncanny doubles of U.S. soldiers and Iraqi insurgents, are productive neither of meaning nor of domination, but only the circulation of what remains untranslatable. It would seem, then, that in the war on terror, translation is at permanent war with itself, and imperialist and anti-imperialist projects seeking to capitalize on this turmoil do so only at the risk of being ensnared and undone by it.

To conclude, I want to return to the analogical relationship between translation and war, with reference to their shared temporality as suggested by the title of this essay. If translation is like war, is there also a way of reversing this association to say that war is like translation? It is possible I think if we consider that the time of war bears some relationship to the movement of translation that leads not to the privileging of meaning but to emergence of the untranslatable. "Wartime" spreads what Nietzsche called in the wake of the Franco-Prussian War "an all consuming fever" that creates a crisis in historical thinking. So much of the way we think about history, certainly in the Westernized parts of our planet since the Enlightenment, is predicated on a notion of time as the succession of events leading toward increasingly more progressive ends. Wartime decimates that mode of thinking. Instead, it creates mass disorientation at odds with the temporal rhythms of progress and civilization. In this way, wartime is what Samuel Weber refers to as "pure movement." It is a "whirlwind that sweeps everything up in its path and yet goes nowhere. As a movement, the whirlwind of war marks time, as it were, inscribing it in a destructive circularity that is both centripetal and centrifugal, wrenching things and people out of their accustomed places, displacing them and with them, all [sense] of place as well. Wartime thus wrecks havoc with traditional conceptions of space and time and with the order they make possible."[14] It is precisely this disordering effect of war on our notions of space and time that brings it in association with translation that, as we saw, scatters meaning, displaces origins, and exposes the radical undecidability of references, names, and addressees. Put differently, translation in a time of war intensifies the experience of untranslatability. It is arguably this stark exposure to translation's limits that we see, for example, in the uncanny body of the Iraqi interpreter. Such a body, now ineradicably part of our own imperial body politic, generates the sense of severe disorientation, sending back to us an interminable scattering of discourses and opinions about the war. Just as civilizational time engenders the permanent possibility of wartime, the time that is out of joint and out of whack, so translation is haunted by untranslatability, the feverish circulation of misrecognition and vengeance from which we can find neither safety nor security, national or otherwise.

Notes

1 Michael Janofsky, "Bush Proposes Broader Language Training," *New York Times*, January 6, 2006. For more details on the National Security Language Initiative, see Bureau of Educational and Cultural Affairs, U.S. Department of State, "National Security Language Initiative," exchanges .state.gov/NSLI/; Dina Powell and Barry Lowenkron, "Fact Sheet: National Security Language Initiative," Office of the Spokesman, U.S. Department of State, January 5, 2006, www.state. gov/r/pa/prs/ps/2006/58733.htm; and U.S. Department of Education, "Press Release: Teaching Language for National Security and Global Competitiveness: U.S. Department of Education Fact Sheet," January 5, 2006, www.ed.gov/news/ pressreleases/2006/01/01052006.html. It is unclear, however, how much of the funding for this program has actually been released as of the date of this writing. I am grateful to Mary Pratt for referring me to this story on Bush's language initiative.
2 For an extended discussion of the politics of translation in the Spanish empire, see, e.g., Vicente L. Rafael, *Contracting Colonialism: Translation and Christian Conversion in Tagalog Society under Early Spanish Rule* (Durham, N.C.: Duke University Press, 1993); and *The Promise of the Foreign: Nationalism and the Technics of Translation in the Spanish Philippines* (Durham, N.C.: Duke University Press, 2005).
3 The following argument on translation as a telecommunicative technology draws largely from Rafael, *The Promise of the Foreign*.
4 John Koopman, "Interpreter's Death Rattles Troops," *San Francisco Chronicle*, August 1, 2004; Moni Basu, "Iraqi Interpreters Risk Their Lives to Aid GI's," *Cox News Services*, November 2, 2005; Howard LaFranci, "Remembering Allan: A Tribute to Jimm Carroll's Interpreter," *Christian Science Monitor*, March 6, 2006.
5 Charles Levinson, "Iraq's 'Terps' Face Suspicions on Both Sides," *Christian Science Monitor*, April 17, 2006, www.csmonitor.com/2006/0417/p01s01-woiq.html. See also Nick Wadhams, "Iraqi Interpreters Face Death Threats from Countrymen, Alienation from U.S. Troops," *Associated Press*, January 23, 2006.
6 Levinson, "Iraq's 'Terps' Face Suspicions on Both Sides." See also Ann Scott Tyson, "Always in Hiding, an Iraqi Interpreter's Anguished Life," *Christian Science Monitor*, September 15, 2004.
7 John M. Glionna and Ashraf Khalil, " 'Combat Linguists' Battle on Two Fronts," *Los Angeles Times*, June 5, 2005; Matthew D. LaPlante, "Speaking the Language;

A Vital Skill; Interpreters in High Demand in Iraq," *Salt Lake Tribune*, October 13, 2005; C. Mark Brinkley, "Translators' Fears Disrupt Vital Lines of Communication," *Army Times*, December 8, 2004.

8 Glionna and Khalil, " 'Combat Linguists' Battle."

9 Levinson, "Iraq's 'Terps' Face Suspicions on Both Sides."

10 David Washburn, "Dangerous Work of Contractors in Iraq," *San Diego Union-Tribune*, November 22, 2006.

11 The term "foreign in a domestic sense" comes from Amy Kaplan, *The Anarchy of Empire in the Making of U.S. Culture* (Cambridge, Mass.: Harvard University Press, 2002).

12 Levinson, "Iraq's 'Terps' Face Suspicions on Both Sides."

13 Washburn, "Dangerous Work of Contractors in Iraq"; Jim Krane, "Translators Dying by the Dozens in Most Dangerous Civilian Jobs in Iraq," *Associated Press*, May 21, 2005.

14 Samuel Weber, "Wartime," in *Violence, Identity, and Self-Determination*, ed. Hent de Vries and Samuel Weber (Stanford, Calif.: Stanford University Press, 1997), 92. I also owe the reference to Nietzsche to Weber's essay.

56

WAR, TRANSLATION, TRANSNATIONALISM[1]

Interpreters in and of the war (Croatia, 1991–1992)

Zrinka Stahuljak

Source: paper written for this collection (2009).

Abstract

In the current global world order, the conduct of war, its success and legitimation, as well as the success and legitimation of
peace-making efforts, largely depend on and are conducted in
translation; as Baker argues, 'translation and interpreting are
part of the *institution of war*' (2006: 1). The analysis of interviews with Croatian wartime interpreters offered in this article
builds on recent work on interpreter agency and activism and
challenges presuppositions of neutrality in the interpreting
process. Complex issues of interpreter positioning, structural
constraints, neutrality, activism and volunteerism vs professionalism – all of which have to be negotiated by interpreters
in any interpretation structure – are analysed, not outside but
within an ongoing armed conflict. The article first explores the
structural violence facing interpreters when the two conditions
that make interpreting in and of a war possible – namely, the
desire to bear witness (volunteerism) and the obligation to
mediate linguistically between primary interlocutors (professionalism) – come into conflict with each other. It then examines
the discursive violence to which interpreters are exposed in
situations of armed conflicts when these conflicts exceed their
local frameworks and enter the larger geopolitical arena in
which arbitration is undertaken by a purportedly neutral third
party. Finally, interpreter activism is examined in its complex
relations to volunteerism and professionalism.

The case of interpreters working for the European Community (EC) in the 1991–1992 war in Croatia, during the break-up of Yugoslavia, brings together several issues of concern to scholars of translation and interpreting. First, it questions the presumed neutrality of interpreters in order to high-light the constraints inherent in the translation structure within which interpreters have to operate on a daily basis. Based on Felman and Laub (1992: 211), I understand wartime translation as a structure within which the interpreter acts as an 'intermediary' between the interviewer and a witness (with 'witness' understood here to encompass an eye-witness, a refugee, an asylum-seeker or any victim of armed aggression). As intermediaries, interpreters and translators play a vital role in the gathering and trans-mission of testimonies (Felman and Laub 1992; Barsky 1996; Stahuljak 1999; Jacquemet 2005), but the responsibility to which they respond and on account of which they intervene, and the kinds of structural violence and trauma to which they may be subjected in the process, have only begun to be addressed recently (Inghilleri 2005; Maier 2007; Moeketsi 2007; Tipton 2008).

Second, beyond the question of structural constraints, the case of the Croatian interpreters demonstrates that wartime interpreters do not merely lend their voices as interpreters in the conflict but are also agents in it; in this respect, the analysis offered here contributes to studies of interpreter agency and activism. Recent work in translation studies has shown that interpreters in war conflicts, most notably in Iraq, have to grapple with a host of conflictual issues and negotiate their positions in relation to them (Inghilleri 2008; Kahane 2007; Maier 2007; Palmer 2007). Among the most important of these issues is the question of trust and credibility (Inghilleri in press, Rafael 2007), but other issues also come up, such as interpreter reflex-ivity (Tipton 2008), agency (Inghilleri 2005), ethics (Baker 2008; Inghilleri 2008, in press) and, most importantly for the case of Croatian interpreters, activism in the context of volunteer interpreting and translation (Baker 2006a; 2006b, in press; Boéri 2008; Tymoczko 2000, 2007). Activism should not be understood here as necessarily involving a conscious distortion and mani-pulation of source materials, for, as Baker argues, 'we may well find that accuracy acquires an additional value in this context and that much of the "political" work is done through the selection of material to be translated and through various methods of framing the translation' (Baker 2006b: 477); this will become clear in some of the examples I analyse later in this article. Ultimately, interpreter activism merely renders visible what is inher-ent in translation, that is, that interpreters, whether explicitly activist or not, do not occupy neutral, in-between positions, that they do not reside outside cultural or ideological systems.

Finally, while the question of the violence that interpreters perform against witnesses has occasionally been raised in the literature (Jacquemet 2005; Inghilleri 2008), I wish to consider here the discursive violence to which interpreters themselves are exposed in an armed conflict, in order to further our understanding of issues of political neutrality and allegiance in wartime translation. The interpreter is not a metaphor here for the physical violence of the war conflict. Rather, the relationship between the Croatian interpreters and Western Europe examined in this article highlights the political and active role of translation as a conflicted battleground in itself, and demonstrates that translation is constitutive of and critical to the political processes of nation-building and international recognition. In this global context, interpreters, as cultural mediators, are subject to the violence of the Western European discourse of conflict arbitration.

The data analysed in this article are drawn from an unpublished study of Croatian interpreters by the Croatian social psychologist Ivan Magdalenic. During the 1991–1992 war, Croatian interpreters for the European Community were organized through the Croatian Liaison Office. At the invitation of the main administrator of the Croatian Liaison Office, Magdalenic conducted interviews with them from 11 September to 18 October 1993, but was later dismissed by the Office without explanation (personal communication, 23 September 1996). Although they were never intended for publication, and were used only as one element in the clinical diagnosis, Dr Magdalenic was willing to share his records of interviews with me in September 1996. The interviews constituted confidential material, and at his request I have withheld the names of interpreters. They were conducted in Croatian; all translations from Croatian into English in the analysis that follows are mine. The interviews were partly transcribed and partly summarized by Magdalenic, which explains the occasional occurrence of indirect speech in quotations from the interviews. Magdalenic interviewed twenty-five Croatian interpreters, and some were evaluated on two different occasions. Ten were female, ages 19–50, and fifteen were male, ages 18–41. In an attempt to protect their privacy, but still indicate the diversity of their opinions, I have 'coded' them as Interpreter A, Interpreter B, etc.

The interpreters responded to a series of questions in a face-to-face interview with the psychologist (see Appendix: interpreter questionnaire). Magdalenic's primary objectives, in his role as clinical psychologist, were to look for the kind of specific trauma that interpreting in and of the war may have produced and to propose an optimal way for dealing with the length of assignments and their potential effects. Each interview was followed by an informal conversation with Magdalenic that was not summarized in the study, but in lieu of which Magdalenic offered his psychological assessment of each subject (personal communication). While clearly designed to identify signs of psychological distress, what emerges from Magdalenic's questions is that, apart from talking to each other, the psychologist was the first to provide these interpreters with a space to tell their story. These interviews demonstrate that interpreters are full-fledged participants in the testimonial process, not merely a communication channel, and in the wartime context –

as in refugee, asylum and court proceedings – they are under severe pressure to perform accurately and professionally, as well as conform to various norms and live up to (self-)expectations (Inghilleri 2005; Jacquemet 2005; Moeketsi 2007; Tipton 2008; Wadensjö 1998). Finding ways to narrate their experience, as Magdalenic's questions enabled them to do, may relieve the pressure and help make sense of the lived experience.

In addition to the accounts provided by Magdalenic's interviewees, some of whom are my former colleagues, I also draw in the following analysis on my own personal experience as someone who has worked as a volunteer interpreter in the same context.[2]

The war in Croatia

The 1991–1992 war in Croatia has been largely occulted, first, by the immensity of the events in Bosnia and Herzegovina (1992–1995) and the role Croatia played in them, along with Serbia, which came to light in the late 1990s and in the early years of the twenty-first century through the work of the International War Crimes Tribunal for the former Yugoslavia in the Hague; and, second, by the war conflict and NATO strikes in Kosovo (1998–1999). Given the limitations imposed by my source material, which was gathered in the autumn of 1993 by Magdalenic, I restrict my comments in this section of the article to the war in Croatia, outlining the situation as experienced by the interpreters in 1993, without the hindsight of Bosnian events.

The 1991–1992 war in Croatia erupted as the result of a conflict over borders between Croatia and Serbia during the break-up of the Socialist Federal Republic of Yugoslavia. The Socialist Federal Republic of Yugoslavia, as its name denotes, was a federation of republics. The republics constituting the Yugoslav federation from 1945 to 1992 were Slovenia, Croatia, Bosnia and Herzegovina, Serbia (with two autonomous provinces of Voïvodina and Kosovo), Montenegro and Macedonia. The 1974 Yugoslav constitution had secured for the republics the right to secede from the federation. However, in the Communist one-party system and for the duration of the Cold War, this kind of self-determination was ideologically and practically inconceivable. The freedom of choice to form or not form a federation with other republics became available only after 1989; multi-party elections were first held in Slovenia and Croatia in the spring of 1990, and then later in other republics of the former Yugoslavia. Initially, a proposal for the confederation of sovereign states, modelled on the European Community, was put forward. After the refusal of the Republic of Serbia and the Republic of Montenegro to form a confederation with other republics that constituted federal Yugoslavia, the Republic of Croatia, along with its western neighbour the Republic of Slovenia, exercised the right to self-determination granted by the Yugoslav constitution and proclaimed independence on

25 June 1991. Independence from federal Yugoslavia was declared following a democratic referendum in which 94 per cent of the Croatian population expressed support for this option in the event that the confederation with other republics was not formed.

Serbia, the republic bordering Croatia to the east, took the position that, in the case of secession, borders between republics were to be reconsidered and renegotiated, because it claimed that all the Serbs of the former Yugoslavia could live only within the national borders of Serbia. In the former federal Yugoslavia, all the Serbs lived in one state in which they constituted the majority. In July 1991, the Yugoslav Army, led by Serbs, mobilized its units and began a strategically developed military campaign on the territory of the former Yugoslav Republic of Croatia, claiming that the Serbian minority in Croatia was now physically and legally 'endangered' and in need of protection from 'secessionist' Croats. The Yugoslav Army dropped the adjective 'national' from its old federal name, Yugoslav National Army, since in the course of the war its commanding chain and soldiers became uniquely of Serbian and Montenegrin nationality, and all other nationalities either gradually deserted the army or were released from duty at the beginning of the war. From the beginning, and in its entirety, the war took place on the territory of the Republic of Croatia; fourteen ceasefires did not hold as they were violated by the Yugoslav Army. By the time the *fifteenth* ceasefire took effect (on 3 January 1992) and the independent Republic of Croatia began to gain international recognition (15 January 1992), one-third of the Croatian territory was under the occupation of the Yugoslav Army (in three different, non-contiguous areas of Eastern Slavonia, Western Slavonia and Krajina). The Yugoslav Army and Serbian paramilitary units first made use of the technique of 'ethnic cleansing' in Croatia, soon to become infamous for its use in Bosnia and Herzegovina. The occupied territories were cleansed of the Croat ethnic presence, with the exception of small numbers of elderly people. All non-Serbian minorities were expelled alongside the Croat population. In January 1993, the numbers stood at 330,100 Croatian civilians who were displaced or took refuge elsewhere, 2,181 killed, 6,762 injured and 14,805 missing out of the total population of Croatia, which then stood at 4,784,265 (*Bulletin* 1993). The occupied territories were populated, and in the years to follow continuously settled, by Serbs coming from Serbia proper and from Bosnia and Herzegovina. The interpreters interviewed in Magdalenic's study, from which the data for this paper are drawn, belonged primarily – but not exclusively – to the Croat population.

This first major armed conflict on European soil since the Second World War commanded the immediate attention of the European Community. At the time of the conflict, the EC had not yet expanded its membership or changed its name to the European Union (EU). The EC consisted of twelve member countries: Germany, France, United Kingdom, Spain, Portugal, the Netherlands, Belgium, Ireland, Italy, Greece, Denmark and

Luxembourg. However, the EC was unable to intervene, for as long as the borders of Croatia were not internationally recognized international law could not view the Serbian military invasion as a war between two sovereign countries, but only as an internal settling of accounts, a civil war. Before adjudicating, the EC wanted to establish the real aggressor in the conflict. In spite of the urgency of the continuing Serbian occupation, as a precondition of Croatia's international recognition the European Community also chose to scrutinize the constitution and the legislature of Croatia in order to verify the status and the rights which the Croatian constitution granted its minorities. According to the 1991 census, there were a number of larger minority groups living in Croatia: Czechs (0.27 per cent), Slovaks (0.46 per cent), Hungarians (0.46 per cent), Italians (0.44 per cent), Muslims (0.90) and Albanians (0.25 per cent).[3] There were also 2.2 per cent of Yugoslavs in 1991.[4] To this list can be added fifteen other nationalities with a population of fewer than 10,000 declared. Among all the nationalities residing in Croatia, Serbs were the largest minority group (12.15 per cent). In its constitution, drawn before the proclamation of independence, Croatia guaranteed all groups the status of minority, enjoying full rights. Only the Croatian Serbs refused the minority status and questioned the status of Croats as the only constitutional majority (representing 78 per cent of the population at that point). The other minority groups in Croatia did not make similar constitutional claims, or any claims in the war fought on the Croatian side. Although interpreters working for the Croatian Liaison Office were mostly ethnic Croats, there were also ethnic Serbian, Macedonian and Albanian interpreters, all citizens of Croatia. Magdalenic's interviewees reflect the diversity of the Croatian population, hence the choice of the Croatian (rather than ethnic Croat) label to refer to the interpreters discussed in this article.

In order to facilitate the work of the EC Arbitration Commission as well as to follow the developments and negotiate the conflict on the ground, the European Community set up the European Community Monitor Mission (ECMM) in July 1991, an international task force with direct access to the conflict. The EC adopted what it referred to as a position of neutrality. 'Neutrality' comes from the Latin word *neuter* and stands for 'neither one nor the other, taking neither side, neither active nor passive, intransitive'. The European arbitration in the conflict was thus intended to proceed neutrally, 'taking neither side', and therefore to be independent of the two governments in question for information which it transmitted to the EC. Fifteen countries participated in the work of the ECMM: the twelve member countries of the European Community plus Canada, the Czech Republic and Slovakia. ECMM's objective was to achieve peace and bring all war activities in Croatia to a halt. The negotiation of a ceasefire, however, focused on freezing the situation on the battlefield while leaving aside the question of enabling the Croatian side to reinstate borders as they were

350

prior to the outbreak of war. In addition, one of ECMM's tasks was to implement confidence-building measures – in other words, to ensure the protection of the rights of minorities. ECMM's function was thus to neutrally monitor the ceasefire(s) it negotiated and to monitor the respect of minority rights in Croatia. The EC monitors collected testimonies from Croats and Serbs alike, both civilians and military personnel, on and close to the front lines. ECMM needed interpreters who could translate these oral testimonies consecutively into English, the *lingua franca* of the organization, and only occasionally into French and German. Thus the triangular structure of translation was set: the interviewer (an EC monitor), the witness (a Croat or a Serb) and the interpreter, a Croatian national.

Its declared position of neutrality allowed the EC to pose as an unengaged, and thus by definition objective and just, arbiter in the conflict, but an arbiter nevertheless. The EC Arbitration Commission in charge of this process took seven months to complete the review. The European Community and several other countries recognized Croatia on 15 January 1992; full international recognition followed on 22 May 1992, when Croatia became a member of the United Nations. Twelve out of the twenty-five interpreters interviewed by Dr Magdalenic started interpreting during the open conflict in the summer and autumn of 1991 and in early 1992 (before the international recognition of Croatia in May 1992), nine began interpreting for the ECMM after May 1992, and four in 1993. It is important to note that, notwithstanding the fifteenth ceasefire and the international recognition of Croatia, the state of war continued until 1995, as the Croatian territories remained occupied. Thus, interpreters who joined in 1992 still experienced war conditions on the front lines similar to those at the peak of the conflict in the autumn and winter of 1991, and conditions of interpreting on the front lines were occasionally life-threatening. The major change for the interpreters was ECMM's decision in autumn 1992 to begin paying for interpreter services: seventeen of the twenty-five interpreters interviewed started working as volunteers; eight (Interpreters J, L, M, P, S, V, W, X) joined in autumn 1992 as paid interpreters.

Wartime translation

Wartime translation began as a purely volunteer, small-scale operation, improvised at first by the Croatian Liaison Office. As the demand grew, so did the number of volunteers. The data gathered from the interviews shows that Croatian interpreters volunteered to translate the war for the ECMM, a politically neutral organization, but their decision to do so was not neutral or disinterested.

Interpreters volunteered out of 'patriotism' (Interpreters B, E, F, G, L, N, R), 'a feeling of responsibility' (Interpreter D), because they 'didn't want to stay on the sidelines' (Interpreter V), because they wanted 'to do something'

(Interpreters A, B, E, H, I, K, N, O, S, T, X), 'to help' (Interpreters C, D, M, P, U, Y), by using their highly valued linguistic skills: 'I believe to be doing a useful job,' says Interpreter Q, echoed by Interpreter P. For these interpreters, translation is a privileged site in which they can exercise their agency, a weapon that can be used to alert the international community to the Croatian position in the conflict:

> INTERPRETER V: An interpreter cannot and should not be just a 'transmitter'.

They refuse to be seen as mere linguistic intermediaries, as invisible go-betweens, 'transmitters' without a voice, and instead exercise their agency at a time when Croatia is under attack. They volunteer out of the desire to witness: Interpreter D 'wanted to see for herself what is really happening on the front-lines',[5] as did Interpreter H, with the intention of bearing witness before the ECMM. In the urgency of a war conflict toward which the EC adopted a position of neutrality, without an internal consensus on who is the aggressor and who is the victim, interpreter volunteering was a form of activism, an attempt to persuade individual monitors of the ECMM to take sides, to show them who the real aggressor is. Translation is not a neutral zone, and in this case became a war zone in itself, one in which Croatia can be defended against the aggression of the occupying Serb forces. To translate here is to be at war, to be on a 'mission'. This is also evident in the way the interpreters interviewed here often resort to the use of military terminology: they are a part of a 'civilian army', 'soldier[s]'. They feel the bond of being 'brothers in arms' (Interpreter D). It is not surprising, then, that many of the volunteer interpreters also call themselves 'veterans' (Interpreters B, L, M, P, S).

But within the structure of translation set up by the EC, interpreters are supposed to function as the conduit of an address between the witness and the EC monitor, an address from which they themselves are excluded. Through the interpreter, the EC monitor and the witness address each other; they become interlocutors. The interpreter, as the third element in the inter-action, must remain outside the address; he or she is the 'intermediary' through whom the address can take place. Despite their original motivation to become witnesses for the ECMM, Croatian interpreters appear to respect the existing structure of translation, which does not allow them to be the patriotic, engaged witness that they thought they could be. I wish to under-line the difference here between conscious interventions in the translation zone, premeditated and intended to manipulate the meaning of the original, and the unconscious alteration or renarration (Baker 2006a) which is always at work in translation – among other things, because of the lack of equivalence between languages and cultures. The interpreters' discourse itself distinguishes between the two: they claim to refrain from manipulating the utterances of the primary interlocutors and take great pride in the accuracy of their translations and their professionalism, as will become clear in the examples that follow.

Some of the interpreting occurred on visits to Serb villages in the remaining free territory of Croatia in order to monitor their status, and very often in tripartite meetings and negotiations between the Croatian military, the Serbian military, and the EC monitors. Here, interpreting clearly involved translating for the enemy party. According to the interpreters interviewed, irrespective of the context, even in cases when the interpreters themselves were personally offended, linguistic neutrality was maintained:

> INTERPRETER G: I translated all of her words [insults] calmly.
> INTERPRETER W: One of the monitors was saying bad things about Croatian politics. I did not participate in the debate.

To translate 'calmly' indicates that the interpreter is focused exclusively on language. On the other hand, not to 'participate in the debate' testifies to an attempt to keep the interpreters' linguistic performance free from political contamination. Interpreters transmit the words of the witness without performing any evaluative or interpretative acts – at least as far as their linguistic output is concerned. Indeed, interpreters persist in translating in the most taxing situations:

> INTERPRETER F: It is embarrassing to have to admit that [Croats] did it [that they blew up Serbs' family houses].
> INTERPRETER H: It is unpleasant to translate [Serbian] lies.
> INTERPRETER N: Situations when one must translate rude comments about [Croatian] interlocutors are unpleasant.
> INTERPRETER V: It is unpleasant to translate rude comments about the ECMM.

They translate professionally in the hope that contradictory evidence will lead the EC monitor to see through those 'lies':

> INTERPRETER S: When Serbs say that their children are working as 'mechanics' on the other side [in the occupied territory], even monitors laugh it away.

They resist the temptation to manipulate other interlocutors' utterances intentionally and fight the impulse to give their own counter-testimony in the name of the 'truth'. Although they know that a partial and faulty translation could completely alter the meaning in their favour, they insist that they observe the principles of professionalism and accuracy and avoid conscious manipulation:

353

INTERPRETER O: Translation is a job of responsibility. [Similar comments are made by Interpreter D.]

INTERPRETER R: I try to maintain objectivity, professionalism . . . Even though I am a volunteer, I am still a professional.

INTERPRETER T: I take it all as a part of the job. [Similar comments are made by Interpreter U.]

Because they are 'professionals', interpreters must accept a form of erasure, at least while interpreting. Rather than distortion and inaccuracy, it is their professionalism which is seen as the best testimony to the fact that Croatia has nothing to hide about its treatment of the Serb minority, nothing to do with violating (one of) the ceasefire(s). ECMM's political neutrality is perceived only as a temporary methodological device, necessary only until the EC monitors find the evidence and themselves witness the war, on the front lines and in the occupied territories, as Serbian territorial expansion. As far as the interpreters are concerned, then, they and the ECMM are working for the common goal of collecting the evidence to determine who the aggressor is in this conflict:

INTERPRETER A: I feel I am a part of the ECMM team. [Similar comments are made by Interpreter Q.]

For Interpreter A, there is an 'us' – the EC monitors and the interpreters are on the same side.

This self-erasure is a violence that the interpreting structure imposes on interpreters and that they feel they have to conscientiously respect. In other words, interpreters who volunteered to translate in order to testify are denied the very possibility of testimony. The two conditions that make interpreting in and of a war possible, the desire to bear witness (volunteerism) and the obligation to mediate linguistically between primary interlocutors (professionalism), come into conflict with each other, since the positions of the witness and of the interpreter are mutually exclusive. The very demand for interpreter activism/intervention from within the structure of translation, contradicted by the structural impossibility of testifying from within, produces an internal conflict in the interpreter to which Interpreter I's personal story testifies:

INTERPRETER I: I wanted to do something because my brothers too were volunteers in the Croatian Army.

Unlike her brothers, who could be simultaneously volunteers and professionals when they joined the Croatian Army, the interpreter is split between being *either* a professional *or* a volunteer, between the task of translating

Croatian and Serbian testimonies professionally and allegiance to Croatia. As Interpreter C puts it succinctly:

> INTERPRETER C: It is not clear to me whom I have to obey when on a mission – the directions from the [Croatian Liaison] Office or the orders of the head of the [ECMM] team.

Torn between political allegiance and professionalism, interpreters literally embody the violence of the conflict that they translate for the international community. While translating the violence of the war, they themselves become the site of a violent conflict.

Just how did Croatian interpreters negotiate their position between volunteerism (bearing witness) and professionalism (providing linguistic mediation)? Here, I wish to differentiate between translations which consciously alter elements of the source material and the particularity of the interpreting context on the front lines, which often provides opportunities for other types of intervention. In the current case, interpreters often went with the same ECMM teams on multiple missions, which lasted anywhere between one day and two weeks. This created suitable conditions for familiarity, with prolonged mutual exposure ultimately serving the interpreters' aim of bearing witness. The interviews show that the interpreters' interventions in the testimonial process constitute a conscious effort to persuade, while simultaneously refraining from altering the original testimonies that they are asked to translate. This attempt to 'persuade' in some respects resembles the kind of political activism that has developed since 2002 (Baker 2006b, in press; Boéri 2008). Rather than changing any aspect of the original testimony, interpreters in this context retain the original testimony intact but supplement it with their own when the opportunity arises. Moreover, the passage between the two is marked, without attempting to pass one for the other. Interpreters act as witnesses when they perform 'switching', as they call it. They 'switch' from the position of 'interpreter' to the position of 'interlocutor' in 'unofficial' situations, 'when personal opinions can be expressed' (Interpreter P) – outside the translation structure, but within the translation war zone, during off-hours:

> INTERPRETER D: Regardless of the official function, I try to play the role of an unofficial representative of the Republic of Croatia, I explain the situation in this part of the world to the monitors.
> INTERPRETER E: We talk a lot, exchange opinions. I try to influence them.
> INTERPRETER O: [There are] unofficial conversations, explanations of the situation, etc. [Similar comments are made by Interpreter M.]
> INTERPRETER V: One needs to have unofficial conversations – that is how mutual trust and respect are built.

'Switching' even occurs at the monitors' request:

> INTERPRETER C: One needs to help introduce the new monitors to the situation here – they even ask for advice.
> INTERPRETER F: Many are poorly informed.
> INTERPRETER Q: There are elements of guided tours, history lessons.

To translate the war means to testify to the war in their own voice, that is, to demonstrate to the EC monitors who is the aggressor and who is the victim. It is an opportunity to elaborate the narrative of one's own culture and history – because for most of the twentieth century Croatia was part of Yugoslavia, its past had been obscured in the communal Yugoslav history. The interpreters represent their country; they are 'ambassador[s]' of Croatia, says Interpreter D, just as they hope to make EC monitors 'into unofficial ambassadors of the Republic of Croatia'.

However, 'switching' becomes more difficult as the tension between professionalism and volunteerism in the interpreters' double position is gradually put under additional strain. With time, some interpreters perceive the European Community as unwilling to act politically or militarily on the basis of physical evidence and testimony that the ECMM collected while investigating the nature and progress of the conflict, and as unable to stop the attacks that continued beyond the fifteenth ceasefire, despite international recognition of Croatia. Indeed, the occupation of Croatia not only continued despite international recognition of its sovereignty, but also advanced unhindered, as Croatian territories were resettled. As Interpreter D put it (corroborated by Interpreter K), 'our side has more and more difficulty in dealing with the EC missions, it is harder than before'. Interpreter X confirms that the '[EC] missions have recently become less popular', an assessment with which interpreter T agrees, and Interpreter O observes that 'there used to be more enthusiasm'. There is no point in continuing the EC monitor mission, according to Interpreter F, since 'monitors have no [other] jurisdiction except monitoring'. Other interpreters express their impatience in similar terms. Often, they find their skills wasted on 'idle talk' (Interpreter M, Y), while 'nothing is being done' (Interpreter M). Interpreter U elaborates:

> INTERPRETER U: I often feel useless. For example, I am at [their] disposal for ninety-six hours (four days), I translate for two to three hours, and the rest of the time I am on stand-by. I spend time in the hotel . . . but that is not why I went on the mission. [Similar comments are made by Interpreter M.]

It is because of the growing absurdity of this situation, in which, despite their professed 'political neutrality', it becomes clear that not to implement and enforce a political decision is in fact to favour the aggressor, that interpreters at times experience difficulties, especially when they witness emotionally charged situations:

> INTERPRETER A: The most difficult moment took place in a refugee centre when a child died and the refugees accused us [the ECMM].
> INTERPRETER B: [I] saw ten-month-old corpses [of Croatian civilians].
> INTERPRETER D: The most difficult are the stories of [Croatian] refugees and displaced persons.
> INTERPRETER E: [I] went into an unmarked minefield with another monitor.
> INTERPRETER G: Six buses with [Croatian] refugees were arriving, and they [the Serbs] were shooting at them, the situation was very tense, and I was hiding with the monitors in a ditch.
> INTERPRETER M: Destroyed Croat villages are particularly difficult to see.
> INTERPRETER N: A meeting with the parents of a child born in the refugee camp was very moving.
> INTERPRETER T: On several occasions, I was at an exhumation (from the well, from the corn field) and at the exchange of corpses, and I translated the identification procedure. It was sickening to look at the corpse taken out of the well.
> INTERPRETER Y: I saw massacred bodies of [Croatian] soldiers and civilians . . . I also watched a village burning at night.

The stress involved in such situations was exacerbated by the fact that counselling was not provided for the interpreters. Instead, they developed their own internal support system, with the idea of a 'community of veterans' composed of volunteers who worked for the ECMM from an early stage being one such system. At any rate, it was in such highly charged situations that, occasionally, the 'switch' occurred not *outside* but *within* the structure of translation, in the course of an official interview. Here, instead of simply translating the witness's testimony, the interpreter 'jumps in' and intervenes. Interpreter J had to be recalled from duty after '[m]ostly interpreting, although I was explaining to them what was happening there'. Interpreter B admits:

> INTERPRETER B: I 'jump in', it's more than interpreting: conversations with monitors, discussions about everything that is going on, explanation of our [Croatian] situation.

The structure of address within which interpreting takes place is exploded. Interpreters become subjects speaking in their own voice, no longer mere intermediaries with no personal history. They become witnesses through their intervention, in their very failure to be interpreters. Precisely because 'switching' can at any given moment disrupt the structure, it reveals the inherent precariousness of the interpreter's 'professional', 'neutral' and 'self-erasing' stance.

In acting as witnesses in their own right, interpreters fail to render the testimony of the original witness faithfully. They divert the address to themselves and respond in lieu of the original witness. This disruption is undeniably a violence committed against witnesses and their testimony. However, the parallels that I have drawn out between professionalism, activism and the breakdown of the translation structure allow us to distinguish between conscious activism and unconscious disruptions in interpreting. 'Switching' may be considered a form of activism; however, the interpreters' testimony is not part of the recorded, official evidence. They may be interlocutors to the EC monitors but they are still not admitted as official witnesses to the ECMM; the ECMM are not interested in allowing the interpreters to be witnesses, to tell their story. The ECMM do not acknowledge interpreters as 'knowledgeable' interlocutors (Tipton 2008: 12). In addition, the structure of testimony conditions the marginality of interpreters – they do not participate in the war in a personal capacity since their interpreting lends voice to someone else. They are interpreters and not witnesses, intermediaries erased from the official history of witnessing. This structural violence and exclusion from the testimonial process create disruptions in particularly challenging situations, but we should not dismiss such interventions on their part as 'distortions', as Felman and Laub do when they argue that 'the interpreter . . . in some ways distorts and screens [the visual/acoustic information] because the translation is not always absolutely accurate' (1992: 212). Rather than a contamination of testimony, the type of 'distortion' described here can be read precisely as interpreters' testimony: to themselves and to their task (Stahuljak 2000).

The 'distortion' of translation should be read here not as 'failure', as the term implies, but as a speech act. At the moment when interpreters do violence to witnesses, they are bearing witness to the violence that was done to them. The violence involved in working within a conflict that is forcibly neutralized becomes audible when translation breaks down. The interpreters' internal conflict between professionalism and volunteerism erupts in the breakdown of 'neutral' translation and demands acknowledgement. The interpreters bear witness to the fact that, as interpreters, they can never testify, politically or structurally – the former undermines their professionalism and the latter disrupts the transmission of the original testimony. Furthermore, their speech act also reveals that they cannot identify from within the structure of translation. Precisely because translation and testimony are mutually exclusive, interpreters can only recognize themselves *outside* and *apart from* the act of translation. The interpreter 'emerges' from the speech act – it is a moment of self-witnessing, making the fact of there-being-a-translation audible, but it is also an assertion of one's own voice. It constitutes a moment of recognition that the interpreters are not outside history, culture or ideology, not simply mechanical transmitters or inter-mediaries, but always within interaction, as witnesses and participants. Their speech act reveals that translation as mediation is always already an intervention (Baker 2008; Inghilleri 2005; Maier 2007; Munday 2007).

Translation and neutrality

But interpreters' speech act, their attempt to act as witnesses in their own right, *is* read as a deliberate distortion and therefore political disobedience, a cause for mistrust and a compromise of credibility (Baker 2008; Inghilleri in press; Rafael 2007). To intervene in the original testimony is a scandalous gesture, because it is perceived as undermining ECMM's proclaimed neutrality:

> INTERPRETER C: I told them that it [bringing medication across the border] wouldn't work, but they got angry at me and reported me [to the manager of the Croatian Liaison Office].
> INTERPRETER U: The EC monitor strongly reprimanded me for not doing my job as I should.

The interpreter's speech act as witness reveals the impossibility of neutral transmission beyond the 'neutrality' of the immediate interpreting situation. If the interpreters' intervention is scandalous, it is not so because of com-promised trust and credibility, but because it gestures toward the very position taken by the ECMM. In other words, interpreters here are both the figure and the channel for the kind of neutral transmission that the ECMM claims to perform. There is an uncanny similarity between the position of inter-preters and the position of the ECMM. Interpreters 'process' an otherwise incomprehensible minor Slavic language into the 'literal meaning of testi-monies' (Felman and Laub 1992: 213). Likewise, in providing information that is essential for arbitration in and later resolution of the conflict, the ECMM plays the role of an interpreter of a potentially incomprehensible conflict. It engages in translation as historical transmission, as the passing-on of a historical event, the war, which it is trying to make intelligible to the international community. The interpreters' concrete linguistic perform-ance is reiterated in the kind of translation into meaning that the ECMM performs.

As we saw, interpreting requires a neutralization of the interpreter as witness. The ECMM imposes a structural (linguistic) neutrality on the interpreter as part of grounding its own political (historical) neutrality. As a consequence of this enforced linguistic neutrality, the ECMM can claim to provide a neutral and all-inclusive overview of the war. When the issue is observed from all sides because neither side is taken, arbitration can pose as a comprehensive, closed and understandable account of the event of the war. Neutrality can lay claim to justice because it wills itself as all-inclusive. This 'all-inclusive' vision, however, manages to overlook the interpreter, whose role is underestimated even as it gives rise to concerns about 'neutrality':

> INTERPRETER D: My PhD degree confuses them [the monitors] – one of them remarked that I could be of more help to my country at my regular job.
> INTERPRETER I: Monitors do not have enough appreciation for the interpreters.

In another example, the ECMM left the selection of interpreters entirely at the discretion of the Croatian Liaison Office. Its neutrality could have been easily compromised from the outset had the Croatian Liaison Office selected only ethnic Croats for interpreters. The ECMM is there to observe the war, yet it manages not to recognize the interpreters' conflicted body and their war efforts. Interpreters are its blindspot: the ECMM denies them the position of a historical witness while at the same time claiming to be all-inclusive. Since interpreters are not outside the war but part of it, the ECMM fails to see in them the war that it came to observe. In this, already, it is missing the war.

But the ECMM is missing the war in yet another way. As we saw, the ECMM 'neutralizes' interpreters in order to ground its own political neutrality. Interpreters must erase themselves, their own history, in order to provide a smooth translation. Translation, where the interpreter remains self-erased throughout, makes itself transparent and performs what Jean-François Lyotard described as the 'dream of a pre-Babel state, of an ideal form of interlinguistic communication in which there is no need for translation. That is every translation's ideal. To render itself useless, impossible even, and to erase the interlinguistic gap which motivates it' (Lyotard 1989: xi). Just as the interpreters erase themselves, make their physical presence transparent, so the translation erases itself from the testimony that it translates. Born out of an interlinguistic gap, it aims to make us forget this gap. At the moment of the interpreter's intervention, what becomes visible and *audible* is that in translation, because of the gap that motivates it, something always remains inaccessible, untranslatable (Stahuljak 2000, 2004; Rafael 2007). Smooth, transparent, neutral translation, on the other hand, would be an accessible, coherent historical narrative that 'pretends to reduce historical scandals to mere sense and to eliminate the unassimilable shock of history' (Felman and Laub 1992: 151). With the self-erasure and neutralization of the interpreter, what is erased and neutralized is the fact that the war is accessed only through translation, through mediation. But the ECMM plays on the notion of the romanticized bridge-builder and neutral transmitter, despite the fact that its neutral position is inherently question-able: the EC is the arbiter in the conflict. As Roland Barthes reminded us, 'le ni-ni tient le discours du maître: il sait, il juge' (the 'neither-nor' holds the master discourse: it knows, it judges), and this 'ni-nisme' (neither-norism) is far from the 'neutral' position that 'ne sait pas' (does not know) (Barthes 2002: 115).

This double erasure enacted by neutrality is what the interpreters do not allow the monitors to forget when they resist a smooth translation. Their speech act may bear witness only to a personal truth, to a personal histor-ical conflict. Yet this personal truth partakes of history to the extent that it reminds the EC monitors that their access to the event is indeed mediated, translational and personal. Second, it underscores the fact that, since the medium, that is the interpreter, is not neutral, not outside the history that he or she translates, the ECMM itself is not outside the history it translates, but is part of it. The ECMM's neutrality plays a historical role in the war; it is a form of engagement. Interpreters reveal the violence that ECMM's disavowal of engagement commits, since they remind the EC monitors that, even when proclaiming their neutrality, they are not beyond/outside their own or someone else's history but rather active participants in it:

INTERPRETER D: I had political contacts with the English and the French, who strongly represented their respective countries' politics, who are unfavourable to us [Croatians].
INTERPRETER I: Some monitors speak badly of Croatia.

By 'strongly representing' their countries, the EC monitors do not abandon an active and engaged stand for a neutral stand in relation to the war in Croatia:

INTERPRETER L: Monitors' partiality is disturbing.
INTERPRETER R: Many are big nationalists, yet they find the same fault with us.

Likewise, because of their engagement in their own Western narrative, Interpreter Q points out that sometimes '[t]here are minor conflicts with monitors, for instance when they talk of Yugoslavia without the attribute "former"'. That some EC monitors are unaware of or unwilling to recognize the official change in the status of Yugoslavia is explained thus:

INTERPRETER I: Most are here only for the money. Some do not know what to ask their interlocutors when on a mission.
INTERPRETER V: Some are here only for the money, they are completely uninterested.

Interpreters report a general lack of interest (Interpreters D, I, L, K, V) or information (Interpreters T, X):

> INTERPRETER L: Some come thinking there is war in Zagreb. They are not interested to know whether what they hear is true; they take everything literally.

They are 'uninterested' because they already 'know' all there is to know about the ancient ethnic conflicts in the Yugoslav region:

> INTERPRETER D: Many come with prejudice about the 'Balkan' people.
> INTERPRETER R: [S]ome behave with superiority, look down on us as 'wild Balkan' people.

Others still, says Interpreter Y, are here 'for tourism', visits to the Croatian Adriatic coast; Interpreter R claims there is more and more of such behaviour. This manner of being above and outside history causes the ECMM to be violently oblivious to the situation on the front lines and to its own historical and cultural position in the conflict; while it is taking its time to arbitrate, temporality becomes de-historicized, thereby privileging the law of the stronger. Finally, even when the ECMM participates by not participating, the interpreters' speech act as witnesses in their own right reminds them that their neutral position is not above or outside violence but is itself a violence: neutral transmission requires a violent erasure of interpreters and their history. Hence, the speech act brings to light the fact that transmission occurs through an erasure. Transmission of history erases the traces of the medium of its transmission and of the history of the medium. Paradoxically, neutral historical transmission requires that one participate in the fiction of a de-historicized transmission.

The ECMM ultimately acknowledges that the interpreters', and their own, neutrality is a fiction when they suspect the interpreters of being spies:

> INTERPRETER C: A Czech monitor searched my belongings, looking for spying equipment, and he did the same to another [female] interpreter.
> INTERPRETER D: Some think that we were 'assigned' to this job – they consider us to be official representatives of the Republic of Croatia.
> INTERPRETER U: Some of them are intelligence officers, and so they think we are too – one of them invited me to talk as 'colleagues'. One of the monitors admitted to an interpreter that he searched her personal belongings for spying equipment . . . Some monitors think that I moonlight as a spy.
> INTERPRETER V: The most difficult situation is when the team leader mistrusts the interpreter, thinking that, as a Croat, he will be partial.

While claiming that it, the ECMM, is neutral, the ECMM suspects that the interpreters' very willingness to translate may be, after all, politically motivated. Conversely, the recognition of the interpreter's fictional neutrality undoes ECMM's own neutrality. Yet the ECMM does not question the political, historical motivation behind its own willingness to provide a neutral translation of the war. Consequently, the fiction of a de-historicized, neutral transmission is a violent and even traumatic one. The trauma can be severe and manifest itself not only as an occasional intervention in translation but also as mental illness. One interpreter, himself a refugee, who was taken off duty after suffering from severe psychological stress, was reported to have no longer been able to bear ECMM's neutrality toward the events on the front lines (reported by Interpreter F and Interpreter S).

War is a proof of history that is too complex to lend itself to smooth de-historicization. Ultimately, the interpreters' intervention within translation reminds us that the shock, the violence of an event such as war, cannot be translated or processed without 'shocking' the very structure of its transmission, and especially its claim to neutrality. A neutral arbitration wills the catastrophic event of the war to be rendered accessible through a smooth, neutral and all-inclusive narration. It seeks to make complete sense of the war. But translation as speech act alerts us to the fact that war is unassimilable to a smooth, non-disrupted translation. The scandal of war cannot be neutrally translated. It may even be that the war, as an interpreter claimed, *should* not be neutrally translated, for to do so would be to miss the event itself. What distinguishes this event is that it does not leave room for neutrality, that it 'shocks' one out of any possible neutral stance, precisely because the breakdown of translation is unavoidable: either the interpreter 'jumps in' or a smooth, uninterrupted translation fails to convey the fact that history is passed on in erasure. The only ethical position may then be to disrupt or undermine the 'neutral' arbiter, a practice that Cronin labels '*translation as resistance*' and describes as 'the ways in which originals can be manipulated, invented or substituted, or the status of the original subverted in order to frustrate the intelligence-gathering activities of the Imperial Agent' (2000: 35), or, in this case, of an intelligence officer in the skin of an EC monitor.

Interpreter activism: between volunteerism and professionalism

Not only does the ECMM suspect the interpreters of being spies, but Croatia also looks at them with suspicion. Interpreters are left out of the history of the international community because, as volunteers, they are always marked as politically motivated, volunteer-patriots or even worse: nationalists. They might then at least hope to be recognized as patriots in the history of their country. Instead, they are perceived as 'double agents' (Rafael 2007), with the Croatian side accusing them of treason:

> INTERPRETER A: [T]he animosity towards monitors is transferred onto the interpreter.
> INTERPRETER D: It affects me that [Croatians] identify us with the monitors, so that sometimes waiters refuse to serve us, children yell or throw stones at us.
> INTERPRETER H: The lack of sympathy towards monitors is partially transferred onto us.
> INTERPRETER I: Sometimes they [Croatians] throw stones at cars.
> INTERPRETER K: Sometimes [Croatians] yell at me for what angers them in monitors.

The interpreters' linguistic neutrality is misinterpreted as political neutrality. Croatia perceives their professionalism as a neutralization of their political allegiance rather than as a structural responsibility – it misreads their volunteerism as betrayal. For Croatia, interpreters remain anonymous. By definition volunteerism is a gift that is neither documented nor recognized. Paradoxically, then, interpreters' patriotism is compromised by their volunteerism, because records that might testify to their participation in the war and their patriotic political allegiance are non-existent.

In addition to the fact that their volunteerism erases them, then, Croatia also refuses to recognize translation as an act of patriotism; already as volunteers, the fact that they are working for a politically neutral organization compromises them. And any remaining patriotic intention to which they could lay claim is definitely jeopardized when this politically neutral organization starts paying interpreters for their work, perhaps in an attempt to develop staff loyalty. In the autumn of 1992, the ECMM started to remunerate the interpreters. A number of new interpreters joined in, but with a motivation radically different from that of the volunteers:

> INTERPRETER I: Most new translators are here for the money; nothing else interests them.
> INTERPRETER N: It is not good that earnings are the only motivation – when on a mission, they try to work as little as possible.
> INTERPRETER T: The newcomers are coming only for the money, so the old ones, who are interested in something else, do not have enough work.

From then on, the interpreters distinguished between those 'who are interested in something else', something other than money, that is, the original volunteers or the 'veterans', and the 'newcomers' or, as they were also called, the 'mercenaries' (Interpreters B, S). Interpreter B openly expressed his anger, which is 'connected to the change of atmosphere at work', a thought further developed by Interpreter L:

> INTERPRETER L: The atmosphere has changed since payments started, there is less enthusiasm and more tension, less cameraderie than before.

Interpreters F and N expressed a similar viewpoint concerning tension among interpreters, and Interpreter M felt that

> INTERPRETER M: Deserving veterans often do not get the job because of them [the newcomers].

At the same time, "mercenaries" complain that 'veterans feel more valuable' (Interpreter P). But outside the Croatian Liaison Office, this internal distinction between volunteers and 'mercenaries' collapsed. The work of the 'veterans' was now documented, along with the work of the 'mercenaries', in contracts and ECMM payroll records. Thus, once the 'veterans' started being paid, their previous volunteerism was occulted. This paradox, the fact that the volunteer-interpreters who are the most engaged and active in the war are also the most erased in the history of their country, is the ultimate violence connected with interpreting in and of the war.

The memory of interpreters' volunteerism faded as volunteers were conflated with 'mercenaries':

> INTERPRETER Q: Some think we [the 'veterans'] only work for the money.

It is within this context that the then Croatian Minister of Education declared that the 'patriotism' of those who worked for international organizations 'is questionable'. That the reference in the minister's statement was to the issue of money as well as the activity of interpreting was proven by the fact that her words provoked strong public reactions from various associations of interpreters in Croatia, even though her statement did not single them out. Interpreters' 'patriotism is questionable' because they are on the ECMM's payroll. The minister assumed that interpreters were 'only work[ing] for the money'. And to be paid by an organization whose proclaimed neutrality was perceived as acting against Croatia's interests defined the interpreters' political allegiance as unpatriotic. On the other hand, for the Minister of Education their 'patriotism is questionable' because translation, surely, constituted a betrayal: the interpreters had not compelled the party on the receiving end of translation to take the Croatian side, and its continuing neutrality prohibited it from championing or, at the very least, recognizing the Croatian rights to the recovery of the occupied territories. Failing to convince the ECMM finally compromised the interpreters' patriotism.

For interpreters, on the other hand, this betrayal of Croatia was unavoidable. If Croatia wanted international recognition, its voice had to be heard. In order to achieve this, interpreters had to translate into the language of the organization upon which Croatia's recognition depended, while at the same time wishing to bear witness to the victimization of their country. But interpreters were condemned to treason because of the incommensurability of the positions of interpreter and witness in a war context. Wartime translation is a double bind: the double bind of having to translate in order to convey the urgency of political recognition of Croatia, but failing to voice this imperative themselves, failing to be a witness in their translation. The neutrality inherent in translation bars the interpreters from ever giving full recognition to Croatia in their translation. On the other hand, this neutrality prevents Croatia from recognizing interpreter volunteerism as a form of patriotism – interpreters will always be locked in another timeframe: they lose their place in the future because they have been erased in the past. They do not have a place in history when the Minister of Education calls them traitors and the ECMM excludes them as witnesses. Earlier we saw that at least one interpreter suffered a trauma because her patriotism could no longer bear ECMM's neutrality. But at this point, interpreters are exposed to another kind of trauma, that of (historical) non-recognition: non-recognition of their testimonial stance by the ECMM and non-recognition of their patriotism by Croatia. In December 2005, fourteen years after their service began, after many appeals and with a centre-right government in power, Croatia recognized the work of some twenty volunteer-interpreters from the Croatian Liaison Office by awarding them a medal of honour for their war efforts. The ceremony, ironically, took place in the offices of the now-defunct Ministry for European Integration (currently part of the Ministry of Foreign Affairs).

The question of interpreter activism thus emerges in a different light when the variable of professionalization (in the sense of paid service) is introduced; in other words, volunteerism may be a more 'acceptable' form of interpreter activism, one that does not lead to situations that demand ethical choices compromised by financial transactions. Baker (2008) argues that 'just because the client is paying doesn't mean they are entitled to more loyalty or respect from the translators – translators . . . should not behave like mercenaries'; but, as we have seen, the fact that the interpreter is being paid by a client does compromise their position in the eyes of others. This is one lesson that the Babel's interpreter-activists seem to have learnt: 'following the unhappy experience of a two-tier workforce of voluntary and paid interpreters in Florence, Babels now makes the principle of 100 per cent volunteer interpretation and translation a precondition of its involvement' (Hodkinson and Boéri 2004). However, as I argue below, while complicating notions of interpreter allegiance both professionalism and volunteerism nevertheless open up a unique space for interpreter activism.

Translating 'the Balkans': transnational translation

As we saw, translation as a speech act always involves the interpreter as a participant, an 'intervenient being' (Maier 2007). But the assertion of one's voice also transcends the individual and becomes an instance of reverse interpellation at the international level, from the minor, obscure language to the hegemonic, major arbiter in the conflict.[6] The interpreters' activism in the testimonial process testifies to a complex and plural past and resists its hegemonic and univocal representation. 'Switching' is consistent with the need to tell one's story, to emplot one's past and thus to challenge the neutral narrative – which is also the dominant narrative, because the ECMM is the arbiter in the conflict. Translation as speech act also points to the need to historicize wartime translation. Interpreters' intervention revealed that, despite ECMM's seeming interest only in the facts of the conflict, these 'facts' are equally part of monitors' own pre-existing narrative about the history of Yugoslavia. If the ECMM does not acknowledge interpreters as 'knowledgeable' interlocutors, it may be because they can only acknowledge them as 'native informants', precisely because of their vision of Western superiority in arbitrating over the fratricidal, tribal ' "wild Balkan" people' (Interpreter R). The Western narrative of former Yugoslavia and its wars in the 1990s reifies cultural and religious differences that inevitably produce conflict among indistinguishable and indistinct ethnicities; in return, the 'balkanization of Europe' can only be a violent process of unstoppable and contagious fragmentation spreading throughout Europe and undermining the stability and unity of its nation-states (Mestrovic 1994). Translation then is a site, not only of identity formation for a minor culture, but of identity legitimation and resistance to a hegemonic, superior vision of the arbiter: a site for reframing the Western European master narrative (Baker 2006a) and for recasting the 'Balkan' discourse. The popular catchphrase 'balkanization of Europe' may be understood, then, not as a threat to European political stability, but as a fragmentation of the hegemonic, master narrative of the 'Balkans'.

During the Yugoslav wars, 'the Balkans' were reduced to Yugoslavia, even though the former Yugoslavia shunned any Balkan labels. The socialist Yugoslavia (1945–1992) was a second version of the country first pieced together in 1918 under the name of the Kingdom of Serbs, Croats and Slovenes, renamed in 1929 the Kingdom of Yugoslavia. All this was meant to resolve the problem of a region located at the crossroads of the former Austro-Hungarian and Ottoman Empires. But the West spoke, not of the specificity of this Austro-Hungarian-Ottoman hybrid, encompassing the former borderline between the East and the West, but of 'the Balkans', a much larger and somewhat vague and shifting geopolitical unit of South-East Europe that included Albania, Bulgaria, Greece, Romania and part of Turkey. In speaking of 'the Balkans', the West evoked an immutable,

367

'Oriental' image of Ottoman legacy, one in which the 'inhabitants do not care to conform to the standards of behavior devised as normative by and for the civilized world' (Todorova 1997: 3). This image was first established in the wake of the two Balkan Wars (1912–1913), precursors to the First World War, traditionally thought to have been triggered by the murder of Archduke Franz-Ferdinand by a Serbian nationalist, Gavrilo Princip, in Sarajevo. Maria Todorova demonstrated masterfully 'How . . . a geographical appellation [of the Bulgarian mountain range could] be transformed into one of the most powerful pejorative designations in history, international relations, political science, and, nowadays, general intellectual discourse' (1997: 7). The term 'Balkan'

> was used alongside other generalizing catchwords, of which 'Oriental' was most often employed, to stand for filth, passivity, unreliability, misogyny, propensity for intrigue, insincerity, opportunism, laziness, superstitiousness, lethargy, sluggishness, inefficiency, incompetent bureaucracy. 'Balkan', while overlapping with 'Oriental', had additional characteristics [such] as cruelty, boorishness, instability, and unpredictability. Both categories were used against the concept of Europe symbolizing cleanliness, order, self-control, strength of character, sense of law, justice, efficient administration.
>
> (Todorova 1997: 119)

In short: civilization was opposed to barbarism. The term 'balkanization', signifying fragmentation into ever-smaller states in the wake of the Balkan wars and the First World War, added to the mix the crucial ingredient of violence, incomprehensible to the civilized Westerner. Archaic aspects of culture, including the cultural tradition of the 'warrior ethos', were naturalized as the essence of 'Balkan' behaviour, epitomized by the Yugoslavs; Yugoslavs just couldn't help themselves, and war was the only path to dialogue, since war is the true expression of the 'Balkan' spirit. In essence, nothing had changed since the Middle Ages, an image frozen in time that the Balkans had already embodied in nineteenth-century travel literature.

It is here that interpreter activism can make a difference. It is, first of all, a demand for recognition. It may have taken a war for the minor to become *audible* and to begin to translate the plural history of what was occulted behind the 'Balkan' narrative. While the war appears to confirm it, the audibility of the minor in wartime translation challenges the Western European discourse of 'the Balkans'. Translation balkanizes Europe not because it directly threatens its political stability and unity, but because it undermines and undoes its hegemonic master narrative. This is the sphere of transnational translation, as defined at the beginning of this article (see note 1): interpreters offer an interpretation of politics, history and culture,

directed vertically at the hegemonic arbiter. When they intervene as interpreters of culture and history, they challenge the narrative of neutrality
at a personal level and resist the oversimplifying and hegemonic Western
discourse of Croatia as a barbaric and 'wild Balkan' nation. But they also
remind the arbiter not to ignore his or her own inscription in the event.
At the same time, a transnational translation agenda horizontalizes and
flattens vertical relations, since the minor becomes a partner in inter-
locution. Regardless of the major or minor status of languages from and
into which translation occurs, all parties in a war conflict depend on the
efficiency of translation: war democratizes the status of languages and
allows for mutual interpenetration of the 'Western' and the 'Balkan'.
Transnational translation plays here a major role: translations correct the
mutual discursive violence of narratives and shift conflicting discursive loyalties in an ongoing process of negotiation through what Sampson (2006)
calls 'cultural translation'.

But interpreters perform yet another kind of translation and negotiation
of discursive violence, this time 'at home'. For they do not hesitate to criticize their own fellow citizens and Croatia's civil servants:

> INTERPRETER D: Regular folks make a better impression (on the monitors
> as well) than some extremists among civil servants.
> INTERPRETER F: Certain situations are uncomfortable when our inter-
> locutors talk politics too much, give lessons in history and such – those
> things are unpleasant to translate because they annoy monitors.
> INTERPRETER N: Our people occasionally talk too much.
> INTERPRETER Q: Occasionally I feel ashamed by what some of our rep-
> resentatives say and how they speak.
> INTERPRETER T: I am occasionally saddened by the way some of our
> people behave; by applying primitive politics and unnecessary [reason-
> ing], they are creating a poor impression of Croatia.
> INTERPRETER X: Sometimes the poor impression that some of our rude
> interlocutors leave on the monitors makes me sad. I think they hurt the
> image of Croatia.

The overall feeling of sadness that the interpreters report is matched by
their feeling of powerlessness in a situation that surpasses their intermediary
position and reminds them of their lack of agency. The ethical responsibility
that they assume in becoming interpreters in and of the war puts them in a
position which is neither strictly political nor national, nor entirely 'neutral'
or 'objective'. It is this in-between space, the double agency of the interpreters' ethical responsibility that Interpreter P struggles to define:

> INTERPRETER P: I think [my work] helps the homeland and it also helps
> in a more general sense.

The interpreters' relationship to history points in at least two directions – toward the "homeland", and also 'in a more general sense'. The interpreters' allegiance to their 'homeland' is not absolute then; they are neither patriots nor traitors, and they are both volunteers and professionals. The case of Croatian translators shows that the ethical responsibility of interpreters in and of the war involves another kind of allegiance to history that situates them beyond their political, national, ethnic, gender, religious or linguistic affiliations, but at the same time not exclusively in the realm of the universal, or the all-inclusive, or the neutral – speaking from the local to the transnational.

Indeed, my emphasis on the interpreters' intervention could be taken to imply a universal claim that interpreters have a privileged relationship to history and ethics, a claim that I do not wish to make, much as I believe that translation and interpreting are a means of destabilizing hegemonic, dominant discourses (Baker 2006a, 2006b, 2008, in press; Cronin 2000, 2002; Stahuljak 2004; Rafael 2007). Just as translators and interpreters are not in-between (Tymoczko 2003) or outside any event, translation itself cannot be used as a metaphor of pure translatability (Stahuljak 2004) or as a 'bridge' between different cultures (Baker 2005, in press). Interpreters do not occupy a position of 'elsewhere' that harmonizes or hybridizes contradictory and conflictual positions; rather, they are very much inscribed in their specific time and place (geographical and ideological). Likewise, their interventions, even activism, are not to be privileged as the ultimate access to history, since the interpreters themselves are a product of a particular set of intersecting narratives which, while potentially transcending particular ethnic, national, gender, religious or linguistic affiliations, remain local. Their power and impact lie, not in any claim to universality, but in their geographic and temporal location and their ability to pose a local challenge to the discourse of arbitration. Only by speaking from within, as the Croatian interpreters did, by having a position rather than occupying a place on the outside, by identifying 'what makes specific examples of engaged translation effective' (Tymoczko 2000: 34) and by formulating an ethics of translation that is 'guided by the nature of the ethical encounter itself' (Inghilleri 2008:222), that is, by the social and political conditions of the event, can interpreters hope to effect geopolitical and social change, the stated goal of activist interpreting.

Appendix: interpreter questionnaire

Interviews were conducted in Croatian between 11 September and 18 October 1993, by Ivan Magdalenic, psychologist, at the premises of the Croatian Liaison Office, Hotel 'I', Zagreb, Croatia. All translations from Croatian into English are provided by the current author.

1   How long have you been working for the Office?
2   What motivated you to join, what are your main motives?
3   How many times have you gone on a fact-finding mission?
4   Where?
5   What is the average length of a mission? What was the length of your longest mission? And the shortest one?
6   With whom did you talk (on our side and on the other)?
7   Generally speaking, what are the impressions left by our interlocutors and by the interlocutors from the other side? Try to describe, without naming, a person from each side who left the best and who left the worst impression on you.
8   What is the impression left by the people for whom you are translating [EC monitors]? Describe, without naming, the most pleasant and the most unpleasant of them.
9   Generally speaking, what do you like best about them [EC monitors] and what bothers you the most? Give an example for each.
10 What duties other than interpreting are assigned to you while on a mission?
11 What do you like best about your job and what do you dislike the most? What is the most burdensome?
12 When on a mission, how do you feel: (a) in general; (b) while interpreting?
13 Have you ever felt that you were in danger while on a mission, whether in the context of a life-threatening situation, particularly unpleasant events, or social situations? Describe the most uncomfortable event you have experienced while on a mission.
14 While on a mission, are you free and able to be alone or to do something of your own choice (except the time reserved for sleep)? Do you have a daily break? If not, do you feel a need to be alone, to have free time and daily breaks?
15 After how many days on a mission do you begin to experience: (a) physical fatigue; (b) psychic fatigue?
16 How do you feel when you return from a mission? How long does this feeling last?
17 In your free time in Zagreb, when you are not at the Office, do you have recurrent thoughts or feelings about what you saw and experienced? Do you dream about it? Do you have nightmares?
18 Do you feel a need to speak with someone about the events experienced on missions? If so, whom do you talk to? Do these conversations bring you relief? Is there an experience about which you don't wish to speak to anyone?
19 Do you feel a need to speak about all of this with a psychologist or a similar specialist? What do you think about the usefulness of collective or group conversations and exchange of impressions among interpreters? Would you have such conversations conditional upon your choice of participants?
20 What would you personally suggest in order to improve your working conditions, that is, to ease the difficulties encountered by you and your colleagues?
21 Are you under the impression that some of your colleagues are not up to the task they are asked to perform? Based on your experience, what kind of selection process of candidates should be implemented? Or should those who show themselves not to be up to the task be discharged?
22 For how long do you intend to continue doing this job? Under what conditions?
23 How do you feel after this conversation? Do you wish to meet again?

Notes

1 By 'transnational' and 'transnationalism' I refer throughout to linkages and networks among people and groups across national boundaries, as opposed to 'international' cooperation among governments and multinational corporations. Transnationalism is an appropriate term to understand circulation within global systems of political, cultural and economic exchange, which can no longer be contained within a state-centric definition of exchange and communication. Translator and interpreter activism is a transnational undertaking in this sense.
2 The title of the first article I wrote on this topic (Stahuljak 1999) referred to 'translators', reflecting the high value of the term 'translation', when it should have been about 'interpreters', the term that the recent focus on interpreting in translation studies has validated as equal to 'literary translator' in importance and that I now use throughout.
3 One of the peculiarities of the communist ex-Yugoslavia was the denomination of 'Muslim' as an ethnic group. The designation of 'Muslim' as a nationality was intended to strip the term of all religious significance. It was applied to Bosnian Muslims; this explains why Albanians, for instance, who are mostly Muslim, constituted a separate nationality.
4 Along with being able to choose from 'Serb', 'Croat', 'Muslim', 'Hungarian', etc., people identifying with Yugoslavia, rather than with particular ethnic groups which made up the country, could choose the national designation of 'Yugoslav'.
5 As explained earlier, these interviews were partly transcribed and partly summarized by Magdalenic, hence the occasional use of indirect speech.
6 I understand 'minor' here as any group whose culture, language and history have been perceived as inferior and subordinate, whose culture has been ignored or essentialized.

References

Baker, Mona (2005) 'Narratives in and of Translation', *SKASE Journal of Translation and Interpretation* 1(1): 4–13.

Baker, Mona (2006a) *Translation and Conflict: A Narrative Account*, London and New York: Routledge.

Baker, Mona (2006b) 'Translation and Activism: Emerging Patterns of Narrative Community', *The Massachusetts Review* 47(III): 462–484.

Baker, Mona (2008) 'Ethics of Renarration. An Interview with Andrew Chesterman', *Cultus* 1(1): 10–33.

Baker, Mona (in press) 'Resisting State Terror: Theorising Communities of Activist Translators and Interpreters', in Esperança Bielsa Mialet and Chris Hughes (eds) *Globalisation, Political Violence and Translation*, Basingstoke: Palgrave Macmillan.

Barsky, Robert F. (1996) 'The Interpreter as Intercultural Agent in Convention Refugee Hearings', *The Translator* 1(2): 45–64.

Barthes, Roland (2002) *Le Neutre. Cours au Collège de France (1977–1978)*, edited by Eric Marty, Paris: Seuil/IMEC.

Boéri, Julie (2008) 'A Narrative Account of the Babels vs. Naumann Controversy', *The Translator* 14(1): 21–50.

Bulletin of the Office for Refugees and Displaced Persons (January 1993), Zagreb.

Cronin, Michael (2000) 'History, Translation, Postcolonialism', in Sherry Simon and Paul St-Pierre (eds) *Changing the Terms: Translating in the Postcolonial Era*, Ottawa: University of Ottawa Press, 33–52.

Cronin, Michael (2002) 'The Empire Talks Back: Orality, Heteronomy and the Cultural Turn in Interpreting Studies', in Edwin Gentzler and Maria Tymoczko (eds) *Translation and Power*, Boston and Amherst: University of Massachussets Press, 45–62.

Felman, Shoshana and Dori Laub (1992) *Testimony. Crisis of Witnessing in Literature, Psychoanalysis and History*, New York and London: Routledge.

Hodkinson, Stuart and Julie Boéri (2004) 'Social Forums after London: The Politics of Language', *Red Pepper*, http://www.redpepper.org.uk/article267.html, consulted 29 April 2008.

Inghilleri, Moira (2005) 'Mediating Zones of Uncertainty: Interpreter Agency, the Interpreting Habitus and Political Asylum Adjudication', *The Translator* 11(1): 69–85.

Inghilleri, Moira (2008) 'The Ethical Task of the Translator in the Geo-political Arena: From Iraq to Guantánamo Bay', *Translation Studies* 1(1): 212–223.

Inghilleri, Moira (in press) 'Translators in War Zones', in Esperança Bielsa Mialet and Chris Hughes (eds) *Globalisation, Political Violence and Translation*, Basingstoke: Palgrave Macmillan.

Jacquemet, Marco (2005) 'The Registration Interview. Restricting Refugees' Narrative Performances', in Mike Baynham and Anna de Fina (eds) *Dislocations/ Relocations. Narratives of Displacement*, Manchester: St Jerome, 197–220.

Kahane, Eduardo (2007) 'Intérpretes en conflictos: los límites de la neutralidad', AIIC (International Association of Conference Interpreters), http://www.aiic.net/ community/print/default.cfm/page2690, consulted 15 February 2008.

Lyotard, Jean-François (1989) 'Foreward', in Andrew Benjamin (ed.) *The Lyotard Reader*, Oxford: Blackwell Publishers, vi–xiv.

Magdalenic, Ivan (1993) 'Interviews with Interpreters from the Croatian Liaison Office', unpublished paper.

Maier, Carol (2007) 'The Translator as an Intervenient Being', in Jeremy Munday (ed.) *Translation as Intervention*, New York: Continuum, 1–17.

Mestrovic, Stjepan G. (1994) *The Balkanization of the West: The Confluence of Postmodernism and Postcommunism*, London and New York: Routledge.

Moeketsi, Rosemary M. H. (2007) 'Intervention in Court Interpreting: South Africa', in Jeremy Munday (ed.) *Translation as Intervention*, New York: Continuum, 97–117.

Morris, Ruth (1995) 'The Moral Dilemmas of Court Interpreting', *The Translator* 1(1): 25–46.

Munday, Jeremy (ed.) (2007) *Translation as Intervention*, New York: Continuum.

Niranjana, Tejaswini (1992) *Siting Translation: History, Post-Structuralism and the Colonial Context*, Berkeley: University of California Press.

Palmer, Jerry (2007) 'Interpreting and Translation for Western Media in Iraq', in Myriam Salama-Carr (ed.) *Translating and Interpreting Conflict*, Amsterdam and New York: Rodopi, 13–28.

Rafael, Vicente L. (2007) 'Translation in Wartime', *Public Culture* 19(2): 239–246.

Sampson, Fiona (2006) 'Heidegger and the Aporia: Translation and Cultural Authenticity', *Critical Review of International Social and Political Philosophy* 9(4): 527–539.

Stahuljak, Zrinka (1999) 'The Violence of Neutrality: Translators in and of the War (Croatia, 1991–92)', *College Literature* 26(1): 34–51.

Stahuljak, Zrinka (2000) 'Violent Distortions: Bearing Witness to the Task of Wartime Translators', *TTR* 13(1): 37–51.

Stahuljak, Zrinka (2004) 'An Epistemology of Tension: Translation and Multi-culturalism', *The Translator* 10(1): 33–57.

Stahuljak, Zrinka (2007) 'Traduire la Honte (Le Tribunal pénal international pour l'ex-Yougoslavie et son deuxième monde)', in Bruno Chaouat (ed.) *Lire, Écrire la Honte*, Lyon: Presses Universitaires de Lyon, 165–183.

Tipton, Rebecca (2008) 'Reflexivity and the Social Construction of Identity in Inter-preter-Mediated Asylum Interviews', *The Translator* 14(1): 1–19.

Todorova, Maria (1997) *Imagining the Balkans*, New York and Oxford: Oxford University Press.

Tymoczko, Maria (2000) 'Translation and Political Engagement. Activism, Social Change and the Role of Translation in Geopolitical Shifts', *The Translator* 6(1): 23–47.

Tymoczko, Maria (2003) 'Ideology and the Position of the Translator. In What Sense Is a Translator "In Between"?', in María Calzada Pérez (ed.) *Apropos of Ideology*, Manchester: St Jerome, 181–205.

Tymoczko, Maria (2007) *Enlarging Translation, Empowering Translators*, Manchester: St Jerome.

Wadensjö, Cecilia (1998) *Interpreting as Interaction*, London and New York: Longman.

57

IDEOLOGY AND THE POSITION OF THE TRANSLATOR

In what sense is a translator 'in between'?

Maria Tymoczko

Source: María Calzada Pérez (ed.) (2003) *Apropos of Ideology – Translation Studies on Ideology – Ideologies in Translation Studies*, Manchester: St Jerome, pp. 181–201.

The ideology of a translation is complex, resulting from the layering of the subject of the source text, the speech acts of the source text, the representation of the content by the translator, and the speech acts of the translation itself, as well as resonances and discrepancies between these aspects of the source text and target text as 'utterances'. If such ideological aspects of a translation are inextricable from the 'place of enunciation' of the translator, which is as much ideological as geographical and temporal, how does the discourse of 'in between' relate to an analysis of the ideology of translation? Why is this trope popular at present? After considering reasons for the use of the trope, this article argues that the discourse of 'between' is ultimately misleading and even retrograde with respect to understanding both the role of the translator and the notion of ideological engagement itself.

Some of the most searching and revealing discussions of translation in the last decade have focused on questions of ideology; indeed, there has been a productive, ongoing academic dialogue about various facets of the issue, extending for years now, with contributions from people on all parts of the globe. Raised principally by those who have an investment in social engagement, questions about the translator as an ethical agent of social change have gone to the heart of both the practice of translation and the theory of translation.[1] Part of the ongoing conversation, this essay is an attempt to

375

clarify issues pertaining to the position of the translator by teasing out some philosophical implications of contemporary discourses about translation. Although successful cultural programs do not necessarily depend on clear and logical philosophical premises, in my experience a firm cognitive and theoretical foundation makes it more probable that a cultural project will draw together groups of people and inspire them to work in concert.

For at least a quarter century now, it has been generally agreed that translation is a text about a text or, to put it another way, a form of metastatement.[2] If we put this seemingly innocuous observation in an ideological context, then we must recognize that the ideology of translation is quite complex. A translation's ideology is determined only partially by the content of the source text – the subject and the representation of the subject – even though this content may itself be overtly political and enormously complicated as a speech act, with locutionary, illocutionary, and perlocutionary aspects of the source text all contributing to the effect in the source context. The ideological value of the source text is in turn complemented by the fact that translation is a metastatement, a statement about the source text that constitutes an interpretation of the source text. This is true even when that metastatement is seemingly only a form of reported speech (cf. Jakobson 1959:233) or quotation uttered in a new context, for in quoting a source text, a translator in turn creates a text that is a representation with its own proper locutionary, illocutionary, and perlocutionary forces which are determined by relevant factors in the receptor context. Thus, even in a simplified model, the ideology of a translation will be an amalgam of the content of the source text and the various speech acts instantiated in the source text relevant to the source context, layered together with the representation of the content, its relevance to the receptor audience, and the various speech acts of the translation itself addressing the target context, as well as resonances and discrepancies between these two 'utterances'.[3]

A concrete example of this layering is found in the well known rewriting and staging of Sophocles's *Antigone* by Jean Anouilh, produced in Paris in 1944 during the Nazi occupation of France. Clearly Sophocles's text had its own ideological significance in its original context. Produced for the Great Dionysia festival held annually in Athens, as a *statement* about the dangers of tyranny and the importance of heroic resistance to tyrants, *Antigone* implicitly *celebrated* Athenian democracy and attempted *to instill independence and moral responsibility* in its audience, as well as *pride in and allegiance to* the city-state of Athens itself, among other things.[4] When Anouilh transposed Sophocles's play into French and staged it for his own time, however, those early ideological meanings were overwritten with contemporary meanings: he was implicitly commenting on the Nazi occupation of France, *inciting* his contemporaries and *encouraging resistance* against the Nazis, *calling for them to act out* against Nazi usurpation. Here I've tried to emphasize the words associated with the illocutionary and perlocutionary dimensions of Sophocles's work and Anouilh's refraction, as well as to indicate briefly some of the relevant contextual dimensions that must be considered in determining the ideology of Anouilh's play.

Ideological effects will differ in every case of translation – even in translations of the same text – because of the translator's particular choices on all these various levels – on the levels of representation of the subject matter, as well as representation of the relevant locutionary, illocutionary, and perlocutionary effects of the source text, and on the relevant locutionary, illocutionary, and perlocutionary acts in his or her own name as translator. That is, the ideology of a translation resides not simply in the text translated, but in the voicing and stance of the translator, and in its relevance to the receiving audience. These latter features are affected by the place of enunciation of the translator: indeed they are part of what we mean by the 'place' of enunciation, for that 'place' is an ideological positioning as well as a geographical or temporal one. These aspects of a translation are motivated and determined by the translator's cultural and ideological affiliations as much as or even more than by the temporal and spatial location that the translator speaks from.

Although more extensive and more precise vocabulary pertaining to the ideology of translation has been developed in the last few decades, these issues of enunciation have been implicitly recognized for years in writing about translation, even if not stated explicitly in the terms that I have used above. Thus, for example, the affiliation and place of the translator were a concern in translation theory as early as 1813 when Friedrich Schleiermacher stated that "just as a man must decide to belong to one country, just so [a translator] must adhere to one language", affiliating himself thus with one particular culture, assumed by Schleiermacher to be the translator's native land.[5] The issues behind Schleiermacher's concerns have continued to be central in translation scholarship and theory. More than 150 years later, for example, in attempting to delineate a descriptive approach to translation, Gideon Toury took up questions pertaining to the position of translation and translators, stating categorically that translated texts are 'facts' of one language and one textual tradition only, namely the target culture's (1980:82–83), and that translators are 'persons-in-the-culture' of the target system (1995:40)[6]. Although one might contest Toury's argument on these points, disagreement should not obscure the importance of his addressing issues of positionality for the evolution of translation studies.

A very nice – albeit brief and circumspect – pragmatic survey of the variety of places the translator can write from is found in an early essay by Norman Simms (1983). Simms shows how the politics of translation intersects with the translator's position. This is true, he indicates, no matter whether the translator is a member of a postcolonial culture using translation into an imperial language as a means of cultural advocacy, or whether the translator holds one of the many possible subject positions within which translation is produced for members of the target culture itself in a specific ideological complex. Descriptive studies and theoretical arguments by many writers, including Simms, illustrate that the translator can be positioned within the receptor culture (the most common case), within the source culture (as, for example, authorized translations of Mao's writings into English that were undertaken in the People's Republic of China during the period 1949–79), or elsewhere (as in a third culture, the case when German philologists translated Irish literature into English and published them in German series, or when U.S. Bible translators translate the New Testament into South American native languages).

Despite the fact that the affiliation and orientation of the translator have been a continual topic in writing about translation for more than a century, the issues remain an active concern in the field, particularly as they impact on questions of the ideology of translation. These questions about the place of enunciation of the translator – both the ideological positioning and the geographical and temporal positioning – are related to the recent development within translation studies of a tendency to speak of translation itself as a place or space somehow disjoined from (or mappable over) the actual physical and cultural space that the translator occupies, and somehow distinct from the ideological position of the translator as well. Particularly employed by progressive and engaged writers on translation theory and practice, translation has been characterized as a place or a space *in between* other spaces. The locution *between* has become one of the most popular means of figuring an *elsewhere* that a translator may speak from – an elsewhere that is somehow different from either the source culture or the receptor culture that the translator mediates between – as well as the culture the translator lives in – an elsewhere that is often seemingly not simply a metaphorical way of speaking about ideological positioning, but that ipso facto affords a translator a valorized ideological stance. An exploration of this discourse – including aspects of its origin, logic, rationale, usefulness, and import – takes us to the heart of the ideology of translation[7].

Let us begin by considering specific recent instances of the figuration of translation as *a place between*. Sherry Simon offers convenient examples in her excellent and provocative book entitled *Gender in Translation* (1996). She speaks (1996:162), for example, of "the blurred edge where original and copy, first and second languages, come to meet. The space 'between' becomes a powerful and difficult place for the writer to occupy". She compares the domain of translation to the domain of a person with multiple cultural affiliations: "the space which Bhabha works in is the liminary terrain of the translational, that hybrid space which stands between the certainties of national cultures but does not participate in them" (1996:153). In her usage Simon follows Gayatri Spivak, whose essay "The Politics of Translation" (1992) has become one of the most influential explorations of the ideology of translation. Spivak alludes to translation as an activity "where meaning hops into the spacy emptiness between two named historical lan-guages" (1992:178), clearly using spatial figurations. Similarly, in "Translation and the Postcolonial Experience", Samia Mehrez asserts, "these texts written by postcolonial bilingual subjects create a language 'in between' and therefore come to occupy a space 'in between'" (1992:121). Although examples could be multiplied[8], these instances suffice to indicate the type of usage that has proliferated. Why are scholars and theorists inclined to use the metaphor of translation as a space – a space 'in between' – in talking about the ideology of translation and in delineating a valorized position for the translator to occupy?[9]

Before addressing this question directly, we must make a brief detour to consider what sorts of answers might be considered adequate. We should note that a question like "why do scholars use the spatial metaphor of between?" admits different responses, depending on the different types of causality to be considered. There are many types of causality. As a start-ing point on the types of answers provided for the question 'why?', we can consider the sorts of causes that might be given for natural phenomena, say the phenomenon of a sneeze. In this case we could note, first, the proxi-mate cause; in the case of a sneeze, the proximate cause is the contraction of the muscles involved in producing a sneeze. Second might be the ultimate cause or the functional cause; the ultimate cause of a sneeze is to expel material from the breathing passages. Third could be the ontogenetic cause, the developmental reason for a phenomenon; in the case of a sneeze, the ontogenetic cause is that the organism is exposed to irritants which must be ejected from the organism. Fourth might be the phylogenetic cause. In biological phenomena, the phylogenetic cause is the causality associated with the characteristics of the organism's nearest relatives; thus, in the case of a human sneeze, the phylogenetic cause is that primates sneeze, hence human beings sneeze. There would be other ways to respond to such a physiological question as well, but these answers suffice for the present context[10].

As is apparent, within the domain of this simple biological example, there are many different ways to answer the question 'why?'. Moreover, other natural sciences would recognize forms of causality proper to their own domains, with adequate explanation differing from one domain to another (Salmon 1998:323). In addition to the types of causes admitted by the natural sciences, also to be considered are the types of causalities accepted by other disciplines, including the social sciences and the humanities. There are anthropological answers to the question 'why?', philosophical answers, and so forth. These various ways of approaching causality – and the ques-tion 'why?' – are not mutually exclusive, nor do the answers invalidate one another (cf. Salmon 1998:74). Thus, in trying to answer the question before us in the domain of translation studies, we should expect a number of dif-ferent ways to respond that are at once disparate and yet do not necessarily undermine or contradict each other. We must also implicitly delineate a theory of causality for translation studies itself.

To turn to the main question before us, therefore, one way to answer the question "why has speaking of translation as a *space between* become popular in translation studies?" is, of course, to seek answers within these established frames of causality. We might, for example, turn to phylogeny and seek a phylogenetic cause. That is, because primates are imitators, humans are imitators: as the English proverb puts it, 'monkey see, monkey do'. Thus, with respect to an academic discourse of the sort we are considering, we see our colleagues using a particular figure of speech, a trope, or a discourse, and as imitators we tend to take up such things ourselves without much reflection. Perhaps the phylogenetic cause in this instance has to do with the specific behavior of our nearest relatives and ancestors in an intellectual or critical sense. From an individual's point of view, the reasoning behind the use of these expressions goes something like this: *between* is a trendy term; if critic X can use the phrase, so can I; indeed perhaps, so should I, insofar as I see myself in her lineage – or phylum – of thinkers. Clearly in the case of intellectual pursuits, a phylogenetic cause for behavior, while perhaps good for accruing patronage, is not the best intellectual reason to adopt a mode of thinking or speaking: we might want to be careful in such circumstances of the impulse to imitate without critical reflection. Moreover, from a phylogenetic perspective, particularly the phylogenetic perspective of creatures who can elect their intellectual lineages and choose their critical and theoretical forebears, we must ask ourselves whether there are other lineages, other contemporary thinkers, whom we as translators and translation theorists might wish to claim as close 'relatives' or 'ancestors', who must be considered as we approach these questions regarding translation as being a *space between*. Obviously, a phylogenetic reason for spatializing translation is not the strongest rationale for the use of these tropes.

A second reason for the easy acceptance of the discourse of translation as a space between may reside in the actual physical location which the translator assumes in the archetypal translation encounter, namely the position of the translator-as-interpreter. In many situations of interpretation, from community interpretation to certain affairs of state, the interpreter literally stands between two speakers, performing the necessary vocalizations of interpretation, turning physically back and forth as the work proceeds, occupying a physical space between the principals. This physical positioning we might identify as the proximate cause for considering translation as a space between and for conceptualizing the translator as speaking from *in between*.[11] Although this proximate cause deserves our consideration in assessing the idea of translation as a space between, we should be wary of an uncritical generalization of one physical aspect of the interpreter's role to other domains of the activity, particularly the symbolic domain of language transfer. Moreover, it is questionable how far the physical location of the interpreter can serve as a literal or metaphorical guide to the ideological positioning of a translator of written texts.

Perhaps a stronger reason for conceptualizing translation in spatial terms has to do with the meaning and history of the words used for translation in certain Western languages. Such a reason may be looked on as the ontogenetic – or developmental – reason for translation being figured in terms of space in Western translation theory. The source of the English word *translation* is the Latin word *translatio*, which means 'carrying across'. Used originally in the very concrete sense of moving things through space, including both objects like the relics of saints and cultural phenomena like learning and power, its meaning was extended relatively late in time, during the fourteenth century, and applied to the activity of interlingual translation in English (OED s.v.). This usage was pioneered by Bible translators in what seems to be a metaphoric extension of more central semantic meanings of the word, which included the movement from earth to heaven, as well as the transference of things from one spot to another on earth.

This lexical shift is interesting in the context of earlier usages in Western tradition. In Old French in the twelfth century, for example, *to translate* in the sense of textual mediation between languages was to put '*en romanz*'; this was standard usage all over the francophone world, which at the time included the British Isles, and such textual mediation could be rather literal, as indicated in certain saints' lives, but more typically involved fairly free adaptation permitting radical shifts of all sorts in vernacular materials[12]. When the term *translation* comes into use in English in the fourteenth century, it seems to be associated with a new esthetic of translation, one more text based, more oriented to the source text, more literal, and less associated with the informal standards of medieval vernacular literature, ad hoc oral interpretation, and other sorts of refractions: in short, with translation strategies that are seen as more appropriate for the growing movement to translate the Bible into the vernacular languages. In this regard, the earliest citation of the word in the OED is suggestive: in 1340 in his prologue of his translation of the Psalms, Hampole writes, "in the translacioun i folow the lettere als mykyll as i may".

Implicit, then, in the English word *translation*, and as well in the words used for *translation* in the Romance languages deriving from the Latin root *trans-ducere*, 'to lead across',[13] is the idea of a *between*, a *space*, that such an act of mediation will cross or bridge. In this historical sense of the word *translation*, there are similarities with the Greek concept of *metaphorein*, which gives the English term *metaphor* and which also involves the etymological sense of carrying across, namely a carrying across of an idea or relationship from one field of reference to another. Both terms – *translation* and *metaphor* – involve extensions of a known concept (specifically the physical act of carrying across) to new ideas, respectively the transposition of texts from one language to another and the transposition of an idea or relationship from one conceptual field to another.

When we explore the rationale for these words denoting interlingual translation as involving a *between* in a concrete sense, we can hypothesize that these modes of speaking derive from an implicit recognition that ideas and knowledge, modes of understanding and learning, are all ultimately local, bound to a specific place, a specific cultural framework, and a specific linguistic mode of construing the world. Indeed, stated this way, such a view seems singularly modern, congruent as it is with contemporary views that meaning is language specific; these arguments have been developed within translation studies by scholars such as J. C. Catford (1965). Such a framework is also stressed by contemporaries writing about the phenomena of globalization. Anthony King, for example, argues that the "autonomy of cultural competence exists at the local level" (King 1997:17; cf. Hannerz 1997:124) and "meaning only exists within a language game, a discourse, practices, etc., negotiated locally and discontinuously" (King 1997:159).

In earlier times, however, before the modern age, the local nature of knowledge and ideas to be translated was less abstract and philosophical. Indeed, translation of such local knowledge might involve a very concrete crossing of space, for it often presupposed physically transporting yourself (*translating* yourself or *carrying yourself across*) to a new place so as to learn about the ideas current in that place, as a precondition of transposing those ideas from one language to another, from one local cultural system to another. As an alternative to translating yourself across space, of course, you could choose to translate some source of knowledge across space to yourself; such a source of knowledge might take a variety of forms – it might be a scroll, a codex, or even a learned person (such as a wise man, captive, slave, or other native of the source culture), who could then serve as a source and interpreter of that distant local knowledge. Some mixture of the two alternatives was also possible: you might undertake a journey to secure a relic and bring it through space to your own land, so as to have leisure in your own space to make the transposition from one language to another. This idea of translation is graphically illustrated in the ancient Chinese legend about the journey to secure Buddhist scriptures from India so they could be translated into Chinese; this tale is at the heart of the legend of Monkey, one of the most popular and productive literary complexes of Chinese culture, but it intersects with actual historical practice as well. In fact the Chinese versions of Buddhist scriptures were textually translated in the Great Wild Goose Pagoda, still standing in Xi'an at the eastern terminus of the ancient Silk Road, after copies of the Buddhist scriptures had been physically translated along that road to China. The legend of Monkey memorializes for us the material conditions of a time when translation East or West involved travel and transport across and through space.

This conceptualization of translation, then, derives from a time when the movement of religious relics through space was not in fact so very different from the transportation of the precious physical and material bases of new knowledge to be transposed into a receiving language. Such a source of learning – whether a scroll, a codex, or a person – was itself a relic of another culture, another time or space. Because in former times the translator himself might have to undertake or to underwrite a dangerous journey across space in order to secure a precious document or source for translation, to undertake translation was to undertake adventure: the translator was a culture hero, one who would brave danger for the sake of knowledge. (The appropriation of this concept of translator as culture hero in itself might be an attractive feature of the current discourse in translation studies of *between*, especially when used by translators themselves.)

A reason for the appeal of the discourse of translation as a space between, therefore, is our continued awareness of the residual sense of these older meanings associated with words in Western languages pertaining to translation, such as *translation* in English or *traduction* in French, as well as our historical sense of the difficulty in ancient times of transposing and expanding cultural knowledge everywhere in the world. In this regard, skilled speakers of English still know what the translation of a saint is, and most people are still aware that *trans-* in *translation* means 'across', a meaning we retain cognitively in part because of our knowledge of other words with the same formant, words such as *transcontinental* or even the automobile name *TransAm*.[14] Although it is suggestive to consider these old meanings and associations of the Western words for translation, we must nevertheless be careful of simply and uncritically accepting such old ideas. Not only do old concepts sometimes cease to be relevant as time passes, but they do not always offer theoretically useful perspectives.[15] We should also be especially careful about claiming as universal a theoretical assertion that is based on the particularities and histories of a few Western European languages. It is not at all certain that such a claim would hold for other languages where the words for translation have different meanings and historical associations[16].

A more compelling attraction of the notion of translation as a space between – a reason that might be seen as a functional or final cause – is the importance of the concept of *between* per se in poststructuralist thought. In challenging the binary conceptualizations of structuralism which dominated critical thought in the mid twentieth century in Europe, poststructuralists emphasized alternatives to the oppositional structures and polar opposites of the structuralists. The concept of *between* epitomizes those alternatives – it suggests that not only the poles but also all the positions in between the poles are open for occupation. Moreover, poststructuralists were not alone in mounting such critiques and in searching for alternatives to binaries; they were part of widespread and generalized developments in intellectual history that explored similar issues in many domains. Perhaps the most notable intellectual development in this regard is an alternative to classical logic that goes by the name of 'fuzzy logic'; proponents of fuzzy logic advocate alternate ways of viewing basic logical principles, rejecting a fundamental principle of classical logic which says that a proposition cannot be both *a* and *not-a*, a principle called the law of the excluded middle. Fuzzy logic, by contrast, allows that a proposition can be both *a* and *not-a*. The standard example usually offered of the difference between fuzzy logic and classical logic is the glass half full of water. Is such a glass full or not full? For fuzzy logic such an entity poses no problem, whereas it does for classical logic. Along with poststructuralism and fuzzy logic, developments that reject absolute contrasts can be seen as part of the intellectual shift associated with the breakdown of positivism in the West.

Although the views of poststructuralists have been enormously useful in undermining structuralist binaries, there are limitations in the concept of *between* as a solution to the problems of structuralism, for not all alternatives to a polarity or a binary figuration lie on a line between the two contrasted elements. For example, not all the alternatives to Claude Lévi-Strauss's famous contrast between *le cru et le cuit* ('the raw and the cooked'), can be placed on a single linear scaled.[17] Thus, not all polarities have a single continuum that we could call *in between*. Moreover, it should be remembered that there are some things that do indeed operate on binary principles – for example, digital computers – and some properties that do follow classical logic.[18]

Whatever its logical limitations, as a metaphor *between* has other values for poststructuralists. Poststructuralist thought has been notable in opposing the idea of an absolute origin, the idea that values, cultural concepts, or systems of knowledge are grounded on a bedrock of certainty, that they rest on essentialist cultural foundations upon which all else can be built with security. Instead critics in this tradition view ideas, knowledge, thought, language, and culture as all being in process, between the uncertainties of the constructions of the past and the uncertainties of the constructions of the future. Rather than being founded upon fundamental or essential realities, such human constructions as language and culture rest upon a chain of signifiers and in turn generate a succeeding chain of signifiers. This conceptual framework has made the term *between* useful, signifying the uncertainty that is inevitably associated with cultural constructions.

There is a third value of *between* as well, related to a more personal and political domain of motivation, that has made this metaphor appealing to poststructuralists. The emergence of poststructuralism is associated with the generation of 1968, and the politics of that generation have coalesced with its critical stances. Motivated by a desire to escape collusion with unsatisfactory political systems and rejecting the compromised, polarized politics of the Cold War, some poststructuralists sought an alternative positioning for their ideological stance, repudiating affiliation with either side in the Cold War. In the period before the dissolution of the Eastern bloc, this desire to escape from and to avoid being trapped by the polarized dominant political alternatives came to be symbolized in certain circumstances by the concept of a *space between*. This is part of the reason for the attraction of the discourse in translation studies as well.

There have been many compelling reasons, thus, for criticism to fasten on the expression *between* and for the term to suggest positive ideological connotations. The concept has been absorbed into translation studies not only because of its use by poststructuralist theorists of translation but also because of its congruence with other aspects that make spatial metaphors congenial and that make gaps in time and space relevant to the activity and process of translation: the physical dimension of interpretation, the history of translation in the West, and the history of words for translation in certain Western languages. Although there are no doubt many other causes for the popularity of the discourse of translation as a *space between*, this brief survey suffices to establish its attraction to scholars. Let us turn then to an evaluation and critique of the discourse to assess its implications for the ideology of translation.

An imperative question is whether this concept of translation as a space between is applicable to all facets of translation, particularly the linguistic dimension of translation. In this regard, we must ask whether poststructuralism is the only intellectual lineage to consider in applying the concept of a space between to translation and in using the notion in the discipline of translation studies. Here I think we must acknowledge that if language is seen in part as a formal system, a code (as it generally has been in modern linguistics), then a spatial concept of translation – the concept of the translator as bridging a gap, a *between*, which the translator can be located within – has a very limited utility in translation theory. That is, when translation is conceptualized in terms of transfer between languages as *systems*, this spatial metaphor of translation breaks down.

In very schematic terms, here is why. In theories of systems, one is seen as acting or operating within a system. In the event that one transcends the limits of a given system, one does not escape systems altogether or fall between systems, but instead one enters another system, generally a larger system that encompasses or includes the system transcended. This is not simply a view of contemporary systems theorists (cf. Luhmann 1995). It can be traced back to the work of Kurt Gödel, whose insights and formulations on mathematics have influenced all of twentieth-century intellectual history. In the incompleteness theorem Gödel demonstrates that questions can always be posed within any formal system (say, arithmetic) which cannot be answered in terms of the formal system itself, and that answers to such questions are formulated not outside of systems altogether but within the framework of another more encompassing formal system.

Such views are not restricted to the domains of mathematics and logic as Gödel has articulated them, or to the domain of systems theory per se. This is also the direction that anthropology and ethnography have taken: these disciplines have come to acknowledge that an ethnographer or anthropologist can never stand in a neutral or free space between cultures, but of necessity operates within some cultural framework, notably the constraints of his or her own primary cultural system. Increasingly in the social sciences such cultural frameworks within which research is conducted are expected to be acknowledged and specified in the work in some fashion.[19] Indeed, it is only by recognizing the position that the investigator holds within a system, that one can understand the ideological contingencies and presuppositions of the investigation itself.

Clearly these arguments have relevance for both translators and writers about translation. In extending such arguments and applying such models to translation, we must recognize, for example, that insofar as translators mediate between cultures, the concerns of anthropology and ethnography are relevant to translation; insofar as languages are formal systems, the findings of logic and systems theory should apply to linguistic activities like translation. Thus, one can argue that in the act of translation, when a translator interrogates a source text on the basis of a target language, the translator transcends the source language as a formal system, without simply switching to the target language as a formal system. Conversely, when the target language is interrogated using the source text as the basis of the examination, the translator transcends the target language as formal system without simply reverting to the system of the source language. The transcendence of both linguistic codes in fact puts the translator into a formal system that encompasses both languages, rather than being restricted to either. How large such an encompassing system will be has to do with the closeness of the two languages and two cultures in question, the breadth of the linguistic purview of the materials translated, and so forth. Whatever the extent of these parameters, however, the translator doesn't altogether leave the system of language *per se*, nor does the translator strictly speaking leave the domain of either or both languages. That is, one must conceptualize the translator not as operating *between* languages, but as operating either in one language or another, or more properly in a system inclusive of both SL and TL, a system that encompasses both.[20] With respect to a theory of formal systerns, there can be no *in between*, no free space that exists outside systems altogether, separate from a more encompassing system: any inquiry or statement or position will fall within the framework of such a larger system. Thus, we can think of systems as a series of Chinese boxes, so to speak, with given systems always nested inside more inclusive ones.

To insist upon a *between* existing with respect to languages is to abandon what the modern age has agreed upon with respect to systems. Such a view of a *between* as occurring in translating from one language to another or from one culture to another *as systems*, is, therefore, incompatible with a view of languages as formal systems that actually *construct* meaning rather than as structures that merely reflect external, language-free meaning. This is the heart of the argument I am making here, and the point must be emphasized and underscored. Spatial metaphors of translation may be useful and even perhaps natural in some contexts having to do with translation, as the ontogenetic and proximate causes considered above indicate; moreover, the concept of *between* may be useful in certain considerations of language as a (single) system, as poststructuralist arguments about the binaries of structuralism indicate. From the perspective of translation as movement from one system of language and culture to another, however, the philosophical implications and limitations of the concept of *between* which have been discussed here must be clearly understood. They return us to retrograde Platonic notions of meaning that were ascendant in the nineteenth century, in which meanings and ideas were thought to exist apart from and above any linguistic formulations.[21]

In her 1987 work entitled *Borderlands*, focusing on identity questions of the Spanish-speaking community that lives in the Southwest of the United States, near the Mexican/U.S. border, Gloria Anzaldúa writes:

> Alienated from her mother culture, alien in the dominant culture, the woman of color does not feel safe within the inner life of her Self. Petrified, she can't respond, her face caught between *los intersticios*, the spaces between the different worlds she inhabits.
>
> (1987:20)

As in the quotes we began with from Simon, Spivak, and Mehrez, Anzaldúa here conceives of a *space between* cultures, from which one can (or cannot) speak – or, *mutatis mutandis*, translate. Although Anzaldúa is not writing primarily about translation, her writing demonstrates the tendency to use a spatial figuration of between for cultural interface, and her work has in fact been used by writers in translation studies as a means of elucidating the positioning of the translator. Anzaldúa returns us to the central topic of this essay. In view of what has been said about both the causes for its popularity and the critiques that can be leveled against it as a concept, what are the implications for the *ideology* of translation in the use of the discourse of translation as a space between?

Certainly a first implication is that this discourse grows out of Western views of translation – notably the history of the words in the Romance languages and in English for the concept of translation. Thus, *prima facie* this is not a discourse that is easily transferable to other cultural systems – including cultures with other European languages. The view of translation as a space between is a model, moreover, that grows out of a particular Western capitalist paradigm of the translator as an isolated individual worker

who independently acts as mediator of languages. It does not fit other paradigms of translation, including the practices used in the People's Republic
of China, for example, or practices in China throughout time for that
matter, where teams of translators have traditionally worked together, with
each member of the team operating primarily within a single linguistic and
cultural framework. In the latter paradigm of translation practice, the first
stage of translation is performed by a person with primary knowledge of and
even loyalties to the source language and culture, followed by a polishing
stage undertaken by someone with clear loyalties to the receptor language
and culture (for example, a native in the receiving language often with
minimal or no knowledge of the source language), with the whole process
under the eye of an ideological supervisor.[22] Such teams and their members
are *ipso facto* together and severally rooted in a specific cultural context and
even an institutional framework. One could even argue that the primary
translation situation throughout history everywhere and still today in most
developing countries – namely oral interpretation – can hardly be modeled
as occurring in a space between, where space is understood in terms of
culture rather than the physical location of the interpreter. Thus, it is problematic to ground an ideological theory of translation in the historical
linguistics and practices of a specific group of Western languages and cultures: *between* is a questionable premise for those seeking ethical geopolitical
change for it is a model based on a framework primarily grounded in a
rather limited range of Western experiences.

Equally problematic are the traces of romantic sensibility lurking behind
this discourse. Rather than promoting a view of a translator as embedded
in and committed to specified cultural and social frameworks and agenda,
however broad, the discourse of translation as a space between embodies
a rather romantic and even elitist notion of the translator as poet. If the
place of enunciation of the translator is a space outside both the source and
the receptor culture, the translator becomes a figure like romantic poets,
alienated from allegiances to any culture, isolated by genius. This view of
the translator is obviously congenial and perhaps even welcome to models
of translation that efface the difference between translating and (original)
writing, between translator and writer. It also coalesces with the model of
the translator as a declassé and alienated intellectual cut loose from specific,
limiting cultural moorings and national affiliations, suggesting in turn comparison with the political meanings of *between* to poststructuralists who
rejected the political polarizations of the Cold War.[23] Again, however, we
may question whether such ideas about the translator are in fact typical of
translators and translation practices worldwide, and whether they are likely
to result in the use of translation for progressive ideological purposes.

Moreover, the concept of the translator as occupying a space between is
hardly one that fits with historical research in translation studies, nor does it
fit with materialist analyses of translation. Over and over again descriptive

studies of translation have demonstrated the connection of all facets of translation – from text choice to translation strategy to publication – with ideology, and they have established how translations are grounded in the politics of particular places and times. Rather than being outside cultural systems, descriptive and historical research on translation indicates that translation is *parti pris* and that translators are engaged, actively involved, and affiliated with cultural movements.[24] Historical research rarely supports the view that translators are characterized by romantic alienation and freedom from culture, whatever their place of enunciation.

In part the (intentional) alienation implicit in the model of translation as a space between reflects dissatisfaction with dominant discourses in dominant cultures, a feeling one can sympathize with. However, to suggest that the only alternative to dissatisfaction with dominant discourses is departure from a culture is, ironically, to affirm implicitly or explicitly the view that culture is a homogeneous construct. Here Sherry Simon's definition of 'the translational' as "that hybrid space which stands between the *certainties* of national cultures but does not participate in them" (1996:153, my emphasis) stands as an example of the dubious implications of translation as a space between: we must note that Simon's trope depends on national cultures being monolithic, homogeneous, and characterized by 'certainties'. These implications of a cultural *between* contrast markedly with contemporary ideas about culture that stress the heterogeneity of culture and that assert that any culture is composed of varied and diverse – even contradictory and inconsistent – competing viewpoints, discourses, and textures,[25] which, paradoxically, Simon herself elsewhere espouses and enjoins in translation studies (Simon 1996:137). Recent scholarship in many fields has delineated the coexistence and maintenance of minority and divergent views within cultures. Clearly, from a logical point of view, the introduction of or adherence to ideas and values from another culture does not *per se* eliminate a translator – or anyone else, for that matter – from being part of her own culture. The suggestion that such influence – or even commitment to 'foreign' ideas – moves a person to a position outside her culture (without even granting the subject a position in the other culture, as the use of *between* suggests) is a very peculiar notion that contravenes work about heterogeneity and hybridity that has emerged in recent explorations of the conditions of the diasporic modern world and that can be projected backward in time as well. One can, of course, choose to reject such views and assert that the only discourses of a culture that count are dominant discourses, but to do so would put one very much out of the mainline of current explorations of culture as a varied and heterogeneous construct. Such a position would clearly not be a step forward for translation theory. It is important therefore to look at the logical implications of vocabulary before it is adopted, interrogating in this regard the ideological discourse of translation as a space between.

Finally, from the point of view of the ideology of translation, the discourse of translation as a space between is problematic because it is misleading about the nature of engagement *per se*. Whether translation is initiated for political purposes from a source culture, from a receptor culture, or from some other third culture, translation as a successful means of engagement and social change – like most political actions – requires affiliation and collective action. The discourse of a space between obscures the necessity of such collective work – even if it is the minimalist collective action of attending to the practical needs of getting a translation published and distributed. Effective calls for translators to act as ethical agents of social change must intersect with models of engagement and collective action. This the discourse of translation as a space between abandons.

As Anthony Pym has chronicled (1992: ch. 7), the loyalty of translators is a leitmotif in translation history. Questions about the loyalty of a translator arise not because the translator inhabits a space between, with affiliations to that space between, but because the translator is in fact all too committed to a cultural framework, whether that framework is the source culture, the receptor culture, a third culture, or an international cultural framework that includes both source and receptor societies. Loyal to dissident ideologies internal to a culture, or to affiliations and agendas external to a culture, the translator can easily become the traitor from within or the agent from without. The problem with translators for dominant centers of power is not that translators are between cultures and cultural loyalties, but that they become all too involved in divergent ideologies, programs of change, or agendas of subversion that elude dominant control. The ideology of translation is indeed a result of the translator's position, but that position is not a space between.

Notes

1 See Hermans 1999a; Pym 1998; and Tymoczko 2000, as well as sources cited.
2 See, for example, Holmes 1994:23–33; Lefevere 1985, 1992.
3 On speech act theory see Austin 1975, Searle 1969, and Sperber and Wilson 1995. The ideological aspects of reported speech have been discussed by Vološinov 1971:149.ff. and Parmentier 1993. A comprehensive study of translation as reported speech is found in Folkart 1991; see also Gutt 2000; Hermans 2000:269: Mossop 1998; and sources cited.
4 *Antigone* is the first of the Theban plays written by Sophocles, performed in Athens probably in 442 or 441 B.C. At the time the democratic system was firmly entrenched in Athens and the prevailing ideology emphasized free speech, free association, and open access to power, limited by loyalty to the laws of the *polis*. These ideals were being actively negotiated with the Delian League and Samos, in particular, having been established in Samos initially by a campaign of 40 ships from Athens. At the period of Sophocles's play, however, the oligarchs of Samos were seemingly fomenting secession from pro-Athenian rule. In 441–40, after the staging of the play, Athens responded with a second expedition to

Samos, this time a hosting of 60 ships under the leadership of Pericles and Sophocles himself, designed to remove the rebels and restore democratic, pro-Athenian rule to the island. Thus the play was staged against a highly politicized historical background and its discourses were probably ideological in very specific ways, in addition to the general ones emphasized here. See Sophocles 1999:1–4; 1973:3–4.

5 Trans. in Lefevere 1977:84; cf. the discussion in Pym 1998:181 ff.

6 These notions have been hotly debated. See, for example, Pym 1998:179 ff. and Hermans 1999:40 ff., as well as sources cited. The impact of translation on many contemporary writers – from Borges to Kundera – whose status 'at home' was immediately enhanced by the translation of their works into English or French is a trivial refutation of Toury's view, despite the importance of his insights about descriptive approaches to translation in general.

7 This is a topic that more people than myself have set their minds to. I am particularly indebted to Annie Brisset with whom I've had conversations on this topic and who has herself published on this topic (1997). Although we come to similar conclusions, we approach the issues from somewhat different directions. The importance of understanding the implications of discourses and metaphors about translation for both the history of translation and the theory of translation has been increasingly recognized. Groundbreaking studies with implications for the ideology of translation are found in Hermans 1985 and Chamberlain 1992. On the general significance of metaphors for the structuration of thought, see Lakoff and Johnson 1980. Because metaphors have ideological power and also structure our thought and our lives, it is important to investigate their implications and to ascertain that they have intellectual integrity.

8 For example, the trope is integral to the argument in Iser 1995. Brisset (1997) offers an excellent critique of Iser's position, arguing that his view is ultimately utopian rather than programmatic for translation per se.

9 Translation studies is not alone in using spatial metaphors. They have become popular in other domains contemporary culture and are perhaps most remarkable in language pertaining to computer activities, as exemplified by such terms as *cyberspace, chat rooms, Web sites*, and so forth. Koppell (2000) suggests that spatial vocabulary has been adopted in the domain of computers to give it status, notably to avoid comparisons with television, to avoid downgrading it to the status of a mere medium, and to avoid the suggestion that Web denizens are passive recipients of electronic signals. Metaphors of space make the Internet seem more intriguing and exciting, helping to sell computers and related products. Moreover, spatial metaphors are part of what has allowed the government to consign decisions about the Internet to profit-seeking companies and commercial interests, skewing its development to favor the corporation rather than the individual or society as a whole.

10 Also troubled by issues of causality, Pym rests a similar discussion on the types causalities distinguished by Aristotle: the material cause, the final cause, the formal cause, and the efficient cause (cf. Pym 1998:144–59). I am adopting a somewhat broader framework than Pym does, incorporating current thinking about causality in the contemporary sciences. For a general discussion of causality and explanation see Salmon 1998; I am also indebted to Julianna Tymoczko for aspects of the argument, as well as to Irven DeVore.

11 This is perhaps one factor inspiring the title *Between* for Christine Brooke-Rose's novel about a simultaneous interpreter, who literally mediates in the sound channel between the speaker's voice and the audience's ear. In written studies about translation, it is also related to the graphological representation of the translator

(and the translator's mediation) as positioned between the source language and text on the one hand, and the target language and text on the other, realized variously in diagrams, such as the following: ST + SL > Translator > TT + TL.

12 Tymoczko 1986; vernacular translation procedures in the Middle Ages show certain congruences with the processes of translation in oral tradition (cf. Tymoczko 1990).

13 E.g. French traduction, Spanish traducción.

14 That is, we don't simply take the current dominant semantic meaning of *translation* as an opaque arbitrary sign.

15 E.g. Descartes's view that animals (but not humans) are machines is one that few would be inclined to accept in a post-Darwinian period, in light of the vast evidence built up by the life sciences in the last century, illustrating the essential continuities between human beings and other animals.

16 For example, Arabic *tarjama*, originally meaning 'biography'.

17 The structuralists' dichotomy of the raw and the cooked no longer convinces in part because experience in our own kitchens shows other options. The raw, the cooked, and the rotten. The raw, the cooked, and the burnt. The raw, the marinated, and the cooked. The raw, the fermented, the salted, the pickled, the dried, and the cooked. Or, when things are *à point*, the perfectly raw-and-cooked. While I take sides with the poststructuralists here, at the same time, it's also clear that these alternatives do not fall on a single scale between the raw and the cooked. Is the dried more or less cooked than the salted, for example? And how does each of those relate to the rotten? Impossible to say, because there is no single criterion that would govern such assignments. See my treatment of these issues as they relate to translation in Tymoczko 1999: ch. 4.

18 Logicians often offer as an example the property 'pregnant': a person is either pregnant or not pregnant – you can't be half-pregnant, or a little pregnant, or on the continuum between pregnant and not-pregnant.

19 See, for example, the arguments in Clifford and Marcus 1986.

20 This is what lies behind Pym's concept of an interculture (1998:ch. 11). His diagram of the translator's position (1998:177) indicates that the translator inhabits the junction or union of two linguistic and cultural systems, represented as the space shared by two overlapping circles, but one could perhaps more accurately diagram the situation as two small circles enclosed within a larger one, a schema more compatible with some conceptions of bilingualism explored in translation studies (see, for example, Oksaar 1978). Actually both representations are very schematized and ultimately inadequate representations of the complexity of human cultures and languages which are open systems rather than closed ones, as the circles in such diagrams would suggest.

21 The implications for an assessment of Spivak, for example, are, thus, clear: although she is at the cutting edge of bringing French poststructuralist theory into an English-language context, her views of translation as a movement between formal systems are paradoxically fairly regressive philosophically and at the same time somewhat naive, ironically implying a Platonic view of language.

22 In the early days of translation in China, there were often even more stages, with oral recitation or reading of the source text by a speaker of the source language conjoined with ad hoc oral transation of the text passage by passage by a bilingual. The material was then transcribed into written language by a third team member, and polished and finalized by yet a fourth, the latter two of whom might not know the source language at all.

23 Not to mention the drop-out mentality of the generation of '68 in the United States.

24 See, for example, the overview in Lefevere 1992:ch. 5; cf. Tymoczko 2000.

25 See, for example, the arguments in Hall 1997.

References

Anzaldúa, G. (1987) *Borderlands=La Frontera: The New Mestiza*, San Francisco: Spinsters.

Austin, J. L. (1975) *How to Do Things with Words* (2nd edition) (ed. by J. O. Urmson and M. Sbisà), Cambridge: Harvard University Press.

Brisset, A. (1997) "La Traduction: Modele d'hybridation des cultures?", *Carrefour* 19(1): 51–69.

Catford, J. C. (1965) *A Linguistic Theory of Translation: An Essay in Applied Linguistics*, London: Oxford University Press.

Chamberlain, L. (1992) "Gender and the Metaphorics of Translation", in L. Venuti (ed.) *Rethinking Translation: Discourse, Subjectivity, Ideology*, London: Routledge.

Clifford, J. and G. E. Marcus (1986) *Writing Culture: The Poetics and Politics of Ethnography*, Berkeley: University of California Press.

Folkart, B. (1991) *Le conflit des énonciations: traduction et discours rapporté*, Candiac, Quebec: Éditions Balzac.

Gutt, Ernest-A. (2000) *Translation and Relevance: Cognition and Context*, Manchester: St. Jerome.

Hall, E. T. (1997) "The Local and the Global: Globalization and Ethnicity", in A. D. King (ed.) *Culture, Globalization, and the World-System: Contemporary Conditions for the Representation of Identity*, Minneapolis: University of Minneapolis Press.

Hannerz, U. (1997) "Scenarios for Peripheral Cultures", in A. D. King (ed.) *Culture, Globalization, and the World-System: Contemporary Conditions for the Representation of Identity*, Minneapolis: University of Minneapolis Press.

Hermans, T. (ed.) (1985) *The Manipulation of Literature: Studies in Literary Translation*, London and Sydney: Croom Helm.

—— (1999a) *Translation in Systems: Descriptive and System-oriented Approaches Explained*, Manchester: St. Jerome.

—— (1999b) "Translation and Normativity", in C. Schäffner (ed.) *Translation and Norms*, Clevedon: Multilingual Matters.

—— (2000) "Self-reference, Self-reflection and Re-entering Translation", in D. de Geest, O. de Graef, D. Delabastita, K. Geldof, R. Ghesquiere and J. Lambert (eds.) *Links for the Site of Literary Theory: Essays in Honour of Hendrik van Gorp*, Leuven: Leuven University Press.

Holmes, J. (1994) *Translated! Papers on Literary Translation and Translation Studies* (2nd edition), Amsterdam: Rodopi.

Jakobson, R. (1959) "On Linguistic Aspects of Translation", in R. A. Brower (ed.) *On Translation*, Cambridge: Harvard University Press.

King, A. D. (ed.) (1997) *Culture, Globalization, and the World-System: Contemporary Conditions for the Representation of Identity*, Minneapolis: University of Minneapolis Press.

Koppell, J. G. S. (2000) "No 'There' There", *Atlantic Monthly*, August: 16–18.

Lakoff, G. and M. Johnson (1980) *Metaphors We Live By*, Chicago: University of Chicago Press.

Lefevere, A. (1985) "Why Waste our Time on Rewrites? The Trouble with Interpretation and the Role of Rewriting in an Alternative Paradigm", in T. Hermans (ed.) *The Manipulation of Literature: Studies in Literary Translation*, London: Croom Helm.

—— (1992) *Translation, Rewriting, and the Manipulation of Literary Fame*, London: Routledge.

Luhmann, N. (1995) *Social Systems* (transl. by J. Bednarz Jr. and D. Baecker), Stanford: Stanford University Press.

Mehrez, S. (1992) "Translation and the Postcolonial Experience: The Francophone North African Text", in V. Lawrence (ed.) *Rethinking Translation: Discourse, Subjectivity, Ideology*, London: Routledge.

Mossop, B. (1998) "What is a Translating Translator Doing", *Target* 10(2): 231–266.

Oksaar, E. (1978) "Interference, Bilingualism and Interactional Competence", in L. Grähs, G. Korlén, and B. Malmberg (eds.) *Theory and Practice of Translation*, Bern: Peter Lang.

Parmentier, R. J. (1993) "The Political Function of Reported Speech: A Belauan Example", in J. A. Lucy (ed.) *Reflexive Language: Reported Speech and Metapragmatics*, Cambridge: Cambridge University Press.

Pym, A. (1992) *Translation and Text Transfer: An Essay on the Principles of Intercultural Communication*, Frankfurt: Peter Lang.

—— (1998) *Method in Translation History*, Manchester: St Jerome.

Salmon, W. C. (1998) *Causality and Explanation*, New York: Oxford University Press.

Searle, J. R. (1969) *Speech Acts: An Essay in the Philosophy of Language*, Cambridge: Cambridge University Press.

Simms, N. (1983) "Three Types of 'Touchy' Translation", *Nimrod's Sin* (ed. by N. Simms) *Pacific Quarterly Moana* 8(2): 48–58.

—— (1996) *Gender in Translation: Cultural Identity and the Politics of Transmission*, London: Routledge.

Sophocles (1973) *Antigone*, (transl. by R. E. Braun), New York: Oxford University Press.

—— (1999) *Antigone*, (ed. by M. Griffith), Cambridge: Cambridge University Press.

Sperber, D. and D. Wilson (1995) *Relevance: Communication and Cognition* (2nd edition), Oxford: Blackwell.

Spivak, G. C. (1992) "The Politics of Translation", in M. Barrett and A. Phillips (eds.) *Destabilizing Theory*, Oxford: Polity Press.

Toury, G. (1980) *In Search of a Theory of Translation*, Tel Aviv: Porter Institute for Poetics and Semiotics.

—— (1995) *Descriptive Translation Studies and Beyond*, Amsterdam: John Benjamins.

Tymoczko, M. (1986) "Translation as a Force for Literary Revolution in the Twelfth-Century Shift from Epic to Romance", *New Comparison* 1: 1–16.

—— (1990) "Translation in Oral Tradition as a Touchstone for Translation Theory and Practice", in S. Bassnett and A. Lefevere (eds.) *Translation, History and Culture*, London: Pinter.

—— (1999) *Translation in a Postcolonial Context: Early Irish Literature in English Translation*, Manchester: St. Jerome.

—— (2000) "Translation and Political Engagement: Activism, Social Change and the Role of Translation in Geopolitical Shifts", *The Translator* 6(1): 23–47.

Vološinov, V. N. (1971) "Reported Speech", (transl. by L. Matejka and I. R Titunik), in L. Matejka and K. Pomorska (eds.) *Readings in Russian Poetics: Formalist and Structuralist Views*, Cambridge: MIT Press.